let the flames begin

let the flames begin

TIPS, TECHNIQUES, AND RECIPES
FOR REAL LIVE FIRE COOKING

CHRIS SCHLESINGER

and

JOHN "DOC" WILLOUGHBY

COLOR PHOTOGRAPHY BY WILLIAM MEPPEM

LINE ILLUSTRATIONS BY JOHN BURGOYNE

W. W. NORTON & COMPANY | NEW YORK · LONDON

For information about permission to reproduce selections from this book, write to Permissions,
W. W. Norton & Company, Inc., 500 Fifth Avenue, New York, NY 10110

The text of this book is composed in Filosofia with the display set in Meta Bold
Composition by Barbara Bachman
Manufacturing by The Maple-Vail Book Manufacturing Group
Book design by Abby Weintraub
Production manager: Andrew Marasia

ISBN 0-393-05087-4

W. W. Norton & Company, Inc., 500 Fifth Avenue, New York, N.Y. 10110
www.wwnorton.com

W. W. Norton & Company Ltd., Castle House, 75/76 Wells Street, London W1T 3QT

3 4 5 6 7 8 9 0

a c k n o w l e d g m e n t s

We've been writing cookbooks for a while now, and along the way we have been helped by more people than we can possibly thank here. But in particular we want to give a nod to these folks:

FROM CHRIS:

First of all I want to thank my wife, Marcy, for her inspiration, tolerance, never-ending good humor, and willingness to put up with all that smoke and fire. Thanks also to Chester and Roscoe, our ever-present companions. At the East Coast Grill, my thanks to Maureen, Kristin, Kathy, and Kate in the International Headquarters office, and to Eric, Elmer, Acar, and all the boys in the kitchen. At the Back Eddy, thanks to Sal, Aaron, Sally, Dan George, and the whole wonderful staff. As always, thanks to my friends, mentors, and tormentors Bob Kinkead and Jimmy Burke.

FROM DOC:

My thanks to Ruth Reichl, Larry Karol, and all the rest of the folks at *Gourmet* as well as to Chris Kimball, Jack Bishop, and the staff at *Cook's Illustrated* for putting up with my preoccupation with live fire. Thanks, too, to Mark Bittman for those many hours of consultation and idle chat, to Nardor and Nancy for their inspiration, to Tom Huth for his wit and optimism, and to the ever-enthusiastic Sherman for his faithful company and unvarying cheerfulness during the writing of the book.

FROM BOTH OF US:

Once again, thanks to our agent, the irrepressible Doe Coover, who guided this book through some rocky shoals, as well as to her colleagues Francis and Amanda, who cheerfully tolerated more than the usual folderol from us. And of course, thanks to our ineffable editor, Maria Guarnaschelli—it's good to be back together again. Our heart-felt thanks also to Nancy Kohl and Kirsten Mikalson, who did much of the heavy lifting involved in getting these recipes onto the page. At W. W. Norton, we also want to thank the hyper-efficient Erik Johnson; Abby Weintraub, who effortlessly came up with a design that thrilled us all; and our marvelous copy editor Katya Rice, who not only clarified our language and thoughts but also discovered confusions and misstatements that no one else noticed over the dozen or so years we've been writing about grilling. Thanks to John Burgoyne for his very helpful illustrations (and a special thanks to Chris Kimball for his help in this regard), and to William Meppem for giving our recipes a beautiful visual life.

Finally, thanks to our close friends, family, and dinner companions: Rick and Susan, Tom and Lizzie, Steve, and Ihsan and Valerie, who not only provided companionship, love, and humor but also were the critical tasters for most of the recipes in this book.

—Chris Schlesinger and John Willoughby

contents

Color photographs appear between pages 240 and 241

east Asia—from these and many more such casual tropical meals came my inspiration to cook with plenty of spices and to create stronger, bolder, louder, brighter flavors.

So these are the three legs that support my grilling inspiration: the good-humored, casual approach taught to me by my dad; the serious technique based on classical French dogma; and the never-ending resources of hot weather cultures, where cooks have many more centuries of grilling experience than we do.

These all came together in 1985 when I opened my first restaurant, the East Coast Grill, in Cambridge, Massachusetts. Since I was in charge, it fell to me to train, teach, and help other cooks understand live-fire cookery in the same way that I did. At that point I began to pay more attention to the techniques that I had picked up over nearly twenty years of grilling so that I could pass them along. I have kept refining my understanding over the nearly two decades since then.

By now I think I've got it down pretty well, and I want to convey it to you. What you have before you in this book is my effort, along with that of my coauthor, Doc, to share with you the joys, good times, and many ways to create tasty food that we have encountered along the grilling trail. It's all here, and it's all fun. So let the flames begin!

—Chris Schlesinger

FROM DOC:

GREAT-TASTING FOOD IS A PRETTY POWERFUL INCENTIVE, all by itself, to haul out the grill. But there is also an undeniable romance to grilling, a kind of fascination that makes it different from any other cooking method. Oh, hell, I'll just come right out and say it: It's fun to play with fire.

In fact, this may be the time to admit that it was me who, some forty-odd years ago, came close to burning down our neighbor's garage. I don't think my parents ever knew about this little peccadillo (sorry, Mom), and in fact it wasn't immediately clear to me that I was the responsible party. When the fire trucks pulled up next door in the middle of our Thanksgiving dinner, sirens screaming, I had forgotten all about my morning of playing pirates. And why would the two be associated, you might ask? Well, pirates, as everybody knows, spend a lot of time putting the torch to various items—merchant ships, port cities that resist their demand for bribes, what have you. To simulate these exercises in mayhem, I had thrown lit matches into the metal garbage cans in the neighbor's garage; the flames were suitably inspiring, wild and free and completely untrammeled. Too untrammeled, as it turned out. When I heard my brother calling me for dinner, it didn't occur to me that those flames, left alone to express their true nature, were dangerous. Fortunately, our neighbors saw little ten-twelve I had pretty much assumed all grilling responsibilities for the family; by sixteen I was courting the disdain of my pizza-ordering buddies by cooking dinner just for myself on the grill; and when I got to culinary school years later, I routinely eschewed the dorm kitchen and fired up the outside hearth even in winter.

But it was not the fire alone, mesmerizing though it was, that drew me to grilling. Essentially, prior to starting my professional cooking career, I was living the grilling lifestyle. To me, summertime, the beach, and grilling all go together, with a mental association so strong that even if you only have two of these elements, the third is inferred. So when I think of grilling, what automatically pops into my mind is a life that involves wide, sandy beaches, cutoff jean shorts, cold drinks, plenty of laughs, good pals, best friends, an absence of formality, and a lot of really good, tasty, solid, unfussy food. This mental attitude toward grilling is present to some degree any time a grilling fire is lit anywhere in the world, but at heart it is quintessentially American. What I mean is that grilling can be a kind of apotheosis of what is best in our national spirit. It is by its very nature fun and casual; its ethos is laid back and wholly unpretentious; and it is always surrounded by good fellowship.

So up until I was twenty-two or so, living the grilling life was my main relationship to live-fire cookery. Then, during my time at the Culinary Institute of America, I added another aspect to my appreciation of grilling: the technical side.

That is to say, I discovered that my dad did not invent grilling. I learned that it, along with braising, sautéing, and so on, is a bone fide cooking method, with practices and procedures laid out by Escoffier and other great experts of Western cooking, and I realized that grilling too is governed by traditional culinary laws. I already knew, for example, that there are right and wrong ways of sautéing and braising, that you need to get the fat in the pan very hot to sauté properly, and that your braise does not come out right if you let the liquid boil rather than simmer. I had also learned, through endless trial-and-error experiences, that these dynamics, rules, and principles went a long way toward dictating the quality of the outcome. Now I understood that the same was true of grilling. So to my formidable base in the goodwill alacrity approach to grilling, I added another paradigm: the classic French technical approach.

The next step in my grilling education came during my misspent mid-twenties, when I was able to parlay my skills as a line cook into a means of traveling around the world. As any of you who have been in the restaurant business know well, line cooks come and go, but a good one is always welcome. So, in addition to taking major time off for the epic surf trip that I had planned since I was sixteen, I also did numerous stints in restaurants located in warm climes with overhead waves. Barbados, Costa Rica, Peru, Hawaii, Southeast Asia, Mexico—they were all part of the travel epoch of my third decade.

During my travels I came to understand one more perspective on grilling, the out-look of cooks from cultures where most of the everyday cooking is done over live fire. Vertical grilled *tacos al carbone* in Mexico, red snapper and mahi-mahi grilled on beaches in Costa Rica, smoky jerk chicken in Jamaica, the ubiquitous satay of South-

flames flicker over the briquettes and then die, and I'd look closely to see if there was any white on any of the charcoals. Dad had taught me if even just one briquette way down at the far end had a little white ash on it, my work was done, because eventually the whole batch would catch. Like many of my father's precepts, this one went against the common backyard wisdom of the day. But I had observed the phenomenon many times and knew it to be true. So when I was at my friends' houses and saw their dads impatiently squirt on more and more lighter fluid in their attempt to get all the coals lit, I would smile quietly, feeling smug and superior. That didn't mean I wouldn't sometimes splash more juice on the charcoal for the fun of it, then jump as the flame followed the stream back up to the can. But at other times I would just watch as the fire crept slowly across the grill from briquette to briquette.

Periodically my dad would stroll out to the back deck, drink in hand, to ask me what I thought about the readiness of the fire. We'd concur that it would probably be another ten or fifteen minutes, and he'd return to the house. After a few more minutes he'd come back out with the steaks on a platter and go through his precooking ritual. He would carefully put the platter down and stare meaningfully off toward the horizon, then glance at the clouds in the sky, wet his finger, and hold it up to test the wind direction.

I never asked why he did this, sensing that it required a deep understanding that would become clear to me at a later age. And indeed I would eventually come to appreciate that artifice of this type is one of the main tools of professional chefs everywhere. The more mystical, the more peculiar, the more arcane the task, then the more skilled the cook has to be. So Dad could not just look at the coals and put the food on the grill. No, no. He had to assess and overcome the mysterious combination of wind, clouds, and barometric pressure, an undertaking that required all his years of experience combined.

When Dad gave the okay we'd slap the steaks on the grill and cook, sometimes adding small pieces of driftwood to the fire for smoky flavor. The fire was always hot, and before long the steaks were black on the outside and basically unchanged on the inside. At that point we'd scoop them onto the platter and, very proud of ourselves, bear them inside, where we'd brag to my mom and sister that we had once again conquered the wilds and uncertainties of the back deck to deliver yet another perfectly grilled meal.

It was so easy—there was never any fuss, mess, or tension, and it always turned out great. True, the food was sometimes a little burned or a little raw, but we always ate it and it always tasted good. This calmness, this total willingness to deal with pretty much whatever comes off the grill, this unflappable acceptance and good-humored approach to the always challenging vicissitudes of live-fire cooking—all of this is at the heart of being a skilled griller. Dad never said this in so many words, but the knowledge passed from him to me as surely as if the words were chiseled in stone.

With Dad's attitude as inspiration, my infatuation with live fire began in earnest. And, unlike many other youthful enthusiasms, it just kept on growing. By the age of

FROM CHRIS:

I AM A GRILLER. I THINK MY RÉSUMÉ QUALIFIES ME AS AN EXPERT IN THE field, and indeed I have made my living by specializing in this unique and tasty brand of cooking.

But there's a lot more to it than just those bald facts. Grilling, to me, is a way of life, and it has been ever since I was a kid. I attribute this primarily to my father. At this stage of my life I often wonder what his reaction would be to my accomplishments. Dad was happy to see me set out on my career path with early restaurant jobs, but unfortunately he wasn't around to witness what came later. There's one thing, however, that I'm quite sure of—he would be amazed and, even more, amused that anybody could make a living from grilling.

The fact is, though, that he is largely responsible for it. He taught me his secrets and showed me the heart of grilling, a cooking method at once easy and complex, endlessly fascinating and rewarding. He lit a fire that burned so deeply and brightly inside me that I turned it into a lifestyle.

How did it happen? Well, imagine this scene. I was eight years old. It was summer, we were at our beach house, and every night was grill night. Even at that young age I was trained to bring out the rusty old grill, pour in the nasty charcoal, squeeze the old-school lighter fluid all over the briquettes, light a match, throw it at the grill, and run, looking over my shoulder at the fireball shooting up into the sky. It's a wonder I was never severely burned.

Smelling of lighter fluid, dirty from the charcoal dust, I would sit and watch the

drils of fire curling out of the garage windows and called the fire department before the building was seriously damaged.

Since those days I've learned a thing or two about safety, responsibility, and keeping fantasy and reality straight. But I still love live fire. Fortunately, the arc of my life has led me to a place where that is not only acceptable but actually rewarded.

It took quite a few years, though, to get from that childhood firebug incident to an understanding of the broad culinary applications of such tendencies. In the rural Iowa town where I grew up, grilling was called "barbecuing," and it was something you did a half-dozen times each summer on a wobbly, slightly rusted metal grill in the back yard or, for picnics or family reunions, on those brick fireplaces ubiquitous in public parks throughout the Midwest. The fact that men almost always were the cooks on those occasions was not very surprising to me, since my father (who loved food and actually read cookbooks just for the pleasure of it) did his share of the cooking in our household anyway.

So my true appreciation of grilling didn't take root until about sixteen years ago. Specifically, it began in earnest at the point when I quit a public service job to protest the gutting of the program where I had worked for years. Somewhat disillusioned, I sold my old yellow Fiat and used the proceeds to indulge in an open-ended journey that started in London and eventually snaked its way to Istanbul via France, Spain, Portugal, the three Magreb countries of northern Africa, Italy, and Greece.

Since the trip was to last until my friend Guido and I ran out of money, we were on a very tight budget. We took third-class trains and local buses; we slept in the open in campgrounds when we happened to find them, in parks and on beaches (and on one occasion in a traffic circle) when we didn't. As always happens when you travel, eating and talking about food occupied a large percentage of our waking hours. We would think and plan and salivate for at least a week before indulging in a splurge like b'istilla in a fancy hotel restaurant in Fez, homemade ravioli in a trendy trattoria in Florence, or classic lamb dishes in an ancient dining room overlooking the Bosporus in Istanbul. For the most part, though, we ate in the inexpensive cafés, bars, and street stands where the ordinary folks ate.

In these places, grilling was the cooking method of choice. I still remember with total clarity the sardine grilled over a wood fire in a little shack on a beach in the Algarve of Portugal; the first grilled fish I ever ate, it was a gustatory revelation. This was followed by a whole panoply of grilled meals, one better than the next: the lamb skewers that we ate with pots of mint tea at rickety tables in the streets of Fez and Marrakech; the spicy wood-grilled rabbit we sampled while stranded in Tunis waiting for a boat to Naples; the grilled tomatoes and bell peppers offered to us by our neighbors in a campground on the outskirts of Rome; the amazing grilled leg of lamb drizzled with honey and studded with fresh apricots that we were lucky enough to taste in an open-air café on a beach on the Greek island of Ikaria; and the plush, smoky grilled eggplant dishes that were everywhere in Istanbul.

That was the true beginning of my love for the rich, deep, smoky, seared flavor of food cooked over live fire. When I returned from the trip I began grilling myself, although I didn't acquire any real skill at the method until my friend Chris (with whom I had long shared a fondness for travel in the tropics and the loud, bright flavors of the foods found there) opened the East Coast Grill and I began working in the kitchen a few nights a week. Chris introduced me to the rudiments of real barbecue, smoke-roasting, and all the other live-fire cooking methods that are explored in this book. I also continued to hone my appreciation of this type of food by traveling and eating in hot weather climates from the Caribbean to North Africa, Central America to South-east Asia.

Then one Tuesday night after the Grill had been open a little over two years, a young woman walked up to Chris at his grill station in the open kitchen, said she was a literary agent, and asked if he wanted to write a cookbook. Since I had more experience writing than he, he suggested to her that the two of us work on it together. She agreed, and we did. Much to our surprise, not only was the book published, but people actually seemed to like it.

That was *The Thrill of the Grill* back in 1990, and I've been writing about grilling ever since. Fortunately, during that same period of time grilling has come into its own throughout the United States. Instead of the hot dogs and hamburgers of my youth, America's backyard grillers are now comfortable putting lamb skewers, whole fish, vegetables of all kinds—all those wonderful foods that inspired my love of grilling on that long-ago trip—over the fire.

And when you get right down to it, the fire is still the important part. Building it, shaping it, enjoying its unpredictability and uniqueness, is all a big part of the pleasure of grilling. Grilling may not be quite as exciting as playing pirates, but it's almost as much fun, it's a lot safer, and you end up with a great meal.

So get out the food, light the fire, and let's go.

—*John Willoughby*

let the flames begin

introduction

THE SKILL OF THE GRILL

Techniques, Fuels, Tools, and
Rules for Live-Fire Cooking

TECHNIQUES

This book is all about cooking over live fire—cooking with a fire you've built yourself from wood or charcoal, rather than one you've ignited by turning a knob. Unlike the uniform and continuous fire of a gas flame, each live fire has a distinct personality, with complex layers of heat and veins of coal and flame that make it subtly different from any other fire you have ever built. And each live fire has a finite life, lasting only while the fuel is being consumed and then disappearing from existence. It is this unique, idiosyncratic quality that makes cooking over live fire challenging, stimulating, and basically just plain fun. Not incidentally, putting food over live fire is the only way to get that true, ineffable grilled flavor.

Not so long ago, all cooking was defined by the qualities of live fire. If you look, for example, at the works of Escoffier, the eighteenth-century French master chef who codified Western cooking techniques, you'll find that each of his primary cooking methods was described as the product of live fire. These days, of course, most cooking is done with heat provided by electricity or gas or even microwaves, so all cooking done with live fire has come to be lumped together. In fact, though, there are quite a few variations of this primal style of cooking.

If you want to master live-fire cooking, you need to understand some definitions and be familiar with some rules. We kind of hate to say that, because in general we are not in favor of constrictions and guidelines. But true success in the live-fire world does require a basic understanding of the techniques, of which there are a full dozen we want to define and discuss here. A dozen techniques may seem like a lot, but if you want the skills—and we know you do—you need to know the drills. Then you can go out in the back yard and act as if your awesome culinary performance is no big deal.

So here they are. The first six consist of the basic live-fire cooking methods, complete with explanations of why and when you might use each one. With these, you will understand the result that almost any live-fire recipe will produce. The subtleties are important. Ask people who grew up in the South or Texas, and they'll tell you that there are very distinct differences among the various live-fire techniques. Unfortunately, many well-meaning folks tend to blur these boundaries. Emblematic of this confusion is the muddle surrounding grilling and barbecuing. In much of the country these labels are used interchangeably, as in "Let's go out in the back yard and barbecue a burger." In fact, grilling and barbecuing are as different as sautéing and braising. While sautéing and braising are similar in that both are done in pots on top of the stove, no one would ever say they are the same thing.

Next come three fundamental techniques that are key to all live-fire cooking—starting the fire, getting yourself organized, and knowing when your food is done. Finally, there follow three methods for adding big flavors to grilled foods. Get these all down pat, and you'll be a bona fide grill master.

THE SIX BASIC LIVE-FIRE COOKING TECHNIQUES

Here are your six options for live-fire cooking, moving from lowest heat to highest, along with an indication of what type of food you might want to cook with each method.

1. **Cold Smoking**. This technique is somewhat risky; if you don't do it just right, you can end up with food that will make you sick rather than happy. But we figure you should know what it is, even though we won't use it in this book.

Cold smoking is done by smoking food very slowly in some kind of confined space at temperatures lower than 90°F. Its main purpose is to preserve food. You can create products that last a long time without refrigeration—cured sausages, beef jerky, Virginia-style country hams, and smoked salmon, for example. To do cold smoking properly, however, you need a scientific knowledge of food technology, you need to use brines, and in general you need to be very careful, because you're operating in a temperature range in which bacteria can easily get out of control. In the modern age there are alternative ways of preserving food and less dangerous ways of getting that smoke flavor. We recommend that you leave this technique to the professionals.

2. **Hot Smoking.** For the home cook, this is a much more accessible technique than cold smoking. Hot smoking involves cooking in a not terribly hot, high-smoke environment where the goal is to bathe the food in as much smoke as possible. The purpose here is not so much to preserve the food as to flavor it with smoke. The fire will be of a

higher temperature than with cold smoking, between 80° and 160°F.

Like all forms of smoking, this technique involves an indirect use of fire. You light a fire over to one side of a covered grill using a fairly small amount of charcoal, only about enough to fill half a shoebox. Then you place the food to be smoked on the other side of the grill, put on the cover, and settle down for a long cooking session. With this technique you might take one or two other steps to enhance the flavor. Brining the food before it goes on the grill will not only prevent it from drying out during the prolonged cooking time but also give it a deeper flavor, while aromatic fuels like hardwood chunks or even chips will give the smoke a particular flavor nuance.

This method would be properly used for smoking a chicken or a piece of meat of that size—something that will cook in three hours or less. It should not be used for a ham or any other really large item that would take longer to cook. When you reach four hours at this temperature, you create a possibly dangerous situation with regard to bacteria. So just to be safe, we set three hours as our limit for hot smoking. (For a large item like a ham, we like to hot-smoke it on the grill for a period of time and then pile on more fuel so we can finish cooking the ham at a higher temperature. That way we get all the smokiness with none of the danger.)

Amount of charcoal
for hot smoking

Setup for indirect heat

Hot smoking a chicken

3. **Barbecuing.** In the South and Texas, barbecue is practically a way of life. Down there "barbecue" refers both to the cooking method itself and to the food created by that method. But as anyone there would hasten to tell you if you should misuse the word, it does *not* refer to food cooked directly over the flames of a charcoal fire. No, indeed.

To barbecue means to cook food slowly over the indirect heat and smoke from a hardwood fire. Like braising, barbecue was invented to deal with tough pieces of meat such as pork shoulder, the favorite of North Carolina aficionados; beef brisket, the preferred barbecue of Texans; and ribs, which are found all through the southern half of the country. The barbecue motto, "Slow and Low," says it all: you are cooking food slowly at a low temperature—the temperature of a barbecue pit should be somewhere between 180° and 240°F. As you do so, the tough connecting tissue in the meat, known as collagen, dissolves into gelatin, and the meat itself becomes delectably tender.

As with cold smoking, the method involves building a fire on only one side of your covered grill, this time using about enough charcoal to fill a large shoebox. You place the food on the opposite side and cover the grill, and then you just let the meat cook, adding a handful of coals every half hour or so to keep the temperature in the proper range (see drawing, page 11). The technique of barbecue is simple, primarily involving patience, but it yields a remarkable end result, as generations of dedicated Southern barbecue cooks can testify. (For more information on the lore and language of barbecue, check out our first book, *The Thrill of the Grill*.)

One other important thing while we're talking barbecue: You don't use temperature to judge when your barbecue is ready to eat, because you are looking to go beyond mere doneness all the way to tenderness. Instead, use the "fork test": stick a large fork into whatever you're cooking and try to pick it up. If the fork slides out of the meat without grabbing onto it, it's done; otherwise, keep cooking.

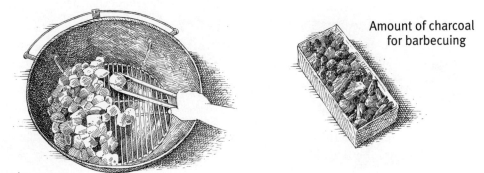

Amount of charcoal
for barbecuing

Indirect heat setup

4. **Smoke-Roasting**. The last of the indirect live-fire cooking methods uses the highest temperature. Here you are cooking at 300° to 450°F. In other words, you are basically roasting in a smoky environment. This method is perfect for roasts of all kinds as well as chickens, turkeys, ducks, and any other large but tender item. If you were cooking a nice piece of beef loin, for example, you'd want it to be rare, so you would smoke-roast it rather than barbecue it.

The fire for this method is similar to that used in the other indirect techniques, but this time you use more charcoal for the fire you build on one side of your grill, enough to fill about 1½ shoeboxes. After that, the technique is the same as with barbecuing, except that you'll need to add a similar amount of charcoal at each refueling. This should take place about every beer or every half-hour, whichever timing method you prefer.

Indirect heat setup

Amount of charcoal for
smoke-roasting

5. **Grilling.** The simplest of all live-fire cooking methods, grilling is no more (and no less) than cooking food directly over flames. It is very similar to sautéing, with the added benefit of that wonderful smoky char. When food is exposed to the direct heat of live fire, a seared crust develops on its exterior, and it is this flavor-packed crust, rather than the fuel used for the fire, as many believe, that is most responsible for the characteristic grilled flavor.

The method is just as direct and simple as you might think—you build a fire, put the grill grid over the fire, put the food on the grid, and cook the food until it's done— but there are a couple of niceties of technique that will pay off in perfectly grilled food.

First, *always build a multi-level fire*. When you set up the fire, leave about one-quarter of the grill free of coals, and bank the coals in the remaining three-quarters of the grill so that the coals are three times as high on one side as on the other. Setting up the coals this way is important because if your food begins to burn on the outside before it's done on the inside, or if there are flare-ups, you can move the food to the cooler portion of the fire or even the area with no fire at all. The multi-level arrangement also provides varying levels of heat in the same fire if you want to cook, for instance, a steak over a very hot fire and asparagus over a medium fire at the same time.

Multi-level fire setup

For these reasons our recipes usually advise you to build a multi-level fire even if what you are cooking in that particular recipe doesn't seem to require it.

Second, *check the fire's temperature before you put the food on the grill.* Allow the flames to build up and subside; when the coals are uniformly gray, put your hand about 5 inches above the grill grid, over the deepest portion of the coals, to check the temperature. If you can hold your hand there for 6 seconds or more (go ahead and count it out: one-one-thousand, two-one-thousand . . .), you have a low fire; 5 seconds is medium-low; 4 to 5 seconds is a medium fire; 3 to 4 seconds is in the medium-hot range; 2 seconds or less means you have a hot fire. Each of our recipes indicates how hot a fire you need.

Because grilling is a direct-cooking method using high heat, it is used for relatively small, tender items, like steaks or chops or chicken breasts that will cook through on the inside before they are incinerated on the outside. Even when we get up to the really thick pork chops and steaks, we do a bastardized grilling technique, in which we sear the meat really well over a hot fire, then move it to the side and cover it with a pie plate for a kind of smoke-roasting finale.

Checking fire temperature

6. **Hobo Pack Cookery.** What we're talking about here is a high-heat steam-roasting technique, in which food is wrapped in foil and cooked in the coals of your fire. It may be the second-oldest cooking method of all (after grilling); certainly people have been encasing food in leaves and putting it in pits lined with coals since before the dawn of recorded history. Ours is a modern version of that ancient approach—in our case inspired by experiences in the Boy Scouts.

For this method, simply wrap up some food in foil—either foil wrap or a disposable foil pan with foil wrap covering it—and toss it in the coals. There are three important things to remember in the process. First, be sure that the food to be cooked is fairly moist; otherwise it might dry out from contact with the hot coals. Second, fashion the package carefully (don't worry, there are instructions with each recipe) so that the juices don't leak out. Finally, place the package on the outside edge of the coals. You don't have to cover it completely. Just nudge it *in* at the edge of the coals so they come partway up the sides of the packet.

Hobo packs may seem a little odd to our modern tastes, but they are actually a great

Positioning a hobo pack

idea because they allow you to cook a number of side dishes *in* the fire at the same time as the main course cooks *above* the fire. And here's another reason for building a multi-level fire—on the side that has fewer coals, you'll always have room under the grill grid for a hobo pack or two. Whenever you're about to grill, check in your refrigerator or pantry and see what vegetables you have got that you could fashion into a hobo pack to go along with the rest of the meal. That way you can stay out of the kitchen, enjoy yourself out on the deck or in the back yard, and still have a complete meal.

THREE FUNDAMENTAL TECHNIQUES ESSENTIAL TO ALL LIVE-FIRE COOKING

1. **Starting the Fire.** Once you understand how easy it is to light a live fire, you'll be inclined to do it much more often. The quickest way to accomplish it is with a *chimney starter*. Also known as a flue, this is a wonderful tool because it is incredibly simple to use and yet 100 percent effective.

A chimney starter is a sheet metal cylinder, open at both ends, with a ring of ventilation holes around the lower end, a grid located inside the flue several inches from the bottom, and a wooden handle. To use the starter, set it in the middle of the fire grate, fill the small section under the grid with crumpled newspaper, fill the section above the grid with charcoal, and light the newspaper. The flames will sweep up through the chimney, igniting the charcoal. When the charcoal is red-hot, which should take about five minutes, dump it out and put as much additional charcoal as you want on top of or around the burning coals.

It really is that easy, and it works every time. This technique comes as a big surprise to folks who think lighting a grilling fire necessarily involves lighter fluid, twigs, a lot of huffing and puffing at the coals, and so on. A couple of years ago a photographer came to take some pictures of us grilling food. After seeing how effortless it was to light a hardwood charcoal fire with a chimney, she confessed that she wished she hadn't spent a good chunk of her money on a gas grill the week before.

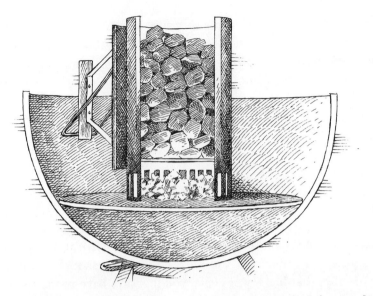

Chimney starter

Despite its bad reputation as a source of chemical fumes, *lighter fluid* is also an excellent choice for lighting your grilling fire. If you wait until the coals are all lit before you start cooking (which you should do in any case), the fluid will have burned off, so the taste of the food won't be affected.

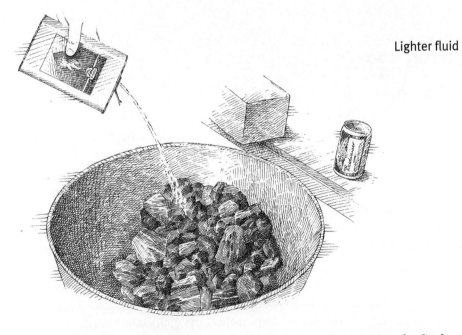

Lighter fluid

An *electric coil starter* is another acceptable option. It consists of a thick, oval electrical coil with a plastic handle. To use the starter, put it right on the fire grate, mound charcoal on top of it, and plug it into a grounded outlet. The coil will soon become red hot, igniting the charcoal in contact with it. At this point, unplug the starter and remove it; the hot coals will ignite the others. After you take the starter out of the coals, set it aside on a fireproof surface to cool, making very sure it is out of reach of children.

Whichever fire-starting method you use, it will take about half an hour or slightly longer for the fire to work up to the fiery-red stage and then die down to the point where all the coals are covered with a fine, gray ash. That's when you start measuring the fire's temperature (see page 8).

And here's another hint to make the whole process easy: There's no need to fuss and worry about getting every piece of charcoal going before you consider the fire lit. All you have to do is get a few pieces of charcoal partially lit—just a corner that is white on each so you know they are really going—and you can stop working at it. Those coals will light the pieces next to them, which in turn will light the ones next to them, and before too long all of your coals will be glowing hot. (Of course, if you're using a chimney starter this won't be an issue, because the whole chimney will be glowing in just a few minutes). Once you get to that point, you can continue to add fresh coals as needed throughout the cooking process.

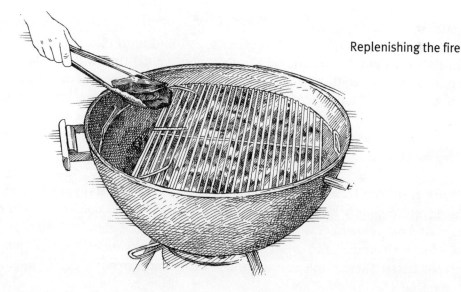

Replenishing the fire

2. **Getting Yourself Organized,** *or Getting Your Mise en Place in Place.* We mention this next because the best time to get yourself organized is after you've started your fire and are waiting for it to reach the right temperature for cooking. *Mise en place* is a French phrase that means something like "put in place." Go into any professional kitchen just before service, look around at each cook's station, and you'll see all the items that he or she is going to need in the course of service—salt, pepper, oils, spices, chopped vegetables, herbs, what have you—all neatly arranged. All the working cooks we know take great pride in having everything completely ready to go before they start to cook, and we want you to feel the same way. It guarantees a clean, quick, and enjoyable cooking process.

When you're grilling it's particularly important to be organized, because you never want to have to leave the fire to race back into the house for something you for-

Grilling *mise en place*

got. Right after you light the fire, spend a few minutes mentally running through the cooking process, note everything that you're going to need, and get it all out there and organized. It may sound a little compulsive, but you're going to have a lot more fun grilling if you do this, and you're going to look very cool when you're out by the fire because you'll be calm and collected. By the way, don't forget to include a good supply of your favorite beverage.

3. **Checking Food for Doneness.** If you know how to judge when your food is perfectly done, you've gone a long way toward being a really good cook. When you're checking your food, remember that it is going to be underdone for a long time, perfectly done for just a minute, and overdone for the rest of its existence. You can't put it back and cook it less. There's only a small window of perfect doneness, and it's important that you find it.

This is especially true with grilling. Since each live fire is somewhat different from every other, the cooking times provided in our recipes are approximations based on our experience. Testing for yourself is crucial, and we recommend that you do it early and often.

There are three ways to test doneness, based respectively on internal temperature, feel, and appearance.

For large cuts of meat or whole fowl—basically anything you grill-roast—the best option is to check the internal temperature with a meat thermometer. Just be sure you use it correctly. With a roast, you want to take the temperature right in its middle. Poke the thermometer all the way through to the other side of the roast, then draw it back to the midpoint. Wait for 5 seconds, and the reading should be accurate. When you're cooking bone-in roasts, be sure you're not touching the bone, because it will give you a false reading. To check the doneness of a whole bird, insert the thermometer at an angle into the area between the drumstick and the breast, aiming for the thickest part of the thigh.

	TEMPERATURE TO REMOVE FROM THE FIRE	APPEARANCE
Meat		
Rare	120°	Raw center
Medium-rare	126°	Red center, slightly warm
Medium	134°	Pink center
Medium-well	150°	Hint of pink in center
Well done	160°	Cooked throughout; no pink in center
Fowl		
	165°–170°	No hint of pink

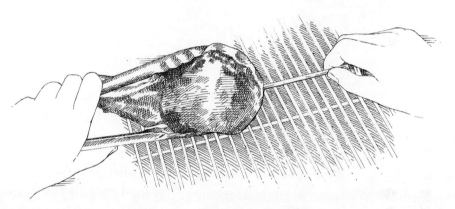

Testing temperature

For other cuts, such as steaks or chops—as well as cut-up chicken, other fowl, and even fish—you have two choices for testing doneness. The first is the "hand method"; the second is what we like to call "nick, peek, and cheat."

The hand method is the one used by many professional chefs. It rests on a basic scientific principle: When proteins, which are like little coils, are subjected to heat, they uncoil and bond with each other, squeezing closer together in a kind of lattice. This is called coagulating. The more the proteins coagulate, the firmer the texture of the food. Professional cooks can judge the degree of doneness of a piece of meat simply by pushing on it with a finger and assessing its firmness. Next time you go to a restaurant with an open kitchen, check it out—you'll see that the grill chef, or the sauté chef if there's no grill, is always poking at the meat or fish to see whether it's ready to come off the heat. (Incidentally, it's called the "hand method" not because you poke with your hand but because, in teaching young cooks, chefs have a system of comparing the texture of the food to the texture of various parts of your hand.) The basic thing to remember is that the firmer the meat or fowl or fish, the more done it is.

The only problem with this method is that you have to have a certain amount of experience to use it with any degree of accuracy. When you're cooking twenty or thirty steaks every night, five or six nights a week, and you're poking each one several times, it soon becomes second nature to know when a steak is anything from rare to well done. You don't even have to think about it. But for home cooks, who may cook a steak once a week, it takes longer to get that feel into your fingers.

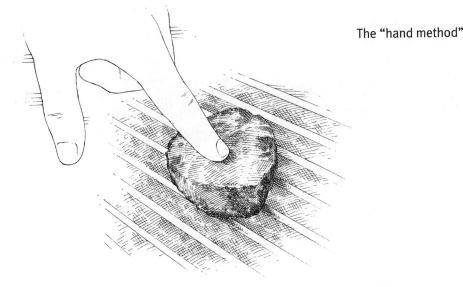

The "hand method"

We recommend that you practice the hand method every time you grill. But we also recommend that you rely on our old tried-and-true method, "nick, peek, and cheat," until you are completely comfortable with the hand method. As the name implies, you

Nick, peek, and cheat

simply pick up whatever you are cooking (or one piece of it), nick it slightly with a knife so you can look inside, and check its state of doneness. That's all there is to it. No guesswork, no intricate techniques. You couldn't get much easier or much more accurate.

Many home cooks think there is something wrong with the "nick, peek, and cheat" method and are reluctant to use it, probably because of the old-school culinary myth that cutting into a piece of food lets all the juices run out. It's true that when you cut into a piece of meat, some juices do escape. But it's not like putting a hole in a balloon; the very small amount of juice you may lose pales in comparison to serving raw or burned food.

Just remember that food continues to cook a bit even after it's off the fire. To allow for this carryover cooking, take that steak off when it looks rare if you want it medium rare, and remove the fish from the flames when it has a tiny trace of transparency in the middle, since your ultimate aim is a fish that is just translucent in the center. When it comes to poultry, though, we like to leave it on the fire until it is completely opaque and there is no pink at all near the bone.

THREE METHODS FOR ADDING FLAVOR TO GRILLED FOOD

1. **Using Salt and Pepper Properly.** The ability to use salt properly is one of the skills that separates the really great cook from a merely good one. Most cooks don't use enough. As for pepper, it is the spicy underpinning of all Western cooking. So when our recipes say to "sprinkle generously with salt and pepper," we mean exactly that. Be a little more generous with these two old standbys and you'll likely find your cooking notably improved. Of course, this is all a matter of taste, which is why we rarely call for specific amounts of either of these seasonings. You know what you like; we're simply suggesting that you try a somewhat bolder approach and see what you think. (Incidentally, if you are worried about the health effects of using more salt, think about the fact that more than 75 percent of the sodium consumed by the average American comes from processed food. Cut down on things like luncheon meats, hot dogs, chips, canned foods, and frozen meals, and you can add more salt to your cooking without a worry.)

We've included detailed discussions of both salt and pepper in our The Flaming Pantry (pages 387 to 389), so we'll say only a few things about them here. Our basic preference is for kosher salt rather than table salt. Kosher has fewer additives and a deeper flavor, and its large crystals make it easier to judge just how much salt you're adding when you use your fingers, which is the best and most fun way to do it. (By the way, when you're following a recipe of ours that calls for a set amount of salt, as opposed to salt "to taste," be aware that regular table salt has about twice as much salt per volume as kosher salt.) And please forget the old saw that says you shouldn't salt food prior to cooking because it draws out moisture. The very slight loss of juices that are drawn to the surface by salt is more than offset by the salt's amplification of flavors when it interacts with the food. Because the moisture drawn to the surface contains proteins, early salting intensifies the browning process, which is also a good thing for flavor.

Freshly ground pepper is one of the few ingredients for which there is no substitute. It is an entirely different creature from preground, and well worth the small amount of extra effort. Personally, we like to grind our peppercorns very coarsely so the large chunks explode with flavor and heat when you bite into them. You can achieve this effect with one of several tools, depending on the desired coarseness. For the coarsest grind, crack the peppercorns by rolling a heavy sauté pan or skillet back and forth over them while bearing down on the pan. For a somewhat finer texture, pulse the peppercorns three or four times in an electric coffee grinder. (This is a particularly useful method when grinding large quantities.) Or you can simply use the coarsest setting of your pepper grinder.

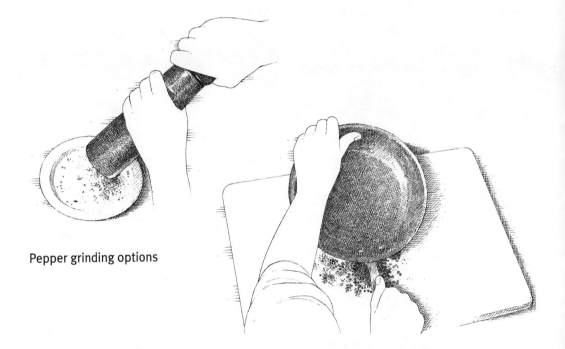

Pepper grinding options

2. **Using Spice Rubs and Pastes.** Grilled food has plenty of flavor in and of itself, but it also takes well to other flavor enhancers. Our favorite among these are spice rubs, which we use as freely as some other grilling guys use marinades. There are several reasons why we like rubs better. Rubs contain a far more concentrated dose of spices than marinades do, so the resulting flavors are more intense. And with spice rubs you don't have to plan in advance—just give the food a rub with those spices and start cooking. Rubs also tend to stick to the surface of foods better than marinades, which again gives them the edge on flavor intensity. Finally, with rubs there is no oil to drip into the fire and cause flare-ups.

Spice rubs can be used with other cooking methods, of course, but they're especially good when you're grilling, because the high heat of the fire causes them to form a deep, dark, incredibly flavorful crust on the outside of the food. Not surprisingly, given our enthusiasm for spice rubs, you'll find lots of them used throughout this book, not to mention ten mix-and-match rubs in the Flavor Spikes chapter.

You'll also find a number of spice and herb pastes, which are basically like spice rubs that include some liquid. Picture them as being about a quarter of the way along the rub-to-marinade continuum. We tend to use them when we want to impart Mediterranean flavors to our food, since olive oil is one of the basic ingredients.

Any time you're using spice rubs or pastes, it pays to use whole spices. Toast them and then grind them yourself in a mortar and pestle or an electric coffee grinder that you keep specifically for this purpose. The difference in flavor is amazing.

Grinding spices fresh

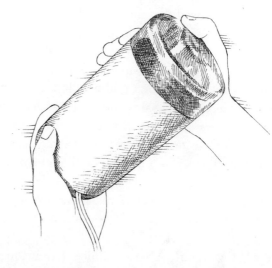

3. **Using Glazes and Barbecue Sauces.** Spice rubs and pastes add flavor to grilled food at the beginning of the cooking process; glazes and sauces add flavor at the end, either just before the food leaves the fire or after it's done cooking. Glazes are reduced, syrupy mixtures that include sugar as one of their primary components. This makes them ideal for adding a little caramelized flavor to food at the end of cooking. However, because of their sweetness, you want to be sure that you don't put them on the food too early; if you do, the sugar will burn. This is also true of barbecue sauces, which almost always contain sugar. In fact, for our money, barbecue sauces are best used as dipping sauces. That means you can apply a little to the food during the last few minutes of cooking, but basically you should just pass the sauce along with the meat.

FUELS, TOOLS, AND RULES

Now that you know the techniques of live-fire cooking, you need to know something about what fuels can be used for the fire and what tools are required for the task. Finally, there are a few rules of the live-fire world, some dos and don'ts that will make your grilling life easier and more fun. And isn't that what we're always looking for?

THE FUELS

Charcoal Briquettes. Briquettes are by far the most common live-fire fuel. In fact, they are so widely used that most people assume that when it comes to grilling you're talking briquettes if you're not talking gas. This is not a terrible thing. Those little pillow-shaped carbon composites provide a good hot fire if you use enough of them, and they have the distinct advantage of being available just about everywhere during the summer. But there is one real problem with charcoal briquettes—they're not all charcoal. Powdered charcoal is combined with binders so it can be easily shaped into those little pillows, and sometimes chemicals are added so the briquettes will light more readily. The thing to be aware of is that you are burning chemicals until the briquettes are completely lit. Concretely, this means you don't want to put any food over them until every briquette is completely covered with gray ash. When you add briquettes to boost or sustain your fire partway through cooking, you should wait until the new briquettes are completely lit to continue cooking.

Hardwood Charcoal. A better choice than briquettes is hardwood charcoal. Fortunately, this more traditional form of charcoal is increasingly available. Made by the age-old process of burning hardwood in a closed container with very little oxygen, this charcoal comes in irregularly shaped lumps, as you might expect since it is made from branches of hardwood. Because it is almost pure carbon, hardwood lump charcoal lights more quickly and is more responsive to changes in oxygen level. You can therefore regulate it more easily. It also burns cleaner and hotter than briquettes. Finally, since it contains no impurities, you can add more of it to the fire at any time and go right on cooking. (This is good, since it tends to burn faster than charcoal briquettes.) We highly recommend this as your standard grilling fuel.

Hardwood Logs. We've become increasingly fond of the original grilling fuel, hardwood logs. We like to use regular fireplace logs, although if you have a smaller grill you may need smaller pieces. As for what type to use, we recommend you go with whatever hardwood is most prevalent in your part of the country. In New England, for example, we get mostly oak or maple with the occasional bit of hickory. But any hardwood will do. You should be aware, though, that using logs can be tricky. They don't burn as evenly as charcoal, and they create a much more unpredictable bed of coals. That said, we still think that if you have the opportunity, and if you are a true griller at heart, you will always enjoy the challenge of going back to where it all began.

There are two basic approaches to constructing wood grilling fires. In the first, you simply build a log fire in your grill just as you would in your fireplace. The only drawback is that you will have to wait at least an hour, maybe more, for the fire to die down to coals suitable for cooking. The second approach is slightly less purist. First you light a small amount of charcoal, then you place three long logs or five fireplace-length logs on top of them and let them burn down to mostly coals. This will take 20 to 40 minutes less—a grand total of maybe 45 minutes—because the charcoal accelerates the process. To refuel either type of wood fire, use relatively small chunks of wood, which catch more readily and reduce to coals more quickly than logs.

Dual Fuel: The Charcoal–Hardwood Log Combo. If you don't feel up to tackling a fire composed completely of logs, we urge you to place a single log in your charcoal fire. We find that it works best to start with the log as a kind of border along the edge of the charcoal. Once your charcoal fire is completely lit, locate a small log along one edge of the coals. Then, using tongs or some other tool, shove the log about a third of the way across the bottom of the grill, bunching up the coals as it goes. This produces something near to the ideal setup for grilling: You have some smoke coming from the wood, you have a portion of the fire that keeps going much longer than charcoal, and you have a natural multi-level fire because most of the coals will be on one side of the wood. At the same time, you have the predictable, steady heat of the charcoal. Try it, and we're betting you'll start using this dual-fuel fire a lot.

A duel-fuel fire

Wood Chips and Dried Vines. We don't use wood chips or aromatic vines very often. Most of the time they're a waste of money. The grilled taste—the ineffable flavor that makes grilling such a popular cooking method—results from the direct, high heat of the flames and not from aromatics in the smoke. Chips, vine trimmings, dried herbs, and such are fine for perfuming the atmosphere in the vicinity of the grill, but they do little or nothing to affect the flavor of what you're cooking. The food simply doesn't spend enough time in contact with the smoke to really absorb it.

It does make sense, though, to use wood chips when you are hot-smoking. In that situation the food and the smoke do have enough time to intermingle. For maximum smoky flavor, wrap the chips tightly in heavy-duty foil, poke a few holes in the top of the package, and place it directly on top of the hot coals. The foil slows down the burn rate of the chips, making the smoke last longer. On page 120 you'll find a list of some types of hardwood chips that are commercially available, along with a description of their major flavor characteristics.

Wood Chunks. Wood chunks are smallish hunks of hardwood, usually about the size of a baseball. We prefer them to the smaller chips because they serve as actual fuel while producing smoke. And somehow the smoke from a burning chunk of wood is just different from the smoke you get off smoldering chips. In fact, if you happen to have hardwood trees in your own yard, branches from them are even better than chunks. When you trim the trees—cherry, apple, peach, maple, or whatever—keep the branches that are about an inch thick, cut them into sections six or eight inches long, and you've got some fantastic flavor boosters for the next time you're doing covered live-fire cooking. You don't even have to dry the wood, since the greener it is, the more smoke it produces and the smokier the food will taste.

THE TOOLS

Grilling, the original cooking method, was never fancy—some cave person just figured out that food tasted better if it spent some time over flames. Simplicity is still a big part of its appeal to us, so we don't go in for a lot of fancy grilling tools and accoutrements. A few tools, though, are worth having. Here they are.

The Grill Itself. A store-bought grill is not absolutely essential for live-fire cooking—we've made pretty tasty meals using an oven grate perched on rocks. But it sure does make the job easier.

The particular grill you select is largely determined by personal preference, your budget, and the space you have available. We encourage you to think of your grill as you would your stove: a fancy one may feature more conveniences, but it's not really going to change how you cook. That's a matter of technique, not equipment.

Of course, the gas grill is a bit of an exception to that rule. These days a lot of people are buying them, for their obvious convenience and speed. We don't have much to say about gas grills because we never use them. The fun and challenge of building a live fire and cooking over its unpredictable flames are key reasons we love grilling. But we do understand the gas grill's appeal. Our only bit of advice is that you buy the most powerful one you can afford. Your food will not taste the same as if you were using live fire, but with a high-powered grill at least you'll be able to get some char onto it.

When you're buying a charcoal grill, buy one with a cover. Without it, you can't hot-smoke or smoke-roast, and why limit your options? Because of their versatility, covered grills have largely taken over the backyard grilling scene and are available just about anywhere. Some people consider it a disadvantage that the distance between the grill grid and the fuel can't be adjusted on most covered grills. We don't find that an important drawback, since you can regulate the heat by the size of the fire you build. The single most important piece of advice we can give you about buying a grill is to get the one with the largest possible grilling surface.

A couple of years ago I (Chris) got a Weber Ranch Kettle. Working with this four-foot-diameter beauty has been a revelation. If you've got the room, I encourage you to get one; they're not cheap, but they're less expensive than most gas grills. I have recommended this grill to all my friends, and people have actually called me to tell me that it has literally changed their life. I don't know about that, but it has definitely at least changed my grilling.

I realized one important thing when I started cooking on this giant grill: It's really tough to cook a meal for six people on a standard home grill, which is just plain too small. But with this baby I can do whatever I want. I can build a small fire off to the side and cook a couple of fish fillets or a few pieces of chicken, or I can build a large fire and cook eight chickens or a leg of lamb. I can cook with logs, I can barbecue, hot-smoke, smoke-roast, or basically do any kind of cooking that involves live fire. It is the ultimate example of the fact that the larger the grill, the more flexibility you have. Not only can you decide how much you want to cook, but you can regulate your cooking by moving food around to hotter and cooler parts of the fire or even off to the side where there is no fire at all. So we strongly recommend that you buy the largest grill your space can accommodate.

On the other hand, don't think you're doomed to a grill-less existence if you have only a balcony or tiny terrace. You can make excellent grilled food on a hibachi. Just keep in mind that you'll be limited in the amount of food and size of the pieces you put on it. You won't be grilling any suckling pigs, but you can turn out some mighty tasty skewers.

If you have a working fireplace, we encourage you to consider buying a so-called Tuscan grill. This handy device consists of a grill grid mounted on iron legs that allows you to grill in your fireplace. It's fun, it keeps the grilling season going all year round, and dinner guests really love it.

Above all, remember what we said at the beginning of this section: It's not about the grill, it's about technique. If you doubt this, I (Chris) challenge you to a cook-off. You can use the grill of your choice, and I'll use an oven rack and two bricks. Unless your technique is better, you're not going to come out on top.

Heavy-Duty, Long-Handled, Spring-Loaded Tongs. Tongs are the one tool a griller can't do without. We each have a half-dozen or so, strategically placed around the kitchen and the grilling area, so that there is always one at hand. Once you start using them, you'll find them indispensable for placing food on the grill, moving it around while it's cooking, picking it up to check for doneness, and removing it from the grill, all without dropping anything or burning your arms. Make sure you get tongs that are heavy-duty so they will not bend when you lift big pieces of food; have long handles so you can work over a hot fire without burning your arms; and are spring-loaded so they are always action-ready, rather than having to be manually opened each time.

Wire Metal Brush. You can pick up one of these for about $2.76 at your local hardware store. Use it to clean the grill grid as soon as possible after you finish cooking, before any grease has congealed and while there are hot coals to take care of any food residue that falls in. You'll find this brush to be your biggest ally in the war against sticking, because food really doesn't stick to a clean, hot grill. The brushes do tend to wear out, though, so you might as well pick up a couple while you're at it.

Disposable Foil Pans. These are great for transporting raw materials to the grill and cooked food from the grill to the table. Since they are inexpensive, you can have plenty on hand and you won't be tempted to mix raw and cooked ingredients. They are also perfect for covering that thick pork chop or the piece of bluefish that's not quite done and had to be moved to the cooler side of the fire to finish cooking. And if that's not enough, they're ideal for making large hobo packs. These are virtuous pans, indeed.

Inexpensive Kitchen Towels. These towels are very handy for picking up hot dishes or skewers, and it's a lot quicker to grab a couple of towels than to fit your hand into a mitt. Just be sure they're not wet, since wet cloth is a great heat conductor. Towels are also very useful for wiping up spills and generally keeping your grill area clean.

Thermometers. We recommend that you have two types of thermometers—a small, shirt-pocket thermometer for checking the interior doneness of roasts, chickens, or anything else that's more than 2 inches thick, and an oven thermometer to put inside the grill if your grill doesn't have one and if you're going to do smoke-roasting, hot smoking, or barbecuing.

Beverage of Your Choice. Grilling is always fun, but it's even more enjoyable with your favorite beverage close at hand. Since you don't want to be running inside to get a refill, we recommend that you have an ice bucket filled with your favorite beverage right by your side. Even better, bring a big cooler out to the grill so you can serve your guests without their having to go inside either.

THE RULES

These rules are basic to good grilling and can't be overstressed, plus it's nice to have a list to refer to. So here are some grilling dos and don'ts.

GRILLING DOs

- DO concern yourself with fire safety. Grilling is fun and you want to look cool and casual, but this is live fire. It is unpredictable and can be dangerous. Always set up your grill on level ground in the largest possible open space, away from walls, wooden fences, overhanging eaves or tree branches, or anything else that might easily catch fire. Never light your fire with gasoline, and never spray lighter fluid onto lit coals. It's a good idea to have a fire extinguisher handy; we always have one around when we're grilling, although of course we put it out of sight so nobody knows. If you don't have a fire extinguisher, try to have a garden hose or bucket of sand nearby. Watch out for kids and dogs—that grill is really hot. And finally, always close down your grill, including the vents, when you're done.
- DO use plenty of charcoal. Skimping to save a few pennies just doesn't make sense, since you are spending a lot more on the food you're grilling, and having a hot enough fire is crucial to ending up with the best possible dinner.
- DO make the right type of fire. A multi-level fire is always a good idea. Not only does it make it easier to get your food to the correct doneness, it allows you to deal calmly with flare-ups.
- DO use the right technique for the right food. A bone-in half chicken should be smoke-roasted rather than grilled directly over the coals.
- DO be aggressive about adding flavor to your food. One of the great things about grilling is that it results in food with strong flavor that can stand up to other powerful ingredients. So use plenty of salt and pepper, layer on those spice rubs and pastes, be generous with the chiles, and go ahead and squirt some citrus juice over that food when it comes off the grill.
- DO start checking for doneness well before you think the food is ready. It won't hurt anything, and it may well save you from a dry, tasteless, overcooked dinner.
- DO get used to disposable foil containers. They have more uses than you think.

GRILLING DON'Ts

- DON'T cover your grill when you are cooking directly over the coals. This is the #1 mistake that we see grillers making. How many times have you seen this? A guy builds a big, hot charcoal fire, he throws a bunch of burgers or chops on the grill, and as the fat drips onto the coals the fire flames up. So what does he do? He covers the grill to douse the flames. Meanwhile, there's a tremendous amount of fat dripping down onto the coals, and that fat is being transformed into bad-tasting, acrid smoke. With the grill covered, the food is being bathed in that unpleasant smoke, so when it comes off the grill it has a definite "off" flavor. This is a technique that has been pushed on us by manufacturers who think we don't have enough skill to handle flare-ups any other way. We urge you to build a multi-level fire, keep your eye on what you are grilling, and just move it to the cool part of the grill when flare-ups threaten. Of course, when you are smoke-roasting or otherwise cooking by indirect heat on your grill, covering is required. Just leave that cover off when you're doing direct-heat grilling.

• DON'T use a water squirter to put out flare-ups, as so many books recommend; when you do, you send up a plume of ash that gets all over your food and gives it— surprise—an ashy flavor.

• DON'T marinate food in sweet sauces or marinades and then put them over direct fire. The sugar will burn and give your food an unpleasant, ashy flavor.

• DON'T dump marinades onto foods that you have put on the grill; it will cause flare-ups. Instead, pick the food out of the marinade (use those tongs), dry it off, and put it on the grill.

• DON'T cook over charcoal briquettes that are not fully lit. The chemicals in the briquettes may impart a slightly "off" flavor to your food.

• DON'T worry too much about it all. Remember, by the time the food comes to the table you've already had a lot more fun than you would have had if you were cooking your dinner any other way, so you're ahead of the game before anyone even takes a bite. Enjoy yourself.

THE ONE THING THAT ALL THE DISHES IN THIS CHAPTER have in common is that they are smaller than entrées. That's because, in the traditional way of thinking, starters are designed as something rather light to go in front of a main course. But coming first is only one of the roles they can play. They are also fully capable of standing on their own as mini-entrées, which together can make a meal. That's what both of us tend to do when we go out to eat—we order two or three "apps" and make them our dinner.

There are a couple of reasons we like to do this. First, appetizers tend to be a little more daring in conception than entrees. The development and the structure and the flavor combinations are usually a bit more interesting because there is no unwritten law, as there is with main courses, that a single larger piece of protein has to be present. So when you eat, say, three starters as your dinner, you are likely to get more gustatory entertainment. Second, eating several apps instead of one app plus one entrée simply gives you the opportunity to sample a wider range of tastes, flavors, and approaches. In other words, it's just more fun to try a bunch of dishes than to stick with only one or two. And fun in cooking and eating is what we're all about.

The dishes in this chapter can also serve another cool function—they allow you to bring a little of that wonderful grilled flavor to the table in the "off" months of winter. You don't have to grill the whole dinner. Instead, you can go outside, even on a cold, snowy day, grill up some little lamb skewers or clams or eggplant on your hibachi, then come back inside with a great smoky starter to use in front of a roast or a stew.

However you decide to use them—and whether you choose to call them starters, appetizers, palate teasers, or even "little plates"—these dishes cover a wide range of ingredients and flavor combinations. There are many that use grilled fish and shellfish, others that feature grilled chicken, vegetables, fruits, even cheeses. And there are a whole raft of recipes featuring grilled bread, something we've really gotten into and spent a lot of time working with. The bread is made from a yeast dough so there is some kneading and rising time involved, but if you make the dough earlier in the day and have it out by the grill, you'll find yourself turning to it all the time, just as we did, eventually inventing your own toppings and uses.

These starters also range pretty widely in their fanciness quotient. There are some rather upscale options, like Grilled Red Onions with Lobster, Truffle Oil, and Scallions, for example, or Curried Grilled Quail with Dried Grapes, Ginger, and Mint. When you make one of those you may want it to be the focus of the meal, following it with pasta or a plain grilled meat or fish. Then there are others, like Grilled Clams on the Half Shell with Tabasco, Lemon, and Garlic, or Grilled Figs with Blue Cheese, that are quite simple and work well as the prelude to something more complex. Many of these dishes can also slide up or down the scale depending on your mood and your cooking time frame. Crispy Prosciutto-Wrapped Asparagus with Saffron-Crab Mayonnaise, for instance, is still going to be great if you drop the mayo. We figure that we'll give you the works and you can pare down if you want.

Lots of the recipes in this chapter also work very nicely as cocktail snacks, something that will come as no surprise to anyone who has been to either of our houses for dinner. Grilled Chile Chicken Wings with Peanut-Ginger Sauce and Cucumber Spears, Ihsan's Grilled Cheese in Grape Leaves, Grilled Peel-and-Eat Colossal Shrimp with Garlic-Tabasco Butter, EZ Grill Bread with Personality and flavored oils for dipping—put them out there, serve the drinks, and you'll have a party going on.

So you could think of the recipes in this chapter as all-purpose utility players, but without any of the dullness that title implies. They fill many roles, but each is designed to make any meal, cocktail party, or just-hanging-around time interesting as well as tasty.

VEGETABLES (AND ONE FRUIT)

silky turkish eggplant dip

SERVES 4 TO 6 AS A DIP

Cooking eggplant on the grill is particularly fun because it's one time when you can feel free to burn your food to cinder. Only when the skin is completely black and charred will the interior have the proper near-mushy consistency that you're looking for. When we went to Istanbul with our friends Ihsan and Valerie Gurdal, we spent a lot of time sampling eggplant mixtures. After we came back, I (Doc) made dozens of different versions to see which people liked best. This is the winner—simple enough to allow the deep, smoky taste of the eggplant to shine but complex enough to avoid being boring. It keeps well, and is just as excellent on sandwiches as it is as a dip.

2 medium eggplants
1 tablespoon minced garlic
Juice of 1 lemon
1/2 cup plain yogurt (whole milk
    if possible)

1/3 cup olive oil
Kosher salt and freshly cracked black
    pepper to taste

1. Build a multi-level fire in your grill: Leaving one-quarter of the bottom free of coals, bank the coals in the remaining three-quarters of the grill so that they are three times as high on one side as on the other. When the coals are all ignited and the temperature has died down to medium (you can hold your hand about 5 inches above the grill grid, over the area where the coals are deepest, for 4 to 5 seconds), you're ready to cook.

2. Prick the eggplants all over, in 6 places or so on each one, with a fork (to let the steam out as they cook), then put them on the grill directly over the coals. Cook, rolling them around every once in a while so all sides get exposed to the heat, until the skins are charred black and the eggplants are very soft, about 20 minutes. They will look like little black balloons that have lost about half of their air.

3. Remove the eggplants from the grill and, as soon as they are cool enough to handle, peel away the blackened skin, being careful to get as much as possible of it off, since it's quite bitter. Place the flesh into a food processor, add the garlic, lemon juice, yogurt, and olive oil, and process until smooth. Season with salt and pepper to taste.

COOK TO COOK: Once the eggplants have reached the proper blackened, burned-on-the-outside state, they're pretty floppy. To remove an eggplant from the grill without breaking it, get a good grip on one end with your tongs and slide a spatula under the other end.

grilled fresh mozzarella and bread skewers with tomatoes, red onion, and pesto vinaigrette

SERVES 4 AS AN APPETIZER

These are neat little Italian-inspired appetizers. We throw them on the grill to soften the cheese and firm up the bread (an interesting dichotomy, and we are big fans of dichotomies), then take them off the skewers and toss them with a pesto vinaigrette. In fact, this dish could be described as bread salad on a stick, so if you want, you can toss some arugula in the pesto vinaigrette and slide the grilled food from the skewers onto it.

1 pound fresh mozzarella cheese, cut into 1-inch chunks
16 1-inch cubes of crusty bread
1 red onion, peeled and cut into 1-inch cubes
16 cherry tomatoes
1/4 cup olive oil
1 tablespoon minced garlic
Kosher salt and freshly cracked black pepper to taste

for the vinaigrette:
1 cup fresh basil leaves
1/4 cup pine nuts, roasted in a 350°F oven until light brown, about 5 minutes
1 tablespoon minced garlic
1/2 cup extra-virgin olive oil
1/4 cup grated Parmesan cheese
2 tablespoons balsamic vinegar
Kosher salt and freshly cracked black pepper to taste

1. Build a multi-level fire in your grill: Leaving one-quarter of the bottom free of coals, bank the coals in the remaining three-quarters of the grill so that they are three times as high on one side as on the other. When the coals are all ignited and the temperature has died down to medium (you can hold your hand about 5 inches above the grill grid, over the area where the coals are deepest, for 4 to 5 seconds), you're ready to cook.

2. Thread the mozzarella cubes, bread cubes, onion sections, and cherry tomatoes onto 4 skewers, alternating as you go. In a small bowl, combine the olive oil and garlic and mix well. Brush this mixture onto the skewers, using just enough to coat the skewers lightly with oil. Sprinkle generously with salt and pepper.

3. Using a mortar and pestle or food processor, mush the dressing ingredients together until they form a nearly smooth paste, then transfer it to a large bowl. For a more rustic dressing, you can just toss the dressing ingredients together in a large bowl.

4. Grill the skewers, turning once, until the bread is toasty, the cheese has started to soften, and the vegetables are tender and nicely seared, about 2 to 3 minutes per side.

Gently push the onions, tomatoes, and cheese off the skewers into the bowl with the dressing, then toss gently to coat.

5. Divide the salad among 4 plates and serve.

COOK TO COOK: To get the proper final texture for this dish, you want the bread to be nicely toasted. So make sure your fire is medium rather than hot before you put the skewers over the flames. That way, the bread will toast rather than burn on the outside.

lightly grilled hearts of romaine with figs, blue cheese, and honey-mustard dressing

SERVES 4

⚶ ⚶ ⚶ ⚶ ⚶ ⚶ ⚶ ⚶ ⚶ ⚶ ⚶ ⚶ ⚶ ⚶ ⚶ ⚶ ⚶

What we like about this dish is that romaine hearts are very crispy, which means they can take a little smoky sear on the grill and still retain a nice crunch. After grilling them lightly along with some fresh figs, we add some blue cheese and a honey-mustard dressing, ending up with a dish that is at once succulent and refreshing. If it seems odd to you to be grilling hearts of lettuce, think of them as a vegetable rather than a salad ingredient. And if you can't find hearts of romaine in the supermarket, buy whole heads of romaine and reserve the outer leaves for a Caesar salad.

for the dressing:	4 romaine lettuce hearts
2 tablespoons grainy mustard	4 fresh ripe figs of your choice,
1 tablespoon honey	halved lengthwise
1/4 cup balsamic vinegar	3 tablespoons olive oil
1/2 cup extra-virgin olive oil	Kosher salt and freshly cracked black
Kosher salt and freshly cracked black	pepper to taste
pepper to taste	8 ounces blue cheese of your choice

1. Build a multi-level fire in your grill: Leaving one-quarter of the bottom free of coals, bank the coals in the remaining three-quarters of the grill so that they are three times as high on one side as on the other. When the coals are all ignited and the temperature has died down to medium (you can hold your hand about 5 inches above the grill grid, over the area where the coals are deepest, for 4 to 5 seconds), you're ready to cook.

2. In a medium bowl, whisk together the mustard, honey, and vinegar until smooth. Add the olive oil gradually, whisking constantly, until the mixture is smooth and even, then season to taste with salt and pepper and set aside.

3. Rub the romaine hearts and the figs all over with the olive oil and sprinkle generously with salt and pepper. Place them on the grill with the figs cut side down. Cook the figs until they are golden brown, about 2 to 3 minutes, then remove from the grill; cook the romaine until it also is golden brown, about 2 to 3 minutes per side, then remove from the grill.

4. Cut the romaine heads in half lengthwise and place each half on an individual salad plate. Arrange the figs, cut side up, next to the romaine. Crumble the blue cheese and scatter it over the romaine and figs, then drizzle with dressing. Serve with crusty bread and additional freshly ground black pepper.

COOK TO COOK: To make sure your blue cheese crumbles rather than mushes, put it in the freezer about 5 minutes before you put the romaine and figs on the fire.

grilled figs with blue cheese

SERVES 8 AS AN APPETIZER

You can't go wrong with figs on the grill. Here you halve the figs, then grill them cut side down until they are just nicely browned; when you take them off the grill and bite into them, it's almost like eating warm jam. To finish off the dish, we top the figs with a little blue cheese, which has a musky sharpness that provides the perfect foil for the sweetness of the figs. We like Maytag or Hubbard blue cheese here because they have sharp, deep flavors and they are American-born, but you can use whatever type you like. For another taste approach, leave out the blue cheese and sprinkle the figs with a little grated Parmigiano Reggiano right after you remove them from the grill.

8 fresh ripe figs of your choice, halved lengthwise
3 tablespoons olive oil
Kosher salt and freshly cracked black pepper to taste

6 ounces blue cheese of your choice, crumbled (about 3/4 cup)

1. Build a multi-level fire in your grill: Leaving one-quarter of the bottom free of coals, bank the coals in the remaining three-quarters of the grill so that they are three times as high on one side as on the other. When the coals are all ignited and the temperature has died down to medium (you can hold your hand about 5 inches above the grill grid, over the area where the coals are deepest, for 4 to 5 seconds), you're ready to cook.

2. In a medium bowl, toss the figs with the olive oil and sprinkle with salt and pepper to taste. Place on the grill, cut side down, and cook until just nicely browned, about 2 to 3 minutes.

3. Arrange the figs cut side up on a serving dish, sprinkle with the cheese, and serve warm or at room temperature.

COOK TO COOK: Figs are wonderful on the grill, but they are also delicate, particularly when very ripe. Be sure you cook them cut side down so the heat penetrates them quickly. To get them off the grill, pick them up gently with your tongs.

ihsan's grilled cheese in grape leaves

SERVES 6 AS AN APPETIZER

This is a great appetizer for spring, when fresh wild grape leaves appear. Wild grapes grow everywhere around my (Chris's) house in Westport, Massachusetts, so my wife Marcy and I like to pick the leaves, pickle them, and keep them around all summer. When our friends the Gurdals come visit they usually bring wonderful cheeses, and I love to wrap different ones up in the leaves and toss them on the grill to give them a slight smoky flavor.

Make sure your fire is of medium temperature so that the cheese melts rather than liquefying and running out of the leaves. (Don't worry about trying to fasten the grape leaves around the cheese; the packets will stick together on their own pretty well.)

A wide variety of cheeses will work in this dish. Some that we have used to good effect are buttons of Coach Farm goat cheese from New York; Grafton Village Cheddar from Vermont; cave-ripened Gruyère from Formaggio Kitchen in Cambridge, Massachusetts; and (Doc's favorite) Erhaki, a sheep's milk cheese from the Pyrenees. We like to serve these cheeses with crackers or grilled toast and some cornichons or other briny pickles.

20 pickled grape leaves, homemade
    or store-bought
20 pieces of cheese, each about the
    size and thickness of a match-
    book, and weighing about
    2 ounces

EZ Grill Bread (page 77)
    or crackers

1. Build a multi-level fire in your grill: Leaving one-quarter of the bottom free of coals, bank the coals in the remaining three-quarters of the grill so that they are three times as high on one side as on the other. When the coals are all ignited and the temperature has died down to medium (you can hold your hand about 5 inches above the grill grid, over the area where the coals are deepest, for 4 to 5 seconds), you're ready to cook.

2. Rinse the grape leaves well to remove the salt, but do not dry them after rinsing; the wetness helps them adhere to the cheese.

3. Lay one grape leaf on the work surface and place a piece of cheese in the center. Fold the leaf up to enclose the cheese completely. Repeat with remaining leaves and cheese.

4. Grill the cheese packets 3 to 4 minutes per side, until they feel soft to the touch. Carefully transfer them to a serving plate and unwrap them. (Don't eat the grape leaves—they are just for flavoring.) Pass crackers or grilled bread on the side.

COOK TO COOK: Don't cut the cheese too thick here—if you do, it won't melt completely.

chopped grilled vegetables with tomato, olives, hard-cooked eggs, and oil-soaked parmigiano reggiano

SERVES 6

A nice summer antipasto, this dish is a collection of both fresh and cooked vegetables topped with one of our new favorite treats, small chunks of Parmesan soaked in olive oil. We like it because the olive oil picks up some of the Parmesan's sharp flavor, while it imparts its own smoothness and unctuousness to the cheese. To get the full effect, buy the real thing, authentic Parmigiano Reggiano.

For the vegetables, we use a straight-up grilling technique; the key is to cut them into inch-thick lengthwise slices (we call them "planks") so they will get browned on the outside prior to getting cooked to mush on the inside. Then when they're grilled we chop them up and mix them with some peppery arugula, juicy tomatoes, briny olives, and rich hard-cooked eggs, and we top it all off with that delicious oil-soaked cheese.

If you have any of this left over, pile it into a pita and sprinkle it with a little balsamic vinegar for a great grilled-vegetable sandwich.

1 pound Parmesan cheese
   (Parmigiano Reggiano if you can
   get it), cut into 1-inch cubes
1/2 cup extra-virgin olive oil
1 small eggplant, unpeeled, cut
   lengthwise into planks 1 inch
   thick
1 medium zucchini, unpeeled, cut
   lengthwise into planks 1 inch
   thick
1 medium summer squash, unpeeled,
   cut lengthwise into planks 1 inch
   thick
1 red onion, peeled and cut into rings
   about 1 inch thick

1/4 cup olive oil
Kosher salt and freshly cracked black
   pepper to taste
1 bunch arugula, washed, dried, and
   cut into long, thin strips
2 ripe tomatoes, about the size of
   baseballs, cored and cut into
   wedges
4 hard-cooked eggs, quartered
1/2 cup pitted brine-cured black
   olives such as Kalamata or Gaeta
1/4 cup balsamic vinegar

1. Place the cheese cubes in a dish just large enough to hold them all in a single layer (one of those square glass casserole dishes works well), drizzle on the extra-virgin olive oil, and stir to coat all the cubes well. Cover and refrigerate for 2 to 5 days, stirring several times a day if you remember.

2. Build a multi-level fire in your grill: Leaving one-quarter of the bottom free of coals, bank the coals in the remaining three-quarters of the grill so that they are three times as high on one side as on the other. When the coals are all ignited and the temperature has died down to medium (you can hold your hand about 5 inches above the grill grid, over the area where the coals are deepest, for 4 to 5 seconds), you're ready to cook.

3. Coat the planks of eggplant, zucchini, and squash and the onion rings all over with the olive oil, sprinkle them generously with salt and pepper, then put them on the grill and cook until they are golden brown and slightly charred, about 4 to 5 minutes per side for the eggplant and onion rings, 6 to 10 minutes for the zucchini and summer squash. Cool to room temperature, then dice medium.

4. To serve, divide the diced vegetables among 6 plates and top with the arugula. Arrange the tomatoes, eggs, and olives on top, and scatter some of the soaked cheese over each. Drizzle with balsamic vinegar and the oil left in the cheese dish, and season with salt and pepper.

COOK TO COOK: There are two common mistakes people make when grilling vegetables— the first is not cooking them enough, so they are too crunchy; the second is cooking them too much, so they are mushy. To avoid these, cut the planks or rings relatively thick, get a nice char on them, and then get them off the fire so they keep a bit of texture inside.

grilled pumpernickel bread salad
with feta, tomatoes, and green olives

SERVES 4

Feta and green olives are a wonderful combination. In this Greek-inspired salad we combine them with big cubes of toasted pumpernickel bread, which has the character to stand up to the strong tastes of the cheese and the olives. You want to leave the bread on the grill just long enough for it to get good and crunchy on the outside while staying soft on the inside for a nice contrast in texture.

1/2 cup olive oil
1/4 cup red wine vinegar
1 teaspoon minced garlic
1/4 cup roughly chopped fresh oregano (or substitute fresh basil)
Kosher salt and freshly cracked black pepper to taste
4 slices of pumpernickel bread (1 inch thick) crusts removed

1 ripe tomato about the size of a baseball, cored and diced large
1 cucumber, diced medium
1/2 red onion, peeled and diced small
1/2 cup pitted green olives such as cracked Moroccan, Manzanilla, or Sevillano
8 ounces feta cheese, diced large

1. Build a multi-level fire in your grill: Leaving one-quarter of the bottom free of coals, bank the coals in the remaining three-quarters of the grill so that they are three times as high on one side as on the other. When the coals are all ignited and the temperature has died down to medium (you can hold your hand about 5 inches above the grill grid, over the area where the coals are deepest, for 4 to 5 seconds), you're ready to cook.

2. In a small bowl, whisk together the oil, vinegar, garlic, oregano, and salt and pepper to taste. Set aside.

3. Put the bread slices over the fire and grill until browned and crisp, about 2 to 3 minutes per side. Remove from the heat, cut into large cubes, and put the cubes into a large bowl. Add the tomato, cucumber, onion, olives, and feta, and pour on enough of the dressing to just coat the ingredients. (If you overdress, you're going to end up with soggy bread.) Toss gently, then season to taste with salt and pepper and serve.

COOK TO COOK: Making a good piece of toast on the grill is actually not that easy. You want it to get really toasted—not just grill-marked—but to stay tender on the inside. So cut the pumpernickel thick and make sure the fire is medium, not hot.

grilled eggplant, mozzarella, and tomato towers with basil-corn relish

SERVES 4 AS AN APPETIZER

A combination of Mediterranean flavors, this dish is another in our vast grilled eggplant repertoire. Instead of cooking the eggplant very thoroughly, as you do for Silky Turkish Eggplant Dip (page 29), here you cut it into thick slices that you grill just until they're brown on the outside and still have some density on the inside. Then you make a little tower by alternating the grilled eggplant slices with slices of mozzarella and tomato, and you top the tower with a simple corn-basil-olive oil mixture to provide extra flavor. Depending on your fondness for stacked food, you can make the tower as high as you like.

1 small eggplant, sliced into
    circles 1 inch thick
1/4 cup olive oil
Kosher salt and freshly cracked black
    pepper to taste
4 tomatoes about the size of
    baseballs, each sliced into
    2 or 3 circles about 1 inch thick
About 8 ounces fresh mozzarella
    cheese, sliced into 1-inch-thick
    pieces

For the relish:
2 ears corn, blanched in boiling
    salted water for 2 minutes,
    drained, and kernels cut off the
    cob (about 1 cup of kernels)
1/3 cup extra-virgin olive oil
1/4 cup balsamic vinegar
1/2 cup julienned fresh basil
Kosher salt and freshly cracked black
    pepper to taste

1. Build a multi-level fire in your grill: Leaving one-quarter of the bottom free of coals, bank the coals in the remaining three-quarters of the grill so that they are three times as high on one side as on the other. When the coals are all ignited and the temperature is medium-hot (you can hold your hand 5 inches above the grill grid, over the area where the coals are deepest, for 3 to 4 seconds), you're ready to cook.

2. Rub the eggplant circles on both sides with the olive oil, sprinkle them generously with salt and pepper, and place them on the grill. Cook until golden brown and slightly charred, about 3 to 4 minutes per side.

3. While the eggplant is on the grill, combine the relish ingredients and mix well.

4. Place an eggplant slice on each plate. Top with a tomato slice, then some cheese, and then another slice of eggplant, repeating the layers as many times as you like. Spoon the relish over the towers and serve immediately.

COOK TO COOK: When you're going to grill vegetables, leave the peel on so they retain their shape. This also helps maintain their textural integrity—in other words, they don't get mushy.

prosciutto-wrapped grilled peaches with a balsamic drizzle

SERVES 8 AS AN APPETIZER

My (Chris's) friend Bob Kinkead, chef/owner of Kinkead's in Washington, D.C., claims that I put prosciutto and peaches together in every possible way, and that it is in fact the only creative food combination I have ever come up with. He may be right, so I dedicate this recipe to him.

This is a simple but tasty appetizer, the perfect thing to serve your guests with glasses of white wine while you cook the rest of the meal. To make it, you wrap prosciutto around peach wedges and grill them up briefly; you don't need to really cook anything here, you're just looking to get a little flavorful browning going on. Then you drizzle on a little reduced balsamic vinegar to finish the dish. Balsamic gets its flavor from being aged in barrels of different woods, which makes it a very appropriate enhancer of grilled food. Some folks have gone so far as to call it the catsup of grilled food.

You can substitute many different fruits in this recipe. We like pineapples, pears, or apricots.

- 1 cup inexpensive balsamic vinegar
- 1 teaspoon sugar
- 1 tablespoon freshly cracked black pepper
- 4 ripe but firm peaches, halved, pitted, and each half cut into 3 wedges

- 12 slices prosciutto, cut in half lengthwise
- 3 tablespoons olive oil
- Kosher salt and freshly cracked black pepper to taste

1. Build a multi-level fire in your grill: Leaving one-quarter of the bottom free of coals, bank the coals in the remaining three-quarters of the grill so that they are three times as high on one side as on the other. When the coals are all ignited and the temperature has died down to medium (you can hold your hand about 5 inches above the grill grid, over the area where the coals are deepest, for 4 to 5 seconds), you're ready to cook.

2. In a small saucepan over medium-high heat, bring the vinegar and sugar to a boil and cook at a steady boil until the mixture is reduced by half, 20 to 25 minutes. (It will be tacky but not quite syrupy.) Stir in the pepper, remove from the heat, and set aside.

3. Meanwhile, wrap each peach wedge with a piece of prosciutto, securing it with a toothpick. Brush with the olive oil and sprinkle lightly with salt and pepper. Put the peaches on the grill and cook until the prosciutto is lightly seared and the peaches are hot and slightly softened, about 2 to 3 minutes per side.

4. Remove the toothpicks, transfer the prosciutto-wrapped peaches to a serving dish, drizzle with the balsamic reduction, and serve immediately.

COOK TO COOK: When grilling fruit, you are not looking to cook the fruit completely—after all, fruits are delicious eaten raw—but just giving it a nice flavorful sear on the outside. So use a medium fire and leave the fruit over the flames for only 2 to 3 minutes.

balsamic reductions, or making the cheap stuff taste like the good stuff

* * *

We are big fans of balsamic reductions. Reducing not only thickens the flavorful vinegar to a rich, mahogany-colored glaze that easily coats fish, meat, fruit, or whatever, it also intensifies its signature sweet-and-sour nature. It's a great way to boost flavor quickly and easily.

Fortunately, making a balsamic reduction is incredibly simple. All you do is bring a relatively large quantity of vinegar—say, a cup—to a boil, then reduce the heat and let it simmer vigorously until it has boiled down by about two-thirds and is thick and syrupy enough to coat the back of a spoon. This might sound costly or even wasteful, but it really isn't, because you're not using the good stuff here. Reduction makes lower-priced vinegars taste more interesting and complex, but it destroys the delicate, mellow flavors of true Aceto Balsamico Tradizionale. That means you want the cheap version for this—something off the supermarket shelf, not that tiny corked bottle from Italy.

There's a quick and easy way to keep track of how much the vinegar has been reduced, which is helpful if you're slightly absent-minded when you cook as we are. When you put the vinegar on the stove, place a chopstick or wooden spoon into it vertically, then use a pencil to lightly mark the point the vinegar comes up to. To check the amount of reduction, put the chopstick or spoon back into the vinegar and you'll be able to compare the current level with the original mark. Pretty easy, eh?

So unscrew a bottle of the cheap stuff, cook it down, and brush it on meat, vegetables, or even fruit right before it comes off the grill. Just be sure that you don't brush it on too early, or the sugar in it will burn.

curried grilled quail with dried grapes, ginger, and mint

SERVES 6 AS AN APPETIZER

We love these grilled game birds because you get to tear them apart, eat the meat with your fingers, and then gnaw on the bones, which reminds us of those wild medieval banquets you see in the movies.

Because the birds are so small, you can use a straightforward over-the-coals grilling technique. But it's still a good idea to build a multi-level fire in case a bird starts to get too dark on the outside and needs to move to a lower fire to finish cooking. Drying the grapes is interesting and easy, but if you forget to do it or don't want to take the time, you can just substitute fresh grapes, which will work fine.

Served with some crusty bread to soak up the juices, this dish works particularly well combined with several other starters for a kind of pupu platter situation.

1 cup red or green seedless grapes
3 tablespoons Sherwood or other
    good-quality curry powder
1 tablespoon freshly cracked white
    pepper (or substitute black
    pepper)
1 tablespoon kosher salt
6 quail, either semi-boneless or
    butterflied with the backbone
    removed

4 tablespoons olive oil, divided
1 red onion, peeled and diced small
2 tablespoons peeled and minced
    fresh ginger
1 cup orange juice
1/3 cup red wine vinegar
1/3 cup roughly chopped fresh mint
Kosher salt and freshly cracked white
    pepper to taste (or substitute
    black pepper)

1. Put the grapes on a rack set on top of a baking pan on the middle shelf of a 200°F oven and let them dry there until they resemble plumped raisins, about 4 to 6 hours. Remove from the oven and set aside. (Grapes can be dried up to 4 days ahead, then covered and refrigerated.)

2. Build a multi-level fire in your grill: Leaving one-quarter of the bottom free of coals, bank the coals in the remaining three-quarters of the grill so that they are three times as high on one side as on the other. When the coals are all ignited and the temperature has died down to medium-hot (you can hold your hand about 5 inches above the grill grid, over the area where the coals are deepest, for 3 to 4 seconds), you're ready to cook.

3. In a small bowl, stir together the curry powder, white pepper, and salt. Coat the butterflied quail with 2 tablespoons of the oil, then rub it all over with the curry mixture.

4. In a large sauté pan or skillet over medium-high heat, heat the remaining 2 table-spoons of oil until hot but not smoking. Add the onions and sauté, stirring occasionally, until golden brown, 11 to 13 minutes. Add the ginger and cook, stirring frequently, for 1 minute. Add the orange juice and vinegar, stir a couple of times, then simmer until reduced by half, about 15 to 20 minutes. The mixture should be thick and slightly syrupy. Remove from the heat, stir in the dried grapes and the chopped mint, and season to taste with salt and pepper, then cover to keep warm while you grill the quail.

5. Put the quail on the grill and cook until just cooked through, about 4 to 6 minutes per side. To check for doneness, first poke with your finger to test firmness level (see page 13). Then, to be sure, nick, peek, and cheat: Cut into the thickest part of one of the thighs and peek to see that there is no more than a hint of pink near the bone; check the breast too, which can have a hint of pink throughout. When the birds are done, remove from the heat and serve hot, accompanying each bird with a generous spoon-ful of the sauce.

COOK TO COOK: Unlike chicken, quail breast is fine medium-rare. But the legs and thighs need to be cooked to medium or medium-well. To accomplish this, place the birds with the leg/thigh area over the hottest part of the grill and the breast over a slightly cooler portion. Then be sure to check *both* breast and thigh areas for doneness.

grilled chile chicken wings
with peanut-ginger sauce and cucumber spears

SERVES 4 TO 6 AS AN APPETIZER

❧ ❧ ❧ ❧ ❧ ❧ ❧ ❧ ❧ ❧ ❧ ❧ ❧ ❧ ❧ ❧ ❧ ❧

I (Chris) really like cooking chicken wings because at my dinners I like to have at least one course that requires eating with your hands. I'm also kind of nutty about coriander seed, which I see as a great near-universal spice that exemplifies the idea that "spicy" food can be exotic and way flavorful without being hot. So here we coat the wings with coriander to get that perfumey taste, grill them, toss them with a combination of Southeast Asian flavorings, and serve them up with a peanut-ginger dipping sauce and some cucumber spears to cool them off. I guess you could call them Southeast Asian Buffalo Wings. Under any name they provide a very flavorful and dynamic beginning for a party.

For the dipping sauce:
1/3 cup roasted unsalted peanuts,
    roughly chopped
1/3 cup molasses
1/3 cup soy sauce
1/3 cup water
1/4 cup peeled and minced
    fresh ginger

3 pounds medium-size chicken wings
Kosher salt and freshly cracked white
    pepper to taste (or substitute
    black pepper)
1/4 cup freshly cracked coriander
    seeds, toasted in a dry sauté pan
    or skillet over medium heat,
    shaking, until fragrant, about 2
    minutes (or substitute 2 table-
    spoons ground coriander)

1/4 cup prepared Asian chile-garlic
    paste (available in Asian markets
    or large supermarkets)
1/4 cup *nam pla*, Southeast Asian fish
    sauce (or substitute soy sauce)
1/3 cup fresh lime juice (about
    3 limes)
1/4 cup roughly chopped fresh
    cilantro
1/4 cup roughly chopped fresh basil
1/4 cup roughly chopped fresh mint
4 cucumbers, peeled and cut
    lengthwise into spears

1. Build a multi-level fire in your grill: Leaving one-quarter of the bottom free of coals, bank the coals in the remaining three-quarters of the grill so that they are three times as high on one side as on the other. When the coals are all ignited and the temperature has died down to medium (you can hold your hand about 5 inches above the grill grid, over the area where the coals are deepest, for 4 to 5 seconds), you're ready to cook.

2. In a small bowl, combine all the ingredients for the dipping sauce and whisk together well. If the mixture is too thick to pour easily, whisk in a tablespoon or so of water. Cover and set aside.

3. Cut each wing into its 3 sections. Discard the wing tips or save them for stock.

4. Rub the wing pieces with the coriander and sprinkle generously with salt and pepper. Place on the grill and cook, turning occasionally, until they are golden brown, about 5 to 7 minutes. (To check for doneness, nick, peek, and cheat: Cut into one of the wings and peek to be sure there is no redness near the bone.)

5. While the wings are cooking, make the sauce: Combine the chile-garlic paste, fish sauce, lime juice, and herbs in a large bowl and give the mixture a few stirs. When the wings are cooked through, add them to the bowl, tossing them to coat with the mixture.

6. Serve the wings on a big platter with the peanut sauce for dipping and the cucumber spears as a coolant.

COOK TO COOK: You have a lot of wing sections on the grill here, so don't let them get away from you. Make sure you have your long-handled tongs right there and are ready to juggle the wings between hotter and cooler parts of the fire so you don't burn any of them before they're cooked through. You've got a challenging 10 minutes of action here.

real-deal barbecued drumsticks
with sweet-and-sour squash pickles

SERVES 8 AS AN APPETIZER

Chicken drumsticks are often relegated to the kids' table. That's a shame, because they're fun to cook and you can do some pretty tasty, sophisticated things with them. They are meatier than wings, and their dark meat is far more flavorful than the white meat of breasts. In any case, when I (Chris) think of barbecued chicken, I think of drumsticks because that's what my mom used to make for me when I was a kid.

So here we are using the real-deal Southern barbecue technique, indirect covered cooking at very low heat, between 180° and 220°F. What you want to do is cook the chicken past doneness to the point of extreme tenderness, just as you do when you're barbecuing beef brisket or pork ribs. To continue the Southern approach, we serve the drumsticks with summer pickles and pass the sauce on the side in the traditional barbecue manner.

We recommend that you make a lot of these little guys, maybe even double the recipe, because having leftover barbecued drumsticks in the refrigerator is a very good thing.

1/4 cup ground paprika	16 small to medium chicken
2 tablespoons packed light or dark	drumsticks
brown sugar	1 cup catsup
2 tablespoons ground cumin	1/2 cup cider vinegar
2 tablespoons dry mustard	1/3 cup molasses
1 tablespoon powdered ginger	10 dashes Worcestershire sauce
1/4 cup freshly cracked black pepper	(or substitute 1/4 cup
2 tablespoons kosher salt	A1 Sauce)

1. Build a fire well over to one side of a large kettle grill, using about enough coals to fill half of a shoebox. When the coals are all ignited and the temperature has died down to medium (you can hold your hand about 5 inches above the grill grid, over the coals, for 4 to 5 seconds), you're ready to cook.

2. In a small bowl, combine the paprika, brown sugar, cumin, mustard, ginger, pepper, and salt and mix well. Rub the drumsticks all over with this spice rub.

3. Place the drumsticks on the side of the grill away from the coals, being careful that none of them are directly over the coals. Put the lid on the grill with the vents one-quarter of the way open, and cook for 40 minutes.

4. While the chicken is cooking, combine the catsup, vinegar, molasses, and Worcestershire sauce in a small bowl. After 40 minutes of cooking, brush some of the sauce on

the drumsticks and give them a turn. Sauce the other side, close the lid, and cook until the chicken is very tender, at least another 10 minutes. (To check for doneness, stick a fork into one of the drumsticks. The drumstick should fall off when you try to lift it.)

5. Serve the drumsticks accompanied by the pickles on the next page.

sweet-and-sour squash pickles

YIELD: ABOUT 2 QUARTS

1 1/2 pounds each zucchini and
    summer squash, unpeeled, ends
    trimmed, cut into very thin
    rounds
2 medium red onions, peeled and cut
    into thin slices
3 fresh chile peppers of your choice,
    cut into thin rounds
1/4 cup kosher or other coarse salt
1/2 cup golden raisins
2 3/4 cups white vinegar
3/4 up dry sherry
1 1/2 cups orange juice

2 cups sugar
1 1/2 tablespoons Sherwood or other
    good-quality curry powder
1 1/2 teaspoons cayenne pepper
1 teaspoon whole cloves
3 garlic cloves, peeled and cut into
    slivers
A piece of fresh ginger the size of
    your thumb, peeled and cut into
    thin coins

1. In a large glass or stainless steel bowl, combine the squash, onions, chiles, and salt, and let the mixture stand for 1 hour. Drain and rinse twice to remove the salt, then add the raisins and set aside.

2. In a medium-size nonreactive saucepan, bring all the remaining ingredients except the ginger to a boil over high heat. Reduce the heat to low and simmer for 3 minutes, stirring once or twice to dissolve the sugar.

3. Pour the hot liquid over the squash mixture; the squash should be amply covered or slightly afloat. Allow to cool to room temperature, then cover and refrigerate. These pickles develop great flavor within a couple of hours and will keep well, covered and refrigerated, for 3 to 4 weeks.

COOK TO COOK: Remember when you cook the chicken that you're barbecuing, not grilling, so be sure there is no chicken directly over the coals. Remember, too, that you are cooking the drumsticks beyond ordinary doneness, until they're very tender.

prosciutto-stuffed grilled chicken tenderloins with fresh figs and pesto butter

SERVES 4 AS AN APPETIZER

Chicken tenderloins are one of those items that people are puzzled by—they don't quite know what to do with them. We know many folks who trim them off chicken breasts when fashioning cutlets, freeze them for later use in stock, and then forget all about them until they've been in the freezer so long they have to be thrown out.

So here's a cool way to use them. For this Mediterranean-style dish we pound the tenderloins to flatten them out a bit, then lay prosciutto inside, roll them up, and put them on skewers with fresh figs. If you've never had grilled figs or prosciutto with a little smoke on it, the taste will be a revelation.

I (Chris) cooked this dish a lot last summer because my wife Marcy became an expert on pesto and we used it in tons of ways. If you don't want to make the pesto butter, substitute a little blue cheese instead.

8 chicken tenderloins, tendons
    removed, about 2 ounces each
8 very thin slices prosciutto
Kosher salt and freshly cracked black
    pepper to taste
4 large fresh figs, halved lengthwise

For the pesto butter:
4 tablespoons unsalted butter,
    softened
1/2 teaspoon minced garlic
3 tablespoons roughly chopped
    fresh basil
2 tablespoons pine nuts, toasted
    and roughly chopped

1. Build a multi-level fire in your grill: Leaving one-quarter of the bottom free of coals, bank the coals in the remaining three-quarters so that they are about three times as high on one side as on the other. When the coals are all ignited and the temperature has died down to medium (you can hold your hand about 5 inches above the grill grid, over the area where the coals are deepest, for 4 to 5 seconds), you're ready to cook.

2. Put the chicken tenderloins between two sheets of plastic wrap or wax paper and pound them until they are roughly twice their original size. Lay one slice of prosciutto on your work surface, place a flattened tenderloin on top of it, and roll them up together from one of the short ends to form a kind of cigar shape. Repeat with the remaining prosciutto and tenderloins, then thread them crosswise onto 4 skewers, alternating them with the fig halves. Sprinkle the skewers generously with salt and pepper.

3. In a small bowl, combine all the ingredients for the pesto butter and mash with a fork until the mixture is evenly mixed and spreadably soft.

4. Put the skewers on the grill and cook until the chicken is just opaque all the way through, 4 to 6 minutes per side. (To check for doneness, nick, peek, and cheat: Cut

into one of the chicken rolls and make sure that the chicken is opaque throughout.) As soon as the skewers are done, brush them generously with the pesto butter and serve immediately.

COOK TO COOK: Take your time pounding the tenderloins, since they rip easily. Once the chicken is on the grill, check it frequently for doneness; the most common mistake people make with low-fat ingredients like these tenderloins is to overcook them, which dries them out.

new-school grilled buffalo wings
with blue cheese dressing and cucumber spears

SERVES 6 AS AN APPETIZER

Food that makes people eat with their hands provides a welcome antidote to formality. So when we're cooking for a bunch of people, we like to have these wings working on the grill when people arrive; when the wings are done, we just toss them in the bowl with the hot Buffalo sauce and let people munch on them while we cook the main course. They are "new-school" wings because they are slightly updated—check out the curry powder we put on them, for example—but they follow the basic mold of the original. We have you choose your own hot sauce for the Buffalo mixture here. We go with Tabasco, but let your taste buds be your guide. Be aware, though, that if you use the larger amount of hot sauce, this is going to be one fiery dish.

For the dressing:
1/4 cup sour cream
1/4 cup cider vinegar
1/3 cup crumbled blue cheese of your
    choice
1/2 cup olive oil
Kosher salt and freshly cracked black
    pepper to taste

For the wings:
3 pounds medium-size chicken wings
2 tablespoons Sherwood or other
    good-quality curry powder
Kosher salt and freshly cracked black
    pepper to taste

For the Buffalo sauce:
2 tablespoons minced garlic
1/4 to 1/2 cup hot sauce of your
    choice (we like Tabasco)
3 tablespoons chopped fresh oregano
    or marjoram
1 tablespoon chopped fresh sage
1/4 cup olive oil
Juice of 2 limes
4 cucumbers, peeled and cut length-
    wise into spears

1. Build a multi-level fire in your grill: Leaving one-quarter of the bottom free of coals, bank the coals in the remaining three-quarters of the grill so that they are three times as high on one side as on the other. When the coals are all ignited and the temperature has died down to medium (you can hold your hand about 5 inches above the grill grid, over the area where the coals are deepest, for 4 to 5 seconds), you're ready to cook.

2. In a food processor or blender, combine the sour cream, vinegar, and blue cheese and process until smooth. With the machine running, add the oil through the feed tube in a thin stream; the dressing should become thick and creamy. Add salt and pepper to taste. Transfer the dressing to a small bowl, cover, and refrigerate.

3. Cut the wings into 3 sections (see below). Discard the wing tips or save them to use in stock. Rub the remaining wing sections with the curry powder and sprinkle them generously with salt and pepper. Place them on the grill and cook, turning occasionally, until they are golden brown, about 5 to 7 minutes. To check for doneness, nick, peek, and cheat: Cut into one of the wings and peek to be sure there is no redness near the bone.

4. While the wings are cooking, combine all the ingredients for the Buffalo sauce in a bowl large enough to hold all the chicken. As the wings come off the grill, drop them into the sauce and turn to coat.

5. Serve the wings right out of the bowl or on a big platter, accompanied by the blue cheese dressing for dipping and the cucumber spears to cool things off.

COOK TO COOK: If you are making these as an appetizer before a grilled entrée, you will probably need to add some more fuel and let the fire build up again before you cook the entrée.

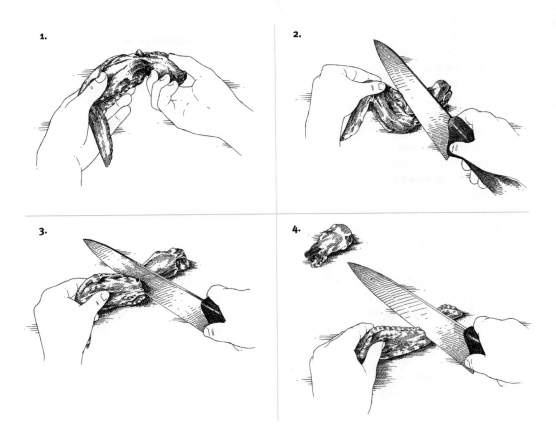

soy-glazed chicken thighs with grilled pineapple and a macadamia power pack

SERVES 4 AS AN APPETIZER

The Hawaiian Islands are a culinary crossroads. They've got it all—Japanese, Korean, Chinese, West Coast American, Filipino, what have you. Now, we're not big fans of so-called fusion cooking, but when it occurs naturally, as it does in Hawaii, it works out fine. So this is a little Japanese-Hawaiian thing using chicken thighs. We prefer them to bone-in chicken breasts because their smaller size makes them cook more quickly and their semi-dark meat is more flavorful. To pep up this dish, we add an Asian-flavored "power pack"—that's our term for an intensely flavored little dish that lands somewhere between a salsa and a relish. If you want to stick with a straight Japanese-influenced dish you can skip the power pack, but it's easy to make and it adds a ton of flavor.

For the glaze:
1 1/2 cups soy sauce
2 tablespoons sugar
1 tablespoon red pepper flakes

For the power pack:
1/4 cup toasted macadamia nuts, roughly chopped
1/4 cup finely chopped scallions, white and green parts
2 tablespoons peeled and minced fresh ginger
3 tablespoons fresh lime juice (about 1 1/2 limes)

2 tablespoons roasted sesame oil
———
3 tablespoons cracked toasted coriander seeds
3 tablespoons cracked white pepper (or substitute black pepper)
Kosher salt to taste
4 large or 8 small boneless, skinless chicken thighs (about 1 1/2 pounds total)
3 tablespoons vegetable oil
2 peeled pineapple slices, each 1 inch thick

1. Build a multi-level fire in your grill: Leaving one-quarter of the bottom free of coals, bank the coals in the remaining three-quarters of the grill so that they are three times as high on one side as on the other. When the coals are all ignited and the temperature has died down to medium (you can hold your hand about 5 inches above the grill grid, over the area where the coals are deepest, for 4 to 5 seconds), you're ready to cook.

2. In a small saucepan over medium-high heat, bring the soy sauce, sugar, and red pepper flakes to a vigorous simmer, stirring until the sugar dissolves. Continue to simmer until the mixture has reduced by about half and coats the back of a spoon, 30 to 40 minutes. Remove the glaze from the heat and set aside.

3. While the glaze is reducing, combine the ingredients for the power pack in a small bowl and mix well.

4. In another small bowl, combine the coriander, white pepper, and salt and mix well. Brush the chicken thighs with 2 tablespoons of the oil, then rub them all over with the spice mixture, pressing gently so it adheres.

5. Put the thighs on the grill over the hotter part of the fire and cook until opaque all the way through, about 4 to 6 minutes per side, brushing with the soy glaze during the last 30 seconds of cooking on each side. To check for doneness, poke the chicken with your finger to test its firmness level (see page 13). If you're unsure, nick, peek, and cheat: Make a cut down to the bone in the thickest part of one of the thighs and check to be sure that it is opaque all the way through, with no red near the bone.

6. While the chicken is cooking, rub the pineapple with the remaining tablespoon of oil and grill until golden brown, 3 to 5 minutes per side. Brush the pineapple with the glaze during the last 30 seconds of cooking on each side as well.

7. Arrange the pineapple slices on 4 plates, top each with a chicken thigh, brush with the rest of the glaze, top with a spoonful of the power pack, and serve.

COOK TO COOK: Keep a close eye on your soy reduction after the first 20 minutes or so. It goes from a thin liquid to a syrupy glaze rather slowly, but from syrupy to burned more quickly than you might think.

barbecued duck legs with peaches, green olives, and sherry

SERVES 4 AS AN APPETIZER

We like to cook duck breast medium-rare, but duck legs taste best cooked all the way through. We chose the barbecue method here, cooking the legs for an hour over indirect heat and smoke, so they would take on a super-smoky flavor and become fall-apart tender. The cracked coriander seed on the skin develops a crunchy crust that contrasts with the tender meat inside. To top it off, the peach-olive relish has strong flavors to stand up to the smoky, rich duck meat.

4 duck legs
Kosher salt and freshly cracked black
     pepper to taste
4 tablespoons freshly cracked
     coriander seeds
2 ripe but firm peaches, pitted and
     diced small
1 red bell pepper, seeded and
     diced small

1/2 cup pitted brine-cured green
     olives such as Manzanilla or
     Sevillano
1/4 cup raisins
3 tablespoons olive oil
2 tablespoons dry sherry
1 tablespoon red wine vinegar
3 tablespoons roughly chopped
     fresh oregano

1. Start a fire well over to one side of your grill, using about enough coals to fill a large shoebox.

2. Sprinkle the duck legs generously with salt and pepper and rub them all over with the coriander, pressing gently to be sure it adheres.

3. When the fire dies down and the coals are covered with gray ash, place the duck legs on the grill on the side away from the coals, being careful that none of the meat is directly over coals. Put the lid on the grill with the vents one-quarter of the way open and cook, adding a handful of hardwood charcoal after 30 minutes, until the legs are done all the way through, about 45 minutes to 1 hour. To check for doneness, poke the meat with your finger to check its firmness level (see page 13). If you're unsure (and really, even if you're not), nick, peek, and cheat: Make a cut down to the bone in the thickest part of one of the legs and check to be sure that it is cooked all the way through, with no red near the bone.

4. Meanwhile, combine the remaining ingredients in a medium bowl and mix well. When the duck is done, put one leg on each plate, spoon some of the peach mixture on top, and serve.

COOK TO COOK: You want duck thighs to be well cooked, so we recommend that you check them with the infallible "nick, peek, and cheat" method rather than the more subjective hand method.

skewered boneless chicken thighs with sweet-and-pungent soy baste and spicy cashews

SERVES 4

We are big fans of chicken thighs because they are more flavorful than breasts and, given their higher fat content, it's easier to grill them without drying them out. For this dish you rub strips of chicken with a spice mixture, thread them onto skewers, and cook them over medium heat, then baste them with a sweet soy baste and scatter some spicy roasted cashews over the top. The recipe was inspired by the Japanese yakitori tradition, which is a combination of the words for grilled (*yaki*) and chicken (*tori*). The practitioners of this informal charcoal grilling style also grill vegetables, but not surprisingly they make admirable use of skinless chicken thighs.

1/2 cup roasted unsalted cashews
2 tablespoons prepared Asian chile-garlic paste (available in Asian markets or large supermarkets)
1/2 cup soy sauce
1/4 cup light or dark brown sugar
2 tablespoons peeled and minced fresh ginger
3 tablespoons roasted sesame oil
2 tablespoons ground coriander

2 tablespoons freshly cracked white pepper
2 tablespoons hoisin sauce
2 tablespoons kosher salt
2 pounds boneless, skinless chicken thighs, cut into strips about 1/2 inch wide
Juice of 1 lime
3 scallions, both white and green parts, sliced thin

1. Preheat the oven to 300°F.

2. In a small bowl, combine the cashews and chile-garlic paste and stir until the nuts are well coated. Transfer the cashews to a small baking pan, place in the preheated oven, and roast until they are dry, about 20 minutes. Transfer to a plate to cool. When the nuts are completely cool, crush them with the bottom of a heavy frying pan until they are like coarse gravel, then set aside.

3. Build a multi-level fire in your grill: Leaving one-quarter of the bottom free of coals, bank the coals in the remaining three-quarters of the grill so that they are three times as high on one side as on the other. When the coals are all ignited and the temperature has died down to medium (you can hold your hand about 5 inches above the grill grid, over the area where the coals are deepest, for 4 to 5 seconds), you're ready to cook.

4. In a small bowl, combine the soy sauce, brown sugar, and ginger and whisk until the sugar dissolves.

5. In a medium bowl, mix together the sesame oil, coriander, white pepper, hoisin, and salt. Add the chicken and toss to coat well. Thread the chicken onto skewers, place

on the grill, and cook until opaque all the way through, about 3 to 4 minutes per side, basting liberally with the soy mixture during the final 30 seconds of cooking. To check for doneness, nick, peek, and cheat: Make a 1/4-inch cut into one of the pieces to be sure it is opaque all the way through, with no redness inside.

6. When the chicken is done, transfer the skewers to a serving platter and sprinkle with the crushed cashews. Add the lime juice and sliced scallions to the remaining soy base, then pass it separately as a dipping sauce for the chicken.

COOK TO COOK: This is a glazing situation. Because the soy baste has sugar in it, put it on for only the last 30 seconds of the cooking time and watch the skewers carefully after that. You want the sugar to caramelize, which creates a deeply flavored glaze on the chicken, but you don't want it to stray over the line to burned, which will result in a bitter, acrid taste.

west indies grilled chicken thighs
with grilled banana and your favorite hot sauce

SERVES 8 AS AN APPETIZER, 4 AS AN ENTRÉE

Jerk chicken is coated with a mixture of garlic, herbs, spices, and chiles that are caked on the chicken before it is very slowly grilled. We are doing something like that here, but with a fire that's a little hotter. Even so, you don't want the chicken to cook *too* fast, because you want the spicy coating to have enough time to set up and make a really thick, crunchy, super-flavorful crust while the inside stays juicy. You can use either bone-in or boneless thighs here, but we particularly like bone-in, because you can cook them until the meat almost falls off the bone.

To continue the tropical theme, we halve some bananas and cook them right in their skins so the flesh stays intact, and then splash on a little glaze just before they come off the fire. To finish up the presentation, we let you show off your favorite bottled hot sauce to your guests, who will no doubt have a favorite of their own that they will need to tell you about.

1/2 cup fresh lime juice (about
   4 limes)
1 tablespoon minced garlic
3 tablespoons minced fresh chile
   pepper of your choice, or to taste
1/4 cup prepared yellow mustard
2 tablespoons ground cumin
1 teaspoon allspice
Kosher salt and freshly cracked black
   pepper to taste

8 small bone-in chicken thighs
   (about 2 pounds total)
4 ripe but firm bananas, halved
   lengthwise but not peeled
2 tablespoons unsalted butter
1/4 cup molasses
A bottle of your favorite hot sauce

1. In a large glass or stainless steel bowl, whisk together the lime juice, garlic, chile, mustard, cumin, and allspice until well blended. Add the chicken, turning to coat all over, then cover and refrigerate for at least 15 minutes or up to 4 hours, turning the chicken from time to time.

2. Build a multi-level fire in your grill: Leaving one-quarter of the bottom free of coals, bank the coals in the remaining three-quarters of the grill so that they are three times as high on one side as on the other. When the coals are all ignited and the temperature has died down to medium (you can hold your hand about 5 inches above the grill grid, over the area where the coals are deepest, for 4 to 5 seconds), you're ready to cook.

3. Put the chicken thighs on the grill, skin side down, over the side with more coals and cook for 10 minutes; flip the thighs over and continue to cook until opaque all the way through, about 10 to 12 minutes more. To check for doneness, poke the chicken

with your finger to test its firmness level (see page 13); if you're unsure, nick, peek, and cheat: Make a 1/4-inch cut in the thickest part of one of the thighs and check to be sure that it is opaque all the way through, with no red near the bone.

4. Meanwhile, combine the butter and molasses in a small saucepan and cook over low heat, stirring, until the butter is just melted. When the chicken is nearly done, put the bananas on the grill, cut side down, and cook until golden brown and slightly charred, 2 to 3 minutes, then turn over, brush with the molasses mixture, and cook for 30 seconds more.

5. Remove the thighs and bananas from the grill and serve, passing the hot sauce on the side.

COOK TO COOK: It might seem as if we're marinating here, but what we're actually doing is giving the thick, flavorful "jerk" mixture time to dry slightly and cake onto the chicken so it doesn't fall off during cooking. In other words, it's about adhesion, not flavor penetration. We want to keep the intense flavors on the outside and let the interior of the chicken retain its own flavor as a contrast.

MEAT

valerie's grilled lamb kefta
with marcy's tomato-cucumber salad

SERVES 4 AS AN APPETIZER

Recently we were lucky enough to go to Istanbul with our friend Ihsan Gurdal and his wife, Valerie, to visit Ihsan's parents. Istanbul is a fantastic city, and one of the best parts is the amazing food in its street stalls, bars, and cafés. Any time we wanted a quick, simple, and delicious meal, we would stop into one of the little bars that seem to pop up in every neighborhood. Even if the bar had only two small tables, it also had a long charcoal grill where an expert cook was turning out oblong ground lamb patties, called *kefta*, on skewers. A couple of weeks after we came home we re-created a Turkish dinner from memories of our meals in those bars. Valerie prepared these kefta, which were as good as any we'd tasted in Istanbul. Chris's wife, Marcy, contributed a classic Turkish salad, the perfect partner to the slightly spicy kefta.

You have two choices for shaping the kefta—either adopt the traditional approach and form oblongs around skewers, which we recommend because it's fun and authentic, or shape the lamb into patties and grill them as you would little hamburgers. If you can't get hold of Maras and Urfa pepper (although we suggest that you try because both kinds are wonderfully flavorful and have a multitude of culinary uses, and because you can mail-order them from Formaggio Kitchen by calling 888-212-3224), you can substitute a few tablespoons of good-quality paprika plus a dash of red pepper flakes.

For the salad:
1/4 cup extra-virgin olive oil
1/4 cup red wine vinegar
1/2 cup roughly chopped fresh parsley
Kosher salt and freshly cracked black pepper to taste
1 large ripe tomato about the size of a baseball, cored, seeded, and diced small
1 cucumber, peeled and diced small
1/2 red onion, peeled and diced small

For the kefta:
1 pound finely ground lamb (see Cook to Cook)

1/2 red onion, peeled and grated
1/3 cup roughly chopped fresh parsley
2 slices white sandwich bread, crusts removed, soaked in water for 30 minutes and then squeezed dry
1/2 tablespoon ground cumin
Pinch of cinnamon
1/2 tablespoon Maras pepper (or substitute good-quality paprika)
1 tablespoon Urfa pepper (or substitute good-quality paprika)
Kosher salt and freshly cracked black pepper to taste

1. Build a multi-level fire in your grill: Leaving one-quarter of the bottom free of coals, bank the coals in the remaining three-quarters of the grill so that they are three times as high on one side as on the other. When the coals are all ignited and the temperature has died down to medium (you can hold your hand about 5 inches above the grill grid, over the area where the coals are deepest, for 4 to 5 seconds), you're ready to cook.

2. In a large bowl, whisk together the olive oil, vinegar, parsley, and salt and pepper. Add the tomato, cucumber, and onion and toss gently but thoroughly. Taste to adjust the seasoning, then set aside while you make the kefta.

3. Put all the kefta ingredients in a large bowl. Wet your hands with water, then mix the meat and other ingredients together very well with your hands (wet them periodically so the meat doesn't stick to them), until the mixture has a uniform, almost silken consistency. Don't skimp on the mixing—getting the right consistency is key. As you knead, the fat will disappear into the meat, and eventually the mixture will have a consistency almost like wet bread dough: smooth and somewhat shiny and a little tacky. Divide this mixture into 8 to 12 portions, then either form each portion into an oblong sausage shape around a flat-sided skewer or shape it into a small patty.

4. Place the kefta skewers or patties on the grill and cook until they are just cooked through, about 3 to 4 minutes per side. (To check for doneness, nick, peek, and cheat: Cut into one and peek to be sure it is done the way you like it; we like it just barely pink inside.)

5. Remove from the grill. Serve hot or at room temperature, accompanied by the salad. Pita bread and yogurt go well with this meal.

COOK TO COOK: To get ground lamb with just the right proportions of lean and fat, buy a cut from the shoulder or leg and ask the butcher to grind it for you. Prepackaged ground lamb is likely to be from the fattier parts of the lamb, like the breast or belly. But if that is the only option, go ahead and buy it rather than deciding not to make this or other ground lamb dishes.

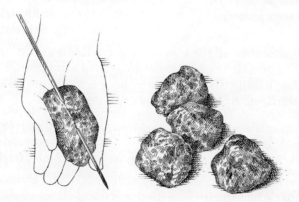

chinese-style ribs with hoisin-mustard sauce

SERVES 8 AS AN APPETIZER

We are not in favor of marinades because they don't really tenderize meat and they are a less efficient carrier of flavor on grilled foods than spice rubs. But every rule has exceptions, and this is one. Somehow the texture of spare ribs and the relative lack of meat on the bones makes them more receptive to marinades than are other meats—and besides, this is a traditional Chinese approach and we like to respect tradition whenever possible. So we let the ribs sit for a few hours in an Asian-flavored marinade that gets an extra punch from the aromatic, almost flowery spiciness of star anise. Then we cook them "slow and low" over the indirect heat and smoke of a low fire, and finally we finish them with mustard and hoisin sauce, a combination that packs plenty of heat and flavor.

We prefer a larger spare rib here, as opposed to the smaller baby back ribs. We've chosen the St. Louis–style cut—ribs with the chine bone (backbone) removed and the tips trimmed—which are easier to deal with, like a meatier version of baby backs. You can substitute baby back ribs in this recipe if you like, but be sure to reduce the cooking time to about 45 minutes. (If you are a fan of ribs, check out page 181 for a fuller discussion of your overall options in this department.)

For the marinade:
1/2 cup dark soy sauce
1/4 cup roasted sesame oil
1/4 cup dry sherry
2 tablespoons light brown sugar
2 tablespoons peeled and minced
   ginger
3 star anise pods, smashed into little
   pieces (optional)
2 tablespoons ground white pepper
   (or substitute black pepper)

1 tablespoon red pepper flakes,
   or to taste
——
2 racks of large (2-down) St. Louis–
   style pork spare ribs (about
   2 pounds)
Kosher salt to taste
1/2 cup hoisin sauce
1/3 cup water
1/4 cup dry mustard

1. In a medium bowl, combine all the marinade ingredients and stir until the sugar is completely dissolved. Sprinkle the ribs generously with salt, arrange them in a single layer in a shallow glass baking dish, and pour the marinade over the top. Cover and refrigerate for between 3 and 6 hours, turning occasionally.

2. In a small bowl, combine the hoisin sauce, water, and mustard, mix well, and set aside.

3. Light a fire well over to one side of a large kettle grill, using about enough charcoal to fill half of a shoebox. When the fire has died down and all the coals are covered with ash, remove the ribs from the marinade and place them on the side of the grill away from the coals, being careful that none of the meat is directly over the coals. Put the lid on the grill with the vents open one-quarter of the way and cook until the ribs are very

tender, about 1/2 to 2 hours, adding another half-shoebox of fresh charcoal every 30 minutes.

4. When the ribs are done, remove them from the grill and brush them generously with the hoisin mixture. Cut the slab into individual ribs, pile them on a platter, and serve, passing the remaining sauce for dipping.

COOK TO COOK: Be very sure that you have enough room on your grill so the ribs are not over the fire. If you have a relatively small grill, go ahead and stack those coals up very steeply on one side—they don't need to be spread out.

balsamic-glazed grilled sweetbreads
with bacon-seared mustard greens

SERVES 4 AS AN APPETIZER

Sweetbreads have always been a tough sell in this country. We think that's partly because they are most often poached, sliced, and sautéed, so they end up with a rather formal appearance and a soft texture. But what we like to do is pull apart the lobes and grill them. For our money, this is the #1 way to cook sweetbreads. The crispy, crusty, flavorful sear that grilling puts on the outside of the sweetbreads is a perfect complement to the mellow, tender, subtle interior.

At the East Coast Grill, the servers refer to this as "the *Green Eggs and Ham* dish"— Would you eat them in a car? Would you eat them in a bar?—and they serve them with a money-back guarantee. I (Chris) would like to continue that tradition here, so if you cook these and don't like them, come on over to the East Coast Grill and I'll buy you an appetizer of your choice. How's that for a personal warranty?

Like most organ meats, sweetbreads are quite perishable. Cook them the day you buy them.

1 cup balsamic vinegar	1 large red onion, peeled and cut into
1 pound very fresh sweetbreads	8 chunks
1 gallon cold water	2 pounds mustard greens, washed,
1 cup white vinegar	dried, and cut crosswise into
2 tablespoons kosher salt	narrow strips (or substitute kale,
12 ounces slab bacon, cut into	collards, turnip greens, beet
12 large, equal pieces	greens, or dandelion greens)
Kosher salt plus freshly cracked	3 tablespoons red wine vinegar
black pepper to taste	1 tablespoon sugar

1. Build a multi-level fire in your grill: Leaving one-quarter of the bottom free of coals, bank the coals in the remaining three-quarters of the grill so that they are three times as high on one side as on the other. When the coals are all ignited and the temperature has died down to medium-high (you can hold your hand about 5 inches above the grill grid, over the area where the coals are deepest, for 3 to 4 seconds), you're ready to cook.

2. In a small, heavy saucepan, bring the balsamic vinegar to a boil over high heat, then reduce the heat and simmer vigorously until it is reduced to 1/4 cup, about 25 minutes.

3. Meanwhile, rinse the sweetbreads thoroughly and place them in a large pot along with the water, the vinegar, and the 2 tablespoons of salt. Bring the water to a boil over high heat, then reduce the heat to very low and simmer gently for 15 minutes. Remove from the heat and let the sweetbreads stand in the liquid for 5 minutes more, then drain them thoroughly and refrigerate until cool.

4. While the sweetbreads are simmering, cook the bacon in a large sauté pan or skillet over low heat until crispy, about 6 minutes. Put the bacon on brown paper bag or paper towels to drain, remove all but about 3 tablespoons of the fat from the sauté pan or skillet, and set the pan aside.

5. Using your fingers, remove the outer film from the cooled sweetbreads and separate them into nuggets. (You should have about 20 nuggets.) Thread the nuggets onto skewers and sprinkle them generously with salt and pepper. Set aside for a few minutes.

6. Put the onion chunks over the coals and cook, turning occasionally, until tender, about 10 to 14 minutes. Halfway through the cooking time for the onions, put the sweetbread skewers on the grill and cook until the sweetbreads are a nice golden brown, about 5 to 7 minutes.

7. When the onions and sweetbreads are done, put the sauté pan or skillet with the bacon fat over medium high heat. When the fat is very hot, add the greens and cook, stirring furiously, until they are wilted, about 1 minute. Remove from the heat and sprinkle with the reserved bacon, the red wine vinegar, the sugar, and salt and pepper to taste. Toss well and divide among 4 plates.

8. Divide the onions and sweetbreads among the 4 plates, placing them on top of the greens; drizzle the balsamic reduction over all, and serve hot.

COOK TO COOK: Sweetbreads are delicate, so handle them gently. Remember, too, that in this recipe they're already cooked when you put them on the grill, so you don't need to worry about cooking them through—get a nice, golden brown exterior and warm them through to the center, and you're set.

grilled lamb skewers with olives, pita, and cucumber-yogurt sauce

SERVES 6

The key to this dish is cutting the lamb chunks quite small, no larger than 1/2-inch cubes. It might seem a little laborious, but what we're trying to do here is re-create a dish that I (Chris) ate when I was eight years old and went to the Oracle at Delphi in Greece with my parents and sister. This is the day to which I trace my love of lamb. It was actually a double lamb day, because we ended up in a tavern where I got to pick my own section from a lamb that was twirling around on a spit over an open fire. But before that we stopped several times on the road to get these skewers of tiny lamb cubes that were grilled over a very hot fire so the fat was crispy but the interior was still rare. To mimic that here, make sure you use a very hot fire. Just grill the lamb over that raging fire, squeeze a little lemon on it, and serve it with cucumber and mint. This is a very simple dish, but when you taste it you will realize why Greece and the Middle East are so renowned for their lamb. You may even become a lamb fanatic like me.

1 cup peeled, seeded, and diced
    cucumber (about 1 small
    cucumber)
1 cup plain yogurt, whole-milk if
    possible
1/2 cup finely chopped fresh mint
Kosher salt and freshly cracked black
    pepper to taste

2 pounds lamb leg or shoulder, cut in
    small chunks (less than 1/2 inch)
1/4 cup plus 2 tablespoons olive oil
1 cup pitted brine-cured black olives
    such as Kalamata or Gaeta
1 lemon, halved
6 slices pita bread

1. Build a multi-level fire in your grill: Leaving one-quarter of the bottom free of coals, bank the coals in the remaining three-quarters of the grill so that they are three times as high on one side as on the other. When the coals are all ignited and the temperature is hot (you can hold your hand about 5 inches above the grill grid, over the area where the coals are deepest, for 2 seconds or less), you're ready to cook.

2. In a medium bowl, combine the cucumber, yogurt, mint, and salt and pepper. Mix well, then cover and refrigerate until serving time.

3. In a medium bowl, combine the lamb with 1/4 cup of the olive oil and salt and pepper to taste (use a lot) and toss to coat. Thread the meat onto skewers, put them on the grill, and cook until the lamb is done the way you like it, 2 to 3 minutes per side for medium-rare. To check for doneness, nick, peek, and cheat: Make a small cut in one of the cubes of meat and peek at the center to be sure it is just slightly less done than you like it.

4. When you put the lamb on the grill, rub the pita with the remaining 2 tablespoons of olive oil, put it on the side of the grill with fewer coals, and cook until nicely toasted and slightly charred in a few places, 2 to 3 minutes. Remove from the grill and slice into quarters.

5. When the lamb is done, push the meat off the skewers into a medium bowl, add the olives, squeeze the lemon halves into the bowl, and toss gently to coat the meat with the juice. Transfer to a serving dish and serve, accompanied by the grilled bread and the yogurt condiment.

COOK TO COOK: Live fires have what you might call "heat lines," seams of coals that provide pretty much the same heat along their length. When you're grilling skewers, keep them parallel rather than perpendicular to these heat lines, so that the food cooks evenly.

grilled sausage with zucchini, red onions, and chipotle-lime vinaigrette

SERVES 6

Today all kinds of great sausages are available in supermarkets and butcher shops, from standard pork sausage to types made with chicken, duck, and even lamb. We urge you to take advantage of them. In fact, when we go to the store before a cookout, we always get a package of sausages to throw on the grill along with whatever else we plan on cooking. That way anyone who wants to can have a sausage or two along with their steak or fish or whatever. It may seem like overkill, but you'd be surprised at how many people slip one onto their plate.

The key to grilling sausages is to cook them slowly over medium heat. That lets all the juices really plump up inside the casing. Here we just grill up the sausages with some planks of zucchini and onion, then serve them together with a little Latin-flavored sauce over the top. Zucchini and sausage are one of those humble combinations that are uniquely satisfying.

If you have any of this left over, it makes a great sandwich.

2 medium zucchini, unpeeled, cut
    lengthwise into planks about
    1 inch thick
2 medium red onions, peeled and cut
    into circles about 1 inch thick
1/4 cup olive oil
Kosher salt and freshly cracked black
    pepper to taste
1 pound fresh pork sausage links or
    another type of your choice

For the vinaigrette:
1/2 cup olive oil
1/4 cup fresh lime juice (about
    2 limes)
1 teaspoon minced garlic
1 tablespoon minced chipotle peppers
    in adobo sauce
1/4 cup roughly chopped fresh
    cilantro
2 teaspoons ground cumin
Kosher salt and freshly cracked black
    pepper to taste

1. Build a multi-level fire in your grill: Leaving one-quarter of the bottom free of coals, bank the coals in the remaining three-quarters of the grill so that they are three times as high on one side as on the other. When the coals are all ignited and the temperature has died down to medium (you can hold your hand about 5 inches above the grill grid, over the area where the coals are deepest, for 4 to 5 seconds), you're ready to cook.

2. Rub the zucchini planks and onion slices with oil and sprinkle them generously with salt and pepper.

3. Put the vegetables and the sausage on the grill and cook until the sausage is cooked through and the vegetables are golden brown and slightly charred, about 6 to 8 minutes for the onions, 8 to 10 minutes for the zucchini, and 10 minutes for the sausage. If flare-ups occur under the sausage, move it to the side with no coals for a few moments to let the flames die down.

4. While the sausage and vegetables are grilling, whisk together the vinaigrette ingredients in a medium bowl until blended.

5. Arrange the zucchini planks on individual serving plates. Cut the sausage into thick slices and spread them on top. Separate the onion slices into rings and scatter them over the sausage. Drizzle the vinaigrette generously over the top, and serve immediately.

COOK TO COOK: When cooking sausages, you need to go on the slow side so they cook through without drying out or getting burned on the outside. Because of their fat content, you also have to be prepared to move them off to the side of the grill if flare-ups occur.

arugula salad with grilled chicken livers, slab bacon, and hard-cooked eggs

SERVES 4 AS AN APPETIZER OR SALAD

I (Chris) always make sure to save the chicken livers, which I really like. They're another one of those items that people are a bit puzzled by, so over the years I've developed lots of applications for them. This is one of my favorites—it's a variation on a fried chicken liver dish that my Grandma Wetzler used to make. Grilling is ideal for cooking chicken livers because, as with sweetbreads, you get a great crispy sear on the outside and they stay medium to medium-rare and creamy on the inside.

- 1/2 pound slab bacon, diced large
- 1/2 cup plus 2 tablespoons olive oil
- 1 1/2 tablespoons honey
- 2 tablespoons grainy mustard
- 1/3 cup balsamic vinegar
- 2 bunches arugula, washed and dried well
- 1/2 red onion, peeled and very thinly sliced
- 8 chicken livers, about 2 ounces each, rinsed and patted dry
- Kosher salt and freshly cracked black pepper to taste
- 2 hard-cooked eggs, roughly chopped

1. Build a multi-level fire in your grill: Leaving one-quarter of the bottom free of coals, bank the coals in the remaining three-quarters of the grill so that they are three times as high on one side as on the other. When the coals are all ignited and the temperature has died down to medium (you can hold your hand about 5 inches above the grill grid, over the area where the coals are deepest, for 4 to 5 seconds), you're ready to cook.

2. In a large sauté pan or skillet, cook the bacon over low heat until it is crispy, 6 to 8 minutes. Remove the bacon from the pan and put it on a brown paper bag or paper towels to drain, then spoon about 2 tablespoons of the bacon drippings from the pan into a large bowl and discard any remaining drippings.

3. Add the 1/4 cup of olive oil and the honey to the bacon drippings and whisk to blend very well. Add the mustard and vinegar and whisk again until the mixture is smooth and uniform. Add the arugula and red onion to the bowl with the dressing, toss to coat the greens well, and then divide this salad among 4 plates.

4. In a small bowl, combine the livers, the 2 tablespoons of oil, and salt and pepper to taste. Toss gently to coat the livers. Place the livers directly on the grill—or, if they're small, first thread them onto skewers—and cook until they are crusty and brown, 2 to 3 minutes per side. (To check for doneness, nick, peek, and cheat: Cut into one of the livers and peek to be sure it is just barely pink inside.)

5. Arrange the grilled livers over the salad, scatter the chopped eggs and reserved bacon on top, and serve.

COOK TO COOK: The success or failure of this dish will hinge on the livers' not sticking to the grill. So make sure you have a clean, hot grill grid; oil the livers lightly before you put them on the grill; and don't move them until they have got a good sear on the first side. You are looking for a nice brown crispiness on the outside but pink tenderness on the inside.

hot latin-style cornbread salad
with grilled sausage and smoky lava dressing

SERVES 4 AS AN APPETIZER

A lot of the best dishes cooked in restaurant kitchens never make it to the dining room. These are the "snacking dishes" made by the kitchen help, usually reflecting their various ethnic backgrounds. We featured quite a few of them in our first book, *The Thrill of the Grill*, and we're still finding new ones. This one was created by Elmer Sanchez and Amilcar Baraca, the El Salvadorean day chefs at the East Coast Grill. They make a lot of cornbread to serve with the barbecue platters at the Grill, and they are not about to let any of the unused bread get tossed out. So they cut it into big croutons and toast it, add some grilled sausage, onion, and tomato, and then toss it all together with a very, very hot dressing fueled by chipotle peppers.

For the dressing:
1/2 cup olive oil
1/4 cup fresh lime juice (about 2
    limes)
1 tablespoon ground cumin
1/4 cup chipotle peppers in adobo
    sauce, puréed
Kosher salt and freshly cracked black
    pepper to taste

——

2 ripe tomatoes about the size of

baseballs, cored and diced large
1/2 red onion, peeled and diced small
1 ripe California avocado, pitted,
    peeled, and diced medium
1/3 cup roughly chopped fresh
    cilantro or parsley
1 pound fresh sausage links of your
    choice (even chicken sausages
    are okay for this one)
2 cups 3/4-inch cubes of cornbread,
    toasted golden brown

1. Build a multi-level fire in your grill: Leaving one-quarter of the bottom free of coals, bank the coals in the remaining three-quarters of the grill so that they are three times as high on one side as on the other. When the coals are all ignited and the temperature has died down to medium (you can hold your hand about 5 inches above the grill grid, over the area where the coals are deepest, for 4 to 5 seconds), you're ready to cook.

2. In a large bowl, whisk together all of the dressing ingredients. Add the tomatoes, onion, avocado, and cilantro and toss gently to combine.

3. Put the sausages on the grill and cook well, about 5 to 8 minutes per side. (To check for doneness, nick, peek, and cheat: Cut into one and peek to be sure it is cooked through, with no trace of pink inside.) When the sausages are done, slice them on the bias neatly, so they keep their shape.

4. Add the toasted cornbread to the salad and toss gently. Divide the salad among 4 plates, fan the sausage slices over the top, and serve.

latin-style bacon, tomato, and chile-cheese dip with grilled pineapple

SERVES 4 AS AN APPETIZER

The pairing of grilled pineapple with cheese in this appetizer might seem odd, but it's another brilliant inspiration from the Latin kitchen staff of the East Coast Grill. Every Saturday afternoon when their prep work is done, these guys celebrate by sitting down to their weekend ritual, the rapid consumption of a pineapple-and-pepperoni pizza. It turns out to be a delicious combination, so we switched the pepperoni to bacon, made the pizza topping into a dip reminiscent of Mexican *queso fundido*, then grilled the pineapple and cut it into wedges to use as dipping sticks.

This is particularly nice when served with a couple of salsas such as Pineapple-Chipotle Salsa (page 330) or Mango–Black Bean Salsa (page 332) in the background.

1 cup shredded Monterey Jack cheese
1/2 cup shredded cheddar cheese
1/2 cup grated Parmesan cheese
1/2 red onion, peeled and diced small
1 ripe tomato about the size of a
   baseball, cored, seeded, and
   diced small
2 tablespoons minced fresh green or
   red chile pepper of your choice,
   or to taste
1/2 cup roughly chopped fresh
   cilantro

6 slices bacon, cooked until crisp,
   drained, and crumbled (or
   substitute 12 slices pepperoni)
1 tablespoon ground cumin
4 slices unpeeled fresh pineapple,
   each 1 inch thick
2 tablespoons olive oil
Kosher salt and freshly cracked black
   pepper to taste

1. Build a multi-level fire in your grill: Leaving one-quarter of the bottom free of coals, bank the coals in the remaining three-quarters of the grill so that they are about three times as high on one side as on the other. When the coals are all ignited and the temperature has died down to medium (you can hold your hand about 5 inches above the grill grid, over the area where the coals are deepest, for 4 to 5 seconds), you're ready to cook.

2. In a small, lightly greased flameproof casserole dish, combine the three kinds of cheese with the onion, tomato, chile, cilantro, bacon, and cumin and toss until well mixed. Cover the dish with foil and put it on the grill grid over the area with fewer coals until the cheese is melted and bubbly, about 15 minutes.

3. Brush the pineapple slices all over with the olive oil and sprinkle them generously with salt and pepper. Place them on the grill grid over the hotter part of the fire and cook until golden brown and slightly charred, 3 to 4 minutes per side.

4. Remove the pineapple circles from the grill and cut each one into 8 wedges. Transfer the warm dip to a bowl and serve with the pineapple wedges for scooping.

COOK TO COOK: Here is a perfect example of the virtues of a multi-level fire: The low heat of the shallow coals gently melts the cheese while the more aggressive heat of the deeper coals sears the pineapple.

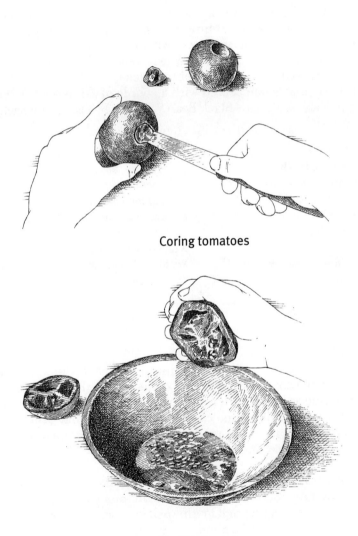

Coring tomatoes

Seeding tomatoes

crispy prosciutto-wrapped asparagus with saffron-crab mayonnaise

SERVES 4 AS AN APPETIZER

We like not only the flavors of this dish but the contrasting textures—the prosciutto gets crispy over the grill while the asparagus stays very tender. For this application, use asparagus spears that are thicker than a pencil but not as thick as a finger; they're big enough that it's easy to wrap prosciutto around them but small enough to cook fairly quickly. Be sure that after blanching the spears you plunge them briefly into ice water so they stop cooking immediately and stay green and crisp.

For some luxe pizzazz, we finish off the dish with a kind of crab salad mayonnaise flavored with orange and saffron. You can use any type of crab in the mayonnaise—blue, Jonah, Dungeness, whatever—but our favorite is blue. You can skip the mayonnaise and still have a very nice dish, of course, but for those more spiffy occasions the mayo is just the thing.

16 large asparagus spears, thicker
  than a pencil but thinner than
  your index finger, trimmed and
  peeled
1/4 pound prosciutto (about 16 slices)
2 tablespoons olive oil
Kosher salt and freshly cracked black
  pepper to taste

For the mayonnaise:
1 egg yolk
1/4 cup olive oil
1/4 cup vegetable oil
1 tablespoon fresh lemon juice (about
  1/4 lemon)
8 saffron threads dissolved in
  1 tablespoon warm sherry
1/2 pound fresh crabmeat,
  carefully picked over
4 tablespoons julienned fresh basil

1. Build a multi-level fire in your grill: Leaving one-quarter of the bottom free of coals, bank the coals in the remaining three-quarters of the grill so that they are three times as high on one side as on the other. When the coals are all ignited and the temperature has died down to medium (you can hold your hand about 5 inches above the grill grid, over the area where the coals are deepest, for 4 to 5 seconds), you're ready to cook.

2. Blanch the asparagus spears in boiling salted water until they turn bright green, about 2 minutes. Drain and immediately plunge them into ice water to stop the cooking, then drain again and pat dry with paper towels.

3. Wind one prosciutto slice around each asparagus spear. Rub the wrapped spears with the olive oil, sprinkle them generously with salt and pepper, and set them aside while you make the mayonnaise.

4. Make the mayo: Put the egg yolk in a blender or food processor, turn on the machine for 10 seconds, and then, with the machine still running, add the two kinds of oil in a thin stream. When the oil is incorporated and the mixture has thickened, add the lemon juice and saffron. Season the mayo with salt and pepper and transfer it to a bowl. Fold in the crabmeat and basil, then cover and refrigerate until serving time. You should have about 1 1/2 cups.

5. Put the asparagus on the grill and cook, gently rolling the spears around occasionally, until the prosciutto is crisp, 3 to 5 minutes. Arrange the hot spears on a platter and serve, passing the mayonnaise for dipping.

COOK TO COOK: Everything in this dish is already cooked before it goes on the grill, which means your goal is to heat it through while providing a flavorful sear on the outside. So decide the heat of the fire according to the thickness of the asparagus: the thicker the spears, the hotter the fire.

crabby, crabby

* * *

Crab, like other seafood, tends to foster regional loyalties. West Coasters swear by Dungeness, Floridians lavish praise on stone crabs, Maine folks are fond of Jonahs, and Southeast Asians delight in the giant hairy crab. Since I (Chris) am from Tidewater, Virginia, my personal opinion is that the best eating crab of them all is the Atlantic blue, which coincidentally is also by far the best-selling variety in the United States.

But whichever kind of crab you choose, it must be cooked while still alive. When buying whole uncooked crabs, don't let anyone tell you they are just sleeping. If they don't raise their claws when you tap on their shells lightly (using something other than your finger), don't buy them. Look for crabs that are heavy for their size, which indicates a high proportion of flavorful meat.

When buying packaged crabmeat, you have several categories to choose from. The top grade, consisting of large, pristine white chunks from the body and the back fin, is variously known as "jumbo," "lump," or "back fin." This is the best choice. Next in order of preference is "flake," smaller pieces of meat from the same parts of the crab. Least desirable is claw meat, which is slightly more fibrous with a brownish hue. All packaged crabmeat is cooked before it is sold, so whatever you buy in stores is ready to use and can be kept, covered tightly and refrigerated, for about three days.

ez grill bread with personality

MAKES 4 FLAT LOAVES

When we cook, we are mostly concerned with making food that tastes good, and we don't worry too much about how it looks. In fact, that's one of the great pleasures of cooking at home rather than in a restaurant. So we call this a bread "with personality" because it tastes great but isn't all that good-looking.

We have long been fans of grilled bread, but in the past we tended to use bread from bakeries, whether pita or thick slices of loaf bread. But over the years, as we traveled around the warm-weather world, we always admired the slightly misshapen, obviously homemade flatbreads that we saw coming off the grill. They just seemed to have more character, and usually more flavor, than store-bought. We were just never *quite* inspired enough to bite the bullet and make our own bread dough on any kind of regular basis. But finally it happened.

What gave us the final push was a trip to Turkey, where we ate all kinds of grilled bread in the kebab joints all over Istanbul. From flat and bumpy to smooth and puffed up with steam that whooshed out when you pricked the surface, the grilled bread was fascinating in its variety and taste. Plus grilling them looked like fun. So when we got back, I (Doc) worked out this recipe. It takes off from a relatively standard version of flatbread, but I added some beer for flavor and a bit of cornmeal for texture. Of course, you can make it without the beer (just use all water for the liquid) and/or without the cornmeal (just use all flour), but this combination is our favorite.

In any case, we had a lot of fun playing around with the bread this past summer, and since we were making it often we ended up serving it with dips, with relishes, with flavored oils, and all kinds of ways. Turns out that, as Middle Eastern cooks have known for centuries, hearth bread is a very easy and versatile appetizer base with a wonderful taste that appeals to people on a very elemental level. When you pull it off the grill, steaming hot and perfectly charred, with that nice faint crunch and deep yeasty flavor, you're going to be a happy griller.

1 tablespoon active dry yeast
3 cups all-purpose flour
1/2 cup warm water
2 tablespoons olive oil, plus more for
    brushing
1/2 cup beer of your choice, at room
    temperature

1/4 cup yellow cornmeal, plus more
    for dusting
1 teaspoon kosher salt, plus more for
    sprinkling

1. In the bowl of an electric mixer, stir together the yeast and 1/2 cup of the flour. Add the warm water and mix until just blended. Cover with a damp towel and let stand in a

warm, draft-free place (inside the oven with the pilot light on, for example) for 30 minutes, until the mixture is thick and foamy and gives off a sound sort of like soda fizz when you stir it.

2. Add the 2 tablespoons of oil and the beer to the yeast mixture and mix well. Now add the 1/4 cup of cornmeal and the teaspoon of salt, then begin adding the remaining 2 1/2 cups of flour, 1/2 cup at a time, to form a soft dough (you may not need all of the flour). Turn the dough out onto a floured board and knead, adding as much of the remaining flour as necessary to prevent the dough from sticking, until the dough is satiny and slightly sticky, about 8 minutes.

3. Place the dough in an oiled bowl, turning once to coat. Cover loosely and let rise in a warm place until doubled in bulk, about 1 to 1 1/2 hours. Divide the dough into quarters, then form each one into a ball. Sprinkle a cookie sheet with cornmeal and put the balls of dough on the sheet, then cover loosely and let rise again for 30 minutes. (Or, if you want, at this point you can cover the dough with plastic wrap and refrigerate until about 1 hour before you want to cook the bread.)

4. Build a multi-level fire in your grill: Leaving one-quarter of the bottom free of coals, bank the coals in the remaining three-quarters of the grill so that they are three times as high on one side as on the other. When the coals are all ignited and the temperature has died down to medium (you can hold your hand about 5 inches above the grill grid, over the area where the coals are deepest, for 4 to 5 seconds), you're ready to cook.

5. Stretch each ball of dough into a rough circle or rectangle about 1/8 inch thick and 10 inches across. Brush with additional olive oil and sprinkle with kosher salt, then place on the grill directly over the coals and cook until black spots form on the bottom and bubbles form on the top, about 4 minutes. Flip the bread and grill the other side until golden and crusty, about 3 to 4 minutes. Remove from the grill and serve.

sometimes ugly is good

* * *

When we say "grilled bread," we're talking about a flat piece of dough that's been licked by flames to its chewy, bumpy, charred-ugly best. While the best-known example in this country is pizza grilled directly on the grill (a technique pioneered by George Germon and Joanne Killeen at Al Forno restaurant in Providence, Rhode Island), not even the Italians can claim grilled bread as their own invention. Folks have been cooking flatbreads over fire in nearly every part of the world for more than six thousand years. In Central Asia and northern China, naan is grilled over the intense, smoky fire of a tandoor. In northern India and Malaysia, soft pappadum are toasted directly over the flames until crisp. Syrian *felaveri* are cooked in wood-burning ovens. Bedouins make *leba*, bread baked in sand under hot coals (sort of like a Middle Eastern hobo pack), and Armenians grill lavash on a *sajj*—a large concave plate—set over a hot fire. In Scotland and Canada, bannocks—traditional cakes made of barley meal and oatmeal—are often cooked over campfires.

Although it's true that cooks in earlier times cooked bread directly over flames because they had no other choice, there has always been a huge side bene-fit that makes it well worth continuing to do today: The smoky, charred flavor that seeps into the dough makes for an unbeatable bread experience. We encourage you to try it early and often.

six flavored olive oils for ez grill bread

Here we draw on the Italian tradition (now very popular in restaurants, too) of setting out bread along with olive oil for dipping. Each of the following recipes makes one cup of flavored oil, enough for a lot of bread, so you are probably going to have some left over. But that's no problem, since the oil will keep for a week if refrigerated. However, because oil partially congeals when it's cold, remember to let it sit out to re-liquefy before you use it with the grilled bread. That doesn't take long—about 15 minutes.

cold oil mix-ins

Add the variation of your choice to 1 cup good-quality extra-virgin olive oil.

Oil with Italian Flavors
1/3 cup roughly chopped oil-packed
    sun-dried tomatoes
1/3 cup lightly packed julienned fresh
    basil leaves
1 tablespoon minced garlic
Kosher salt and freshly cracked black
    pepper to taste

Oil with Mexican Flavors
1/2 cup pitted and roughly chopped
    green olives, preferably cracked
    Moroccan
1 tablespoon freshly cracked black
    pepper
1 tablespoon minced garlic
1 tablespoon freshly grated lime zest
1 teaspoon red pepper flakes
Kosher salt to taste

hot oil mix-ins

In a small saucepan, add the variation of your choice to 1 cup good-quality extra-virgin olive oil and warm over medium-low heat for 15 minutes. Let cool to room temperature before using.

Oil with Mediterranean Flavors
2 tablespoons minced garlic
1/4 cup fresh rosemary needles
Kosher salt and freshly cracked black
    pepper to taste

Oil with Middle Eastern Flavors
2 tablespoons cracked toasted
    cumin seeds
2 tablespoons cracked toasted
    coriander seeds
2 tablespoons freshly grated orange
    zest
Kosher salt and freshly cracked black
    pepper to taste

Oil with Mexican Flavors
2 tablespoons chopped chipotle
    peppers in adobo sauce
1 tablespoon freshly grated orange
    zest
1 tablespoon minced garlic
1 tablespoon cracked toasted cumin
    seeds
3 tablespoons roughly chopped fresh
    cilantro
Kosher salt and freshly cracked black
    pepper to taste

Oil with Sweet Turkish Flavors
1/4 cup minced dates
1/3 cup minced fresh parsley
1/4 cup honey
1/4 cup finely chopped almonds

ez grill bread
with caramelized onions and blue cheese

SERVES 4 TO 6 AS AN APPETIZER

There are hundreds of grilled bread traditions all around the world; this is our version. We grill the bread on one side, then flip it, put onions and cheese on top, and cover it with a foil pan to finish cooking. The pan is important because it helps the cheese melt before the bread burns on the bottom. If you like pizza, you're going to love this.

5 tablespoons olive oil
3 red onions, peeled and sliced into
    thick rings
Kosher salt and freshly cracked black
    pepper to taste
EZ Grill Bread (page 77), shaped into
    4 rounds but not cooked

1/2 cup crumbled Maytag or other
    blue cheese of your choice
1/4 cup roughly chopped
    fresh parsley

1. In a large sauté pan or skillet over medium heat, heat 2 tablespoons of the oil until it is hot but not smoking. Add the onions and reduce the heat to low. Season with salt and pepper and sauté, stirring occasionally, until well caramelized, 20 to 30 minutes.

2. While the onions are cooking, build a multi-level fire in your grill: Leaving one-quarter of the bottom free of coals, bank the coals in the remaining three-quarters of the grill so that they are about three times as high on one side as on the other. When the coals are all ignited and the temperature has died down to medium (you can hold your hand about 5 inches above the grill grid, over the area where the coals are deepest, for 4 to 5 seconds), you're ready to cook.

3. When the onions are ready, brush both sides of the bread rounds with the remaining 3 tablespoons of oil. Put the bread on the grill and cook until toasted and brown on one side. Flip over and top each slice with a pile of the onions. Scatter the blue cheese over the onions, invert a foil pan over the bread, and continue to cook until the cheese starts to melt, about 3 minutes.

4. To serve, cut the bread into smaller pieces using a large, sharp knife, arrange the pieces on a serving platter, and sprinkle with parsley.

COOK TO COOK: It's important to be sure the dough is pretty close to 1/8 inch thick when you put it on the grill—much thicker and it will be hard to get it cooked through without burning it; much thinner and it will tend to droop down between the rungs on the grill grid.

ez grill bread with asiago, prosciutto, and sun-dried tomatoes

SERVES 4 TO 6 AS AN APPETIZER

Make sure you use oil-packed sun-dried tomatoes here, rather than the version that comes dried in a cellophane package. Even when you soak the dried ones in olive oil, they remain too leathery for this particular treatment. Of course, you can always just use thin strips of fresh bell pepper if you like.

3 tablespoons extra-virgin olive oil
EZ Grill Bread (page 77), shaped into
    4 rounds but not cooked
1/4 pound thinly sliced prosciutto
1/4 cup lightly packed fresh basil
    leaves, cut into thin strips
1/4 cup drained oil-packed sun-dried
    tomatoes, cut into thin strips

1 cup freshly grated Asiago or other
    hard Italian cheese such as
    Taleggio or Parmigiano Reggiano
Kosher salt and freshly cracked black
    pepper to taste

1. Build a multi-level fire in your grill: Leaving one-quarter of the bottom free of coals, bank the coals in the remaining three-quarters of the grill so that they are about three times as high on one side as on the other. When the coals are all ignited and the temperature has died down to medium (you can hold your hand about 5 inches above the grill grid, over the area where the coals are deepest, for 4 to 5 seconds), you're ready to cook.

2. Brush both sides of each bread round with oil, place the rounds on the grill, and cook until they are nicely toasted and brown on one side. Flip over and top each one with a strip of prosciutto, a few of the basil leaves, and some strips of tomato. Top it all off with the cheese. Invert a foil pan over the bread and continue to cook until the cheese starts to melt, about 3 minutes.

3. To serve, cut the bread into smaller pieces using a large, sharp knife, season with salt and pepper, and arrange on a platter.

COOK TO COOK: Putting a foil pan over food on the grill creates an oven effect. In this case, that helps melt the cheese without the need for a hot fire that would burn the bottom of the dough. Keep several sizes of foil pans handy—the ideal is to have one that fits rather snugly around the food being grilled, since this creates the most heat inside the pan.

ez grill bread with shrimp, artichoke hearts, and bacon

SERVES 4 TO 6 AS AN APPETIZER

This is the most upscale version of our pizza-style grilled bread options. So if you've got some folks coming to dinner whom you want to impress with your grilling prowess, this may be the one to choose.

1/2 pound cooked shrimp, diced medium
4 bacon slices, cooked and crumbled
3 tablespoons roughly chopped fresh oregano or thyme
3 tablespoons extra-virgin olive oil
1 teaspoon minced garlic, mashed to a paste with the side of a knife

EZ Grill Bread (page 77), shaped into 4 rounds but not cooked
6 artichoke hearts, cut into quarters (either canned or thawed frozen is okay)
Kosher salt and freshly cracked black pepper to taste

1. Build a multi-level fire in your grill: Leaving one-quarter of the bottom free of coals, bank the coals in the remaining three-quarters of the grill so that they are about three times as high on one side as on the other. When the coals are all ignited and the temperature has died down to medium (you can hold your hand about 5 inches above the grill grid, over the area where the coals, are deepest, for 4 to 5 seconds), you're ready to cook.

2. In a small bowl, combine the shrimp, bacon, and oregano and toss.

3. In another small bowl, mix the olive oil and garlic together. Brush both sides of each bread round with this mixture, place the rounds on the grill, and cook until they are nicely toasted and brown on one side. Flip over and top each round with some of the shrimp mixture and a few pieces of artichoke. Season lightly with salt and pepper and invert a foil pan over the bread until the topping is heated through.

4. To serve, cut the bread into smaller pieces using a large, sharp knife, drizzle with a little of the remaining garlic oil, and arrange on a platter.

COOK TO COOK: For any of these topped grilled breads, you can grill the bread an hour or two ahead of time if you want, then add the toppings and heat through (using your foil pan, of course) just before you're ready to serve.

ez grill bread with tomatoes, parmesan, and basil

SERVES 4 TO 6 AS APPETIZERS

This is similar to the classic Pizza Margherita combination, except that we substitute some grated Parmesan for the buffalo mozzarella used in Margherita. That way, the cheese melts more readily so you don't have to leave the bread over the fire too long and risk scorching it.

2 tomatoes about the size of
    baseballs, cored, seeded, and
    diced small
1 cup lightly packed fresh basil
    leaves, cut into thin strips
2 tablespoons minced garlic
1 tablespoon red pepper flakes
1/4 cup plus 3 tablespoons
    extra-virgin olive oil

1/2 cup grated Parmesan cheese
Kosher salt and freshly cracked black
    pepper to taste
EZ Grill Bread (page 77), shaped into
    4 rounds but not cooked
Fresh basil sprigs (for garnish)

1. Build a multi-level fire in your grill: Leaving one-quarter of the bottom free of coals, bank the coals in the remaining three-quarters of the grill so that they are about three times as high on one side as on the other. When the coals are all ignited and the temperature has died down to medium (you can hold your hand about 5 inches above the grill grid, over the area where the coals are deepest, for 4 to 5 seconds), you're ready to cook.

2. In a medium bowl, combine the tomatoes, basil, garlic, red pepper flakes, and 1/4 cup of the olive oil and toss to combine. Add the Parmesan cheese and salt and pepper to taste and toss again.

3. Brush both sides of the bread rounds with the remaining 3 tablespoons of olive oil, place the rounds on the grill, and cook until they are nicely toasted and brown on one side. Flip over and top each round with some of the tomato mixture. Invert a foil pan over the bread until the tomatoes are heated through and the cheese is starting to melt, about 3 minutes.

4. To serve, cut the bread into smaller pieces using a large, sharp knife, arrange them on a platter, and garnish with sprigs of fresh basil.

COOK TO COOK: If you find yourself without disposable foil pans (shame, shame), you can use a baking dish to cover the bread. Just be prepared for some heavy scrubbing.

ez grill bread with middle eastern salad

SERVES 4 AS A SALAD COURSE

꙳ ꙳ ꙳ ꙳ ꙳ ꙳ ꙳ ꙳ ꙳ ꙳ ꙳ ꙳ ꙳ ꙳ ꙳ ꙳ ꙳

We are very fond of *fattoush*, a Middle Eastern salad that includes pieces of grilled pita or other hearth bread. For this appetizer we're working a little change on the concept, piling the salad on top of the grilled bread instead of including the bread in the salad itself.

1/4 cup red wine vinegar
1/4 cup plus 3 tablespoons extra-virgin olive oil
2 tomatoes about the size of baseballs, cored, seeded, and diced small
2 cucumbers, halved, seeded, and diced small
1 red onion, peeled and diced small
1/2 cup brine-cured black olives, such as kalamata, pitted and roughly chopped

5 scallions, both white and green parts, sliced thin
1/2 cup crumbled feta cheese
Kosher salt and freshly cracked black pepper to taste
EZ Grill Bread (page 77), shaped into 4 rounds but not cooked

1. Build a multi-level fire in your grill: Leaving one-quarter of the bottom free of coals, bank the coals in the remaining three-quarters of the grill so that they are three times as high on one side as on the other. When the coals are all ignited and the temperature has died down to medium (you can hold your hand about 5 inches above the grill grid, over the area where the coals are deepest, for 4 to 5 seconds), you're ready to cook.

2. In medium bowl, whisk together the vinegar and the 1/4 cup of olive oil. Add the tomatoes, cucumbers, onion, olives, and scallions and mix well.

3. Brush both sides of the bread rounds with the remaining 3 tablespoons of oil, place the rounds on the grill, and cook until nicely toasted and brown on one side. Flip over and grill on the second side.

4. Place a round of grilled bread on each salad plate. At the last minute, toss the feta cheese with the tomato salad and season with salt and pepper. Top each bread round with a portion of the salad and serve.

COOK TO COOK: It saves a lot of tedium if you buy pitted olives. But we're not talking about those big, mushy ones that come in cans. Look for the brine-cured varieties, which usually come in plastic deli-style containers.

ez grill bread with mango, avocado, and cucumber salad

SERVES 4 AS A SALAD COURSE

Here we use our grilled bread as the base for a substantial salad course with an Indian-influenced dressing. The Tabasco adds a punch to the dish while the mango, cucumber, and avocado all help to cool it down. Of course, if you are not a big fan of heat, you can always just use less Tabasco. You should have some dressing left over, which is a good thing—you can keep it, covered and refrigerated, for up to a week, and it makes a great glaze for any pork or chicken dish you happen to be grilling.

For the dressing:
- 1/2 cup extra-virgin olive oil
- 1/4 cup fresh orange juice (about 1/2 orange)
- 1/4 cup fresh lime juice (about 2 limes)
- 2 tablespoons red wine vinegar
- 2 tablespoons cracked toasted cumin seeds (or substitute 1 tablespoon ground cumin)
- 1 tablespoon cracked toasted coriander seeds (or substitute 1/2 tablespoon ground coriander)
- 8 dashes Tabasco sauce, or to taste
- 1/4 cup roughly chopped fresh cilantro
- Kosher salt and freshly cracked black pepper to taste

For the salad:
- 2 bunches arugula, washed, dried, and trimmed
- 1 ripe but firm mango, peeled, pitted, and diced large
- 1 ripe but firm California avocado, peeled, pitted, and diced large
- 1 cucumber, peeled if you want, diced large

- 3 tablespoons olive oil
- EZ Grill Bread (page 77), shaped into 4 rounds but not cooked

1. Build a multi-level fire in your grill: Leaving one-quarter of the bottom free of coals, bank the coals in the remaining three-quarters of the grill so that they are three times as high on one side as on the other. When the coals are all ignited and the temperature has died down to medium (you can hold your hand about 5 inches above the grill grid, over the area where the coals are deepest, for 4 to 5 seconds), you're ready to cook.

2. In a medium bowl, whisk together the olive oil, orange juice, lime juice, and vinegar until well blended. Add the remaining dressing ingredients and mix well.

3. In a large bowl, combine the arugula, mango, avocado, and cucumber. Stir the dressing once more, then add to the bowl just enough to moisten all the salad ingredients (there will probably be some dressing left over) and toss well to coat.

4. Brush both sides of each bread round with oil, then place on the grill and cook until nicely toasted and brown on one side. Flip the rounds over and grill on the second side.

5. Place a grilled bread round on each salad plate, top with a portion of the salad, and serve.

COOK TO COOK: To get the best from whole spices, toast them before use to bring out the volatile oils. Simply place the seeds in a sauté pan or skillet over medium heat and toast, watching carefully and shaking frequently to avoid burning, until the seeds are aromatic and a shade darker, about 2 to 3 minutes. Believe us, it's worth the time.

ez grill bread with latin caesar salad

SERVES 4 AS A SALAD COURSE

Here we combine the bread salad tradition of Italy and the Middle East with Latin flavors and the romaine-Parmesan combination that is at the heart of the Caesar Salad, the most popular salad in the United States today. This is a relatively robust salad, even suitable for a light lunch for four. You should have some dressing left over, but don't throw it out; it's really good drizzled over grilled vegetables or even mixed with rice.

For the dressing:
1/4 cup sour cream
1/2 cup olive oil
1/4 cup fresh lime juice (about
    2 limes)
1/4 cup roughly chopped fresh
    cilantro
1 tablespoon chili powder, or to taste
1 teaspoon minced garlic
1 tablespoon minced fresh chile pep-
    per of your choice, or to taste
Kosher salt and freshly cracked black
    pepper to taste

For the salad:
2 romaine lettuce hearts, washed,
    dried, and cut crosswise into 2-
    inch pieces
2 ripe but firm California avocados,
    peeled, pitted, and quartered
2 tomatoes about the size of base-
    balls, cored and quartered
1 small red onion, peeled, halved
    lengthwise, and thinly sliced
1/3 cup grated Parmesan cheese
———
3 tablespoons olive oil
EZ Grill Bread (page 77), shaped into
    4 rounds but not cooked

1. Build a multi-level fire in your grill: Leaving one-quarter of the bottom free of coals, bank the coals in the remaining three-quarters of the grill so that they are three times as high on one side as on the other. When the coals are all ignited and the temperature has died down to medium (you can hold your hand about 5 inches above the grill grid, over the area where the coals are deepest, for 4 to 5 seconds), you're ready to cook.

2. In a small bowl, whisk together the sour cream and olive oil. Add the remaining dressing ingredients and mix until smooth. Set aside while you make the salad.

3. In a large bowl, combine the romaine lettuce, avocados, tomatoes, and onion. Stir the dressing well, add just enough to moisten the ingredients (there will be some left over), and toss gently to coat. Sprinkle with the cheese and toss gently again.

4. Brush both sides of each bread round with oil, place the rounds on the grill, and cook until they are nicely toasted and brown on one side. Flip over and grill on the second side.

5. Place a round of grilled bread on each salad plate, spoon a portion of the salad on top, and serve.

three smart grilled quesadilla options

If you are intimidated by the idea of making quesadillas, think of them as tortilla sandwiches. As you might imagine from that description, they are pretty easy to make: You take some fresh flour tortillas, fill them with whatever you choose, put them over the flames for a few minutes to brown them on the outside and melt any cheese in the filling, then cut them into quarters and serve them up. They are an excellent pass-around appetizer, and they taste even better when accompanied by any of the salsas on pages 328 to 332.

Whichever option you choose, be sure to put your quesadillas together on a baking sheet or you may have a messy trip to the grill.

option #1

avocado, bacon, and jack cheese quesadillas

8 6-inch flour tortillas
1 cup shredded Monterey Jack cheese
2 tomatoes about the size of baseballs, cored and thinly sliced
2 ripe but firm California avocados, pitted, peeled, and sliced into thin wedges
8 thick-cut bacon slices, cooked the way you like it and roughly chopped

2 tablespoons cracked toasted cumin seeds
16 fresh cilantro sprigs
Kosher salt and freshly cracked black pepper to taste

option #2

smoked duck quesadillas with pineapple, jalapeños, and scallions

8 6-inch flour tortillas
1 cup shredded Monterey Jack cheese
4 super-thin fresh pineapple rings
1/2 pound smoked duck meat (pulled off 3 legs) (page 00)
2 jalapeños, diced small
1/4 cup sliced scallions, both green and white parts

1/4 cup roughly chopped fresh oregano
Kosher salt and freshly cracked black pepper to taste

duck legs take to smoke

* * *

Smoke-roasting is an excellent way to treat duck legs; they have enough flavor to stand up to the smoke, and the slow cooking makes the meat fork-tender. Unlike duck breast, which seems fancy no matter how you serve it, smoked legs have a dual personality: Served whole on the bone, they can be the first course for a fancy dinner (page 262); pull the meat off the bone, and you've got a rich, tasty filling for quesadillas or barbecue sandwiches. (The pulled meat also freezes well, and all the crispy skin goes to the cook.) But don't plan on using leftover smoked duck to make your quesadillas; unless you throw a few extra legs on the grill, there won't be any. It's that good.

option #3

shrimp, corn, and tomato quesadillas

8 6-inch flour tortillas
1 cup shredded Monterey Jack cheese
1 tomato about the size of a baseball, cored and diced small
1/2 pound cooked shrimp, diced medium
1 ear corn, blanched in boiling salted water for 2 minutes, drained, and kernels cut off the cob (about 1/2 cup kernels)

2 tablespoons cracked toasted coriander seeds
1/4 cup roughly chopped fresh cilantro
Kosher salt and freshly cracked black pepper to taste

1. Build a multi-level fire in your grill: Leaving one-quarter of the bottom free of coals, bank the coals in the remaining three-quarters of the grill so that they are three times as high on one side as on the other. When the coals are all ignited and the temperature has died down to medium to low (you can hold your hand about 5 inches above the grill grid, over the area where the coals are deepest, for 5 to 6 seconds), you're ready to cook.

2. Lay 4 tortillas out on a baking sheet. Divide your Option ingredients among the tortillas, putting them on in the order listed. Top each stack with another tortilla, then gently press down so that everything holds together. Carefully transfer the quesadillas to the grill and cook until the cheese melts and the bottoms are crisp, about 3 minutes. Use a wide metal spatula to turn them over carefully. Cover with a disposable pie pan and toast on the other side.

3. Transfer the quesadillas to a serving plate, cut each one into quarters, and serve.

COOK TO COOK: Because corn tortillas become quite brittle over a fire, flour tortillas are our choice here. Also, note that the mixtures you put into the tortillas should be somewhat wet so that they come together like a hamburger when you press down; if they are all crumbly, they don't stay inside. Tortillas are a little delicate, so be careful when you handle them, and use a spatula to turn them over.

grilled shrimp skewers with plums and hoisin barbecue sauce

SERVES 4 AS AN APPETIZER

We are happy to spring for the extra money to buy humongous shrimp, both because people are not used to seeing shrimp this size and because they come off the grill moister than their smaller brethren. There's a good buying tactic for them, too. The truth is that store owners buy them frozen in five-pound boxes, then defrost them and put them out on ice in the fish counter. If you can get the retailer to sell you one of those five-pound boxes from his freezer, you'll be saving a fair amount of money while getting exactly the same shrimp. At home, defrost them just enough to take them apart, then re-freeze them in smaller portions for cooking.

Here we give the giant shrimp a Chinese-inspired treatment, combining them on skewers with fresh plums and coating them with a hoisin-based barbecue sauce. Hoisin is one of our favorite flavors, and we heartily recommend that you stock it in your pantry. In fact, it's hard to make a dish using hoisin sauce that people don't like.

For the sauce:
1/3 cup hoisin sauce
1 tablespoon catsup
2 tablespoons dry sherry
1/4 cup rice wine vinegar (or substitute cider vinegar)
1 tablespoon brown sugar
1 teaspoon five-spice powder
___
1 pound mammoth (U/12) shrimp, peeled and deveined, with tails intact
3 ripe but firm plums, pitted and cut into quarters

2 tablespoons olive oil
2 tablespoons peeled and minced fresh ginger
Kosher salt and freshly cracked white pepper to taste (or substitute black pepper)
3 scallions, white and bottom 2/3 of green parts, trimmed and cut into thin strips
1 lime, quartered

1. Build a multi-level fire in your grill: Leaving one-quarter of the bottom free of coals, bank the coals in the remaining three-quarters of the grill so that they are three times as high on one side as on the other. When the coals are all ignited and the temperature has died down to medium (you can hold your hand about 5 inches above the grill grid, over the area where the coals are deepest, for 4 to 5 seconds), you're ready to cook.

2. In a small bowl, combine all sauce ingredients and mix well.

3. In a large bowl, combine the shrimp, plums, oil, ginger, and salt and pepper. Toss until the shrimp and plums are well coated, then alternate them as you thread them onto 4 skewers.

4. Put the skewers on the grill and cook for 3 to 4 minutes per side, basting with the sauce during the last 30 seconds of cooking on each side. To check for doneness, poke the shrimp with your finger to check its firmness level (see page 13); if you're unsure, nick, peek, and cheat: Cut into one of the shrimp and check to be sure it is opaque all the way through.

5. Arrange the skewers on a platter, garnish with the scallions, and serve with the remaining sauce for dipping and lime quarters for squeezing.

COOK TO COOK: We don't usually bother with deveining small shrimp, but with the big guys it makes a difference. The easiest way to do it is to take the point of a small, sharp knife or a pair of small scissors and cut through the back of the shell and through just a bit of the meat underneath, from tail to head. Then, using the point of the knife, just drag out the vein.

grilled colossal shrimp and mango skewers with guava-lime glaze

SERVES 4 AS AN APPETIZER

Most recipes that you'll find—and most restaurants as well—use large shrimp, called 16/20s because there are anywhere from 16 to 20 of them per pound. But we recommend that when grilling shrimp you buy the really big guys, known as U/12s, which means there are fewer than a dozen of them to the pound. We think they're worth the extra cash—that extra bit of meat keeps them considerably more tender and moist.

This recipe features the fantastic Southeast Asian fish sauce–sesame oil–ginger combination that we really love, with the guava glaze adding a little exotic sweetness. Guava juice is available in most Latin or Asian grocery stores, but if you can't locate it, you can use all pineapple juice in the glaze.

2 tablespoons peeled and minced fresh ginger

2 tablespoons *nam pla*, Southeast Asian fish sauce (or substitute soy sauce)

2 tablespoons roasted sesame oil

3 tablespoons cracked toasted coriander seeds (or substitute 1 1/2 tablespoons ground coriander)

1 tablespoon red pepper flakes, or to taste

Kosher salt and freshly cracked white pepper to taste (or substitute black pepper)

16 extra-large (U/12) shrimp, peeled and deveined, with tails intact

2 red bell peppers, seeded, halved, and each half cut into 4 pieces

1 large red onion, peeled, halved, and each half cut into 4 pieces

2 firm but ripe mangoes, peeled, pitted, and each cut into 8 chunks

For the glaze:

2 cups guava juice

1 cup pineapple juice

1/2 cup white vinegar

2 tablespoons peeled and minced fresh ginger

1/3 cup fresh lime juice (about 3 limes)

1/4 cup roughly chopped fresh mint

1. In a large bowl, combine the ginger, fish sauce, sesame oil, coriander, red pepper flakes, and salt and pepper and mix well. Add the shrimp, bell peppers, onions, and mangoes, tossing to coat, and thread them onto 4 skewers, alternating as you go. Cover and refrigerate while you make the glaze.

2. In a medium saucepan, combine the guava juice, pineapple juice, vinegar, and ginger and bring to a boil over high heat. Reduce the heat to medium and simmer vigorously until the mixture is reduced by two-thirds and becomes slightly syrupy, about 30 or 40 minutes. Remove from the heat, allow to cool to room temperature, then stir in the lime juice and mint.

3. When you start making the glaze, build a multi-level fire in your grill: Leaving one-quarter of the bottom free of coals, bank the coals in the remaining three-quarters of the grill so that they are three times as high on one side as on the other. When the coals are all ignited and the temperature has died down to medium (you can hold your hand about 5 inches above the grill grid, over the area where the coals are deepest, for 4 to 5 seconds), you're ready to cook.

4. Place the skewers on the grill and cook until the shrimp are just cooked through, about 3 to 4 minutes per side. About 30 seconds before the skewers come off the grill, brush them liberally with the glaze. (To check the shrimp for doneness, nick, peek, and cheat: Cut into one of the shrimp at its thickest point and peek inside to be sure it is opaque all the way through.)

5. Serve the shrimp and mangoes either skewered or taken off, passing any remaining guava glaze in a small bowl as a dipping sauce.

curry-rubbed grilled shrimp
with gingered cucumber relish and minted yogurt

SERVES 4 AS AN APPETIZER

≈ ≈ ≈ ≈ ≈ ≈ ≈ ≈ ≈ ≈ ≈ ≈ ≈ ≈ ≈ ≈ ≈ ≈

This is an Indian interpretation of the grilled shrimp oeuvre, with lots of bright flavors. To get the necessary flavor components, we rub the shrimp with sesame oil and curry powder before grilling, then heat cumin seeds in oil to create a flavored oil for the simple relish. The pungent, oily cucumber relish makes a very nice contrast up against the lemony minted yogurt and the smoky curried shrimp. If you like, you can substitute scallops for the shrimp.

This is great served in front of a vegetarian entrée. It also makes a nice entrée for two when served with rice.

1 pound large (U/20) shrimp, peeled and deveined, with tails intact	3 tablespoons peeled and minced fresh ginger
2 tablespoons roasted sesame oil	2 tablespoons cracked toasted cumin seeds
3 tablespoons Sherwood or other good-quality curry powder	3 tablespoons olive oil
Kosher salt and freshly cracked black pepper to taste	1/2 cup plain yogurt
	1/4 cup roughly chopped fresh mint
2 cucumbers, peeled, seeded, and diced medium	Juice of 1 lime

1. Build a multi-level fire in your grill: Leaving one-quarter of the bottom free of coals, bank the coals in the remaining three-quarters of the grill so that they are three times as high on one side as on the other. When the coals are all ignited and the temperature has died down to medium (you can hold your hand about 5 inches above the grill grid, over the area where the coals are deepest, for 4 to 5 seconds), you're ready to cook.

2. In a large bowl, toss the shrimp with the sesame oil, then add the curry powder and salt and pepper and toss to coat again. Put the shrimp on the grill and cook until just opaque, about 3 to 4 minutes per side. To check for doneness, poke the shrimp with your finger to check its firmness level (see page 13); if you're unsure, nick, peek, and cheat: Cut into one of the shrimp at its thickest point and peek to be sure it is opaque all the way through.

3. While the shrimp are cooking, make the relish: In a small sauté pan or skillet, combine the cumin seeds and olive oil and sauté over medium heat, stirring frequently, until the cumin becomes very aromatic, about 3 minutes. Transfer the oil and cumin to a medium bowl, add the cucumbers and ginger, and mix well.

4. In a small bowl, combine the yogurt, mint, and lime juice and mix well.

5. To serve, arrange the shrimp on 4 plates, spoon the relish over the top, add a spoon-ful of the minted yogurt, and bring to the table immediately.

COOK TO COOK: Indian cooks are geniuses with spices. Here we use one typical Indian tech-nique, cooking a spice in oil to spread its flavor throughout the dish. The key is to get the spice (in this case cumin) hot enough to release its volatile aromatics into the oil but not so hot that it burns. To achieve this, stir often while cooking the spice, and when the aroma becomes very pro-nounced, remove the pan from the heat.

grilled peel-and-eat colossal shrimp with garlic-tabasco butter

SERVES 4 AS AN APPETIZER

This is a gloriously messy dish, but we like it for precisely that reason. To eat it, you stick your hand in the bowl and get some shrimp and peel them yourself, which means your hands get all covered with the garlic butter that's on the shrimp. It's kind of like East Coast crab-eating, where you also have to get involved and touch the food. To us, it makes the whole process more fun.

Here we use the colossal shrimp, known in the trade as U/12 or U/10, meaning that there are under 12 or under 10 to the pound. We slit these giant guys down the back a little bit but keep the shell on, rub them with a little paprika, then grill them and toss them in a bowl with garlic, Tabasco, and a few other tasty ingredients. This is definitely a good-eatin' dish, particularly if you trust us and spring for the big shrimp, which end up being almost like langoustines.

12 colossal (U/12 or U/10) shrimp
2 tablespoons paprika
3 tablespoons olive oil
Kosher salt and freshly cracked black
    pepper to taste
4 tablespoons unsalted butter,
    softened
1 tablespoon minced garlic

1/3 cup roughly chopped fresh
    parsley
Juice of 1 lemon
2 tablespoons Tabasco sauce, or
    to taste
4 dashes Worcestershire sauce
1 lemon, quartered lengthwise

1. Build a multi-level fire in your grill: Leaving one-quarter of the bottom free of coals, bank the coals in the remaining three-quarters of the grill so that they are three times as high on one side as on the other. When the coals are all ignited and the temperature has died down to medium (you can hold your hand about 5 inches above the grill grid, over the area where the coals are deepest, for 4 to 5 seconds), you're ready to cook.

2. Using a small, sharp knife or a pair of small scissors, slit the shell along the back of each shrimp and remove the vein (see p. 94).

3. In a large bowl, combine paprika, oil, and salt and pepper and mix a bit. Add the shrimp and toss to coat. Put the shrimp on the grill and cook until opaque throughout, about 4 to 5 minutes per side. To check for doneness, poke the shrimp with your finger to check the firmness level (see page 13); if you're unsure, nick, peek, and cheat: Cut into one of the shrimp at its thickest point and peek to be sure it is opaque all the way through.

4. While the shrimp are cooking, combine all the remaining ingredients except the lemon wedges in the bowl you originally used for the shrimp. When the shrimp are

done, add them to the bowl and toss gently until the butter is melted and the shrimp are nicely coated with the other ingredients. Serve the shrimp right out of the bowl, with lemon wedges for squeezing and another big bowl for shells.

COOK TO COOK: If you are into neatness, you can adopt a different approach for this dish. Rather than mixing the shrimp with the flavored butter, peel the shrimp first and then dip them into the butter mixture.

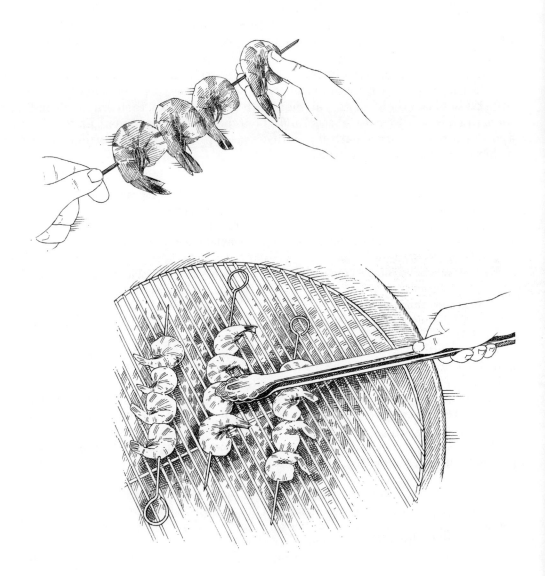

grilled shrimp scampi

SERVES 4

This very straightforward dish, a live-fire takeoff on classic shrimp scampi, is another one of those appetizers that allow you to greet your guests with something right off the grill. These flavorful shrimp are excellent served on toast (drizzle the toast with the butter-tomato mixture) and also go great on a little bowl of pasta, transforming it into an easy entrée.

2 ripe tomatoes about the size of
    baseballs, cored and diced small
3 tablespoons unsalted butter
3 tablespoons dry sherry
1/4 cup roughly chopped fresh
    parsley
Juice of 1 lemon

1 1/2 pounds medium shrimp, peeled
    and deveined, with tails intact
2 tablespoons olive oil
2 tablespoons minced garlic
Kosher salt and freshly cracked black
    pepper to taste

1. Build a multi-level fire in your grill: Leaving one-quarter of the bottom free of coals, bank the coals in the remaining three-quarters of the grill so that they are three times as high on one side as on the other. When the coals are all ignited and the temperature has died down to medium (you can hold your hand about 5 inches above the grill grid, over the area where the coals are deepest, for 4 to 5 seconds), you're ready to cook.

2. In a shallow foil pan large enough to hold the shrimp, combine the tomatoes, butter, sherry, parsley, and lemon juice. Place it on the grill over the side that has no fire, and stir or swirl the mixture around a few times as it heats up.

3. In a medium bowl, combine the shrimp, oil, garlic, and salt and pepper and toss to coat. Thread the shrimp onto skewers, put the skewers on the part of the grill over the deepest coals, and cook until the shrimp are done, about 3 to 4 minutes. To check for doneness, nick, peek, and cheat: Cut into one of the shrimp at its thickest point and peek to be sure it is opaque all the way through.

4. Push the shrimp off the skewers into the butter mixture, toss to coat, and serve.

COOK TO COOK: You don't need to let the shrimp cook in the butter mixture—just toss them in there, get them nicely coated, and serve them up.

grilled garlic new potatoes with shrimp puttanesca

SERVES 4 AS AN APPETIZER

We always think it's fun to take an everyday ingredient like a potato and combine it with a more upscale ingredient like shrimp. Here we grill new potatoes and shrimp separately, and then we toss the shrimp with capers, garlic, and all the other ingredients of the classic Italian puttanesca (whore's) sauce and serve it on top of the potatoes for an outstanding hearty appetizer.

By the way, when you grill the potatoes, make sure they are nice and golden brown on the outside before you take them off the heat. Just because they are inexpensive doesn't mean they don't deserve special attention.

8 potatoes about the size of golf balls
   (new red, Yukon Gold, or other
   medium-starch variety), washed
6 tablespoons extra-virgin olive oil,
   divided
1 1/2 tablespoons minced garlic, divided
Kosher salt and freshly cracked black
   pepper to taste
1/2 pound medium-large (16/20)
   shrimp, peeled and
   deveined, with tails intact
1/4 cup roughly chopped pitted
   Kalamata or other brine-cured
   black olives

3 tablespoons capers, well rinsed and
   drained
2 anchovy fillets, chopped
   (optional)
1/4 cup finely chopped fresh parsley
1 teaspoon red pepper flakes,
   or to taste
1 tablespoon fresh lemon juice (about
   1/4 lemon)
1 lemon, sliced thin for garnish

1. Place the potatoes in boiling salted water and let boil, uncovered, until they are just tender enough to be easily pierced with a fork but still offer some resistance, about 12 minutes. Immediately plunge them into ice water to stop the cooking, then drain well and refrigerate until cold.

2. Build a multi-level fire in your grill: Leaving one-quarter of the bottom free of coals, bank the coals in the remaining three-quarters of the grill so that they are three times as high on one side as on the other. When the coals are all ignited and the temperature has died down to medium (you can hold your hand about 5 inches above the grill grid, over the area where the coals are deepest, for 4 to 5 seconds), you're ready to cook.

3. Cut the chilled potatoes in half and transfer them to a large bowl. Add 2 tablespoons of the olive oil and 1 tablespoon of the minced garlic, along with salt and pepper to taste, and toss until the potato halves are well coated. Thread the potatoes onto skew-

ers, arranging the potatoes to face the same way so that the cut sides will lie flat on the grill. Put the skewers on the grill, cut side down, and cook until golden brown, about 3 to 4 minutes; turn and cook the rounded side for 2 minutes more. Push the potatoes off their skewers onto a serving dish and cover to keep warm.

4. Meanwhile, sprinkle the shrimp generously with salt and pepper, put them on the grill beside the potatoes, and cook until just done, about 3 to 4 minutes per side. To check for doneness, nick, peek, and cheat: Cut into one of the shrimp at its thickest point and peek to be sure it is opaque all the way through.

5. Transfer the cooked shrimp to a large bowl. Add the remaining 4 tablespoons of olive oil and 1/2 tablespoon of minced garlic along with the olives, capers, anchovies, parsley, red pepper flakes, and lemon juice. Toss until the shrimp are well coated, then arrange the shrimp over the potatoes, garnish with lemon slices, and serve.

COOK TO COOK: The thing about grilling potatoes (or beets or any other dense, ovoid vegetable) is that they have to be pre-boiled properly before grilling so they are neither too soft nor too hard. After they have been in the boiling water about 8 to 10 minutes, start testing them by piercing them with a fork; you want to take them out when they are easily pierced but still offer some resistance.

grilled avocados stuffed with shrimp-mango salsa

SERVES 4 AS AN APPETIZER

Here we take the avocado-stuffed-with-shrimp-salad plate off the cafeteria line, dress it up with mango and some other Caribbean flavors, and bring it onto the back patio.

Because you're chopping up the shrimp here, you can use any size. Also, make sure the fire has died down to medium-low before you put the avocado and the limes on the grill. You're not trying to cook either one of them, just get them brown and give them some smoke, so you want to go slow. That makes this a particularly good dish to cook after you have finished grilling an entrée that needs a hotter fire. Just be sure you have everything ready to go when the entrée comes off the grill.

For the salsa:
- 1 pound cooked and peeled shrimp (any size), diced medium
- 1 ripe but firm mango, peeled, pitted, and diced small
- 1/2 red onion, peeled and diced small
- 1/3 cup extra-virgin olive oil
- 1/2 cup roughly chopped fresh cilantro
- 2 tablespoons Tabasco sauce, or to taste
- 1/4 cup orange juice
- 1/4 cup fresh lime juice (about 2 limes)

Kosher salt and freshly cracked black pepper to taste

- 2 ripe but firm California avocados, halved and pitted
- 2 limes, halved
- 2 tablespoons vegetable oil
- 1 tablespoon cracked toasted cumin seeds (or substitute 1 teaspoon ground cumin)

Kosher salt and freshly cracked black pepper to taste

1. Build a multi-level fire in your grill: Leaving one-quarter of the bottom free of coals, bank the coals in the remaining three-quarters of the grill so that they are three times as high on one side as on the other. When the coals are all ignited and the temperature has died down to medium-low (you can hold your hand about 5 inches above the grill grid, over the area where the coals are deepest, for 5 seconds), you're ready to cook.

2. In a medium bowl, combine all the salsa ingredients, mix well, and set aside.

3. Rub the exposed flesh of the avocado and lime halves all over with the vegetable oil, then rub with the cumin and sprinkle with salt and pepper. Place them on the grill, cut side down, and cook until just golden brown, about 5 minutes.

4. Arrange the grilled avocado halves on 4 plates, fill each cavity with some of the salsa, and serve with the grilled lime halves on the side for squeezing.

COOK TO COOK: The key to this dish is getting the right avocados. Look for ones that are firm but ripe—they should give to the touch, but only with a fair amount of pressure.

grilled red onions with lobster, truffle oil, and scallions

SERVES 4 AS AN APPETIZER

If you should ever have any leftover lobster, this is the way to use it—you need only half a pound. But since it is highly unlikely that you will have even that much cooked lobster meat hanging around in the refrigerator, it's fortunate that these days it is available in small amounts in many fish stores and even supermarkets. You'll probably want to stop by a specialty food store to pick up your white truffle oil, too; if you don't have such a store near you, check out our Sources section (page 401) to mail-order this wonderfully flavorful, luxe ingredient.

2 medium red onions, peeled and cut into slices 1 inch thick (keep the rings together)
3 tablespoons olive oil
Kosher salt and freshly cracked black pepper to taste

Juice of 1 lemon
1/4 cup finely chopped scallions, white and green parts
1/2 pound cooked lobster meat, picked over and diced medium
2 tablespoons white truffle oil

1. Build a multi-level fire in your grill: Leaving one-quarter of the bottom free of coals, bank the coals in the remaining three-quarters of the grill so that they are three times as high on one side as on the other. When the coals are all ignited and the temperature has died down to medium (you can hold your hand about 5 inches above the grill grid, over the area where the coals are deepest, for 4 to 5 seconds), you're ready to cook.

2. Rub the onions with the oil and sprinkle them generously with salt and pepper. Put the onions on the grill and cook until golden brown and slightly charred, about 5 to 7 minutes per side. Transfer the onions to a bowl, add the lemon juice and scallions, and toss gently.

3. Divide the onions among 4 plates, arrange the lobster meat on top, sprinkle with the truffle oil, and serve.

COOK TO COOK: Be sure to let the fire die down to medium before you put the onions on the grill. That way, they can stay over the fire long enough to get completely cooked through, which causes them to lose their bite, without burning on the outside. If any start to char before they are fully tender, move them over to the side of the grill with fewer coals.

thai-style grilled scallops with aromatic greens and ginger-chile dressing

SERVES 4 AS AN APPETIZER

The complex layering of sweet, salty, hot, sour, and bitter flavors, along with the use of herbs as greens, clearly marks this as a Southeast Asian dish. It also provides an example of the way that Thai and other Southeast Asian cooks match strong flavors with fish and shellfish, which many Western cooks consider too delicate for this type of treatment.

As usual, we like to use sea scallops rather than the smaller and more costly bay scallops. We have long been fans of these bigger scallops for the same reason we like thick steaks: It is easier to avoid overcooking. They allow you to get a good, hard sear on the outside when sautéing or grilling while keeping the inside moist and tender. Fortunately, a couple of years ago the government reopened large areas of the Georges Bank (the huge and fecund fishing grounds off the coast of New England and Eastern Canada), which has resulted in an upsurge of plump, delicious, extra-large sea scallops. This dish is a first-rate way to take advantage of that bounty.

1 cup loosely packed fresh Thai basil leaves (or substitute regular basil)

1 cup loosely packed fresh mint leaves

1/2 cup loosely packed fresh cilantro sprigs

1 bunch watercress, trimmed, well washed, and dried

1/2 cup thinly sliced red cabbage

1/2 cup julienned carrots

1/3 cup fresh lime juice (about 3 limes)

3 tablespoons olive oil

3 tablespoons *nam pla*, Southeast Asian fish sauce (optional)

3 tablespoons dark soy sauce

2 tablespoons peeled and minced fresh ginger

2 tablespoons prepared Asian chile-garlic paste (available in Asian markets or large supermarkets)

1 tablespoon light brown sugar

1 pound very large sea scallops (about 10 to 12)

3 tablespoons roasted sesame oil

2 tablespoons Sherwood or other good-quality curry powder

Kosher salt and freshly cracked black pepper to taste

2 tablespoons toasted sesame seeds (optional)

1. Build a multi-level fire in your grill: Leaving one-quarter of the bottom free of coals, bank the coals in the remaining three-quarters of the grill so that they are three times as high on one side as on the other. When the coals are all ignited and the temperature has died down to medium (you can hold your hand about 5 inches above the grill grid, over the area where the coals are deepest, for 4 to 5 seconds), you're ready to cook.

2. In a large bowl, gently toss together the herbs, watercress, cabbage, and carrots. In a medium bowl, combine the lime juice, olive oil, fish sauce, soy sauce, ginger, chile

paste, and brown sugar, whisking until the sugar dissolves and the mixture is well blended. Pour the dressing over the greens, tossing to coat. Divide the dressed salad among 4 plates.

3. Rub the scallops with the sesame oil, sprinkle with salt and pepper, and rub all over with the curry powder. Place on the grill and cook until they are completely opaque, 3 to 4 minutes per side. (To check for doneness, nick, peek, and cheat: Cut into one of the scallops and peek inside to be sure it is just opaque all the way through.)

4. Arrange the scallops over the salad, sprinkle with the sesame seeds (if you are using them), and serve.

COOK TO COOK: Scallops are very easy to grill, but there is one occasional drawback—if they are not really large, they can slip through the grill grid every once in a while. So if you get scallops on the smaller side, consider threading them on skewers for grilling. Also, make sure you check for doneness on these early and often, because you definitely don't want to overcook them.

all (or at least a lot) about scallops

* * *

There are basically five varieties of scallops. Largest and most common are **sea scallops**. Harvested year-round from the floor of the Atlantic Ocean off the coast of New England, they are about 1 1/2 inches or more in diameter, weigh from 1/2 ounce up to several ounces, and are very versatile in the kitchen, with a lovely, briny flavor. These are our favorites.

Small, cork-shaped **bay scallops**, about 1/2 inch in diameter, have long been highly valued by gourmands for their exceptional delicacy and sweetness. Owing to their minuscule natural range (basically only the area between Cape Cod and Long Island) and the fact that they are in season only from November through February, they are very expensive.

In recent years farm-raised bay scallops, also known as **Chinese scallops** because most are farmed in China, have become available throughout the United States. Like other kinds of farm-raised seafood, they are not quite as flavorful as the wild version, but they're much less expensive.

Rarest and more expensive are **pink scallops**, found only in small quantities in the Pacific Northwest. Unlike other varieties, they are steamed in their shells, like steamer clams. They are particularly delicate in flavor but are very rarely available outside the Northwest.

Least desirable of the scallop options are **calico scallops**. Found in warmer waters off the Atlantic and Gulf coasts as well as Central America, they are known as southern bay scallops. These specimens look like a somewhat larger version of the erasers on pencils. Because they are too small to be profitably shucked by hand, they are blasted out of their shells with steam, which partially cooks them. Extremely prone to overcooking, they also have a rather dull flavor.

In recent years two new designations for scallops have emerged. Both terms originated in Maine and are most frequently seen on the menus of high-end restaurants. **Day-boat scallops** originally referred to scallops harvested from shoal areas off the Maine coast by scallopers who went out and back in the same day. This term is now also applied to scallops harvested during the final day of the longer trips that are more typical of the industry. **Diver scallops**, harvested individually from ocean shelves off the coast of Maine by divers, are highly valued for their freshness and are very expensive.

In addition to the *varieties* of scallops, there are two *types*, which differ in how the scallops have been processed. To get the full benefit of the gustatory virtues of scallops, it's best to seek out "dry" ones. These are nothing more than scallops that have not been treated in any way. The more readily available "wet" scallops, on the other hand, have been soaked in phosphates, a process that preserves the perishable seafood for an average of four days longer. Unfortunately, it also adds weight and plumps up the scallops with water. As a result, these scallops exude some liquid when cooked, which makes it more difficult to brown them properly.

There are some differences in appearance that may help you distinguish wet from dry. Untreated scallops tend to be ivory, pinkish gray, tan, light coral, or even grayish, usually a mixture of several colors in the same package. They are sticky and rather flabby in texture. Wet scallops, by contrast, are uniformly bright white with a slippery feeling, and they're often sitting in a telltale pool of milky liquid. But it is admittedly difficult for a non-expert to tell by sight whether scallops are dry or wet. The best bet, as with most seafood, is to buy from a fishmonger you trust. Simply say you want unsoaked scallops.

grilled scallops with tomato, corn, and chipotles

SERVES 4 AS AN APPETIZER

At my (Chris's) restaurant in Westport, Massachusetts, about twenty miles from New Bedford, the scallop capital, we take advantage of the nearly endless supply of giant, hyper-fresh sea scallops. This dish features the corn and tomatoes of late summer along with some heat from our favorite chile pepper, the chipotle, but really it's all about the scallops. We like to serve it with tortilla chips as a scallop salsa.

2 ears corn, shucked
1 ripe tomato about the size of a
    baseball, cored and diced small
1/2 red onion, peeled and diced small
2 tablespoons extra-virgin olive oil
1 teaspoon minced garlic
Juice of 3 limes
Pinch of sugar
1/2 cup chopped fresh cilantro

1 tablespoon minced chipotle
    peppers in adobo sauce
Kosher salt and freshly cracked black
    pepper to taste
1 pound large sea scallops
2 tablespoons olive oil
2 tablespoons cracked toasted cumin
    seeds (or substitute 1 tablespoon
    ground cumin)

1. Build a multi-level fire in your grill: Leaving one-quarter of the bottom free of coals, bank the coals in the remaining three-quarters of the grill so that they are three times as high on one side as on the other. When the coals are all ignited and the temperature has died down to medium (you can hold your hand about 5 inches above the grill grid, over the area where the coals are deepest, for 4 to 5 seconds), you're ready to cook.

2. Put the corn on the grill and cook, rolling the ears around occasionally until the kernels begin to brown, 2 to 3 minutes per side. Remove the ears from the grill and slice the kernels off the cobs.

3. In a medium bowl, combine the corn kernels, tomato, red onion, extra-virgin olive oil, garlic, lime juice, sugar, cilantro, and chipotles. Mix well and season to taste.

4. Rub the scallops with the olive oil, then coat them with the cumin seeds and sprinkle them generously with salt and pepper. Place on the grill and cook until just opaque throughout, about 2 to 3 minutes per side. To check for doneness, nick, peek, and cheat: Cut into one of the scallops and peek to be sure it is opaque all the way through.

5. Add the cooked scallops to the tomato-corn mixture, mix well, and serve.

COOK TO COOK: Like fin fish, scallops sometimes have a tendency to stick to the grill. So follow the same three precautions you do with fin fish: (1) make sure you have a very clean, hot grill grid; (2) oil the scallops lightly before you put them on; and (3) don't move them for a couple of minutes after they go on.

grilled oysters on the half shell
with sweet-and-sour bacon dressing

SERVES 4 AS AN APPETIZER

This is a variation on a dish that I (Chris) have enjoyed with my wife, Marcy, at these rustic joints on Bodega Bay, north of San Francisco. What happens at dockside oyster stands is that you buy a dozen or two of their hyper-fresh oysters, and they give you an oyster knife and a bottle of Tabasco so you can shuck and eat your own with as much heat as you desire. It personifies the casual, do-it-yourself approach to food that I really love. So here we take the same approach but add a simple bacon dressing that we think complements the briny oysters very nicely.

The only real trick to making this dish is shucking the oysters. To do this, place the oyster on a flat surface, cupped side down, then slip an oyster knife, can opener, or relatively dull paring knife into the hinge. Twist forcefully until the oyster pops, then twist off the top shell and discard it. Finally, sever the muscle that holds the oyster meat to the bottom shell, and there you have it. Unless you're a real pro, though, we suggest that you shuck the oysters before your guests arrive.

For the dressing:
5 slices thick-cut bacon
2 tablespoons celery seeds
3 tablespoons olive oil
3 tablespoons balsamic vinegar
1/4 cup catsup
2 tablespoons sugar

Kosher salt and freshly cracked black
    pepper to taste

24 oysters of your choice, shells
    scrubbed
1/4 cup roughly chopped fresh
    parsley

1. Build a multi-level fire in your grill: Leaving one-quarter of the bottom free of coals, bank the coals in the remaining three-quarters of the grill so that they are three times as high on one side as on the other. When the coals are all ignited and the temperature has died down to medium (you can hold your hand about 5 inches above the grill grid, over the area where the coals are deepest, for 4 to 5 seconds), you're ready to cook.

2. In a medium sauté pan or skillet over medium-high heat, cook the bacon until crisp, about 6 to 8 minutes. Move the bacon to a brown paper bag or paper towels to drain, leaving 3 tablespoons of drippings in the pan. Remove the pan from the heat and add the celery seeds and olive oil, swirling to combine. Stir in the vinegar, catsup, and sugar and mix until the sugar is dissolved. Season to taste with salt and pepper and transfer to a small bowl. Crumble the bacon into a separate bowl.

3. Shuck the oysters and loosen them in their bottom shells. Arrange the oysters (in their bottom shells) on the grill and cook just until their edges start to ruffle, about 2 to 3 minutes. Transfer the oysters to a serving platter, top each one with a spoonful of the sauce, sprinkle with the bacon and parsley, and serve immediately.

COOK TO COOK: Don't put oysters directly over a very hot fire because that might shatter the shells. The oysters are done when they begin to curl up along their sides.

those beautiful oysters

* * *

In this country, there are four major oyster species that are more or less routinely available: the briny-tasting **Atlantic**, grown along the East Coast as well as the Gulf Coast; the **Europea**, a round, flat-shelled species grown in the Northwest and parts of Maine; the **Pacific**, a species with a very deeply scalloped shell that is grown along the Pacific Coast; and the half-dollar–sized **Olympia**, grown only in the Northeast. Within each of the four species there are dozens of individual varieties corresponding to the particular place the oyster was raised, like Bluepoint and Wellfleet, both of which are Atlantics. The localized names are useful because oysters get much of their individual flavor from the particular character and temperature of the water where they grow, as well as from what they eat.

It's kind of neat to know this stuff, and it's really fun to try all the different oysters to see which you like best. But for us the bottom line is that as long as the oyster is truly fresh and properly shucked, it's going to be a great eating experience.

grill-steamed mussels with chourico and texas toast

This technique, a variation on the original Clams Johnson recipe, is one of our rock-solid favorites. Because it allows you to stand at the fire talking to your guests while you pull stuff off the grill for them to eat, we find it emblematic of what a casual grill meal is all about. And it features the classic Portuguese combination of seafood and sausage, which we are particularly fond of.

So here's the drill: You build a big, hot fire in half of your grill and put a large foil roasting pan on the other side of the grill with some butter and garlic and white wine and parsley in it. After debearding the mussels you put them right over the coals, and as they open you grab them with your tongs and put them into the foil pan with the sauce. You also grill up some chourico and some big slices of toast, and then you give everybody who comes near the grill a little plate with some mussels, a bit of chourico, and some buttered Texas toast. Now that's an appetizer to make just about anybody happy.

4 tablespoons unsalted butter, softened

2 tablespoons minced fresh parsley

3 tablespoons minced garlic, divided

2 cups dry white wine

1 tomato about the size of a baseball, cored and diced small

1 pound chourico, halved lengthwise

5 pounds (about 50 to 60) mussels scrubbed and debearded

Kosher salt and freshly cracked black pepper to taste

1/2 cup chopped fresh parsley

1 lemon, halved

4 slices good bread, 1 inch thick

1. Build a fire on one side of your grill, using about enough coals to fill a large shoebox. When the coals are all ignited and the temperature is medium (you can hold your hand 5 inches above the grill grid for 4 to 5 seconds), you're ready to cook.

2. In a small bowl, combine the butter, the minced parsley, and 1 tablespoon of the minced garlic and set it aside at room temperature.

3. Find a shallow baking pan or foil pan that is large enough to hold all the mussels in a single layer and sturdy enough to withstand the heat of a low fire. Put the wine, the remaining garlic, and the tomato in this pan and place it on the grill over the side that has no fire. As the contents heat up, stir or swirl the mixture around a few times to combine the ingredients.

4. Put the chourico on the grill over the coals and cook until it is crisp and brown, about 3 to 4 minutes per side, then remove from the heat, slice it thin, and add it to the wine mixture in the pan. Place the mussels on the hot side of the grill and cook until they open, about 8 to 10 minutes. As the mussels open, transfer them to the pan. (Discard any that do not open.)

5. While the mussels are cooking, arrange the bread slices around the edge of the fire and toast them lightly, about 2 minutes per side. Spread the hot, toasted slices with the garlic butter.

6. Squeeze the lemon halves over the mussels, sprinkle with the chopped parsley and salt and pepper to taste, and serve the mussels and chourico straight out of the pan, along with the Texas toast to soak up the pan juices.

COOK TO COOK: Make sure that your shallow foil pan is off to the side, with no fire directly underneath it. As soon as the mussels pop open, put them in the pan with the butter-wine mixture and let them cook a couple of minutes before you serve them.

grill-steamed thai-style mussels with ginger-coconut curry sauce

SERVES 4 AS AN APPETIZER

This is a variation of a dish that has been tremendously successful at the East Coast Grill. It features our very favorite way to cook shellfish: Just put them directly on the grill and let them cook. We're fond of this method because it's incredibly simple and direct, which is always a virtue in cooking, and because we love the fact that shellfish have their own built-in timer—when they open, they're done. (Remember, though, that any that don't open in about 10 minutes should be discarded.) Also, cooking the mussels in this way gives them a more individual flavor in the final dish than they would have if you cooked them with all the other ingredients from the beginning. The Thai-inspired sauce of this dish stays separate—heating up on the side of the grill in a foil pan—until the mussels have opened.

Serve these flavorful beauties with an extra squeeze of lime juice and a big hunk of grilled bread for soaking up the sauce.

3 tablespoons peeled and minced fresh ginger

1 tablespoon minced garlic

4 tablespoons roasted sesame oil, divided

2 tablespoons minced fresh jalapeños, or to taste

3 tablespoons hoisin sauce

1 tablespoon Sherwood or other good-quality curry powder

1/2 cup coconut milk (low-fat if you want)

4 whole scallions, trimmed, white part only

4 pounds mussels (about 45 to 50), scrubbed and debearded

Kosher salt and freshly cracked black pepper to taste

1/3 cup roughly chopped fresh cilantro

2 limes, halved

1. Build a fire on one side of your grill, using about enough coals to fill a shoebox. When the coals are all ignited and the temperature is hot (you can hold your hand 5 inches above the grill grid for 2 seconds or less), the fire is ready for cooking this dish.

2. Find a shallow baking pan (a crummy one that you can reserve for grilling) or a foil pan that is large enough to hold all the mussels in a single layer and sturdy enough to withstand the heat of a low fire. Put the ginger, garlic, and 2 tablespoons of the sesame oil into the pan and put it on the grill close to the fire but not directly over it. Cook for 2 minutes, stirring or swirling the mixture around a few times. Add the jalapeños, hoisin, curry, and coconut milk to the pan, then let the mixture come to a simmer, stirring occasionally. As soon as the mixture starts to simmer, push the pan all the way over to the side of the grill with no fire.

3. Place the mussels on the hot side of the grill and cook until they open, about 8 to 10 minutes. As they open, transfer them to the pan. (Discard any that do not open.) Meanwhile, brush the scallions with the remaining sesame oil, place them on the hot side of the grill next to the mussels, and cook, turning occasionally, until they are golden brown and slightly charred, about 2 to 3 minutes. When the scallions are done, cut them into 2-inch lengths and add to the pan.

4. When all the mussels are in the pan, season with salt and pepper to taste and stir the mussels around in the sauce, then remove the pan from the grill. Sprinkle with the cilantro, squeeze the lime halves over the mussels, and serve.

COOK TO COOK: You want a pretty hot fire here so that the mussels open up quickly, but you also have to make sure that the foil pan is not over the fire because the sauce should be just below a simmer. So get those mussels to open up and move them right over into your foil pan.

grilled clams on the half shell
with tabasco, lemon, and garlic

SERVES 6 AS AN APPETIZER

Because we have so enjoyed using this technique with oysters, last summer we tried it with clams. It worked great, so here it is.

One advantage of this method is that because the clams get slightly cooked over the fire, you don't need to use the very small ones that you look for when you're going to serve clams raw on the half shell. You can use any size from littlenecks on up to quahogs in this recipe. On the other hand, if you do have the smaller clams, they will be more tender.

1/3 cup olive oil
3 tablespoons Tabasco sauce, or to taste
Juice of 1 lemon
2 tablespoons Worcestershire sauce
1/4 cup catsup

3 tablespoons roughly chopped fresh thyme and/or oregano
Kosher salt and freshly cracked black pepper to taste
36 littleneck or 24 cherrystone clams

1. Build a multi-level fire in your grill: Leaving one-quarter of the bottom free of coals, bank the coals in the remaining three-quarters of the grill so that they are three times as high on one side as on the other. When the coals are all ignited and the temperature has died down to medium (you can hold your hand about 5 inches above the grill grid, over the area where the coals are deepest, for 4 to 5 seconds), you're ready to cook.

2. In a small bowl, combine all the ingredients except the clams and mix well to combine.

3. Scrub the clams well with a stiff brush, then shuck them (see drawing) and loosen them in their bottom shells. Arrange the clams on the grill and top each one with a bit of the sauce. Cook until the sauce bubbles and simmers for a couple of minutes, then carefully take the clams off the grill and serve immediately.

COOK TO COOK: There are basically three steps in shucking clams: (1) Hold the clam in the palm of your hand, hinge facing toward you, with a towel underneath the clam to protect your hand. (2) Wiggle a clam knife between the two shells, then work it around the edge to separate the shells. (3) Open the clam and use the knife to scrape the meat from the top shell into the bottom shell, then to separate the meat from the bottom shell.

clam up

* * *

Clams come in two basic varieties, soft-shell (also called "steamers") and hard-shell. The hard-shell are given different names according to their size. When there are around 500 in a bushel they're called littlenecks; 300 to a bushel makes them top necks; with 180 in a bushel they're known as cherry-stones; and when you get only 120 to a bushel they become chowder clams or quahogs. Generally speaking, the smaller they are, the more tender and therefore the more expensive.

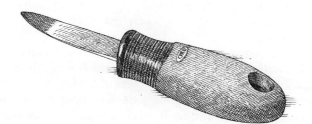

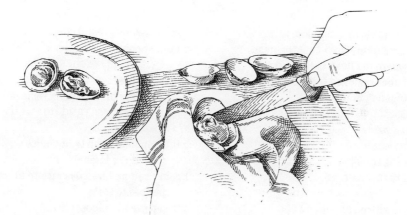

hot-smoked salmon with green grape-garlic sauce

SERVES 8 TO 10 AS AN APPETIZER

We're hot-smoking here, folks. That means it's time to break out the hardwood chips or chunks or tree trimmings because we're going to put some real smoke flavor on the food. As the indirect heat from the small charcoal fire slowly cooks the fish, whatever type of smoke you have coming off that fire has time to actually penetrate the flesh and influence its taste.

There are lots of options for aromatic flavor boosters (see Smoke Flavor Boosters, page 120), but in general we recommend that you use whatever is easiest for you to get hold of. Cut some trimmings from your grape vines or fruit trees if you have them in your yard. Small branches from hardwood trees like hickory or oak also work well, and chunks of hardwood the size of softballs are fine, too. You can also use wood chips wrapped up in tin foil with some holes punched in the foil to release the smoke.

In addition to the smoke, we add other layers of flavor here by brining the fish—a technique that, like smoking, was originally designed for preservation but today is used to add flavor and moisture—and then rubbing it with spices before it goes on the grill. We really like the combination of the salty brine with the sweet rub. A Middle Eastern-inspired sauce with garlic and green grapes provides the perfect complement.

2 16-ounce skin-on salmon fillets (preferably from near the head, where the flesh is thicker), pin bones removed (or substitute bluefish or mackerel)

For the brine:
1 quart water
1 cup sugar
1 cup kosher salt

For the spice rub:
3 tablespoons brown sugar
1 tablespoon kosher salt
3 tablespoons freshly cracked black pepper

2 tablespoons ground cumin
2 tablespoons paprika

For the sauce:
2 slices white bread, crusts removed
5 garlic cloves
1/2 cup olive oil
2 tablespoons fresh lemon juice (about 1/2 lemon)
Kosher salt and freshly cracked black pepper to taste
1/2 cup green grapes, halved lengthwise
1/3 cup roughly chopped fresh parsley

1. In a pot large enough to hold the two pieces of salmon, stir together the water, sugar, and salt until the sugar and salt are dissolved. Add the salmon, making sure that it is completely submerged in the liquid. Cover and allow the salmon to brine in the refrigerator for 3 to 5 hours, stirring the liquid and turning the salmon occasionally. (If you don't have room in your refrigerator, you can do the brining in a large cooler; just be sure to add 3 or 4 freezer packs to keep the temperature down.)

2. In a medium bowl, combine the ingredients for the spice rub and mix well. Remove the salmon from the brine and pat it dry. Rub the flesh side of the fish all over with the spice rub, pressing gently to be sure it adheres.

3. Start a fire well over to one side of a large kettle grill, using about enough coals to fill half a shoebox. When the fire dies down and the coals are well lit, place the salmon on the side away from the coals, skin side down, being careful that none of the fish is directly over the coals, and put the lid on the grill with the vents one-quarter of the way open. Cook, adding a handful of fresh charcoal after the first 30 minutes, until the fish is just done all the way through, about 50 to 70 minutes. To check for doneness, poke the fish with your finger to check its firmness level (see page 13); if you are unsure, nick, peek, and cheat: Cut into one of the fillets at its thickest point and peek to be sure it is opaque all the way through.

4. While the salmon is smoking, make the sauce: Wet the bread thoroughly with water, then squeeze it dry. In a food processor or using a large mortar and pestle, combine the bread, garlic, olive oil, lemon juice, salt and pepper, and grapes. If using the food processor, purée the mixture, using on/off turns, until smooth; if using a mortar and pestle, mash it until smooth. Stir in the parsley, adjust the seasoning, and transfer the sauce to a bowl.

5. We prefer to serve the salmon warm, passing the sauce on the side, but you can also refrigerate the salmon and serve it cold with the sauce.

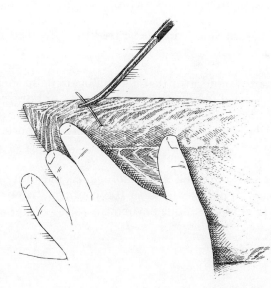

Removing pin bones from salmon

COOK TO COOK: This is a time for patience. You are hot-smoking—your fire should be only somewhere between 80° and 160°F—so it's going to take some time to cook the fish all the way through. Keep the salmon as far from the fire as you can get it, and don't rush the process. If you're using a smoke flavor booster, put it on about a third of the way through the cooking process.

smoke flavor boosters

* * *

It's fine to smoke salmon (or anything else, for that matter) with plain hard-wood charcoal, but it will taste even better if you add a "smoke flavor booster" of aromatic wood. For maximum smoky flavor, wrap wood chips or chunks tightly in heavy-duty foil, poke a few holes in the top of the package, and place it directly on top of the hot coals. The foil slows down the burn rate of the wood, making the smoke last longer. For even longer-lasting smoke, use wood chunks instead of chips.

Here are some options for flavoring chips. Just remember that smoking chips aren't charcoal; they're in there to flavor your food, not as the main source of cooking heat.

Fruitwoods: Apple, cherry, grape, peach, and persimmon are sweet, subtle woods perfect for fish, poultry, and pork chops.

Maple: A sweet, fragrant wood, maple is traditionally used for ham but excellent for salmon as well.

Oak: Oak is a standard wood flavor that doesn't overwhelm the food. It can be used with leaner types of fish or with ham, sausage, or burgers.

Hickory: A strong-flavored favorite for ribs, burgers, and pork, hickory can also be used with leaner types of fish.

Mesquite: Sweeter and more delicate than hickory, mesquite is one of the most commonly used smoking woods in the country. To our taste buds, though, it gives food a slight resinous flavor.

skewers of bacon-wrapped monkfish and radicchio with romesco sauce

SERVES 4 AS AN APPETIZER

This simple skewer dish has its roots in the Catalan region of Spain, where cooks revel in wonderful fish from both Atlantic and Mediterranean shores, often served with a traditional red pepper–almond sauce called Romesco. Monkfish is a particularly good fish for the grill because of its firm consistency. Locating it is sometimes difficult; if you can't get it, substitute steaks of another firm-fleshed fish, like tuna or swordfish.

1 pound cleaned monkfish fillet, cut into 1-inch chunks (or substitute swordfish or tuna steaks)
2 heads radicchio, cut into 1-inch chunks
3 tablespoons olive oil
Kosher salt and freshly cracked black pepper to taste
6 slices thick-cut smoked bacon, cut crosswise into thirds

For the sauce:
2 roasted red peppers (page 290)
1 tablespoon minced garlic
1/4 cup toasted chopped almonds
1/4 cup sherry vinegar (or substitute red wine vinegar)
1/2 cup extra-virgin olive oil
1/3 cup finely chopped fresh parsley

1. Build a multi-level fire in your grill: Leaving one-quarter of the bottom free of coals, bank the coals in the remaining three-quarters of the grill so that they are three times as high on one side as on the other. When the coals are all ignited and the temperature has died down to medium-low (you can hold your hand about 5 inches above the grill grid, over the area where the coals are deepest, for 5 seconds) you're ready to cook.

2. In a medium sauté pan or skillet, cook the bacon over medium heat until about halfway cooked, about 4 minutes. Remove the bacon from the pan and discard the fat.

3. In a large bowl, toss the monkfish and radicchio with the oil and salt and pepper to taste. As soon as the bacon is cool enough to handle, wrap each piece of monkfish with one of the bacon slices, secure it with a toothpick, and thread the wrapped fish and radicchio alternately on skewers.

4. Put the skewers on the grill and cook until the fish is cooked through and the bacon is crisp, 4 to 6 minutes per side. (To check for doneness, nick, peek, and cheat: Cut into one of the monkfish chunks at its thickest point and peek to be sure it is opaque all the way through.)

5. While the skewers are on the grill, make the sauce: Put the peppers, garlic, and almonds in a food processor, purée them, then add the vinegar. Turn the machine on

again and, with the machine running, add the olive oil in a thin stream until it is incorporated; the mixture should be approximately the consistency of mayonnaise. Season the sauce with salt and pepper and stir in the parsley.

6. Arrange the skewers on a platter and serve, passing the Romesco sauce on the side.

COOK TO COOK: To avoid burning the radicchio or the bacon, we use a medium-low fire here, but you still need to keep an eye on the skewers and move them to the cooler part of the fire if any bacon grease drips down into the coals and causes a flare-up.

grilled squid with lemon and toasted garlic

SERVES 6 TO 8 AS AN APPETIZER

This is a variation on one of our favorite recipes from our very first cookbook, *The Thrill of the Grill*. The key to cooking squid is to cook it really quickly or really slowly; otherwise you're going to end up with a pretty tough cephalopod. Grilling is ideal for the really quick method, and the indispensable tool is a foil-covered brick, which we use to ensure that the bodies of the squid stay flat and therefore cook as quickly and evenly as possible.

It's much easier to buy cleaned squid these days than to clean it yourself. In fact, squid, like shrimp, freezes very well, so your best option may be to buy pre-cleaned, frozen squid.

2 pounds cleaned squid
5 cloves garlic, peeled and thinly
    sliced
6 tablespoons olive oil, divided
Kosher salt and freshly cracked black
    pepper to taste

Juice of 1 lemon
4 to 6 dashes Tabasco sauce
1/4 cup roughly chopped fresh
    parsley
1 lemon half for garnish

1. Build a multi-level fire in your grill: Leaving one-quarter of the bottom free of coals, bank the coals in the remaining three-quarters of the grill so that they are three times as high on one side as on the other. When the coals are all ignited and the temperature is hot (you can hold your hand about 5 inches above the grill grid, over the area where the coals are deepest, for 2 seconds or less), you're ready to cook. Wrap a clean brick (yes, a brick) with foil and place it by your grill.

2. Transfer the cleaned squid to a large bowl. Toss the squid with salt and pepper and a few tablespoons of the olive oil, just enough to coat.

3. In a small sauté pan or skillet, sauté the garlic and 1 tablespoon of the remaining olive oil over medium heat until the garlic is just light brown and crispy, about 2 to 3 minutes, being careful not to burn it.

4. In a small bowl, combine the remaining oil with the garlic, lemon juice, Tabasco, and parsley. Rub this mixture all over the squid.

5. Arrange a few squid bodies on the grill and cover them completely with the brick. Cook 1 1/2 to 2 minutes per side, then remove the brick and allow the bodies to cook about 30 seconds longer. Repeat this process until all of the squid bodies are golden brown and crispy. Add the tentacles to the grill (no brick required) with the last batch of bodies and cook for 2 minutes, rolling them around on the grill until they are evenly brown and crispy.

6. To serve, slice the bodies into rings and leave the tentacles whole. Pile the squid on a plate, give it a squeeze of lemon and a good sprinkling of salt, and serve it up.

COOK TO COOK: The brick we're talking about here is a plain old standard-size brick like the ones they use to build houses. It's a great tool for squid grilling, and if it seems odd to you, just think of that old Italian grilled classic, "Chicken Under a Brick." The principle is the same: Whether it's squid or butterflied chicken, the brick keeps it flat so it cooks quickly and evenly.

grilled thai-style squid with lime, chile, and peanuts

SERVES 4 TO 6 AS AN APPETIZER

Whenever I (Doc) eat this dish I am reminded of my friends Laurie Ochoa and Jonathan Gold, both wonderful writers and editors, whose six-year-old daughter Isabel has an advanced taste in food that often confounds waiters. Once when she ordered squid in a restaurant, the waiter very protectively asked if she knew what they were. With a sweet smile she answered, "I really like tentacles." So do I, and you probably will, too, if you try this dish.

Here we just cook the squid very fast—using a foil-lined brick as the enforcer that keeps the squid from curling up and getting away from the heat—and combine it with classic pungent, aromatic, spicy Thai ingredients. Squid is fantastic when grilled very quickly at very high heat, because it develops a nice char and doesn't become rubbery.

This goes great on a bed of greens, piled on top of Asian noodles, or all by itself in front of a light entrée.

For the dressing:
3 tablespoons *nam pla*, Southeast Asian fish sauce
1/4 cup lime juice (about 2 limes)
1 teaspoon peeled and minced fresh ginger
2 tablespoons prepared Asian chile-garlic paste (available in Asian markets or large supermarkets)
1 teaspoon sugar

3 tablespoons roughly chopped fresh cilantro
3 tablespoons roughly chopped fresh mint
_____

2 pounds cleaned squid
1 tablespoon peanut oil
Kosher salt and freshly cracked black pepper to taste
1/4 cup roasted unsalted peanuts, chopped

1. Build a multi-level fire in your grill: Leaving one-quarter of the bottom free of coals, bank the coals in the remaining three-quarters of the grill so that they are three times as high on one side as on the other. When the coals are all ignited and the temperature is hot (you can hold your hand about 5 inches above the grill grid, over the area where the coals are deepest, for 2 seconds or less), the fire is ready for cooking this dish. Wrap a clean brick in foil and set it beside the grill.

2. In a medium bowl, combine the dressing ingredients and mix well.

3. Rub the squid with the oil and sprinkle it generously with salt and pepper. Arrange a few squid bodies on the grill and cover them completely with the brick. Cook 1 1/2 to 2 minutes per side, then remove the brick and allow the bodies to cook about 30 seconds longer. Repeat this process until all of the squid bodies are golden brown and crispy. Add the tentacles to the grill (no brick required) with the last batch of bodies and cook for 2 minutes, rolling them around on the grill until they are evenly brown and crispy.

4. When all the squid are cooked, slice the bodies into rings and add them to the dressing bowl along with the tentacles. Toss well, sprinkle with the chopped peanuts, and serve.

COOK TO COOK: Keep in mind that smaller squid (those with bodies about 4 to 5 inches long, not including the head and tentacles) are more tender than larger ones, so seek those out if you can. Remember, too, that you are cooking quickly over a very hot fire here—get it on, then get it off.

grilled deviled octopus

SERVES 6 TO 8 AS AN APPETIZER

Octopus is one of those foods that many Americans find just too weird. But remember that not so long ago—before fried calamari became one of the most popular appetizers in the land—squid was in that category, too. Octopus is actually terrific seafood, delicate and very tasty. We were lucky enough to discover this on the Tunisian island of Djerba, where we were served a delicious salad of octopus that had been grilled, then marinated in olive oil and lemon juice and tossed with green olives, capers, and a handful of almonds.

The one problem with octopus is that it can be quite tough. There are dozens of folk remedies for this problem, ranging from beating the octopus against rocks (Greece) to kneading it with grated daikon (Japan). The best bet, though, is to get a relatively small octopus, which is usually more tender. In that case, simple parboiling and proper cooking is really all that is required. The market size for these creatures is usually 2 to 4 pounds, with tentacles about 2 feet long.

This is a pretty simple dish in which we devil the octopus up a bit with red pepper flakes and Tabasco and put on a nice crispy sear right over the coals. If you've never tried octopus before, this is a good place to start, because the classic Mediterranean flavors give it a familiar tone. And if we still haven't convinced you of the virtues of octopus—or if you can't get your hands on any—you can substitute squid or even shrimp in this recipe.

1 quart salted water
1 cup white vinegar
1 small octopus, about 2 pounds,
    cleaned, thawed if frozen
1/4 cup olive oil
1 teaspoon red pepper flakes
Kosher salt and freshly cracked black
    pepper to taste

For the dressing:
1/4 cup extra-virgin olive oil
Juice of 1 lemon
1 teaspoon minced garlic
1 plum tomato, cored and diced small
1/3 cup roughly chopped fresh thyme
    or oregano
5 dashes Worcestershire sauce
10 dashes Tabasco sauce
Kosher salt and freshly cracked black
    pepper to taste

1. Build a multi-level fire in your grill: Leaving one-quarter of the bottom free of coals, bank the coals in the remaining three-quarters of the grill so that they are about three times as high on one side as on the other. When the coals are all ignited and the temperature has died down to medium (you can hold your hand about 5 inches above the grill grid, over the area where the coals are deepest, for 4 to 5 seconds), you're ready to cook.

2. In a medium saucepan, bring the salted water to a boil. Add the vinegar, reduce the heat to low, and add the octopus. Simmer for 30 minutes, then drain well.

3. While the octopus is simmering, whisk the dressing ingredients together in a large bowl until well combined, then set aside.

4. Separate the octopus tentacles from the body, then divide each of them crosswise into two sections. Cut the body into strips 1/2 inch wide. Transfer the octopus pieces to a large bowl along with the oil, red pepper flakes, and salt and pepper and toss well to coat.

5. Put the octopus on the grill and cook until it is browned and slightly crisp, about 5 to 6 minutes. Remove from the grill and, as soon as it is cool enough to handle, slice the octopus into bite-sized pieces. Transfer to the bowl of dressing, toss well to coat, and serve hot.

COOK TO COOK: It is difficult to locate fresh octopus in this country; most that you see in seafood cases has been previously frozen and thawed anyway. So you are probably better off buying it frozen, then letting it defrost in the refrigerator or in a bowl of cold water.

crispy pan-fried soft-shell crab sandwich on cheap white bread toast with tartar sauce

SERVES 8 AS AN APPETIZER

We know: If this is a grilling book, why are we giving you a fried soft-shell recipe? The answer is that this recipe is something of a political statement. Grilling is our #1 favorite cooking method and we'll put almost anything over the coals. But there are some things that simply do not thrive on the grill, and soft-shell crabs are one of them. They need to be fried.

In addition, this recipe is a fulfillment of my (Chris's) obligation to the Tidewater area of Virginia, where I grew up and where pan-fried soft shells are a way of life. In fact, there is some reason to believe that when a cook leaves Tidewater, he or she is obliged to sign a statement saying that if he or she ever writes a cookbook it will feature a recipe for pan-fried soft shells. So here it is. If you try it, you'll understand why we had to include it.

1 cup milk
2 eggs
Dash of Tabasco sauce
Kosher salt and freshly cracked black pepper to taste
8 soft-shell crabs, cleaned
1 cup all-purpose flour
1 cup cornmeal

For the tartar sauce:
1 cup mayonnaise
1/4 red onion, peeled and diced small

1/3 cup sweet pickles, diced small (or substitute sweet pickle relish)
1 teaspoon powdered mustard
Juice of 1/2 lemon
12 to 18 dashes Tabasco sauce, or to taste

16 pieces Wonder or other nutritionally worthless white bread
1/2 cup unsalted butter
1/4 cup olive oil

1. In a large bowl, whisk together the milk, eggs, dash of Tabasco sauce, and salt and pepper until smooth. Dredge the crabs in the flour and shake off the excess. Dunk them into milk-egg mixture and then into the cornmeal, turning to coat, and place them on a wire cooking rack to dry.

2. Make the tartar sauce: In a small bowl, combine the ingredients for the tartar sauce, add salt and pepper to taste, and mix well. Smear some on each slice of bread and set the slices aside.

3. In a frying pan over medium-high heat, combine the butter and oil and get it good and hot. Drop in the breaded crabs, working in batches if necessary—avoid crowding them in. Cook until the crabs are golden brown, 3 to 4 minutes per side, then remove and set on newspaper or a brown paper bag to drain.

4. When all the crabs are done, place each one on a slice of bread, top with a second slice, and serve immediately, accompanied by a cold one or a tall glass of iced tea.

COOK TO COOK: If you are frying the crabs in batches—which you should be unless you have a huge pan, because you don't want to crowd them—don't be in too much of a hurry. It's best to give the oil-butter combination a minute or two between batches to come back up to heat.

lime- and chile-soaked black-and-blue snapper with avocado and chips

SERVES 6 TO 8 AS AN APPETIZER

Here's Mexican-influenced variation on the classic Latin American dish called ceviche, in which ultra-fresh fish is marinated in lime juice so the lime juice "cooks" the fish. We're adding flavor dimensions by quickly searing the fish over a very hot fire before its lime bath, so it takes on a little grill flavor and a little crispness as well. We call it "black-and-blue" because when it comes off the grill it's similar to the famous black-and-blue steak—seared hard on the outside, still raw on the inside. At that point, we put the fish in the lime juice and serve it right away so the fish gets "lime-cooked" only a little. This approach avoids a problem common to ceviches left to sit in the lime juice too long: mushy fish.

This is a refreshing summertime dish. Be sure to buy very fresh, sushi-quality fish. And while you're at it, fry up extra tortilla chips, since they make excellent tools for scooping up salsas.

1 cup fresh lime juice (about 8 limes)
1/3 cup plus 3 tablespoons olive oil
1/2 cup roughly chopped fresh cilantro
1 teaspoon minced garlic
1 to 3 tablespoons minced fresh chile pepper of your choice, according to your taste for heat
1 ripe avocado, peeled, pitted, and diced small
1 red onion, peeled and diced small
1 tomato about the size of a baseball, cored and diced small

Kosher salt and freshly cracked black pepper to taste
1 cup vegetable oil for frying
8 corn tortillas, each cut into 6 wedges
2 pounds skin-on red snapper fillets (or substitute grouper, striped bass, or other mild fish fillets)
4 tablespoons freshly cracked toasted cumin seeds (or substitute 2 tablespoons ground cumin)

1. Build a multi-level fire in your grill: Leaving one-quarter of the bottom free of coals, bank the coals in the remaining three-quarters of the grill so that they are about three times as high on one side as on the other. When the coals are all ignited and the temperature is very hot (you can hold your hand about 5 inches above the grill grid, over the area where the coals are deepest, for 1 second or less), you're ready to cook.

2. In a large bowl, whisk together the lime juice, the 1/3 cup of olive oil, cilantro, garlic, and chile. Add the avocado, onion, tomato, and salt and pepper to taste and toss gently to coat. Cover and refrigerate until serving time.

3. In a heavy-bottomed medium-size saucepan, heat the oil to 375°F. (If you don't have a candy thermometer to check the temperature, the oil is ready when a small piece of tortilla dropped into the oil immediately rises to the top, sizzling.) Fry the tortilla

wedges, in batches if necessary to avoid crowding, until they are crisp and most of the bubbling subsides, about 1 minute. Use tongs or a slotted spoon to transfer the chips to a brown paper bag or paper towels to drain. Sprinkle the fried chips with plenty of salt, then hide them from your guests or they'll be gone in the time it takes to cook the fish.

4. Brush the fish fillets lightly with the remaining 3 tablespoons of olive oil, sprinkle generously with salt and pepper, and rub all over with the cumin. Place the fillets on the grill, skin side up, and grill until a dark, crispy crust forms on the bottom, about 3 minutes. When they are cooked on the bottom, take them off the grill—they will still be quite raw in the center.

5. Lay the fillets on a flat surface and remove the skin, then cut the fish into strips about 1/2 inch wide. Transfer to the bowl with the avocado mixture, toss gently to combine, then spoon into individual bowls and serve, passing the warm tortilla chips on the side.

COOK TO COOK: The key to this dish is having a very hot fire so that the fish, with that deeply flavored spice rub on it, gets very crisp.

raw striped bass salad with ginger, sesame, and soy

SERVES 4 AS AN APPETIZER

This dish is a takeoff on *poke*, a Hawaiian raw fish salad that's usually made with tuna. Because we can buy super-fresh striped bass from local New England fishermen in the summer, that's what we use here, but you can substitute snapper, halibut, fluke, or whatever fillet fish you can get that's dead-on super-fresh. With the fiery chile paste, tangy ginger, mellow sesame, and a spark of lime, this is a rich combination of Asian flavors. To provide a little textural contrast and to cool it down a bit, we serve the fish on top of cucumbers.

Although these raw fish dishes (this bass salad and the raw fluke that follows) are obviously not grilled, we associate them with the beach and grilling. Another reason for including them is that they are excellent appetizers in front of heavy grilled meat entrées.

1 pound raw striped bass, cut into matchstick-size pieces

2 tablespoons roasted sesame oil

1 tablespoon prepared Asian chile-garlic paste (available in Asian markets or large supermarkets)

2 tablespoons peeled and minced fresh ginger

5 scallions, white and green parts, sliced very thin

3 tablespoons soy sauce

Juice of 1 lime

1/2 teaspoon sugar

3 tablespoons sesame seeds

1 cucumber, sliced into very thin circles

1. In a medium bowl, combine all of the ingredients except the sesame seeds and the cucumber and mix well.

2. Toast the sesame seeds in a dry skillet over medium heat, shaking frequently, until they just begin to smoke, 3 to 4 minutes.

3. Arrange some cucumber slices on each plate, mound the fish mixture on top, sprinkle with sesame seeds, and serve immediately.

COOK TO COOK: If you see *hajiki* seaweed in Japanese stores, it makes a nice complement to this dish. Or you can cut up the *nori* seaweed in which sushi is wrapped and sprinkle some of that on top. Make sure the bass is on ice from the minute you get it, and serve it on plates that you have had in the freezer for an hour or so.

spicy raw fluke with mangoes, lemon, and lime

SERVES 4 TO 6 AS AN APPETIZER

In the waters off the coast of southern Massachusetts there are a lot of fluke, a flat fish in the flounder family. Our friend Steve Johnson, a highly proficient fluke fisherman who spends much of his summer on a houseboat anchored in the harbor at Westport, Massachusetts, almost never returns from an outing empty-handed. We came up with this dish in trying to use his bounty.

A mild-flavored white fish, fluke works very well in this sashimi-like preparation where we simply cut the raw fish into strips and mix it with mango, citrus juices, chiles, olive oil, and cilantro. The approach is actually quite similar to a ceviche, except we don't let the fish sit in the lime juice long enough to cook. Instead, you put the dish together right before you're ready to serve it, and what you have is a nice raw fish salad. Just make sure that any fish you use in this dish is super-fresh. (If you don't have fluke around where you live, you can substitute halibut, other kinds of flounder, or even striped bass.)

This goes great with soft tortillas cut into wedges and fried up to use as scoops; the textural contrast of the raw fish and crispy tortillas is outstanding.

1 pound super-fresh, sushi-quality fluke, cut into matchstick-size pieces
1 ripe but firm mango, diced small
1 tablespoon minced fresh chile pepper of your choice
Juice of 1 lemon
Juice of 2 limes
1/4 cup extra-virgin olive oil
3 tablespoons finely chopped fresh cilantro
Kosher salt and freshly cracked black pepper to taste

In a medium bowl, combine all of the ingredients, mix well, and serve right away.

COOK TO COOK: This is another case where the freshness of the fish is crucial. If you know a fisherman who can bring you fish right out of the water, that's obviously the best deal. Otherwise, apply the usual tests for fresh fish and tell the fishmonger you are going to eat it raw so he has a chance to warn you if he thinks that's a bad idea. Keep everything very cold here, and (if you have time) put the plates you're going to serve it on in the freezer for an hour or so before serving.

THE BIG GUYS:
MAIN COURSES

GRILLING HAS COME OF AGE IN THIS COUNTRY. WE ARE very happy about that, since it means we don't have to keep explaining that grilling is not just for hot dogs and hamburgers. The average backyard cook no longer thinks that it's weird to put fish over a fire, vegetables have become relatively common in the American grilling vocabulary, and even grilled fruit is not considered beyond the pale.

In other words, grillers are now allowed freer rein than ever before—and the recipes in this chapter take full advantage of that freedom. Here you'll discover a wide variety of pretty much everything you can find in the supermarket, from chicken to fish, shellfish to beef, pork, lamb, and veal, even a few pastas with a grilled component. (Vegetable side dishes come later; check out page 274). You'll also find a whole range of flavors, with a heavy emphasis on tropical ingredients but also a strong representation of Mediterranean, Central and South American, and Middle Eastern flavor footprints. This chapter also includes mini-essays on particular foods that we have several recipes for, such as ribs, steaks, chops, and the so-called oily fish. Be on the lookout for them; we think you'll find them pretty useful.

While the recipes here are definitely for home cooks, the portions are restaurant style—they're larger than the portions you are used to at home. The reason for this is not that the recipes come from restaurants but that we like to eat. But do keep this in mind, because sometimes people say we use more protein per portion in our entrées than they are used to. So what we say serves four, for example, might serve six in your house.

You'll also find that our idea of an entrée is often pretty close to a whole meal. Our version of grilled strip loin steak, for example, comes with a grilled avocado and some chipotle-tinged onions on the side, and when we give you recipes for pork tenderloin, each has two accompanying recipes—cheesy grilled tomatoes and white beans in one case, grilled peaches and black olive relish in another. Grilled swordfish is accompanied by crispy asparagus with a flavored butter, while grilled mahi mahi comes with not only avocado sauce but a salad featuring hearts of palm. At the very least you'll find that every recipe comes with a chutney, a glaze, a sauce, or something that makes the dish special and fills the plate. That's just the way we like to do recipes. You can always pare them down to bare bones if you're in a hurry, of course, but we think it's fun to prepare the whole shebang while you're at it, and most of the supporting dishes are really pretty simple. Besides, when it's all there in the recipe, there's just that much less thinking you have to do about what to serve. So light the grill and let's get going.

BEEF

mustard-slathered grilled flank steak with smoky jalapeño-honey sauce

SERVES 4 TO 6

Flank steak is one of three unusual thin, flat steaks (skirt steak and hanger steak are the other two) that possess marvelous flavor and if cooked right and sliced right are quite tender. That means grilled hot and hard and sliced thin, on the bias, against the grain.

To add a layer of intense flavor, we slather the steaks with a spicy, herby mustard rub and let them sit for an hour before they go on the grill. Grilling will be a little messy, but don't let that deter you. Get the steaks crusty on one side, then pick them up with your tongs and rub them around in the mustard mixture again before you sear the other side. When the steaks come off the grill, we slice them and serve with a spicy sweet-and-sour sauce of grilled onions and jalapeños, which provides another layer of flavor.

If you have any left over the next day, this steak is great for sandwiches or for salads.

1/2 cup grainy mustard	3 tablespoons honey
2 tablespoons ground cumin	3 tablespoons red wine vinegar
3 tablespoons chili powder	1 teaspoon minced garlic
2 flank steaks, about 1 1/2 pounds each (or substitute skirt steaks or hanger steaks)	1/4 cup finely chopped fresh oregano
	1 red onion, peeled and sliced into disks about 1 inch thick
Kosher salt and freshly cracked black pepper to taste	4 jalapeños or other fresh chile peppers of your choice, left whole
2 tablespoons catsup	2 tablespoons vegetable oil

1. In a small bowl, combine the mustard, cumin, and chili powder and mix well. Sprinkle the flank steaks generously with salt and pepper and spread the mustard mixture all over them on both sides. Place the steaks in a shallow baking dish and refrigerate for 1 hour.

2. In a small saucepan over medium heat, combine the catsup, honey, vinegar, and garlic and mix well. Bring to a simmer, stirring to blend, and remove from the heat. Stir in the oregano and set aside.

3. Build a multi-level fire in your grill: Leaving one-quarter of the bottom free of coals, bank the coals in the remaining three-quarters of the grill so that they are three times as high on one side as on the other. When all the coals are ignited and the temperature is medium-hot (you can hold your hand about 5 inches above the grill grid, over the area where the coals are deepest, for 3 to 4 seconds), the fire is ready.

4. Rub the onion slices and jalapeños with the vegetable oil and sprinkle with salt and pepper. Place them on the grill over the cooler half of the fire and cook until just nicely browned, about 5 minutes per side. Remove from the grill and chop them fine before adding to the sauce. (If you want less heat in the sauce, remove the seeds and ribs from the jalapeños before chopping them.)

5. While the onions and chiles are cooking, put the steaks on the hottest part of the grill and sear well on one side, about 4 minutes. Pick each steak up with your tongs and rub the unseared side around in the mustard mixture, then put the steaks back on the grill and sear that second side well, about another 4 minutes. If you like your steak rare, it should be ready at this point; otherwise, continue cooking until it is done to your liking. To check for doneness, poke the meat with your finger to check its firmness level (see page 13); if you're unsure, nick, peek, and cheat: Make a cut in the thickest part of the meat and peek at the center to be sure it is just slightly less done than you like it. Remove the steaks from the grill, cover loosely with foil, and allow them to sit for 5 to 10 minutes.

6. While the steaks are resting, reheat the sauce if necessary. Slice the steaks thinly against the grain on the bias, arrange the slices on a serving platter, and serve, passing the sauce on the side.

COOK TO COOK: The mustard coating makes sticking a bit of an issue here, so take the usual precautions: Make sure the grill grid is very clean and very hot. The easiest way to get the grid hot is simply to put it over the coals as soon as you light them, so it heats up as the coals do.

the tender slice

* * *

Over the years, cooks have come up with lots of ways to try to make tough steaks more tender. The most widely used (primarily in inexpensive restaurants) is a process called "needling," in which a machine pierces the meat all over with tiny needles. It does technically make the meat more tender, but it's not the kind of tenderness you get in, say, a filet mignon. Instead, it's a kind of mushy tenderness, which we find unpleasant.

The reason needling is successful (to the extent that you can consider mushy meat a success) is that short muscle fibers seem more tender than long muscle fibers when you chew them. In fact, a beef industry organization once did a series of expensive experiments to find out the best way to tenderize tough meat. The ultimate method they came up with involved building a sealed chamber, placing a piece of meat on a pedestal inside it, and exploding a bomb in the chamber. No kidding. It worked because the concussive effect of the blast very effectively shortened the muscle fibers—but of course it wasn't exactly practical.

There is one instance, though, in which shortening fibers not only works well for tenderizing but is eminently practical. That is in the case of the thin, flat cuts—skirt steak, flank steak, and hanger steak. All three have a very clear striated grain, and with all three, if you slice them very thin on a steep bias against the striated grain, you shorten the fibers and make the meat much more tender. If you don't believe it, try cutting one piece of flank steak with the grain, not on the bias, and another in the manner we recommend. You'll be amazed at the difference in tenderness.

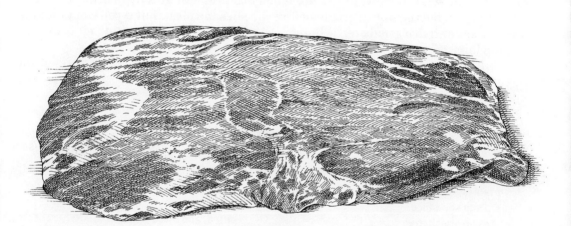

Flank steak

teriyaki-style thin-sliced beef with mango and lime

SERVES 4

꒦ ꒦ ꒦ ꒦ ꒦ ꒦ ꒦ ꒦ ꒦ ꒦ ꒦ ꒦ ꒦ ꒦ ꒦ ꒦ ꒦

We love teriyaki, a classic Japanese technique in which you marinate meat (or fowl, fish, even vegetables) in a sweet-and-sour soy-based sauce and then grill it. In this recipe we ring a little change on tradition by using half the soy mixture first as a light marinade, then adding some ginger and chopped scallions to brighten up the flavor and using the resulting mixture as a finishing sauce. It's a very nice, fresh, light treatment for beef.

Our choice for the beef cut in this recipe is the chuck top blade steak, the ultimate secret weapon of cooks who like tender beef but don't like to pay a lot for it. Unlike other cuts from the chuck, this steak is exquisitely tender; in fact, it's the second most tender cut of beef you can buy, surpassed only by the tenderloin—and it's about half the price of other, less tender steaks. There is a catch, of course. Running smack down the center of each top blade steak is a line of inedible cartilage. But since you're going to thin-slice the steak anyway, this is not much of a problem. After you grill the steaks, you simply cut out the line of gristle before you slice the meat. But if you can't find top blade steaks or if that gristle really bothers you, you can always substitute more expensive top loin strip steaks.

Think about serving this with Sesame-Crusted Grilled Zucchini with Honey-Soy Glaze (page 277).

For the marinade:
1/2 cup freshly cracked coriander
    seeds, toasted (or substitute
    1/4 cup ground coriander)
2 tablespoons powdered ginger
1 tablespoon dry powdered mustard
1/2 cup soy sauce
1/4 cup dry sherry
3 tablespoons roasted sesame oil
3 tablespoons Asian chile-garlic
    paste (available in Asian stores)
2 tablespoons brown sugar

3 pounds chuck top blade steaks
4 scallions, both white and green
    parts, thinly sliced
2 tablespoons peeled and minced
    fresh ginger
2 ripe but firm mangoes, peeled,
    pitted, and diced small
Juice of 2 limes
3 tablespoons roughly chopped
    fresh cilantro

1. Build a multi-level fire in your grill: Leaving one-quarter of the bottom free of coals, bank the coals in the remaining three-quarters of the grill so that they are three times as high on one side as on the other. When all the coals are ignited and the temperature is hot (you can hold your hand about 5 inches above the grill grid, over the area where the coals are deepest, for 2 seconds or less), you're ready to cook.

2. In a large bowl, mix together all the ingredients for the marinade until they are well combined and the sugar has dissolved. Place the meat in a single layer in a shallow

dish, pour half of the marinade over it, and turn several times to coat on both sides. Add the scallions and fresh ginger to the marinade remaining in the bowl, mix well, and set aside.

3. Put the steaks on the hottest part of the grill and cook until just seared, about 5 minutes per side. To check for doneness, poke the meat with your finger to check its firmness level (see page 13); if you're unsure, nick, peek, and cheat: Make a cut in the thickest part of the meat and peek at the center to be sure it is just slightly less done than you like it to allow for carryover cooking. Remove the meat from the grill, cover it loosely with foil, and let it rest for 5 minutes.

4. Slice the meat very thinly against the grain and add the slices to the bowl of ginger and scallion sauce, tossing to coat. Mix together the diced mangoes and the lime juice. Divide the meat among serving plates, garnish with the mangoes and the cilantro, and serve immediately.

COOK TO COOK: You're grilling over a very hot fire here, and you have a little sugar in the marinade, so watch carefully for burning—you want the very dark brown color of a high sear, not the black of burned. The grain of this steak runs parallel to the strip of cartilage in the middle, so slice the meat perpendicular to that strip.

latin-style grilled tips with mojo

SERVES 4

"Tips" is an all-inclusive term for just about any small, boneless pieces of tender meat or chicken. Where do tips come from? Well, when a butcher is sectioning a large cut of tender meat he is often left with rather small pieces as well as some larger bits that don't quite fit the specifications for standard retail cuts, so he slices them all into relatively small pieces and throws them into the tips pile. There are beef or pork tenderloin tips, sirloin tips, and chicken tips. Nowadays you even see packages of "tuna tips" in some stores. I (Chris) have always thought it would be fun to open a tips restaurant, where little chunks of chicken, steak, lamb, and other kinds of meat would be put on skewers and cooked over a fire—which is what we do here. To get the best tips, buy the tenderloin whole and cut it up yourself.

To accompany the skewers of tips, pineapple, and onions, we have the classic Latin Caribbean "mojo," which is a simple lime, garlic, and olive oil combination. While some cooks like to use these ingredients as a marinade, we usually prefer to add them to the dish *after* it's cooked, because that provides a more lively flavor.

Try serving these babies with Cucumber, Tomato, and Mango Salad (page 320) and Grilled Corn (page 286).

---

2 pounds beef or pork tenderloins (or substitute boneless chicken), cut into 1-inch cubes

1/4 cup cumin seeds (or substitute 2 tablespoons ground cumin)

1 small fresh pineapple, peeled, cored, and cut into 1-inch cubes

1 large red onion, peeled and cut into 1-inch chunks

Kosher salt and freshly cracked black pepper to taste

2 tablespoons minced garlic

1/2 cup olive oil

1/3 cup fresh lime juice (about 3 limes)

3 tablespoons minced fresh chile pepper of your choice

1/4 cup roughly chopped fresh oregano

---

1. Build a multi-level fire in your grill: Leaving one-quarter of the bottom free of coals, bank the coals in the remaining three-quarters of the grill so that they are three times as high on one side as on the other. When all the coals are ignited and the temperature is medium-hot (you can hold your hand about 5 inches above the grill grid, over the area where the coals are deepest, for 3 to 4 seconds), you're ready to cook.

2. In a large bowl, combine the meat (or chicken) cubes with the cumin seeds and toss until well coated. Thread the cubes, alternating with the pineapple and the onion, onto skewers, then sprinkle generously with salt and pepper.

3. Make the mojo: In a small saucepan over medium-high heat, sauté the garlic in 2 tablespoons of the olive oil, stirring frequently, until golden but not brown, about 2 minutes. Transfer to a large bowl and add the remaining oil, the lime juice, chile,

oregano, and salt and pepper to taste. Stir until the ingredients are well blended, then set aside at room temperature.

4. Put the skewers on the grill and cook until done to your liking, about 4 to 5 minutes per side for medium-rare. To check for doneness, nick, peek, and cheat: Make a 1/4-inch cut into one of the cubes and peek to be sure that it is slightly less done in the center than you want it to be if you are using beef or pork, or that it is opaque all the way through if you are using chicken.

5. When the tips are done, push everything off the individual skewers right into the bowl of mojo, toss until well coated, and serve.

COOK TO COOK: The key to this dish is to get the tips nicely seared and well cooked while making sure the accompanying onions and pineapple become tender but do not burn. So watch carefully, and move the skewers off to the cooler part of the fire if any ingredient starts to burn before the tips are cooked the way you like them.

high steaks

* * *

Steaks are probably the #1 grilled item in the United States. For all you steak lovers, we offer a lot of different cuts of steak for you to choose from in the recipes that follow:

the top loin, T-bone, and porterhouse for tenderness;
the chuck top blade steak for your undiscovered gem;
the skirt and flank for deep flavor;
the magnificent rib eye for an unmatched combination
of tenderness and flavor.

One of the keys to a great grilled steak is to begin with a steak that is cut thick, at least 1 1/2 inches, so you can get a good, strong sear on the outside without overcooking it on the inside. In our book *How to Cook Meat*, we call this the Prime Steak Directive. And with a really expensive cut such as T-bone or porterhouse, it is worth the extra minutes it takes to go to the butcher and have it custom cut. In most cases you'll be getting a more evenly cut steak, and you're probably just plain going to get better quality as well.

Of course, that "cut 'em thick" advice applies only to the traditional steaks. With thin, flat ones like skirt and flank steak, the key is to cook them quickly, then slice them very thinly against the grain. By doing so, you'll transform a potentially tough cut into a perfectly tender piece of meat.

grilled giant porterhouse (or t-bone) with grilled exotic mushrooms

SERVES 4 TO 6

If you were to poll professional chefs about the steak they themselves prefer to eat, the porterhouse would come in #1. It combines a portion of the ultra-tender tenderloin with a larger portion of the very flavorful top loin.

So here is our recipe for the classic steak-eating experience. For steaks of this size you will probably have to go to the butcher shop, but when you walk away from the counter the butcher is going to have a smile on his face and probably give you a little wink, because he's going to be feeling just a bit jealous. The steaks are so large that each one will feed two or even three people.

With a cut like this, you want to exercise restraint. Just sprinkle the meat generously with salt and pepper. (This is the time to bring out your designer salt and to crack the pepper right before you use it, leaving some nice, large chunks so you get a little heat when you bite into them.) Grilled exotic mushrooms that have been tossed in a little butter, parsley, and sherry provide the right topping.

Serve with Grilled Potato Steaks with Bacon, Sour Cream, and Chives (page 298) and simple grilled onions.

2 giant 2- to 2 1/2-inch-thick porterhouse (or T-bone) steaks, about
2 pounds each
1/2 cup olive oil, divided
Kosher salt and freshly cracked black
pepper to taste
1 1/2 pounds exotic mushrooms
(portobellos, shiitake, creminis,
chanterelles, oyster, or other
kinds), the larger the better,
trimmed

1 teaspoon freshly ground
black pepper
4 tablespoons unsalted butter
1/3 cup roughly chopped fresh
parsley
3 tablespoons dry sherry

1. Build a multi-level fire in your grill: Leaving one-quarter of the bottom free of coals, bank the coals in the remaining three-quarters of the grill so that they are three times as high on one side as on the other. When all the coals are ignited and the temperature is hot (you can hold your hand about 5 inches above the grill grid, over the area where the coals are deepest, for 2 seconds or less), you're ready to cook.

2. Pat the steaks dry with paper towels, then rub them all over with 1/4 cup of the olive oil and sprinkle them generously with salt and pepper. Place the steaks over the hottest part of the fire and cook until well seared on one side, 6 to 8 minutes. Turn and sear well on the second side, again about 6 to 8 minutes. Now move them to the medium-hot part of the grill and cook, turning once, until they are done the way you like them, 10 to 15 minutes more for rare. To check for doneness, poke the meat with

your finger to check its firmness level (see page 13); if you're unsure, nick, peek, and cheat: Make a cut into the center and peek to be sure it is just slightly less done than you like it.

3. While the steaks are cooking, combine the mushrooms, the remaining 1/4 cup of olive oil, and the teaspoon of pepper in a large bowl. Toss gently until the mushrooms are well coated and all the oil is absorbed.

4. When the steaks are done, transfer them to a serving platter, cover them loosely with foil, and let them rest while you grill the mushrooms. Put the mushrooms on the medium-hot part of the grill and cook, turning occasionally, until they are golden brown and moist all the way through, about 8 to 10 minutes. Slice the cooked mushrooms and put them back in the bowl along with the butter, parsley, sherry, and salt and pepper to taste, and toss gently to coat.

5. Cut the meat away from the bone, then cut it into thick slices. Divide them among 4 serving plates, spoon the mushrooms over the top, and serve.

COOK TO COOK: You want giant steaks here, at least 2 inches thick, so that you can get a good, dark sear on the outside and still leave the inside beautifully rare. Dry them well before you put them on the grill (this helps get the sear), and then, since they are *so* big, transfer them to a lower-heat part of the fire after they get that hard sear.

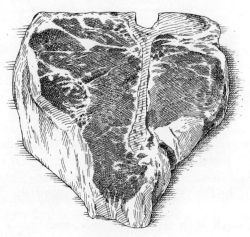

Porterhouse

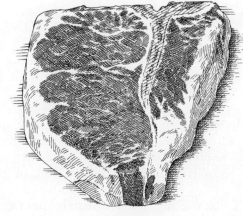

T-Bone

cumin-crusted grilled sirloin strip steak
with grilled avocados and chipotle-coated onions

SERVES 4

We like our grilled beef with lots of other lively flavors to accompany it. This Latin-style dish certainly fills that bill. The strip loin—a very popular cut of beef also known as the New York strip, Kansas City strip, sirloin strip, or club steak, among other monikers, depending on where you buy it—is given a coating of cumin and grilled over a hot fire so it gets nice and crusty on the outside. As usual, we recommend using a very thick piece of beef so it stays rare on the inside while acquiring this seared crust. Then we serve the beef along with a musky, loamy, rich grilled avocado filled with onions that are coated with a lime-soaked mixture fired by the smoky, hot chipotle pepper.

You can substitute any other thick, tender beef steak of your choice in this recipe. Whichever you choose, try serving it with black beans and rice.

3 tablespoons olive oil, divided
Juice of 2 to 3 limes
2 tablespoons orange juice
2 tablespoons minced chipotle
    peppers in adobo sauce
1 red onion, peeled and thinly sliced
1/4 cup finely chopped fresh cilantro

Kosher salt and freshly cracked black
    pepper to taste
4 top loin steaks, 12 to 14 ounces
    each, about 1 1/2 inches thick
1/4 cup cumin seeds
2 ripe avocados, halved and pitted

1. In a medium bowl, combine 1 tablespoon of the olive oil with the lime juice, orange juice, and chipotles and whisk until blended. Add the onions and cilantro and toss until the onions are well coated. Season with salt and pepper to taste, then set aside to marinate for 1 hour, stirring every once in a while.

2. Build a multi-level fire in your grill: Leave one-quarter of the bottom free of coals, bank the coals in the remaining three-quarters of the grill so that they are three times as high on one side as on the other. When all the coals are ignited and the temperature is hot (you can hold your hand about 5 inches above the grill grid, over the area where the coals are deepest, for 2 seconds or less), the fire is ready for cooking this dish.

3. Pat the steaks dry, sprinkle them generously with salt and pepper, and then rub them all over with the cumin seeds, pressing down gently to be sure they adhere. Place the steaks over the hottest part of the fire and cook until well seared, 4 to 5 minutes per side. Move them to a cooler part of the grill and cook, turning once, until they are done to your liking, 10 to 12 minutes more for rare. To check for doneness, poke the meat with your finger to check its firmness level (see page 13); if you're unsure, nick, peek,

and cheat: Make a cut into the center and look to be sure it is just slightly less done than you like it. Transfer the steaks to a serving platter, cover loosely with foil, and let them rest for 5 to 10 minutes.

4. While the steaks are resting, grill the avocados: Rub the cut sides of the avocado halves with the remaining 2 tablespoons of oil and sprinkle them generously with salt and pepper. Place them cut side down on the hot side of the grill and cook until they are golden brown and slightly charred, about 3 to 5 minutes. Remove from the grill and arrange them, cut side up, between the steaks on the platter. Fill the avocado cavities with the chipotle-coated onions and serve immediately.

COOK TO COOK: As always with steaks, be sure to let these rest under a tent of foil for 5 to 10 minutes after they come off the grill. While they rest, juices that were driven out of the protein molecules during cooking will be reabsorbed so they stay in the meat when you cut it, rather than running out onto the plate. To put it simply, patience results in juicier steak.

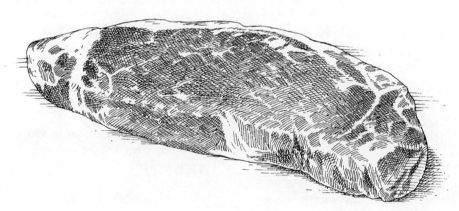

Beef strip steak

grilled bone-in beef rib eye
with aged balsamic and garlic spinach

SERVES 2

Jimmy Burke, a good friend and early mentor of mine (Chris's), owns a number of restaurants in the Boston area and serves a version of this dish that will bring you to your knees. It is this preparation that converted my friend Doug Sharon, a former T-bone booster, to the rib eye camp.

This "huge steak for two" treatment works well with the rib eye because it is so tender and has a wonderful beef flavor. To give you a little perspective, a rib eye is basically a prime rib cut into steaks, so you know it's going to be top drawer. You also know you're going to have to go to your butcher and lay out some cash to get a steak of this size.

We're cooking the beef pretty simply here, with only a few other flavors, so each one needs to be first-rate. Break out your expensive extra-virgin olive oil and fifty-year-old balsamic vinegar, and take care to grill the steak right: Sear it very well, then move it over to the cooler part of the fire to finish up. Finally, be sure you have some crusty bread on hand, because you're definitely going to want to sop up the juices on this one.

Serve this with Grilled Peppered Portobello Steaks with Parmesan Dressing (page 282).

1 bone-in rib eye steak, about 2
    pounds, 2 inches thick
1/2 cup kosher salt
1/2 cup freshly cracked black pepper,
    or to taste
3 tablespoons extra-virgin olive oil
1 tablespoon aged balsamic vinegar
1/4 cup roughly chopped fresh
    oregano

2 tablespoons olive oil
1 pound fresh spinach, trimmed and
    well washed
4 garlic cloves, sliced, cooked in olive
    oil until crisp, and drained well
1 lemon, halved

1. Build a multi-level fire in your grill: Leaving one-quarter of the bottom free of coals, bank the coals in the remaining three-quarters of the grill so that they are three times as high on one side as on the other. When all the coals are ignited and the fire temperature is hot (you can hold your hand about 5 inches above the grill grid, over the area where the coals are deepest, for 2 seconds or less), you're ready to cook.

2. Rub the steak all over with the salt and pepper, pressing down gently to be sure it adheres. Put the steak on the grill directly over the hottest part of the fire and sear very well, about 5 to 8 minutes per side. Now move it to a cooler part of the grill and cook until it is done to your liking, 8 to 10 minutes more per side for rare. To check for done-

ness, poke the meat with your finger to check its firmness level (see page 13); if you're unsure, nick, peek, and cheat: Make a cut into the center and look to be sure it is just slightly less done than you like it.

3. Transfer the steak to a platter, drizzle it with the 3 tablespoons of extra-virgin olive oil and then the vinegar, then sprinkle it with the oregano. Cover loosely with foil to keep warm while you cook the spinach.

4. In your largest sauté pan or skillet, heat the 2 tablespoons of olive oil over high heat. Add the spinach and cook, stirring furiously, for about 1 minute; the spinach should turn bright green and wilt slightly. Add the garlic and continue to cook, stirring rapidly, for 30 seconds. Remove the spinach from the heat, squeeze the lemon over the top, pile it on top of the steak, and serve immediately.

COOK TO COOK: We are convinced, as is virtually every one of the scores of butchers and meat aficionados that we have talked to, that meat tastes better on the bone. The possible scientific reasons are many—the internal composition of bones, their ability to modulate heat transfer, and their position in the midst of a web of cartilage and capillaries are possible contributors—but the proof is in the eating.

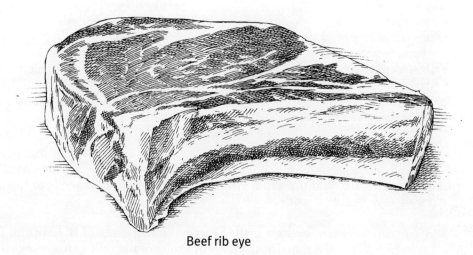

Beef rib eye

parsley- and garlic-rubbed skirt steak with sweet-and-sour marinated red onions

SERVES 4

We have a South American pampas—style situation here, featuring one of our very favorite steaks, the skirt. This thin, flat, heavily grained piece of meat—which became well known in this country because it was the meat originally used in fajitas—has terrific beef flavor. Cooked quickly over high heat and sliced thin against the grain, it is also very tender. In other words, get it on, get it seared, and get it off.

Here we coat the steak with parsley and garlic before it goes on the grill, then serve it with some simple marinated onions to complete the mix of South American flavors. This is a great dish if you're having friends or a crowd over, because the onions are made in advance and the steak cooks very quickly. And people unfamiliar with skirt steak will be amazed by its flavor.

Serve with Grilled Potato Steaks with Bacon, Sour Cream, and Chives (page 298), or check out the Fire-Roasted Peppers with Five Flavor Options (page 290).

For the onions:
1 large red onion, peeled and
    sliced thin
1 cup red wine vinegar
3 tablespoons sugar
Kosher salt and freshly cracked black
    paper to taste
2 tablespoons white vinegar
3 tablespoons extra-virgin olive oil
3 tablespoons freshly cracked
    coriander seeds

3 tablespoons minced garlic
1/3 cup roughly chopped fresh
    parsley
2 teaspoons red pepper flakes,
    or to taste
1/4 cup olive oil
Kosher salt and freshly cracked black
    pepper to taste
4 pieces of skirt steak, 8 to 10 ounces
    each

1. In a large bowl, combine the onions, red wine vinegar, sugar, and salt and pepper to taste, mix well, and let stand 3 to 4 hours at room temperature. Drain the onions, discarding the marinade. Add the white vinegar, oil, and coriander seeds to the onions and stir well. Cover and set aside.

2. Build a multi-level fire in your grill: Leaving one-quarter of the bottom free of coals, bank the coals in the remaining three-quarters of the grill so that they are three times as high on one side as on the other. When all the coals are ignited and the fire is hot (you can hold your hand about 5 inches above the grill grid, over the area where the coals are deepest, for 2 seconds or less), you're ready to put the meat on.

3. Meanwhile, combine the garlic, parsley, red pepper flakes, olive oil, and salt and pepper to taste and mix well. Rub this mixture onto both sides of each piece of steak.

When the fire is ready, put the steaks over the hottest coals and cook until done to your liking, 4 to 5 minutes per side for medium-rare. To check for doneness, poke each steak with your finger to check its firmness level (see page 13); if you're unsure, nick, peek, and cheat: Make a cut in the thickest part of the one of the pieces and peek at the center to be sure it is just slightly less done than you like it.)

4. Thinly slice the steak, cutting on the bias across the grain. Arrange the slices on a serving platter, heap the onions beside the meat, and serve.

COOK TO COOK: These steaks are going to cook very quickly, and you might get a little flare-up action; if you do, move the steaks to the cooler side and let them rest for 15 or 20 seconds.

thai-style white pepper-crusted grilled skirt steak with two sauces

SERVES 4

One of the reasons we are so fond of skirt steak is that its deep, ultra-beefy flavor is powerful enough to stand up to a lot of other bold tastes. That, combined with the fact that it cooks quickly and is less expensive than many other steaks, has made it my (Doc's) fallback dinner. Here we exploit the skirt's accommodating personality and combine it with a lot of pungent, lively, and bold Southeast Asian flavors, including a classic peanut sauce and a chile-basil sauce that resembles an Indonesian sambal. As always, hot, hot, hot and quick, quick, quick is the way you want to cook skirt steaks.

Your choice of the Four Grilled Corn Strategies with Latin Modifiers (page 286) and Grilled Eggplant with Spicy Black Bean Sauce (page 280) would be nice accompaniments.

For the chile-basil sauce:
2 tablespoons roasted sesame oil
2 red onions, peeled and thinly sliced
2 to 3 tablespoons minced fresh chile
  peppers of your choice, or
  to taste
3 tablespoons peeled and minced
  fresh ginger
1 tablespoon prepared curry powder
3 tablespoons *nam pla*, Southeast
  Asian fish sauce (or substitute
  2 tablespoons soy sauce)
1/2 teaspoon sugar
1/2 cup roughly chopped fresh basil
  (Thai basil if you can find it)

Juice of 1 lime

For the peanut sauce:
1/2 cup roasted, unsalted peanuts
1 tablespoon peeled and minced fresh
  ginger
1 teaspoon minced garlic
1/2 cup hot water
1 1/2 tablespoons soy sauce
4 pieces of skirt steak,
  8 to 10 ounces each
Kosher salt to taste
1/3 cup freshly cracked white pepper

1. Build a multi-level fire in your grill: Leaving one-quarter of the bottom free of coals, bank the coals in the remaining three-quarters of the grill so that they are three times as high on one side as on the other. When all the coals are ignited and the temperature is hot (you can hold your hand about 5 inches above the grill grid, over the area where the coals are deepest, for 2 seconds or less), the fire is ready for cooking this dish.

2. Make the chile-basil sauce: In a large sauté pan or skillet over medium-high heat, heat the sesame oil until hot but not smoking. Add the onions and sauté, stirring occa-

sionally, until transparent, 7 to 9 minutes. Add the chiles, ginger, and curry, and sauté, stirring frequently, 1 minute more. Remove the pan from heat, stir in the fish sauce, sugar, basil, and lime juice, and set aside.

3. Make the peanut sauce: In a blender or food processor, combine the peanuts, ginger, and garlic and pulse to chop finely. Add the water and soy sauce and blend until smooth.

4. Sprinkle the skirt steaks generously with salt, then rub them all over with the white pepper, pressing down gently to be sure it adheres. Put the steaks on the grill and cook until well seared on one side, about 4 minutes. Turn and continue to cook to desired doneness, about 2 minutes more for rare. To check for doneness, poke the meat with your finger to check its firmness level (see page 13); if you're unsure, nick, peek, and cheat: Make a cut in the thickest part of one of the steaks and peek at the center to be sure it is just slightly less done than you like it. Remove the steaks from the grill, cover loosely with foil, and allow them to rest for 5 minutes.

5. Slice the steaks thinly on the bias, drizzle generously with the basil sauce, and serve, passing the peanut sauce on the side.

COOK TO COOK: When these steaks come off the grill, be certain that you slice them very thinly against the grain (which is the long way), or they will be tough.

smoke-roasted sirloin butt "london broil style" with tabasco onions and texas toast

SERVES 4

꧀ ꧀ ꧀ ꧀ ꧀ ꧀ ꧀ ꧀ ꧀ ꧀ ꧀ ꧀ ꧀ ꧀ ꧀ ꧀ ꧀

Here's a spice-rubbed and smoke-roasted dish with a ton of rich, dark flavor, the kind of meal you want to serve up with a few bottles of big, bold red wine and the proverbial loaf of crusty bread. We call it "London broil style" because we slice the beef very thinly against the grain before serving it, which is really all that London broil means. To soak up the juices, we provide big slices of garlicky grilled bread.

There are a couple of good options for the cut of beef to use in this dish. Our first choice, the one we specify in the recipe, is top sirloin butt weighing 2 or 3 pounds. This cut, the most tender part of the sirloin, is tender enough to be cooked directly over a hot fire but tough enough to have plenty of beefy flavor. A second possibility is the tri-tip, a triangular roast taken from the bottom end of the bottom sirloin. This tender little roast has gained a lot of favor recently, particularly on the West Coast.

Serve this with Cinnamon Soy-Glazed Grilled Sweet Potatoes (page 295).

For the spice rub:
1/4 cup freshly cracked black pepper
1/4 cup kosher salt
1/4 cup freshly cracked coriander seeds (or substitute 2 tablespoons ground coriander)
2 tablespoons ground cumin
2 tablespoons paprika
2 tablespoons brown sugar
———
1 beef top sirloin butt, 2 to 3 pounds
6 tablespoons olive oil, divided

3 tablespoons roughly chopped fresh parsley
Juice of 2 limes
1/4 cup Tabasco sauce, or to taste
2 tablespoons unsalted butter, softened
1 teaspoon minced garlic
4 thick slices bread
2 large onions, peeled and sliced into rounds about 1 inch thick
Kosher salt and freshly cracked black pepper to taste

1. In a medium bowl, combine all the spice rub ingredients and mix well. Rub the roast all over with this mixture, pressing down gently to be sure it adheres.

2. Start a fire well over to one side of a large kettle grill, using about enough coals to fill a shoebox. When the fire dies down and the coals are well lit, place the roast on the side of the grill away from the coals, being careful that none of the meat is directly over the coals. Put the lid on the grill with the vents one-quarter of the way open and cook until the meat is done the way you like it, about 30 to 40 minutes for medium-rare. To check for doneness, insert a meat thermometer into the center of the roast and let it sit for 5 seconds, then read the temperature: 120°F is rare, 126°F is medium-rare, 134°F is medium, 150°F is medium-well, and 160°F is well-done. (We like to pull the roast at 147°F.) When the roast is done to your liking, remove it from the grill, cover it loosely with foil, and allow it to rest for at least 10 minutes before carving.

3. While the meat is cooking, combine 3 tablespoons of the olive oil with the parsley, lime juice, and Tabasco sauce in a large bowl, mix well, and set aside. In a small bowl, mash together the butter and garlic. Spread some of this mixture on one side of each bread slice.

4. While the meat is resting, rub the onions with the remaining 3 tablespoons of olive oil and sprinkle them generously with salt and pepper, then place them on the grill over the coals and cook until they are golden brown, about 5 to 8 minutes per side. Add them to the lime-Tabasco dressing and toss until well coated. Grill the bread next to the onions, buttered side up, until well toasted, about 5 minutes.

5. Cut the roast into thin slices, fan several slices out on each plate, put a pile of onions on one side of the meat and a piece of grilled bread on the other, and serve. Yeah, boy.

COOK TO COOK: This is an indirect heat situation that also includes a spice rub, so it's particularly important for the meat never to be directly over the coals. You don't want the spice rub to burn or the meat to cook too quickly.

straight-up barbecued beef brisket

SERVES 8 TO 10

What you're doing here is turning a large, gnarly hunk of meat into a tender delicacy by cooking it over the indirect heat and smoke of a low fire, about 180° to 200°F, for as long as you can possibly stand to let it go. This is the straight-up barbecue technique, but we take it a little bit out of the barbecue world by giving the meat a pastrami-esque rub. The inspiration came from Doc's fiftieth-birthday party at Schwartz's Deli in Montreal, where they serve the most awesome smoked brisket sandwiches we ever tasted, with the possible exception of my (Chris's) mother-in-law Shirley Jackson's version.

Make sure to rub the brisket generously with the spice mixture, keep the meat as far off the fire as you can, and exercise patience, taking it one beer at a time. This dish will convince you of the rewards of going slow. You can use a large half brisket instead if you adjust the other ingredients in the recipe in proportion. If you do use a half, try to get the point cut, also known as the thick cut or the nose cut. It's cheaper and fattier than the flat cut, and with this cooking method both of those qualities are advantageous.

One way we love to eat this is to slap the meat between thick slices of good rye bread and slather it with one of our high-flavor homemade mustards (pages 346 to 348). Now that's a sandwich worth eating.

1 cup freshly cracked black pepper	1/2 cup kosher salt
1 cup freshly cracked coriander seeds	1 beef brisket, 10 to 12 pounds
1/2 cup freshly cracked white pepper	

1. Start a small fire well over to one side of your grill, using about enough coals to fill half a shoebox.

2. In a medium bowl, combine the pepper, coriander seeds, white pepper, and salt and mix well. Rub the brisket thoroughly on all sides with this mixture, pressing down gently to be sure it adheres to the meat.

3. When the fire has died down and the coals are covered with white ash, place the brisket on the side of the grill with no coals, being careful that none of the meat is directly over the coals. Put the lid on the grill with the vents one-quarter of the way open and cook, low and slow, adding a handful of fresh charcoal about every 30 minutes. (If your grill has a thermometer, keep the temperature between 180° and 220°F.) Keep the fire going for 8 to 10 hours or even 12 if you can stand it, until the exterior of the brisket is superdark and the meat is very tender.

4. When the meat is cooked past the point of doneness to extreme tenderness—you can test this by sticking it with a fork; if the meat is so tender that the fork just slips out of it when you try to lift it up, the meat is done—pull it off the grill. Slice it very thinly across the grain and serve it with your favorite sauce.

COOK TO COOK: Any brisket you buy will have at least 1/4 inch of surface fat on one side; don't remove it because it will help keep the meat moist. If you can find a brisket with the cap left on, that's your best bet, since the cap contains a lot of fat and connective tissues to keep the brisket moist through the long, slow, dry cooking.

smoke-roasted standing rib roast of beef

SERVES 6 TO 8

Here's the Big Daddy, the supreme monarch of roast beefs. This has been the center-piece of our joint Christmas dinner for the past ten years, and it has been a huge hit every single time. As you no doubt know, the standing rib roast—also called prime rib—is a very expensive, tender, richly flavored piece of beef, so you don't want to muck around with it too much. Just sprinkle it all over with salt and pepper, put it on the grill, cover it up, and let 'er rip. Be sure to use the meat thermometer to check the doneness on this one (we like to pull the roast at 122°F, which is rare, but suit yourself), and let it repose under foil for quite a while after it comes off the heat so the juices redistribute and are reabsorbed. That's all you have to do for a prime rib that you will never forget.

Since this is such an expensive cut, you might want to make a special trip to the butcher shop to buy it. If you do, you'll have a choice to make. A rib roast this size can come either from the large end, near the shoulder, or from the small end, nearer the loin. Many chefs recommend the smaller end, which has a bit less fat and is slightly more tender, but we like the shoulder end, which is marginally less tender but has just a bit better flavor.

We like to accompany this grand roast with horseradish and serve it with—what else?—mashed potatoes, a green salad, and a big, hearty red wine.

1 bone-in beef rib roast with 4 ribs, about 6 to 8 pounds
6 tablespoons kosher salt

6 tablespoons freshly cracked black pepper

1. Build a fire on one side of your grill, using about enough charcoal to fill a shoebox.

2. Rub the roast all over with the salt and pepper, pressing down gently to be sure they adhere.

3. When the coals are well lit and covered with white ash, place the roast on the side of the grill away from the coals, being careful that none of the meat is directly over the coals. Put the lid on the grill with the vents one-quarter of the way open, and cook, adding a handful of fresh charcoal about every 30 minutes, until the roast is done the way you like it, about 1 3/4 to 2 hours for rare. To check for doneness, insert a meat thermometer into the dead center of the roast and let it sit for 5 seconds, then read the temperature: 120°F is rare, 126°F is medium-rare, 134°F is medium, 150°F is medium-well, and 160°F is well done. (We like to pull the roast at 122°F.) When the roast is done to your liking, remove it from the grill, cover it loosely with foil, and allow it to rest for at least 20 minutes before carving.

4. To serve, cut the beef into big, thick slices, and serve with horseradish if you want.

COOK TO COOK: Smoke-roasting requires adding fuel to the fire during cooking. A grill grid with a small section that swings open is ideal for this. If your grill grid doesn't have this feature, keep a big platter on a table right next to the grill so you can lift the food off the grill onto the platter (using your tongs), lift up the grid (tongs again), add the fuel, and get that food back on there.

mustard seed–crusted pork tenderloin with cheesy grilled tomatoes and white beans

SERVES 4

The pork tenderloin, which is essentially a mini-roast, is a super cut of meat. It's widely available, it has good pork flavor, its size makes it quick and easy to cook, and its shape gives it the attractiveness, versatility, and celebratory feel of a roast. It is also eminently suitable for grilling. In fact, grilling tenderloins is an ideal way to hone your doneness-testing skills. It is less intimidating than a larger roast but more amenable to the hand method (see page 13) than smaller cuts like steaks. So each time you cook a tenderloin, make sure you poke the meat with your finger and make a guess at its state of doneness before you nick it and peek inside to be certain.

This particular recipe is basically an upscale version of pork and beans, accompanied by smoky grilled tomatoes topped with melted cheese. You can use canned beans here if you like, but try to get hold of really good, red, juicy, vine-ripened tomatoes.

We might serve this with a Hobo Pack of Sweet Potatoes, Apples, and Sage (page 304) and simple seared greens.

1 1/2 cups dried white beans of your choice (Great Northern, cannellini, navy, etc.), or substitute 2 cans, 15 1/2 ounces each
1 tablespoon fresh rosemary needles
1 tablespoon minced garlic
1/4 cup extra-virgin olive oil
Kosher salt and freshly cracked black pepper to taste
3 pork tenderloins, 12 to 14 ounces each
3 tablespoons vegetable oil

1/4 cup freshly cracked brown mustard seeds (or substitute 2 tablespoons dry yellow mustard)
1/3 cup shredded Asiago or other flavorful hard cheese
1/4 cup roughly chopped fresh parsley
1/3 cup unseasoned fresh breadcrumbs
2 ripe tomatoes about the size of baseballs
2 tablespoons olive oil

1. If using dried beans: Soak the beans overnight in water to cover. Drain the beans, place them in a 3-quart saucepan, and cover with 2 inches of fresh water, then cover the pan and bring to a boil over high heat. Reduce heat to medium-low and simmer until the beans are tender, about 45 minutes to 1 hour. About 10 minutes before you think the beans will be done, stir in the rosemary, garlic, olive oil, and salt and pepper to taste. When the beans are tender, remove them from the heat and cover the pan to

keep them warm. (If using canned beans, rinse and drain the beans, combine them in a small saucepan with the rosemary, garlic, olive oil, and salt and pepper, and bring just to a simmer over medium heat.)

2. Build a multi-level fire in your grill: Leaving one-quarter of the bottom free of coals, bank the coals in the remaining three-quarters of the grill so that they are three times as high on one side as on the other. When all the coals are ignited and the temperature has died down to medium (you can hold your hand about 5 inches above the grill grid, over the area where the coals are deepest, for 4 to 5 seconds), you're ready to cook the meat.

3. Rub the tenderloins all over with the vegetable oil, sprinkle them generously with salt and pepper, and coat them with the mustard seeds, pressing down gently to be sure they adhere. Put the tenderloins on the grill and cook, rolling them around every 3 to 4 minutes to make sure they cook evenly, until they are done to your liking, about 12 to 15 minutes for medium. To check for doneness, poke the meat with your finger to check its firmness level (see page 13); if you're unsure, nick, peek, and cheat: Make a 1/4-inch cut in the thickest part of the meat and peek at the center to be sure it is just slightly less done than you like it. Remove the tenderloins from the heat and cover them loosely with foil to keep warm.

4. In a small bowl, combine the Asiago cheese, parsley, and breadcrumbs and mix well, then set aside. Cut a thin slice off the top and bottom of each tomato and cut them in half horizontally. Rub the halves with olive oil and season with salt and pepper. Put the tomatoes on the grill cut side down and cook for 2 minutes; turn them over and cook 2 minutes more. Gently transfer the tomato halves to the cool side of the grill and top with the cheese mixture. Invert a foil pan over the tomatoes and let them stand until the cheese is melted.

5. To serve, arrange a grilled tomato half and some of the beans on each plate. Cut the pork into 1/2-inch slices, then fan the slices over the beans.

COOK TO COOK: Because pork tenderloin doesn't have any flat sides, the best way to deal with it on the grill is to roll it around every once in a while to ensure even cooking.

bacon-wrapped pork tenderloin
with balsamic-glazed peaches and black olive relish

SERVES 4

We use bacon here to put back a little of the fat that pork breeders have taken out of the tenderloin. To finish the dish, we grill up some peaches and drizzle them with reduced balsamic vinegar, one of our favorite condiments, then we add a straightforward black olive relish. Also, this is one of those times when you might want to toss some hardwood chips on the fire—the pork will have just enough time to absorb the smoky flavor of a particular wood.

Serve the tenderloin with a Warm Salad of Grilled Eggplant, Summer Squash, and Zucchini (page 315) or a Hobo Pack of Squash, Bacon, and Red Onions (page 303).

3 pork tenderloins, 10 to 12 ounces
   each
Kosher salt and freshly cracked black
   pepper to taste
6 slices bacon
1/3 cup roughly chopped black olives
1/4 cup roughly chopped fresh
   parsley

1/4 cup olive oil
3 ripe but firm peaches, halved and
   pitted
3/4 cup balsamic vinegar simmered
   until reduced to 1/4 cup

1. Dry the tenderloins well and sprinkle them generously with salt and pepper.

2. Start a fire well over to one side of your grill, using about enough coals to fill a large shoebox. When all the coals are ignited and the fire is hot (you can hold your hand about 5 inches above the grill grid for 2 seconds or less), place the tenderloins on the hot part of the grill and cook, rolling them around a couple of times to ensure even cooking, just long enough to develop a brown crusty sear on the outside, about 12 to 14 minutes. Remove the tenderloins from the grill and allow them to cool slightly, then wrap 2 strips of bacon around each one, securing them with toothpicks if necessary.

3. When the fire has died down to medium (you can hold your hand about 5 inches above the grill grid for 4 to 5 seconds), place the bacon-wrapped tenderloins on the side of the grill away from the coals, being careful that none of the meat is directly over the coals. Cover them with a 9-inch tin pie plate and cook for 15 to 20 minutes. To check for doneness, poke the meat with your finger to check its firmness level (see page 13); if you're unsure, nick, peek, and cheat: Make a cut in the thickest part of the meat and peek at the center to be sure it is just slightly less done than you like it. When the tenderloins are done to your liking, remove them from the grill, cover them loosely with foil, and let them rest about 10 minutes.

4. While the pork is cooking, combine the olives, parsley, and olive oil in a small bowl and toss well, then set aside.

5. While the pork is resting, put the peaches on the grill, cut side down, and cook until they are well seared, 3 to 4 minutes, lifting them up briefly to brush the cut side with the reduced balsamic glaze during the last 30 seconds of cooking. Remove the peaches from the grill, and when they are cool enough to handle, slice them and put them in a medium bowl. Add the remaining reduced balsamic and toss gently.

6. Slice the pork crosswise on an extreme bias, arrange the slices on plates, and top with a spoonful of the peaches and some of the olive relish.

COOK TO COOK: After the initial searing, we move on to smoke-roasting here so the bacon cooks without getting burned. Because this is an indirect cooking process, it is going to take a little while, so be patient.

good chops

* * *

Just about everybody who likes meat loves pork chops. And why not? They are easy to cook, they have wonderful pork flavor, and they come in many versions—loin chops, rib chops, center-cut chops, even blade chops and sirloin chops. And you can have any of these cut thick or thin.

Although it's fun to have choices, it can also be confusing. The good news is that since all pork chops come from the loin of the hog, which is the most tender part of the animal, they are all quite tender. But there are some differences. Chops taken from the extreme front and back of the loin—blade chops and sirloin chops, respectively—tend to be gnarlier. Any of the three types of chops that come from the center of the loin—loin chops, top loin chops, and rib chops, which are often lumped together as center-cut chops—will be very tender and gristle-free. If you get a loin chop, you'll notice that it contains meats of two slightly different colors. That's because this cut includes portions of the top loin muscle and the tenderloin muscle. A top loin chop, on the other hand, is essentially a loin chop without the tenderloin section. The rib chop, our particular favorite, comes from the section of the loin nearer the shoulder. Because of that, it has a little bit more fat than the other center-cut chops, which makes it more flavorful and less likely to dry out over the grill.

But what about chops from other animals? Well, there are no beef chops. Instead, these same cuts are called steaks. The rib chop, for example, becomes a rib eye steak, while the equivalent of a pork loin chop is a porterhouse, and so on.

When it comes to lamb, on the other hand, chops are the single most popular cut. Loin and rib chops, both of which are very tender and hyper-expensive, are excellent choices. Our favorite, though, is the lamb shoulder chop. It is less tender (and a lot less expensive) than loin or rib chops, but it's excellent for grilling and has more lamb flavor than its tonier cousins.

grilled giant pork chops with sweet peach barbecue sauce

SERVES 4

※ ※ ※ ※ ※ ※ ※ ※ ※ ※ ※ ※ ※ ※ ※

To our minds, there's not much that can beat a grilled giant pork chop. You will prob-ably have to go to your butcher shop to get chops 1 1/2 inches thick, but it's going to be worth it. That fantastic sear on the spice-rubbed outside, that moist, tender, juicy meat on the inside—who could resist it?

Since these chops are so thick, you may well need to use the classic sear-and-move technique, moving the chops to the cooler part of the fire if you see that they're getting too done on the outside before they cook through on the inside. Make sure you have a metal pie pan or disposable foil pan on standby when you put the chops on the grill. That way, if you do need to move the chops you can use the pan to cover them when they're on the cooler part of the fire, getting some convection cooking going.

We really like pork with fruit, so we finish this dish with a little peach barbecue sauce. Serve the chops with Blue Cheese–Stuffed Ash-Roasted Red Onions (page 306) and grilled corn cooked according to your favorite of our Four Grilled Corn Strategies (page 286).

For the spice rub:
3 tablespoons ground coriander
3 tablespoons ground paprika
2 tablespoons ground cumin
1 tablespoon kosher salt
3 tablespoons freshly cracked black
    pepper
1 tablespoon brown sugar

———

4 rib or loin pork chops, about
    1 1/2 inches thick, 12 to 14
    ounces each

For the sauce:
2 tablespoons olive oil

1 small red onion, peeled and
    sliced thin
3 peaches, pitted and diced medium
2 tablespoons peeled and minced
    fresh ginger
2 ripe tomatoes about the size of
    baseballs, diced medium
1/2 cup cider vinegar
1/2 cup orange juice
1/3 cup light or dark brown sugar
1 teaspoon ground allspice
1/3 cup light or dark brown sugar
1 teaspoon ground allspice
Kosher salt and freshly cracked black
    pepper to taste

1. Build a multi-level fire in your grill: Leaving one-quarter of the bottom free of coals, bank the coals in the remaining three-quarters of the grill so that they are three times as high on one side as on the other. When all the coals are ignited and the temperature has died down to medium (you can hold your hand about 5 inches above the grill grid, over the area where the coals are deepest, for 4 to 5 seconds), you're ready to cook.

2. Meanwhile, combine the ingredients for the spice rub in a small bowl and mix well. Rub the pork chops generously on both sides with this mixture and set them aside while you make the sauce.

3. In a large sauté pan or skillet over medium-high heat, heat the oil until it is hot but not smoking. Add the onions and sauté, stirring occasionally, until golden brown, 11 to 13 minutes. Add the peaches, ginger, and tomatoes and cook, stirring frequently, for 2 minutes more. Stir in the vinegar, orange juice, sugar, allspice, and salt and pepper. Bring the mixture to a boil, then reduce the heat and simmer until the mixture is reduced by about half and has thickened slightly, about 20 minutes. Taste for seasoning, then transfer the sauce to a blender or food processor and purée until smooth (be careful with the hot liquid). Reserve 1/4 cup sauce for basting the chops, then pour the remaining sauce into a small serving bowl.

4. Put the chops on the grill over the coals and cook, turning once, until done to your liking, 8 to 10 minutes per side for medium. During the last 30 seconds of cooking on each side, baste the chops generously with the barbecue sauce. To check for doneness, poke the meat with your finger to check its firmness level (see page 13); if you're unsure, nick, peek, and cheat: Make a 1/4-inch cut in the thickest part of one of the chops and peek at the center to be sure it is just slightly less done than you like it.

5. Serve the chops hot, passing the remaining barbecue sauce on the side.

COOK TO COOK: In this recipe, both the spice rub and the sauce have sugar in them. That adds a lot of caramelized flavor, but it also means you have to watch the chops carefully to be sure the rub doesn't burn—you want it to get dark brown but not black—and put the sauce on for only the last bit of the cooking time. If the chops start to burn on the outside, move them to the cooler part of the grill and cover with a metal pie pan or disposable foil pan to finish cooking.

hoisin-glazed grilled thin pork chops with thai-style power pack

SERVES 4

You know how it goes when students catch their teacher in a contradiction and the whole class says, "Oh, but you said . . ." Well, that's what happens to me (Chris) whenever I bring out this recipe at one of my cooking classes. Their glee makes sense, given that I ordinarily stress that when grilling meat you want to use a thick cut so it gets a good sear without overcooking. But to them, and to all you grasshoppers out there, I say, "As knowledge grows, rules fall away."

In other words, the exception proves the rule, and this is the exception. We like thin pork chops because they're easy to find and they have good pork flavor. And as I (Chris) learned by watching street cooks down in Mexico, if you cook them over a really hot fire you can get a pretty good sear on them without getting them too done on the inside. Of course, the fact that we like to cook pork to medium rather than rare also helps here. Brushing a little glaze on the chops during the last few seconds of cooking contributes as well, since it develops the sear more quickly.

Here we put the chops in a Southeast Asian suit consisting of a simple hoisin-lime glaze and a very dynamic, spicy power pack mixture that you sprinkle on the end. We might serve this dish with white rice and steamed or sautéed Asian greens.

For the glaze:
1/2 cup hoisin sauce
1/4 cup fresh lime juice (about 2 limes)

For the power pack:
1/2 cup coarsely chopped roasted, unsalted peanuts
1/4 cup roughly chopped fresh mint
1/4 cup roughly chopped fresh cilantro
2 jalapeños or other chile peppers of your choice, minced

3 tablespoons peeled and minced fresh ginger
1/4 cup scallions, both white and green parts, chopped
Kosher salt and freshly cracked black pepper to taste

———

8 thin (1/2 inch or less) loin pork chops of your choice
Kosher salt and freshly cracked black pepper to taste

1. Build a multi-level fire in your grill: Leaving one-quarter of the bottom free of coals, bank the coals in the remaining three-quarters of the grill so that they are three times as high on one side as on the other. When all the coals are ignited and the fire is hot (you can hold your hand about 5 inches above the grill grid, over the area where the coals are deepest, for 2 seconds or less), you're ready to cook.

2. In a small bowl, whisk together the hoisin sauce and lime juice until smooth, then set aside. In a medium bowl, combine the power pack ingredients, mix well with your fingers, and set aside.

3. Sprinkle the chops generously with salt and pepper, place on the hottest part of the grill, and cook about 3 to 4 minutes per side, brushing with the lime-hoisin mixture during the last 30 seconds of cooking. To check for doneness, poke the meat with your finger to check its firmness level (see page 13); if you're unsure, nick, peek, and cheat: Make a 1/4-inch cut in the thickest part of the meat and peek at the center to be sure it is just barely pink.

4. Arrange the glazed chops on a platter, sprinkle the power pack over them, and serve, passing the remaining glaze on the side.

COOK TO COOK: To keep these thin chops tender and moist but still cook them through, you need to have a hot fire, and you need to get them on and get them off quickly.

grilled thin pork chops (chuletas)
with sweet potato salad and a chile-glazed apple

SERVES 4

We think of these thin chops as *chuletas*, which simply means chops in Spanish. I (Doc) first encountered them in northern Spain about twenty-five years ago. Driving through the incredibly picturesque Picos de Europa mountains south of Bilbao, I stopped at a little restaurant for lunch and was served grilled chuletas with nothing more than salt, pepper, and a sprinkling of smoky dried red peppers that we identified much later as *pimenton de la vera*. In Mexico, the chops are served with fiery salsas.

In any case, thin pork chops are tasty, cook quickly, and are one of the few things you can always count on finding in the supermarket meat section, usually in a big family pack. So it's good to have a bunch of recipes for them. In homage to the chuletas we've eaten in Spain and Mexico, we accompany them here with side dishes inspired by Spanish-speaking countries—a South American—style sweet potato salad and some grilled green apple halves spiced up with molasses and chile peppers.

This dish has real picnic potential. All you need to make it a meal is some bread and a dessert.

For the salad:
- 4 medium sweet potatoes
- 1/4 cup chopped scallions, both green and white parts
- 1/2 cup diced celery (about 1 large stalk)
- 1/4 cup fresh lime juice (about 2 limes)
- 1/4 cup honey
- 1/4 cup extra-virgin olive oil
- 1/4 cup roughly chopped fresh cilantro

- 1/4 cup molasses
- 1 tablespoon minced fresh chiles of your choice, or less to taste
- 8 thin pork chops, about 6 ounces each
- 3 tablespoons ground cumin
- Kosher salt and freshly cracked black pepper to taste
- 2 Granny Smith apples, cored and halved
- 2 tablespoons olive oil

1. Build a multi-level fire in your grill: Leaving one-quarter of the bottom free of coals, bank the coals in the remaining three-quarters of the grill so that they are three times as high on one side as on the other. When all the coals are ignited and the temperature over the side with more coals is hot (you can hold your hand about 5 inches above the grill grid for 2 seconds or less), you're ready to cook.

2. Peel the sweet potatoes and dice them medium (you should have about 3 cups). Cook the diced potatoes in a large pot of boiling salted water until just tender but not mushy, about 8 to 10 minutes, then drain, cool well in running cold water, and drain again. Place them in a large bowl with all the remaining salad ingredients and toss until well mixed. Set aside while you grill the chops and apples.

3. In a small bowl, combine the molasses and chiles, mix well, and set aside.

4. Rub the chops with the cumin, sprinkle them generously with salt and pepper, place them on the grill, and cook until they are well seared on the outside and done the way you like them on the inside, about 3 to 4 minutes per side for medium. To check for doneness, poke the meat with your finger to check its firmness level (see page 13); if you're unsure, nick, peek, and cheat: Make a cut in the thickest part of the meat and peek at the center to be sure it is just slightly less done than you like it.

5. Meanwhile, rub the apples with the oil, sprinkle with salt and pepper, and put them on the side of the grill with fewer coals, cut side down. Cook until they are golden brown, about 5 minutes; during the last 30 seconds or so of cooking, turn them over and brush the cut sides generously with the molasses-chile mixture.

6. Put a chop on each plate along with one of the apple halves and some of the salad and serve.

COOK TO COOK: Thin pieces of meat generally need to be cooked over a hot fire so that they get nicely seared but don't dry out. These chops are no exception. In fact, the twin keys to this dish are very thin chops and a very hot fire.

chipotle grilled pork medallions
with cilantro-peanut sprinkle

SERVES 4

In this dish we use pork loin medallions, a.k.a. fillets or noisettes. They are basically small, boneless pork filet mignons that are very easy to prepare. They are lifesavers when you are challenged by a small grill and many guests, because they don't take up much grill space and they cook quickly. To give the pork plenty of flavor we first coat it with cumin and coriander, and when it comes off the grill we toss it in a mixture of chipotle peppers, citrus, and garlic. A little sprinkling of peanuts and fresh cilantro finishes this Mexican-influenced dish.

To maintain the smoky-heat theme, serve this with Black Bean and Pineapple Salad with Orange-Chipotle Vinaigrette (page 312). Or try it with Slaw "A La Playa" (page 310).

2 to 3 tablespoons chipotle peppers
    in adobo sauce, puréed
1/4 cup fresh orange juice
3 tablespoons fresh lime juice (about
    1 1/2 limes)
1/4 cup extra-virgin olive oil
1 tablespoon minced garlic
Kosher salt and freshly cracked black
    pepper to taste

8 pork loin medallions, about
    3/4 inch thick, 4 ounces each
3 tablespoons vegetable oil
2 tablespoons ground cumin
2 tablespoons ground coriander
1/2 cup roughly chopped fresh
    cilantro
1/2 cup chopped roasted,
    unsalted peanuts

1. Build a multi-level fire in your grill: Leaving one-quarter of the bottom free of coals, bank the coals in the remaining three-quarters of the grill so that they are three times as high on one side as on the other. When all the coals are ignited and the temperature has died down to medium-hot (you can hold your hand about 5 inches above the grill grid, over the area where the coals are deepest, for 3 to 4 seconds), you're ready to cook.

2. In a large bowl, combine the chipotles, orange juice, lime juice, olive oil, garlic, and salt and pepper to taste, mix well, and set aside.

3. Coat the pork medallions lightly with the vegetable oil, then rub them all over with the cumin and coriander and sprinkle them generously with salt and pepper. Put the medallions on the grill and cook them until they are done the way you like them, about 5 minutes on each side for medium-well done. To check for doneness, poke the meat with your finger to check its firmness level (see page 13); if you're unsure, nick, peek, and cheat: Make a small cut in one of the medallions and peek at the center to be sure it is just slightly less done than you like it. Remove from the heat, cover loosely with foil, and let the meat rest for 5 minutes.

4. While the pork is resting, combine the cilantro and peanuts in a small bowl and mix well.

5. When the medallions have rested, add them to the large bowl with the chipotle mixture and toss to coat. Put the medallions on a platter, top with the cilantro-peanut sprinkle, and serve.

COOK TO COOK: Make sure you're cooking over a medium-hot fire here. These medallions are too thick for a hot fire, but a medium fire would not take them where we want them to go, because they would be done in the center before they had that nice sear on the outside.

rosemary-crusted smoke-roasted pork loin with sautéed green grapes and grilled oranges

SERVES 6

In this recipe we put some smoke on a bone-in, center-cut pork loin. Quite lean and fine-grained in texture, the tender center-cut loin is the epitome of the new pork. Be sure to have your butcher cut the chine bone (backbone) off, because once it's removed you can cleanly and easily cut the roast into individual chops after grilling. If you can't get a center-cut roast (or you want to spend a bit less money), you can substitute a pork loin *blade* roast or pork loin *sirloin* roast. The blade comes from the part of the loin near the shoulder, the sirloin from the part nearest the leg. Both have a slightly rougher texture than a center-cut roast, but to offset that disadvantage you'll be getting more pork flavor, because they are a bit fattier.

This dish is ideal if you have a lot of people coming over. You have to think ahead—the brining of the meat, which we recommend that you do, takes 24 hours—but once you put the lid on the grill you can just relax and hang out with your friends. To accompany the roast, we grill up some thick orange slices with the peel still on; they are a little unusual, which is always a good thing, and they get nicely caramelized because of the sugar they contain. As a bonus, they look pretty on the plate with the sautéed green grapes.

This goes well with Ihsan's Grilled Cheese in Grape Leaves (page 34) in front of it and a Hobo Pack of Winter Squash, Bacon, and Red Onions (page 303) alongside.

For the brine (optional):
2 1/2 quarts water
2 packed cups light or dark brown
    sugar
1 cup kosher salt
5 large sprigs fresh rosemary
10 garlic cloves, peeled and crushed
3 bay leaves, crumbled
————
1 bone-in, center-cut pork loin, about
    6 pounds
1/2 cup roughly chopped fresh
    rosemary

2 tablespoons minced garlic
1/4 cup olive oil
1 tablespoon red pepper flakes
Kosher salt and freshly cracked black
    pepper to taste
2 oranges, sliced into 1/2-inch-thick
    rounds (not peeled)
2 tablespoons vegetable oil
3 tablespoons butter
1 1/2 cups seedless green grapes
Juice of 1 orange
Juice of 1 lime
1/3 cup roughly chopped fresh
    parsley

1. In a large bowl, clean bucket, or roasting pan large enough to hold the meat, combine the water, brown sugar, and salt, and stir until the sugar and salt are completely dissolved. Add the remaining brine ingredients and mix well. Add the pork loin, mak-

ing sure that it is completely submerged in the liquid (if not, add enough water to cover). Let the roast brine in the refrigerator for 24 hours, stirring the brine and turning the meat occasionally.

2. Start a fire well over to one side of a large kettle grill, using about enough coals to fill a large shoebox.

3. Remove the pork from the brine and dry it well with paper towels. Discard the brine. Using a mortar and pestle (or a small bowl and a fork), mash together the rosemary, garlic, olive oil, red pepper flakes, and salt and pepper until the mixture forms a loose paste. Rub the pork all over with it.

4. When the fire dies down and the coals are well lit, place the roast on the side of the grill away from the coals, being careful that none of the meat is directly over the coals. Put the lid on the grill with the vents one-quarter of the way open. Cook, adding a handful of fresh charcoal about every 30 minutes, until the pork is done, about 80 minutes. To check for doneness, insert a meat thermometer into the dead center of the roast and let it sit for 5 seconds, then read the temperature: 134°F is medium, 150°F is medium-well, and 160°F is well-done; we like to pull the meat at 147°F. When the roast is done to your liking, remove it from the grill, cover it loosely with foil, and let it rest about 20 minutes.

5. While the pork is resting, brush the orange slices with the vegetable oil, put them on the grill, and cook until slightly browned with some dark brown spots, about 5 minutes per side.

6. Meanwhile, melt the butter in a medium saucepan over medium heat. Add the grapes and sauté, stirring occasionally, just until they are hot, about 5 minutes. Remove the pan from the heat and stir in the orange juice, lime juice, parsley, and salt and pepper to taste.

7. To serve, slice the pork between the bones, arrange the meat and orange slices on a platter, drizzle with a bit of the grape sauce, and serve, passing any remaining grape sauce separately.

COOK TO COOK: Brining is a pretty good idea with today's relatively low-fat pork roasts. The brine not only deepens the meat's flavor, it also helps keep it moist over the fire. If you don't have room in your refrigerator for the container, you can do your brining in a cooler with three or four freezer packs in the brine to keep it cool. Just be sure to put new freezer packs in the solution every few hours so the temperature doesn't rise.

slow-smoked latin-style pork butt
with creole barbecue sauce and roasted corn

SERVES 8 TO 10

≈ ≈ ≈ ≈ ≈ ≈ ≈ ≈ ≈ ≈ ≈ ≈ ≈ ≈ ≈ ≈ ≈

This is kind of a Latin version of the shredded pork barbecue beloved of the American South. It is basically a pork butt—which, oddly enough, comes from the shoulder rather than the rump of the animal—cooked by the traditional slow-and-low barbecue method. When this baby finally comes off the grill, you chop or shred it into tendrils that are soft and tender on the inside, beautifully seared and a little crunchy on the outside.

You should have the Creole-inspired finishing sauce and the corn ready to go by the time the meat is done. You can either pass the sauce separately, in the manner of true barbecue aficionados, or you can mix a bit of it with the shredded pork and pass the rest. Cooking the corn in the ashes gives it a particularly smoky flavor that goes well with the spicy butter, but if you prefer you can cook the corn on top of the grill instead.

All you need to make this a Latin-style feast is Cheesy Chipotle Cornbread (page 323) and Slaw "A la Playa" (page 310) along with rice and black beans.

1 boneless pork butt or other bone-
    less pork shoulder roast, about
    6 pounds
Kosher salt and freshly cracked black
    pepper to taste

For the sauce:
1 cup olive oil
1/2 cup red wine vinegar
1/2 cup tomato juice
3 ripe tomatoes about the size of
    baseballs, cored and diced
    medium
3 tablespoons minced garlic
1/4 cup ground paprika
3 tablespoons ground cumin

2 tablespoons dry mustard
1/2 cup roughly chopped fresh
    oregano
2 limes, halved
Kosher salt and freshly cracked black
    pepper to taste

For the corn:
12 ears of corn, husks peeled back,
    silk removed, and husks
    replaced over the corn
1 cup (2 sticks) unsalted butter at
    room temperature
2 tablespoons ground dried chiles of
    your choice
Juice of 1 lime (about 2 tablespoons)

1. Build a small fire in one side of a covered grill, using about enough charcoal to fill a shoebox. When all the charcoal is completely ignited, wait a few minutes for the fire to die down, then you're good to go.

2. Sprinkle the pork butt generously on all sides with salt and pepper and place it on the grill grid on the side away from the fire. Cover the grill, vent slightly, and cook about 5 to 8 hours, until the meat is very tender and the internal temperature is at least

165°F on a meat thermometer. As the meat cooks, add a handful of charcoal every 30 to 40 minutes, or as needed to keep the fire going. To check for doneness, stick a big fork into the pork and try to lift it up off the grill—if it falls off the fork, it's done.

3. Meanwhile, make the sauce: Combine all the sauce ingredients in a medium saucepan, bring to a simmer over medium-high heat, then reduce the heat slightly and cook until the sauce thickens, about 30 minutes. Remove from the heat and set aside.

4. During the last 30 minutes of the pork's cooking time, lift up the lid and place the corn on the outer edges of the coal bed and roast in the coals until the ears are tender, about 20 to 30 minutes. While the corn is roasting, combine the butter, chile, lime juice, and salt and pepper in a small bowl and mash with a fork until it has an even consistency.

5. Chop or shred the pork and either pile it on hamburger buns or serve it with corn tortillas. In either case, pass the sauce, corn, and chile butter on the side.

COOK TO COOK: As with other barbecues, the length of time you cook this pork butt depends on your patience. It is edible after about 3 hours, but what you really want to do is cook it past the point of doneness to the point of real tenderness, which takes between 5 and 8 hours. You might want to select a favorite beverage to carry you through.

smoke roasted whole fresh ham
with orange-pineapple chutney and grilled mangoes

SERVES 10 TO 12

Sweet, tender, juicy, and full of pork flavor, fresh ham—which we like to think of as "ham in a roast pork suit"—is one of our top favorites among underappreciated cuts of meat. Few people have experienced it, since the usual approach to this part of the pig is to cure and smoke it. As a side benefit, it is considerably less expensive than a loin roast. Try to get one with the skin on; the ultra-crisp skin that results from hours of smoky heat is one of the great pleasures of this piece of meat.

With a cut this large, we use the indirect smoke-roast method, maintaining a fire temperature in the neighborhood of 325°F. To keep the meat moist during roasting, we soak it in a saltwater brine for at least 24 hours prior to cooking. As long as we're going to the trouble, we add some bright Caribbean flavors—rum, cloves, and nutmeg—to the brine. Both the chutney, which can be made ahead, and the mangoes are outstanding accompaniments to the pork.

Serve with a Hobo Pack of Sweet Potatoes, Apples, and Sage (page 304) or Grilled Fingerling Potatoes with Blue Cheese (page 297).

For the brine:
3 quarts water
1 cup sugar
1 cup kosher salt
3 cups dark rum
25 whole cloves
2 teaspoons ground nutmeg

———

1 bone-in fresh ham (half a leg),
    8 to 10 pounds, with skin

For the chutney:
1/4 cup vegetable oil
2 red onions, peeled and thinly sliced
3 tablespoons peeled and minced
    ginger
1 small or 1/2 large pineapple, peeled
    and cut into 1-inch dice
2 cups orange juice
1 cup cider vinegar
1/2 cup brown sugar
1/2 cup golden raisins
1 teaspoon allspice
1 teaspoon cardamom
Kosher salt and freshly cracked black
    pepper to taste

For the spice rub:
1/2 cup of your favorite hot sauce
2 tablespoons minced garlic
1 1/2 tablespoons cumin seeds,
    toasted (or substitute 1 table-
    spoon ground cumin)
1 1/2 tablespoons freshly cracked
    toasted coriander seeds (or
    substitute 1 tablespoon ground
    coriander)
1 1/2 tablespoons kosher salt
1 1/2 tablespoons freshly cracked
    black pepper
1 1/2 tablespoons dark brown sugar

For the grilled mangoes:
3 tablespoons butter
3 tablespoons molasses
5 to 6 firm but fully ripe mangoes
    (depending on the number of
    guests), halved and pitted, skin
    left on
3 tablespoons vegetable oil

1. In a large bowl, clean bucket, or roasting pan large enough to hold the ham, stir together the water, sugar, and salt until the sugar and salt completely dissolve. Add the rum, cloves, and nutmeg and mix well. Lower the ham into the brine, making sure it is completely submerged; add additional water if necessary to cover. Cover and place in the refrigerator for at least 24 hours and up to 3 days, stirring the brine and turning the ham over every 12 hours.

2. Make the chutney: In a large sauté pan or skillet over medium-high heat, heat the oil until hot but not smoking. Add the onions and sauté, stirring occasionally, until transparent, about 7 to 9 minutes. Stir in the ginger and pineapple and sauté, stirring occasionally, 3 minutes more. Stir in the remaining chutney ingredients and let the mixture come to a simmer, then reduce the heat to medium and simmer gently for about 30 minutes, stirring occasionally to keep the mixture from sticking to the pan. When the chutney has thickened, remove the pan from the heat, taste for salt and pepper, and set aside. (The chutney can be made up to 4 or 5 days ahead of time. Keep it covered and refrigerated.)

3. Getting set up for the big event: Start a fire well over to one side of a large kettle grill, using about enough coals to fill a shoebox.

4. In a medium bowl, combine the ingredients for the spice rub and mix well. Remove the ham from the brine and pat it dry with paper towels. (Discard the brine.) Rub the ham all over with the spice rub, pressing down gently to be sure it adheres.

5. When the fire dies down and the coals are well lit, place the ham on the side of the grill away from the coals, being careful that none of the meat is directly over the coals. Put the lid on the grill with the vents one-quarter of the way open and cook, adding a handful of fresh charcoal about every 30 minutes. Start checking for doneness after about 2 hours, but expect that it may take up to 3 hours to cook a piece of meat this large to medium or medium-well. To check for doneness, insert a meat thermometer into the center of the ham and let it sit for 5 seconds, then read the temperature: 126°F is medium-rare, 134°F is medium, 150°F is medium-well, and 160°F is well-done; we like to pull the ham at 147°F. When the ham is done to your liking, remove it from the grill, cover it loosely with foil, and allow it to rest for 20 to 30 minutes before carving.

6. Meanwhile, melt the butter in a small saucepan over medium heat. Add the molasses and stir until well mixed, then remove from the heat. Rub the mango halves lightly with oil, place them on the grill cut-side down, and cook until they have light grill marks, 2 to 3 minutes. Flip them over, brush them liberally with the glaze, and grill for 1 minute more. Remove from the grill and drizzle with any leftover glaze.

7. Cut ham into thick slices and serve, accompanied by chutney and grilled mangoes.

COOK TO COOK: This is a really big cut of meat, so if your grill has a thermometer, keep the heat at the lower end of your smoke-roasting temperature range: 325° to 350°F, rather than 350° to 400°F. And make sure that the meat is never directly over the coals.

grilled country-style pork ribs
with pineapple-chipotle barbecue sauce

SERVES 4

Though the cut we're using here is called country-style ribs, that's a bit of a misnomer. These "ribs" are actually the last few chops, cut in half, from the shoulder of the pig. They cook pretty fast, so they can be placed directly over medium coals. And since they have plenty of flavor, we just rub them with some coriander before they go on the grill, then glaze them during the last half-minute of cooking with a Mexican-influenced barbecue sauce, basically a pineapple, orange, and chipotle reduction. As always, decide for yourself how much of the chipotles to add to the sauce. We like things pretty hot; that's what you'll get if you use the amount we call for.

Try serving these ribs with East Coast Grill Cornbread (page 322) and Slaw "A la Playa" (page 310).

For the barbecue sauce:
- 2 cups pineapple juice
- 1 cup orange juice
- 3 tablespoons minced chipotle peppers in adobo sauce, or to taste
- 1 tablespoon ground cumin
- 1/3 cup fresh lime juice (about 3 limes)
- 1/3 cup roughly chopped fresh cilantro

- 12 country-style pork spare ribs, 4 to 6 ounces each
- Kosher salt and freshly cracked black pepper to taste
- 1/4 cup freshly cracked toasted coriander seeds (or substitute 2 tablespoons ground coriander)

1. In a medium saucepan, bring the pineapple juice, orange juice, chipotles, and cumin to a boil over medium-high heat. Reduce the heat to low and simmer, stirring frequently, until the sauce is thickened, sticky, and reduced by half, about 1 hour. Remove from the heat, stir in the lime juice and cilantro, and set aside.

2. Meanwhile, build a multi-level fire in your grill: leaving one-quarter of the bottom free of coals, bank the coals in the remaining three-quarters of the grill so that they are three times as high on one side as on the other. When all the coals are ignited and the temperature has died down to medium-hot (you can hold your hand about 5 inches above the grill grid, over the area where the coals are deepest, for 3 to 4 seconds), you're ready to cook.

3. Sprinkle the ribs generously with salt and pepper, then rub all over with coriander seeds, pressing down gently to be sure they adhere. Put the ribs on the grill over the coals and cook about 3 to 4 minutes per side, brushing with the barbecue sauce during the last 30 seconds of cooking. To check for doneness, cut into one of the ribs and peek to be sure it is just barely pink at the center.

4. Remove the ribs from the grill and serve, passing the remaining barbecue sauce on the side.

COOK TO COOK: Make sure you don't cook these ribs too long and dry them out; check them for doneness (using the nick, peek, and cheat method) early and often.

ribs galore

* * *

We are huge fans of ribs. They are relatively inexpensive, they possess spectacular flavor, and you get to pick them up with your hands and gnaw on them. What more could you ask of a cut of meat?

In this section we provide recipes for several types of pork ribs, with the exception of one kind, the ones called simply **spare ribs**. These guys come from the belly of the pig right under the bacon, so as you can imagine they have plenty of rich taste—in fact, they're our favorite in terms of pure flavor. But because of their size, they require hours of slow cooking at very low temperatures and you can cook only a few at a time with a home setup, so we reluctantly leave them to those cooks who have professional barbecue pits. We do, however, give you an excellent treatment for their close second in flavor, **St. Louis-style ribs**, spare ribs that have been trimmed by removing the backbone and part of the breastbone. Often called "3 and down" (because each rack is less than 3 pounds), they are a little neater than your regular spare ribs and have the great advantage of taking up less room on the grill. Next are the very popular **baby back ribs**, which come from the loin of the animal. Because they are smaller they can be cooked directly over coals when you can't take the time for the slow-and-low treatment. They're good, of course— after all, they do come from the pig and they are ribs—but their chief advantage over larger ribs is convenience. The pork "rib" entry on page 180 is the so-called **country ribs**. In fact, those are really the last few chops from the shoulder of the pig, just before you get into the rib section, which have been butterflied to resemble a rib. They have more fat and more meat than a true rib but less than what you are used to in a standard pork chop.

We close this pork rib–packed section with a non–pork rib experience, the more unusual lamb ribs, known as Denver rack. They are a little fatty but very tasty if you cook them slow and low.

We strongly encourage you to make the process of cooking ribs over live fire a part of your life. It does take some time, but if you approach it with the right attitude we think you'll find it a very relaxing pastime, on a par with other favorites like fishing or watching sports or strolling along a beach. Plus you end up with something great to eat.

barbecued st. louis–style pork spare ribs with grilled mangoes and curry

SERVES 4

St. Louis–style ribs are pork spare ribs that have had the chine bone removed and the breastbone trimmed. They are "2 and under," meaning that each rack weighs less than 2 pounds, and they resemble baby back ribs but are a little longer, about 4 inches compared to the 3-inch baby backs. You can substitute baby backs if you like; just be sure to adjust the cooking time appropriately, cooking the smaller baby backs less time.

Even with the smaller ribs it's hard to fit enough of them on the grill to justify the effort that slow-and-low barbecuing requires. This has led to the time-honored method of parboiling the ribs before grilling them. We abhor parboiling because it makes the ribs very tough. Instead, we favor what you might call a parbaking approach—we cook the ribs most of the way through in a low oven, then put them on the grill to infuse them with smoke flavor.

When they are cooked, we dress the ribs in an Indonesian-Malaysian suit. This is a little heretical because you don't see a whole lot of pork in these two mostly Muslim countries, but it's a wonderful matchup. Since the ribs are going to get dipped in that strong curry paste at the table, we don't rub them with any spices before grilling, just sprinkle them with salt and pepper. To complete the Southeast Asian theme and cut the strength of the curry paste a bit, we serve the ribs with lightly grilled mangoes, which we crosshatch first so they open up as they cook.

Serve this with Smoky Corn and Tomato Salad with Cilantro Vinaigrette (page 319) and Grilled Eggplant Steaks with Minted Yogurt-Cucumber Relish (page 279).

2 racks St. Louis–style spare ribs, about 2 pounds each
Kosher salt and freshly cracked black pepper to taste

For the curry paste:
1 knob of fresh ginger, about the size of your little finger, peeled
5 cloves garlic, peeled
1/2 cup fresh cilantro leaves
1/3 cup fresh or 1/4 cup dried red chiles, or to taste
2 tablespoons kosher salt

1/4 cup fresh lime juice (about 2 limes)
1/4 cup curry powder
2 tablespoons light or dark brown sugar
2 tablespoons freshly cracked white pepper (or substitute black pepper)
1/4 cup roasted sesame oil
———
2 ripe but firm mangoes, cut in half, pitted, and cut into a crosshatch pattern
2 tablespoons vegetable oil

1. Preheat the oven to 200°F.

2. Sprinkle the racks of ribs generously with salt and pepper and place the racks on baking sheets. Put the ribs in the preheated oven and cook for 3 1/2 hours, turning the

ribs over and switching the baking sheets from front to back at about 1 1/2 hours. Remove the ribs from the oven. At this point you can put them right on the grill, or you can let them sit for a couple of hours until you're ready to grill them, or you can refrigerate them for up to 2 days before grilling them.

3. While the ribs are in the oven, make the curry paste: In a food processor or blender, combine the ginger, garlic, cilantro, chiles, and salt and pulse to chop finely. Add the lime juice, curry powder, brown sugar, and white pepper and pulse until incorporated. With the motor running, add the sesame oil in a stream until a smooth, thick paste forms. Transfer the curry paste to a serving dish and set aside.

4. Build a multi-level fire in your grill: Leaving one-quarter of the bottom free of coals, bank the coals in the remaining three-quarters of the grill so that they are three times as high on one side as on the other. When all the coals are ignited and the temperature has died down to low (you can hold your hand about 5 inches above the grill grid, over the area where the coals are deepest, for 6 seconds), the fire is ready for cooking this dish. Put the ribs on the grill and leave them there, turning once or twice with your tongs, until they get a good sear and take on some color, about 7 to 10 minutes total.

5. Once the ribs are on the grill, rub the mango halves with the vegetable oil, place them cut side down on the grill beside the ribs, and cook until the flesh is golden brown and slightly charred, about 4 to 6 minutes.

6. When the ribs are done, remove them from the grill, cut them apart, and serve them along with the mango halves, passing the curry paste on the side so each person can dip the ribs into it or not, as they please.

COOK TO COOK: The key to this dish is to expose the ribs to as much smoke as possible after they come out of the oven, without letting them get too crusty on the exterior. To do this, you need a super-low fire with maybe some green twigs or even wood chips in there. The longer the ribs are exposed to the smoke, the more flavorful they are going to be.

jerk baby back ribs with banana-guava catsup

SERVES 3 TO 5

We love the jerk cooking technique, but we knew it had gone too far when we ran into "Jerk Pizza" on a menu in a Los Angeles pizza joint not long ago. Developed centuries ago by escaped Maroon slaves in the Blue Hills of Jamaica, jerk has become one of the most widely borrowed, redone, misinterpreted, and ripped-off cooking methods of all time. Throw some chiles on it and grill it, and people will call it "jerk."

That doesn't mean that we know the One True Method, either—and in fact there isn't one. Go down to Boston Bay on the northern coast of Jamaica, the epicenter of jerk cooking, and you'll find about twenty guys down there with totally authentic-looking setups, each making jerk somewhat differently and each claiming to have the original recipe. So this is our version of jerk, which we think features the essential characteristics of the real thing. Our only major shortcut is to use the smaller, more tender baby back ribs so they cook more quickly.

To accompany the ribs, we make a tropical catsup. It may seem strange to you to call it a catsup, since it contains no tomatoes, but until the twentieth century "catsup" referred to a wide range of fruits, vegetables, nuts, and even seafood cooked down and preserved in a mixture of vinegar, sugar, and spices. This one complements a wide range of grilled food and will keep, covered and refrigerated, for up to 6 weeks. You might want to make a double batch while you're at it.

Try serving these ribs with Black Bean and Pineapple Salad with Orange-Chipotle Vinaigrette (page 312) and a Hobo Pack of Yuca, Corn, and Tomatoes (page 302).

3 slabs baby back pork ribs,
   1 1/2 pounds each

For the jerk rub:
1/3 cup yellow mustard
6 to 10 habanero or Scotch bonnet
   peppers
2 tablespoons peeled and minced
   fresh ginger
1 tablespoon minced garlic
4 scallions, both green and white
   parts, finely chopped
1 tablespoon curry powder
1 tablespoon ground coriander
1 tablespoon ground cumin
3 tablespoons freshly cracked black
   pepper
2 tablespoons kosher salt
1 teaspoon ground allspice

For the catsup:
2 tablespoons vegetable oil
1 yellow onion, peeled and diced
   medium
5 ripe bananas (about 2 pounds),
   peeled and cut into large chunks
1/2 cup guava paste blended with
   1 cup orange juice (or substitute
   a 12-ounce can of guava nectar)
2 tablespoons light or dark brown
   sugar
2 1/2 tablespoons raisins
1 tablespoon curry powder
1/2 cup fresh orange juice
2 tablespoons white vinegar
4 tablespoons fresh lime juice (about
   2 limes)
Kosher salt and freshly cracked black
   pepper to taste

1. Start a fire well over to one side of your grill, using about enough coals to fill a shoe-box.

2. Combine all the rub ingredients in a food processor or blender and purée until smooth and even. Coat the ribs all over with the rub. When the fire dies down and the coals are covered with white ash, place the ribs on the grill on the side away from the coals, being careful that none of the meat is directly over the coals. Put the lid on the grill with the vents one-quarter of the way open. Cook the ribs for 30 to 45 minutes, then flip them over and cook them for 10 to 20 minutes more. To check for doneness, cut into one of the ribs to be sure that there is no pink down near the bone.

3. While the ribs are cooking, make the catsup: In a large sauté pan or skillet over medium-high heat, heat the oil until hot but not smoking. Add the onion and sauté, stirring occasionally, until transparent, 5 to 7 minutes. Add the bananas to the pan, reduce the heat to medium, and cook about 5 minutes, stirring constantly to keep them from sticking. Stir in the guava mixture, sugar, raisins, curry, orange juice, and 1 tablespoon of the vinegar. Bring to a boil and simmer the catsup gently, stirring occasionally to prevent scorching, until it reaches the consistency of applesauce, about 15 minutes. Remove from the heat, stir in the lime juice and the remaining tablespoon of vinegar, and season to taste with salt and pepper.

4. To serve, cut the ribs apart and pass the catsup, either warm or at room temperature, on the side.

COOK TO COOK: As with any paste, rub, or marinade that contains sugar, you have to be certain that it does not burn. So be particularly careful that the meat is never directly over the coals. That means, of course, that you'll need a pretty big grill to handle this recipe. Also, try to handle these ribs as little as possible so the paste doesn't fall off.

memphis-style grilled baby back ribs with barbecue shake

SERVES 4 HUNGRY PEOPLE

This is a unique old-school Memphis-style method for cooking ribs. Instead of dry-rubbing the ribs before you grill them, you shake the rub on after they are cooked. There are two benefits to this approach—you don't have to worry about scorching the spice rub while the ribs cook, and you can cook the ribs not by the indirect heat and smoke of a very low fire but by the direct heat of a low fire.

Serve these with the traditional sides: watermelon, baked beans, cornbread, and cole slaw. (For recipes, check out the Old Testament of grilling, *The Thrill of the Grill*.)

4 slabs baby back pork ribs, 1 1/2 pounds each
Kosher salt and freshly cracked black pepper to taste

For the barbecue shake:
1/4 cup paprika
2 tablespoons ground coriander
1 tablespoon ground cumin
1 tablespoon ground chiles of your choice, or red pepper flakes
1 tablespoon powdered mustard
3 tablespoons freshly cracked black pepper
1 tablespoon kosher salt

1. Build a multi-level fire in your grill: Leaving one-quarter of the bottom free of coals, bank the coals in the remaining three-quarters of the grill so that they are three times as high on one side of the grill as on the other. When all the coals are ignited and the temperature has died down to medium-low (you can hold your hand about 5 inches above the grill grid, over the area where the coals are deepest, for 5 seconds), you're ready to cook.

2. Sprinkle the ribs lightly with salt and pepper, place them on the grill, and cook until they have a nice, crusty sear on the outside and are cooked through, about 10 to 15 minutes per side. To check for doneness, cut into one of the ribs and peek to be sure there is no pink all the way down to the bone.

3. While the ribs are cooking, combine all the shake ingredients in a small bowl and mix well. When the ribs are done, remove them from the grill, immediately sprinkle them generously with about half of the shake, cut them apart, and serve. If you like, you can pass any remaining shake separately.

COOK TO COOK: The barbecue shake recipe makes at least twice as much as you're going to need. But since it stores well if covered and kept in a cool, dry place, you might as well make some to spare while you're at it. That way, the ribs will be quicker to make the next time.

basil-crusted barbecued lamb ribs with apricot-balsamic glaze

SERVES 4

Lamb on the grill just can't be beat. So we encourage you to explore some of the lesser-known cuts, such as the ribs. You need to cook them quite a long time to get some of that fat out. You don't tend to see these ribs in supermarkets, but you should be able to find them at your local butcher's.

Serve these with Warm Grilled New Potato Salad with Corn and Chiles (page 316) and grilled asparagus or a salad of Boston lettuce and tomatoes.

4 slabs (racks) lamb ribs, 12 to 14 ounces each
Kosher salt and freshly cracked black pepper to taste
1 cup basil leaves

3 cloves garlic
1/4 cup olive oil
1/2 cup apricot jam or preserves
1/2 cup balsamic vinegar

1. Build a fire well over to one side of your grill, using about enough coals to fill a large shoebox.

2. Sprinkle the lamb ribs generously with salt and pepper. Put the basil and garlic in a food processor or blender and pulse to chop finely. Then, with the motor running, add the oil in a thin stream and process until the mixture is a smooth paste. Season the paste with salt and pepper and coat the lamb with it.

3. When the fire dies down and the coals are covered with gray ash, put the ribs on the grill on the side away from the coals, being careful that none of the meat is directly over the coals. Put the lid on the grill with the vents one-quarter of the way open and cook, adding a handful of fresh charcoal about every 30 minutes, until the meat is so tender it pulls very easily away from the bone, about 1 1/2 to 2 hours.

4. While the ribs are cooking, make the glaze: In a medium saucepan, bring the apricot jam and vinegar to a boil over medium heat. Reduce to low and simmer, stirring frequently to prevent scorching, until the mixture has thickened, about 10 minutes. Brush both sides of the ribs with the glaze during the last 30 seconds of cooking.

5. Serve each person a rack of ribs, passing the remaining glaze on the side.

COOK TO COOK: When you put the glaze on the ribs, you want it to turn dark brown but not black, and it should get very sticky rather than dried out. So watch it carefully.

grilled garlicky lamb skewers with tomato-feta relish

SERVES 4

This is pretty much a straight-up shish kebab situation, in which we rub cubes of lamb with garlic and olive oil, thread the lamb cubes onto skewers with red onions and red peppers, and put the skewers over the flames. We then serve the kebabs with a relish featuring feta cheese, which gives the lamb a definite Greek or Middle Eastern feel.

You can use either shoulder or leg here, depending on whether flavor or tenderness is more important to you. The shoulder has somewhat better flavor than the leg, but it is also chewier. The choice is yours. (You can also use beef in place of the lamb.)

If you want to get fancy, add fresh halved apricots or figs to the skewers. Mix any leftovers with some arugula or other salad greens lightly dressed with vinaigrette and have yourself a little grilled lamb salad.

2 pounds lamb shoulder or leg
   (or substitute beef chuck),
   cut into 1-inch cubes
2 red bell peppers, seeded, halved,
   and each half quartered
2 red onions, peeled, halved, and
   each half quartered
1/4 cup olive oil
3 tablespoons minced garlic
Kosher salt and freshly cracked black
   pepper to taste

For the relish:
2 cucumbers, peeled and diced small
2 ripe but firm tomatoes about the
   size of baseballs, cored and
   diced small
1/2 cup finely chopped Kalamata or
   other brine-cured black olives
1/2 cup roughly chopped fresh
   parsley
1/3 cup extra-virgin olive oil
Juice of 1 lemon (about 1/4 cup)
Kosher salt and freshly cracked black
   pepper to taste

1. Build a multi-level fire in your grill: Leaving one-quarter of the bottom free of coals, bank the coals in the remaining three-quarters of the grill so that they are three times as high on one side as on the other. When all the coals are ignited and the temperature has died down to medium-hot (you can hold your hand about 5 inches above the grill grid, over the area where the coals are deepest, for 3 to 4 seconds), you're ready to cook.

2. In a large bowl, combine the lamb, peppers, onions, olive oil, garlic, and salt and pepper to taste and toss to coat. Thread the meat onto long skewers, alternating with the peppers and onions. Place the skewers on the grill and cook until the vegetables are tender and the lamb is done to your liking, about 3 to 4 minutes per side for rare. To check for doneness, nick, peek, and cheat: Make a small cut in the thickest part of the meat and peek at the center to be sure it is just slightly less done than you like it. Remove the skewers from the grill, cover them loosely with foil, and let them rest for about 5 minutes.

3. While the skewers are cooking, combine the relish ingredients in a medium bowl and mix well.

4. Serve the skewers with the relish on the side.

COOK TO COOK: Recently it has become somewhat fashionable when grilling skewers to put each type of food on its own skewer, so each can be cooked to just the right degree of doneness. To us that benefit pales when compared with the pleasure of tasting the unique flavors created at the point where different ingredients touch. Lamb nestled next to peppers and onions on a skewer, for example, tastes more interesting than lamb grilled by itself. To deal with the varying cooking times of different ingredients on the same skewer, cut slower-cooking foods into smaller pieces.

grilled baby lamb chops with two dipping sauces

SERVES 4

If you ever go to an affair where they're serving grilled baby lamb chops, you know somebody's spending some dough, because these babies are not cheap. What they are, though, is incredibly tender and spectacularly tasty, with that earthy, slightly aromatic lamb flavor that we love. They are also fun to eat, kind of like succulent little meat popsicles.

What you're dealing with here is a rack of lamb cut up into thin, single-rib chops for grilling. We like them rare, which means they go on and off the grill in about 4 minutes; if you like them more done, leave them on longer. Keep a careful eye on them, though, since they cook really fast. With the grilled chops we offer two dipping sauces—a balsamic-mint sauce and an apricot-port reduction reminiscent of the English Cumberland sauce usually served with game. You can double-dip if you like; they work well together.

This is a very special dish that works nicely as either an appetizer or an entrée. You might try it as an appetizer in front of a simple fish or vegetarian main course; as an entrée, it could be served with a salad of tender greens and Grilled Leeks with Chunky Artichoke and Sun-Dried Tomato Dressing (page 284) and/or Grilled Fingerling Potatoes with Blue Cheese (page 297).

For the apricot-port glaze:
1/2 cup apricot preserves
1/2 cup port
1 tablespoon freshly grated orange
  zest
1 tablespoon freshly grated lime zest
Kosher salt and freshly cracked black
  pepper to taste

For the balsamic-mint catsup:
1/3 cup balsamic vinegar
1/4 cup catsup
2 tablespoons tomato paste
1/4 cup finely chopped fresh mint
1 teaspoon minced garlic
Kosher salt and freshly cracked black
  pepper to taste

16 lamb rib chops (2 racks, cut into
  single-rib chops)
Kosher salt and freshly cracked black
  pepper to taste

1. In a small saucepan over medium heat, combine the preserves, port, and orange and lime zest. Bring to a simmer, whisking until the preserves are melted. Simmer gently until the glaze is reduced by half and feels sticky, about 25 to 30 minutes. Remove from the heat, strain into a small bowl, and season.

2. Build a fire in your grill, leave one-quarter of the bottom of the grill free of coals; bank the coals in the remaining three-quarters of the grill so they are three times as high on one side as on the other. When all the coals are ignited and the temperature is

hot (you can hold your hand about 5 inches above the grill grid for 2 seconds or less), you're ready to cook.

3. In a small bowl, combine all the ingredients for the balsamic-mint catsup and mix well.

4. Sprinkle the lamb chops generously with salt and pepper, then put them on the grill and cook until nicely seared on the outside and done the way you like them on the inside, about 2 minutes per side for rare. Brush with the glaze during the last 30 seconds of cooking on each side. To check for doneness, poke the meat with your finger to check its firmness level (see page 13); if you're unsure, nick, peek, and cheat: Make a small cut in the thickest part of the meat and peek at the center to be sure it is just slightly less done than you like it.

5. Fan the chops out on a platter and serve, passing the remaining apricot-port glaze along with the balsamic-mint catsup for dipping.

COOK TO COOK: Remember that food will continue to cook even after you take it off the flames, so the chops should come off the fire when they are one degree less done than you want them to be when you eat them.

curry- and ginger-rubbed grilled lamb shoulder chops with apricot-lime barbecue sauce

SERVES 4

꙳ ꙳ ꙳ ꙳ ꙳ ꙳ ꙳ ꙳ ꙳ ꙳ ꙳ ꙳ ꙳ ꙳ ꙳ ꙳ ꙳

Lamb is superb on the grill, and shoulder chops are a first-rate alternative to the much pricier loin or rib chops. They are a little more chewy and fatty, but they also have a deeper, richer lamb flavor. For this dish the chops need to have that flavor, because we're not backing off here. We're matching up the lamb with a host of strong seasoning competitors—ginger, curry, lime, Tabasco, balsamic, even the sweetness of apricots and raisins. We love the complex levels of flavor that result.

As always when using a spice rub, you can put it on the meat just before it goes on the fire or up to 2 hours in advance, whichever is more convenient.

Try this with Parsley Salad with Tomatoes and Bulgur (page 311) or Orange-Raisin Couscous with Almonds and Parsley (page 321)

.

8 shoulder or arm lamb chops,
    8 ounces each
About 1/4 cup olive oil
1/3 cup prepared curry powder
3 tablespoons peeled and minced
    fresh ginger
Kosher salt and freshly cracked black
    pepper to taste

For the sauce:
2/3 cup apricot jam or preserves
1/4 cup balsamic vinegar
1/4 cup catsup
1/4 cup Worcestershire sauce
1 tablespoon Tabasco sauce
1/3 cup raisins
2 tablespoons fresh lime juice
1/3 cup roughly chopped fresh mint

1. Build a multi-level fire in your grill: Leaving one-quarter of the bottom free of coals, bank the coals in the remaining three-quarters of the grill so that they are three times as high on one side as on the other. When all the coals are ignited and the coals are hot to medium-hot (you can hold your hand about 5 inches above the grill grid, over the area where the coals are deepest, for 3 seconds), you're ready to cook.

2. Coat the chops lightly with the olive oil, then rub them all over with the curry powder and ginger and sprinkle generously with salt and pepper. Set aside while you make the sauce.

3. In a small saucepan over low heat, combine the jam, vinegar, catsup, Worcestershire sauce, Tabasco sauce, and raisins. Stir until the jam is completely melted and the ingredients are well blended, then remove from the heat, stir in the lime juice and mint, and set aside.

4. Place the chops on the grill over the coals and cook until done to your liking, 4 to 5 minutes per side for medium-rare, brushing with the sauce during the last 30 seconds

of cooking on each side. To check for doneness, poke the meat with your finger to check its firmness level (see page 13); if you're unsure, nick, peek, and cheat: Make a small cut in one of the chops and peek at the center to be sure it is just slightly less done than you like it.

5. Serve the chops hot, passing the remaining sauce on the side.

COOK TO COOK: If you buy shoulder chops in the supermarket, they will most likely be blade chops, from the top of the shoulder. If you go to a butcher, ask him for arm chops; they come from the bottom of the shoulder and are a bit less fatty but just as flavorful.

barbecued lamb shoulder with mint-raisin sauce

SERVES 6

❧ ❧ ❧ ❧ ❧ ❧ ❧ ❧ ❧ ❧ ❧ ❧ ❧ ❧ ❧ ❧ ❧

There's something about lamb and smoke that is meant to happen. So even if you think barbecued lamb is bizarre, you ought to give this recipe a try. It is inspired by the classic barbecued mutton of Kentucky, but here we give it a Moroccan accent, rubbing the shoulder with a little bit of spice and then topping it with a simple mint-raisin sauce. The idea for the flavorings came from a day we spent in a souk in Marrakech with our friend Sari Abul-Jeben, owner of the Casablanca restaurant in Cambridge, Massachusetts. We had a lamb jones and spent much of the day searching the intricate alleyways for the best grilled lamb. When we found it, the spicing was simple but just right, and it was served with a minty sauce.

When the lamb comes off the grill and you bite into it, you won't believe the depth of rich but mild lamb flavor and the almost velvety texture. The secret is long, slow cooking, so get your patience on line and your beers (or pinot noir) ready before you start cooking this one.

You might want to try serving this along with Grilled Eggplant Steaks with Minted Yogurt-Cucumber Relish (page 279).

1/2 cup freshly cracked black pepper
1/2 cup curry powder
1/4 cup kosher salt
1 boneless lamb shoulder, about
    5 pounds

For the sauce:
1 cup roughly chopped fresh mint
1/2 cup raisins
1/2 cup molasses
1/2 cup catsup
1/2 cup red wine vinegar
3 tablespoons Tabasco sauce,
    or to taste

1. Light a fire well over to one side of your grill, using enough coals to fill half a shoebox.

2. In a small bowl, combine the pepper, curry powder, and salt and mix well. Rub the lamb all over with this mixture, pressing down gently to be sure it adheres.

3. When the fire has died down and the coals are covered in white ash, place the meat on the side of the grill away from the coals, being careful that none of the meat is directly over the coals. Put the lid on the grill with the vents open one-quarter of the way and cook, adding a handful of fresh charcoal about every 30 minutes, until the meat is super-tender, 3 to 4 hours. To check for doneness, plunge a fork straight down into the meat and try to pull the fork out. If the fork slides out easily, the meat is done; if the meat hangs on to the fork, give it more time.

4. While the lamb is cooking, make the sauce: In a small saucepan over medium heat, combine all the sauce ingredients and mix well. Simmer for 5 minutes, then remove from heat and set aside.

5. When the lamb is done, remove it from the grill, cut it into thin slices against the grain, and serve, passing the sauce separately.

COOK TO COOK: Although the lamb shoulder, unlike the pork shoulder, is a fairly tender piece of meat and could probably be roasted, we are barbecuing it here to take it past doneness to the point of melting tenderness. So this is another of those situations that call for patience, patience, patience.

grilled butterflied leg of lamb
with a platter of greek garnishes

SERVES 6 TO 8

We find the aroma of lamb on the grill intoxicating. In addition to holding out the promise of a great meal, it reminds us of when we first encountered really excellent grilled lamb, Chris as a teenager in rural Greece, Doc in the souks of Morocco. In homage to the grillmasters of our youth, we have you use a rather advanced technique here, in which you put this large piece of meat directly over a medium-hot fire. The goal is to achieve a super sear without burning the meat. You have to pay attention and use your grilling sense to decide when to move the lamb to the cooler part of the fire.

To boost the flavor quotient, we rub the lamb with a slightly hot, oregano-garlic paste before putting the meat on the grill. We serve slices of the grilled lamb with pita and a large selection of classic Greek garnishes, all of which creates a fantastic pita sandwich situation. This is also an ideal summer buffet dish, because the lamb is equally good served hot or at room temperature.

1 boneless leg of lamb, butterflied,
    4 to 5 pounds
Kosher salt and freshly cracked black
    pepper to taste
8 slices pita bread or EZ Grill Bread
    (page 77)

For the rub:
1/2 cup roughly chopped fresh
    oregano (or substitute 3 table-
    spoons dried oregano)
1/2 cup freshly cracked black pepper
1/4 cup minced garlic
1/4 cup kosher salt
2 tablespoons red pepper flakes,
    or to taste
1/4 cup olive oil

For the garnishes:
1 bunch fresh mint sprigs, washed
3 lemons, quartered

2 cups good-quality black olives
3 cucumbers, thinly sliced
3 ripe tomatoes about the size of
    baseballs, cored and diced
    medium
2 red onions, peeled and thinly sliced
1 pound feta cheese, crumbled
2 cups plain yogurt, preferably
    whole-milk

For the dressing:
3/4 cup extra-virgin olive oil
1/4 cup red wine vinegar
1/2 cup roughly chopped fresh
    parsley
2 tablespoons minced garlic
1 tablespoon red pepper flakes, or
    to taste
Kosher salt and freshly cracked black
    pepper to taste

1. Build a fire on one side of your grill, using about enough charcoal to fill a large shoe-box. When all the coals are ignited and the temperature is medium-hot (you can hold your hand about 5 inches above the grill grid for 3 to 4 seconds), you're ready to cook.

2. Use a mortar and pestle or a food processor to blend the ingredients for the rub into a coarse paste. Rub the lamb all over with the paste, pressing down gently to be sure it adheres.

3. Put the lamb on the grill directly over the coals and sear it well all over, about 15 to 18 minutes total. Now move the lamb to the side of the grill with no coals, making sure that none of the meat is directly over the coals. Cover the lamb with a large disposable foil pan or tent it closely with heavy-duty foil, then cook until it is done to your liking, about 10 minutes more for medium-rare. To check for doneness, insert a meat thermometer into the dead center of the roast and let it sit for 5 seconds, then read the temperature: 120°F is rare, 126°F is medium-rare, 134°F is medium, 150°F is medium-well, and 160°F is well-done; we like to pull the lamb at 126°F. Remove it from the grill, cover it loosely with foil, and let it rest for 10 minutes.

4. Meanwhile, whisk all the dressing ingredients together in a small bowl until well blended, then arrange the garnishes and the dressing on a platter.

5. Put the pita bread on the grill and toast lightly, about 1 1/2 minutes per side. Remove from the grill and cut it in quarters.

6. To serve, pile the grilled pita in a basket or bowl, cut the lamb into thin slices against the grain, spoon some of the sauce over the sliced lamb, and let your guests help themselves to the lamb, the garnishes, the bread, and more dressing as they wish.

COOK TO COOK: This is a classic "sear and move" technique, so be on the lookout for the point at which the meat has acquired a good, dark, heavy sear and is ready to be moved (with your tongs and a meat fork) to the cooler part of the fire. Watch for flare-ups here, too.

grilled veal chops with grilled mushrooms and sweet-and-sour shallots

SERVES 4

❊ ❊ ❊ ❊ ❊ ❊ ❊ ❊ ❊ ❊ ❊ ❊ ❊ ❊ ❊ ❊ ❊

We generally don't do a lot of veal on the grill because it is a little out of our price range and kind of out of our flavor range, too, typically calling for more subtle accompanying flavors than we tend to use. But there's one cut of veal that's fantastic on the grill, and that is the chop. You can use either the loin or the rib chop here, although we have a slight preference for the more picturesque rib chop.

To keep the seasoning subtle, we sprinkle the chops with salt and pepper and grill them up alongside some white mushrooms that we mix with garlic, sherry, and parsley. Then, because we can't stand to leave all those mellow, restrained flavors alone, we top off the chops with some sweet-and-sour shallots, almost a light shallot chutney.

We like these chops with Grilled Broccoli Rabe with Sun-Dried Tomatoes, Balsamic Vinegar, and Pine Nuts (page 283).

4 loin or rib veal chops, about 1 1/2
    inches thick, 12 ounces each
Kosher salt and freshly cracked
    black pepper to taste
1 pound white mushrooms, stems
    trimmed
3 tablespoons olive oil
1 tablespoon minced garlic
4 tablespoons butter
3 tablespoons dry sherry
1/4 cup roughly chopped fresh
    parsley

For the shallots:
3 tablespoons olive oil
6 large shallots, peeled and diced
    medium (about 1 cup)
2 tablespoons molasses
1/4 cup red wine vinegar
1/4 cup raisins
Kosher salt and freshly cracked
    black pepper to taste

1. Build a multi-level fire in your grill: Leaving one-quarter of the bottom free of coals, bank the coals in the remaining three-quarters of the grill so that they are three times as high on one side as on the other. When all the coals are ignited and the temperature has died down to medium (you can hold your hand about 5 inches above the grill grid, over the area where the coals are deepest, for 4 to 5 seconds), you're ready to cook.

2. Sprinkle the chops generously on both sides with salt and pepper, then put them on the grill and cook until well seared on the outside and done as you like them on the inside, about 8 to 10 minutes per side for medium. To check for doneness, poke the meat with your finger to check its firmness level (see page 13); if you're unsure, nick, peek, and cheat: Make a 1/4-inch cut in the thickest part of one of the chops and peek at the center to be sure it is just slightly less done than you like it. When the chops are done, remove them from the heat, cover them loosely with foil, and allow them to rest for 10 minutes.

3. Meanwhile, in a small bowl, combine the mushrooms, olive oil, and garlic and toss gently to coat. Put the mushrooms on the grill next to the chops and cook until they are moist all the way through, about 10 minutes, then remove them from the grill, cut them into quarters, and place them back in the same bowl you tossed them in. Immediately add the butter, sherry, and parsley and mix gently until the butter is melted. Season with salt and pepper and cover with foil to keep warm.

4. In a large sauté pan or skillet over medium-high heat, heat the oil until it is hot but not smoking. Add the shallots and sauté, stirring occasionally, until golden brown, about 10 minutes. Add the molasses, vinegar, raisins, and salt and pepper to taste and stir well to combine.

5. Arrange a chop on each plate along with some of the mushrooms, spoon some of the shallot sauce over each chop, and serve.

COOK TO COOK: You've got several things going on here, so here's a step-by-step strategy: Put the chops on the grill; put the mushrooms on the grill next to the chops; take the mushrooms off the grill; take the chops off the grill; make the shallots, which actually you can start while the chops are still cooking unless you are outside with the chops, which you probably are.

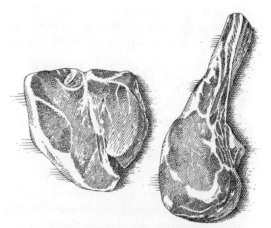

Loin (left) and rib veal chops

'Shrooms on the Grill

* * *

Grilling brings out the deep, rich flavors of mushrooms and adds a smoky flavor dimension you just can't get on the stove. All kinds of 'shrooms are great on the grill, and it's cool to mix together a bunch of different types.

To prepare mushrooms for the grill, rinse them lightly and pat them dry. (Don't worry, the old saw about mushrooms absorbing a lot of water if you rinse them is really not true.) Since mushrooms are mostly water, they're hard to burn, but tossing or brushing them with oil does help keep them moist during cooking. Mushrooms are done when they are dark and moist all the way through rather than dry at the center, most become firmer in texture as they cook.

Mushrooms are used in cuisines all over the world and can be seasoned in many different ways. Simply grilled with oil and salt and pepper is fine, but adding garlic and an herb of your choice makes things interesting. Thyme, rosemary, savory, and parsley all work well; another classic is the combination of soy sauce, salt, and sugar. Remember that acids such as vinegar, wine, or lemon juice can overwhelm the flavor of mushrooms; a little goes a long way.

Here's a quick guide to a few of the fungi you might want to toss on the grill:

White or button mushrooms are sometimes dissed by food snobs, but they are actually great grillers. They can be creamy white to light brown in color, and range in size from small (45 to a pound) to jumbo (15 to a pound). Older ones will have more flavor—look for open veils (the caps have opened at the stem end to expose the gills) and darkened caps, but avoid any that feel soft or slimy or have dark bruises.

Cremini mushrooms are actually portobellos, picked when they are small and tightly closed. (Once their veils have opened, slightly larger creminis are labeled "baby bellas" or "baby portobellas" in supermarkets.) Similar in size and shape to white mushrooms, they have a darker brown color, firmer texture, deeper flavor—and higher price tag.

Portobello mushrooms are the big guys—sometimes up to 6 inches in diameter—with the very earthy, rich taste. Since mature portobellos have the most flavor, look for flatter, darker, slightly wrinkled caps.

Shiitake mushrooms are golden to brown in color, with umbrella-shaped caps and wide-open veils. For the best texture and flavor, look for large, dense mushrooms with domed, dappled caps, edges that curl under, and a distinct mushroomy smell.

Oyster mushrooms are beige to gray, with velvety, fan-shaped caps. They have a mild flavor that pairs well with other mushrooms. Oysters are very perishable; look for dry (not powdery) clusters with no dark or wet areas.

Maitake mushrooms get their nickname, "hen of the woods," from their overlapping clusters of feathery caps, which range in color from bright yellow-orange to tan and brown. Rich and tasty, they have a distinctive, woodsy aroma that fades when cooked.

Wood ear mushrooms are ear-shaped, wrinkled, and shiny, with a purplish gray, semi-translucent color that darkens with age. They have little flavor on their own, but their unusual texture—crunchy and firm, somewhat like cartilage—makes them great for grilling and mixing with other mushrooms.

Chanterelles are golden in color and shaped like the bell of a trumpet. Their fruity scent and mild, nutty flavor goes especially well with chicken or veal. Chanterelles can't be cultivated and therefore have to be gathered, so you probably won't see them in the supermarket—but check out specialty stores in the spring and fall to find them. Chanterelles are very delicate and overcook quickly, which toughens them, so be careful.

grilled fluke johnson with a provençal-style hobo pack
SERVES 2

We are lucky enough to have many friends in the restaurant business, and their constant innovations both in their restaurants and at their homes continue to give us ideas. Our good amigo Esteban Johnson, chef/owner of the Blue Room in Cambridge, Massachusetts, is an expert at catching fluke. Steve cleans them as you would a Dover sole, taking out the feather bones with a sharp knife, and then he simply rubs them with olive oil and tosses them on the grill. To go with Steve's fluke, we make a simple, Provençal-inspired hobo pack that matches up with the delicate texture and mild flavor of the fish. If you can't find fluke, you can substitute red snapper, ocean perch, or striped bass.

Serve this dish with Lightly Grilled Hearts of Romaine with Figs, Blue Cheese, and Honey-Mustard Dressing (page 32).

For the hobo pack:
2 ripe tomatoes about the size of baseballs, cored and quartered
1 head garlic, broken into cloves and peeled
5 fresh herb sprigs: any one or a combination of thyme, oregano, or marjoram
1/4 cup extra-virgin olive oil
1/4 cup dry white wine
Kosher salt and freshly cracked black pepper to taste

2 whole fluke, 2 pounds each before dressing, dressed (have the fishmonger do this for you, or, alternatively, make sure both sides are scaled, remove the head, cut off the fins with scissors, peel back the top, darker-colored skin, and leave the bottom, white-colored skin on)
2 tablespoons olive oil
Kosher salt and freshly cracked black pepper to taste

1. Build a multi-level fire in your grill: Leaving one-quarter of the bottom free of coals, bank the coals in the remaining three-quarters of the grill so that they are three times as high on one side as on the other. When all the coals are ignited and the temperature has died down to medium (you can hold your hand about 5 inches above the grill grid, over the area where the coals are deepest, for 4 to 5 seconds), you're ready to cook.

2. Make the hobo pack: Tear off 4 sheets of heavy-duty foil, each about 2 feet long, and stack them one on top of the other. Arrange the tomatoes, garlic, and herbs on the center of the top sheet of foil. Drizzle with the extra-virgin olive oil and wine and

sprinkle with salt and pepper to taste. Fold up the sheets of foil around the tomatoes, one after the other, turning the package one-quarter turn each time and making sure that each sheet is well sealed around the contents. Place the package in the coals at the periphery of the fire, where the heat is less intense. Pile the coals up around it and cook until the tomatoes are very tender, about 25 minutes.

4. While the hobo pack is cooking, rub the 2 fluke on both sides with the olive oil and season them generously, inside and out, with salt and pepper. When the hobo packs are about half done, place the fish on the grill and cook until it is just opaque throughout, about 6 to 8 minutes per side. To check for doneness, poke one of the fish with your finger to check its firmness level (see page 13); if you're unsure, nick, peek, and cheat: Cut into one at its thickest point and peek to be sure it is opaque all the way through.

5. Remove the fluke from the grill and the hobo pack from the coals. Place each fluke on a plate, then unwrap the hobo pack and spoon half of the tomato mixture onto each plate beside the fish.

COOK TO COOK: A very clean and very hot grill grid are key here. Also, make sure that when the fish is ready to be turned you carefully wiggle each one free with your tongs, then gently roll it over.

fish without sticks

* * *

Many cooks avoid fish on the grill because they're afraid it will stick to the grid when they try to turn it over or take it off. There's good reason for this fear, because fish does often stick. But it doesn't have to. Here are four simple rules for avoiding this potentially meal-destroying phenomenon:
1. Make sure your grill grid is super-clean; any residue from previous cooking will provide a natural sticking point for fish skin.
2. Get the grid very hot before you put the fish on it. The easiest way to accomplish this is simply to put the grid in place as soon as you light the fire and to leave it there as the fire heats up to the proper temperature.
3. Coat the fish with a very thin film of vegetable oil just before cooking it. Be sure, though, that you just moisten the skin, since if you use too much oil it will drip into the fire and cause flare-ups.
4. When you put the fish on the grill, leave it in its original position for at least a couple of minutes before you move it. This allows a sear to develop between metal and flesh, which helps avoid sticking.

learning to love oily fish

* * *

Dark-fleshed fish—often called oily fish—have a bad name among cooks in this country. Since the same high oil content that makes these fish so flavorful also makes them very perishable, we suspect that many people's experience has consisted of consuming slightly rancid specimens.

Whichever variety of dark-fleshed fish you choose, it is important that you buy only the very freshest specimens or you risk perpetuating their bad reputation. Apply the usual visual tests—the eyes of the fish should look shiny rather than dull; the skin should be bright and glistening, with a clear, almost translucent quality; the flesh should be firm and unbruised. But the best test is to sniff the fish. It should smell like fresh seawater, not "fishy" or tinged with ammonia. If you're not sure, go on to the next store.

In addition to their rich flavor and easy grilling qualities, there's another reason to focus on oil-rich fish—their healthfulness. Anyone who has ever been lectured by an overzealous nutritionist (and these days, who hasn't?) can enjoy the ironic fact that the health benefits of seafood come from the bad boy of nutritional policy, fat. Called omega-3 fatty acids, the fats in fish not only help prevent heart problems but also seem to eliminate the symptoms of certain auto-immune diseases, reduce the risk of breast cancer, and even help prevent depression. That last one may seem strange, but it makes more sense when you learn that omega-3s make up most of the fat in the brain. And where do you get omega-3s? Only from fish and seafood, and the fattier the better. Sardines, mackerel, rainbow trout, bluefish, anchovies, and of course the ever-popular tuna and salmon are all prime sources. So start eating those so-called oily fish as often as you get the chance. They could make you happier as well as healthier.

simple cumin-crusted grilled mackerel with lime-chile vinaigrette

SERVES 4

When it comes to grilling, rich-fleshed fish have several advantages over their white-fleshed cousins. Their higher content of healthful fish oil not only keeps them moist over the fire, it also helps prevent them from sticking to the grid. And their heartier flavor gives them the ability to stand up to stronger seasonings. We make full use of that last quality here—we coat mackerel with cumin before grilling, and afterward we dress it with a vinaigrette flavored with lime, garlic, and a generous dose of fresh chile peppers. This is an excellent dish to serve to friends who think they don't like oily fish.

Serve this with Hobo Pack of Plantains and Onions (page 301), Hobo Pack of Yuca, Corn, and Tomatoes (page 302), or Black Bean, Avocado, and Tomato Salad (page 273).

4 mackerel fillets, 8 ounces each (or substitute fillets of bluefish, pompano, or salmon)
3 tablespoons olive oil
Kosher salt and freshly cracked black pepper to taste
3 tablespoons freshly cracked cumin seeds (or substitute 1 1/2 tablespoons ground cumin)

For the vinaigrette:
1/3 cup extra-virgin olive oil
1/4 cup fresh lime juice (about 2 limes)
1 teaspoon minced garlic
2 tablespoons minced fresh chile pepper of your choice, or to taste
1/4 cup roughly chopped fresh cilantro
Kosher salt and freshly cracked black pepper to taste

1. Build a multi-level fire in your grill: Leaving one-quarter of the bottom free of coals, bank the coals in the remaining three-quarters of the grill so that they are three times as high on one side as on the other. When all the coals are ignited and the temperature has died down to medium (you can hold your hand about 5 inches above the grill grid, over the area where the coals are deepest, for 4 to 5 seconds), you're ready to cook.

2. Rub the mackerel fillets all over with the olive oil, sprinkle them generously with salt and pepper, then coat them with the cumin, pressing down gently so it adheres. Put the fillets on the grill over the coals and cook until they are nicely seared on the outside and just opaque on the inside, about 4 to 6 minutes per side. To check for doneness, poke the fish with your finger to check its firmness level (see page 13); if you're unsure, nick, peek, and cheat: Cut into one of the fillets at its thickest point and peek to be sure it is opaque all the way through.

3. While the mackerel is cooking, combine the vinaigrette ingredients in a small bowl and whisk until well blended.

4. Serve each mackerel fillet topped with a generous spoonful of the vinaigrette.

COOK TO COOK: Remember your four points to prevent fish from sticking: a clean grid; a hot grid; lightly oiled fish; and no moving the fish at all for the first 2 minutes.

wine-steamed flounder
with oranges, fennel, and artichoke hearts

SERVES 4

The neat thing about the method we use for this dish is that it solves the problem of how to grill pieces of fish that are too delicate to stand up to the rigors of direct live-fire cooking. We make a little foil pouch, put in some orange slices and fennel and artichoke hearts and white wine along with the fish, seal the pouch, and then basically steam it on the grill. It's kind of like a hobo pack done on the grill grid instead of down in the coals. Another reason we like this method is that it's fun to cook things in little packages. Be careful, though, not to puncture the foil or the juices will run out and you will have lost the beauty of the dish.

You can substitute just about any firm, white-fleshed fish such as cod or grouper in this recipe with good results. Try serving the fish with Extra-Large Grilled Sweet Potato Fries with Shiitake-Parsley Butter Sauce (page 294) and a Warm Salad of Grilled Eggplant, Summer Squash, and Zucchini (page 315).

2 pounds flounder fillets, divided into
    4 equal portions
1/4 cup extra-virgin olive oil
2 oranges, very thinly sliced (including peel)
1 fennel bulb, trimmed and very
    thinly sliced
2 tablespoons minced garlic

1 small red onion, peeled and very
    thinly sliced
6 jarred artichoke hearts, halved
4 tablespoons unsalted butter
4 sprigs fresh oregano or thyme
1/2 cup dry white wine
Kosher salt and freshly cracked black
    pepper to taste

1. Build a multi-level fire in your grill: Leaving one-quarter of the bottom free of coals, bank the coals in the remaining three-quarters of the grill so that they are three times as high on one side as on the other. When all the coals are ignited and the temperature has died down to medium-hot (you can hold your hand about 5 inches above the grill grid, over the area where the coals are deepest, for 3 to 4 seconds), you're ready to cook.

2. Tear off 8 sheets of heavy-duty foil, each about a foot long, and lay them out in 4 stacks of 2 sheets each.

3. Center a serving of fish on each stack of foil, sprinkle with the olive oil, and arrange the oranges, fennel, garlic, onion, and artichoke hearts evenly on top. Dot each stack with butter, then top each with an herb sprig, sprinkle with one-quarter of the wine, and season generously with salt and pepper.

4. Bring the sides of foil up over the fish and seal up the edges to make a snug packet. Repeat with the bottom sheet of foil so that each packet is double-wrapped. (Packets can be made up to this point as much as 3 hours ahead and refrigerated.)

5. Place the packets on the grill and cook until the fish is just opaque, about 12 minutes. To check for doneness, open a packet and poke the fish with your finger to check its firmness level (see page 13); if you're unsure, nick, peek, and cheat: Cut into one of the fillets at its thickest point and peek to be sure it is opaque all the way through.

6. Serve the packets immediately, cutting them open at the table.

COOK TO COOK: This is one of the very few situations where a pair of tongs is probably not adequate for removing something from the grill. We recommend that you slip a large offset spatula under the packets, then lift away.

spice-crusted bluefish "new bedford" with mussels, chourico, and tomatoes

SERVES 4

※ ※ ※ ※ ※ ※ ※ ※ ※ ※ ※ ※ ※ ※ ※ ※ ※

Living off the south coast of New England and having a restaurant there as well, I (Chris) have become increasingly familiar with the Portuguese cooking brought by immigrants to the area around New Bedford, Massachusetts. This dish originated in the classic Portuguese combination of fish and pork.

The sweet, delicate mussels and spicy chourico sausage here match up particularly nicely with the well-defined flavor of bluefish. By the way, if you are one of those people who think they don't like bluefish, you may not have had a very fresh version, because it is a fine eating fish. Its flesh is very tender and flaky, almost like mahi mahi, and it has that distinctive deep, rich bluefish flavor. If you can't find very fresh bluefish, you can substitute fillets of mahi-mahi, mackerel, or striped bass.

Eat this with Grilled Asparagus with Parmesan Cheese and Sweet-and-Sour Bacon Dressing (page 274) and Colorful Grilled Peppers (page 289).

1/4 cup freshly cracked toasted cumin seeds (or substitute 2 tablespoons ground cumin)
1/4 cup freshly cracked toasted coriander seeds (or substitute 2 tablespoons ground coriander)
2 tablespoons kosher salt
3 tablespoons freshly cracked black pepper
4 bluefish fillets, 8 ounces each (or substitute mahi-mahi, mackerel, or striped bass)
3 tablespoons olive oil
3 tablespoons unsalted butter
1/2 pound chourico, diced small (or substitute kielbasa or linguiça)

1 red onion, peeled and diced small
3 tablespoons minced garlic
40 mussels, scrubbed and de-bearded (about 2 pounds)
2 ripe tomatoes about the size of baseballs, cored and diced small
1 1/2 cups dry white wine
Kosher salt and freshly cracked black pepper to taste
5 scallions, sliced thin, both green and white parts
1/4 cup roughly chopped fresh parsely

1. Build a multi-level fire on one side of your grill: Leaving one-quarter of the bottom free of coals, bank the coals in the remaining three-quarters of the grill so that they are three times as high on one side as on the other. When all the coals are ignited and the temperature has died down to medium (you can hold your hand about 5 inches above the grill grid, over the area where the coals are deepest, for 4 to 5 seconds), you're ready to cook.

2. In a small bowl, combine the cumin, coriander, salt, and pepper and mix well. Brush the bluefish on both sides with the oil, then rub it all over with this spice mixture, pressing down gently to be sure it adheres.

3. In a shallow baking pan or disposable foil pan large enough to hold the mussels in a single layer (your standard 10 × 12 × 3-inch pan will probably be about right) and sturdy enough to withstand the heat of a low fire, combine the butter, chourico, onion, and garlic and stir around a few times. Place the pan over the fire until the butter is melted and hot, stirring occasionally, then move the pan to the side of the grill that has no fire.

4. Put the bluefish and the mussels on the hot side of the grill. As the mussels open, transfer them to the pan; discard any that do not open. Grill the bluefish until it is just opaque all the way through, about 5 to 7 minutes per side. To check for doneness, poke the fish with your finger to check its firmness level (see page 13); if you're unsure, nick, peek, and cheat: Cut into one of the fillets at its thickest point and peek to be sure it is opaque all the way through. When the bluefish is done, transfer the fillets to a large, rimmed platter and cover loosely with foil to keep warm.

5. Meanwhile, add the tomatoes, wine, and salt and pepper to the pan with the chourico and mussels, stir to combine, and taste for seasoning. Just before serving, place the pan over the hot side of the grill for a moment to heat the sauce.

6. To serve, arrange the mussels around the fish, pour the sauce over all, sprinkle with the scallions and parsley, and serve hot.

COOK TO COOK: A multi-level fire is a requirement for this dish—the sauce placed off to the side stays just hot enough to keep the butter melted. Make sure that you don't put the pan too close to the hot part of the fire, though; if the liquid starts to simmer, move it a little farther away. When you're getting ready to serve the meal, slide the pan over to the hot side for a minute so that the sauce heats up.

sweet-and-sour grilled salmon steaks with glazed pineapple and mint

SERVES 4

🌾 🌾 🌾 🌾 🌾 🌾 🌾 🌾 🌾 🌾 🌾 🌾 🌾 🌾 🌾 🌾 🌾

We like fish steaks on the grill because they have a bone in them, and in our experience all meat, fowl, or fish somehow tastes a little better when it's cooked on the bone. To give the salmon a little Asian slant we rub it with sesame oil and coat it with coriander (there it is again—we love the stuff) before putting the fish on the grill. If you use whole coriander seeds and crack them yourself, you'll get a much more aromatic spice than if you use preground. Coriander seeds are easier to crack than peppercorns, so it's less work than you think. A sweet soy glaze goes on the fish toward the end. Make sure you wait until the fish has almost finished cooking before you brush on the glaze, because the sugar in it will burn if you apply it too soon.

Try this with a Hobo Pack of Squash, Bacon, and Red Onions (page 303) or Orange-Raisin Couscous with Almonds and Parsley (page 321).

For the glaze:
1/2 cup catsup
1/4 cup soy sauce
3 tablespoons dry sherry
3 tablespoons dark or light brown sugar
1/4 cup pineapple juice
1/4 cup red wine vinegar
3 tablespoons peeled and minced fresh ginger
Juice of 1 lime
1/3 cup roughly chopped fresh mint
———

4 salmon steaks, 1 to 1 1/2 inches thick, 10 to 12 ounces each (or substitute steaks of mahi-mahi, halibut, or bluefish)
3 tablespoons roasted sesame oil
Kosher salt and freshly cracked black pepper to taste
1/4 cup freshly cracked toasted coriander seeds (or substitute 2 tablespoons ground coriander)
4 pineapple slices, 1 inch thick, peeled
1/4 cup vegetable oil

1. Build a multi-level fire in your grill: Leaving one-quarter of the bottom free of coals, bank the coals in the remaining three-quarters of the grill so that they are three times as high on one side as on the other. When all the coals are ignited and the temperature has died down to medium (you can hold your hand about 5 inches above the grill grid, over the area where the coals are deepest, for 4 to 5 seconds), you're ready to cook.

2. In a small saucepan, combine the catsup, soy sauce, sherry, brown sugar, pineapple juice, vinegar, and ginger and bring to a boil over medium-high heat. Reduce the heat to low and simmer until the mixture has been reduced by half, about 15 minutes. Remove from the heat, allow to cool slightly, then add the lime juice and mint.

3. Coat the salmon steaks on both sides with the sesame oil and sprinkle them generously with salt and pepper, then rub them all over with the coriander, pressing down gently so it adheres. Rub the pineapple slices with the vegetable oil. Put the salmon and

the pineapple over the coals and grill until the pineapple is nicely seared, 4 to 6 minutes per side, and the salmon is almost opaque throughout, 6 to 8 minutes per side. To check for doneness, poke the fish with your finger to check its firmness level (see page 13); if you're unsure, nick, peek, and cheat: Cut into one of the steaks at its thickest point and peek to be sure it is almost opaque all the way through. During the last 30 seconds of cooking, brush both sides of the salmon and the pineapple with the glaze.

4. To serve, arrange the pineapple slices on plates, top each with a salmon steak, and drizzle with more of the glaze.

COOK TO COOK: Fish steaks are cross sections of the fish, made by cutting vertically through the fish rather than horizontally, so part of the backbone is included. Because bone holds heat longer than flesh does, steaks continue to cook more after being removed from the fire than fillets do. So take these salmon steaks off the fire while they are somewhat less done than you want them to be when you eat them.

simple grilled salmon fillets with spicy herb sauce

SERVES 4

❧ ❧ ❧ ❧ ❧ ❧ ❧ ❧ ❧ ❧ ❧ ❧ ❧ ❧ ❧ ❧ ❧

This is a dish that puts a great meal on your table 20 minutes after you've got your fire going. You could serve the salmon with White Bean Salad with Grilled Squash, Zucchini, and Roasted Red Pepper Dressing (page 313) or Colorful Grilled Peppers (page 289).

4 salmon fillets, 8 ounces each (or
   substitute fillets of striped bass,
   bluefish, or mahi-mahi)
3 tablespoons vegetable oil
Kosher salt and freshly cracked black
   pepper to taste

For the sauce:
1 bunch fresh parsley, washed and
   dried, large stems removed

1/2 cup fresh cilantro leaves, washed
   and dried
1/2 cup fresh mint leaves, washed
   and dried
1 garlic clove, peeled
2 tablespoons grainy mustard
5 dashes of Tabasco sauce, or to taste
1/2 cup olive oil
1 tablespoon fresh lemon juice

1. Build a multi-level fire in your grill: Leaving one-quarter of the bottom free of coals, bank the coals in the remaining three-quarters of the grill so that they are three times as high on one side as on the other. When all the coals are ignited and the temperature has died down to medium (you can hold your hand about 5 inches above the grill grid, over the area where the coals are deepest, for 4 to 5 seconds), you're ready to cook.

2. Rub the salmon fillets on both sides with the vegetable oil and sprinkle them generously with salt and pepper. Place them over the coals and grill until they are just opaque throughout, 6 to 8 minutes per side. To check for doneness, poke the fish with your finger to check its firmness level (see page 13); if you're unsure, nick, peek, and cheat: Cut into one of the fillets at its thickest point and peek to be sure it is just opaque all the way through.

3. While the salmon is cooking, combine all the sauce ingredients in a food processor or blender and purée until smooth.

4. Serve each salmon fillet topped with a spoonful of the sauce, passing any remaining sauce on the side.

COOK TO COOK: Be particularly careful not to overcook the fish here. And again, to prevent sticking, remember the preheated and very clean grill grid, the lightly oiled fish, and the prohibition against moving the fish during the first 2 minutes of cooking.

grilled double-thick tuna, east coast grill style

SERVES 4

᠉ ᠉ ᠉ ᠉ ᠉ ᠉ ᠉ ᠉ ᠉ ᠉ ᠉ ᠉ ᠉ ᠉ ᠉ ᠉ ᠉

We remember the days, not all that long ago, when tuna was rarely served in restaurants and most people thought of it as a canned pantry item. Then, when tuna made its way onto restaurant menus, it was usually cut quite thin and cooked all the way through. Funny how tastes change—nowadays grilled double-thick tuna is everywhere. That's not a bad thing; it simply means that people have finally caught on to how tasty fresh tuna is. To complement it, we serve it with pickled ginger, wasabi, and soy, the classic accompaniments to sushi.

Serve the tuna with Extra-Large Grilled Sweet Potato Fries with Shiitake-Parsley Butter Sauce (page 294).

4 hyper-fresh tuna steaks, about 3 inches thick, 8 ounces each
4 tablespoons roasted sesame oil
Kosher salt and freshly ground white pepper to taste (or substitute black pepper)
3/4 cup pickled ginger (available at Asian markets)
6 tablespoons wasabi powder, mixed with water to the consistency of wet sand
3/4 cup soy sauce

1. Build a multi-level fire in your grill: Leaving one-quarter of the bottom free of coals, bank the coals in the remaining three-quarters of the grill so that they are three times as high on one side as on the other. When all the coals are ignited and the temperature is hot (you can hold your hand about 5 inches above the grill grid, over the area where the coals are deepest, for 2 seconds or less), you're ready to cook.

2. Brush the tuna steaks lightly with the sesame oil and sprinkle generously with salt and pepper. Put the steaks on the grill and cook until you have a dark brown, crispy crust on both sides, about 4 to 5 minutes per side.

3. Now cook the steaks on each of the 4 edges for about 2 minutes, trying to achieve the same dark brown, crispy effect. Remove the steaks from the grill and serve along with the pickled ginger, wasabi, and soy sauce.

COOK TO COOK: You'll need a good hot fire here, because what you want to do is cook the tuna hard on the outside so it gets well seared while you keep it close to raw at the center. It's also important to have really thick tuna steaks, basically cut like filet mignon.

grilled swordfish and crispy asparagus with smoked salmon-chive butter

SERVES 4

Swordfish may well be the apotheosis of fish on the grill, the absolute easiest kind to cook over live fire because of its steaklike texture. Here we pair it with asparagus, which is one of our favorite vegetables for the grill. To finish the dish, we add a little butter flavored with chives and smoked salmon, another example of the seafood-on-seafood approach we really enjoy.

This is a good springtime dish. We like to serve it with Orange-Raisin Couscous with Almonds and Parsley (page 321), or you might try the Four Grilled Corn Strategies with Latin Flavor Modifiers (on page 286).

4 swordfish steaks, about 1 1/2
    inches thick, 8 to 10 ounces each
    (or substitute steaks of tuna,
    striped bass, or salmon)
20 small asparagus spears
6 tablespoons olive oil
Kosher salt and freshly cracked black
    pepper to taste

1/2 cup unsalted butter, softened
1/4 pound smoked salmon, minced
1/4 cup roughly chopped fresh chives

1. Build a multi-level fire in your grill: Leaving one-quarter of the bottom free of coals, bank the coals in the remaining three-quarters of the grill so that they are three times as high on one side as on the other. When all the coals are ignited and the temperature has died down to medium (you can hold your hand about 5 inches above the grill grid, over the area where the coals are deepest, for 4 to 5 seconds), you're ready to cook.

2. Rub the swordfish and asparagus with the olive oil and sprinkle them generously with salt and pepper. Place the swordfish on the grill over the hotter side and cook for 7 minutes. Flip the fish steaks, put the asparagus on the grill next to the fish, and cook for 5 to 7 minutes more, rolling the asparagus back and forth, until the asparagus spears are lightly browned and the swordfish is cooked through. To check for doneness, poke the fish with your finger to check its firmness level (see page 13); if you're unsure, nick, peek, and cheat: Cut into one of the steaks at its thickest point and peek to be sure it is opaque all the way through.

3. While the swordfish and asparagus are on the grill, put the butter, salmon, chives, and salt and pepper to taste in a medium bowl and mash with a fork until smooth.

4. To serve, divide the asparagus spears among 4 plates and fan them out. Arrange a swordfish steak on top, spread some of the salmon-chive butter on each, and serve hot.

COOK TO COOK: Use the thinner asparagus spears so they are cooked through on the inside by the time they get crisp on the outside. If you can find larger asparagus spears only, plunge them into boiling water for a couple of minutes before oiling and grilling them.

grilled striped bass
with chunky mango-ginger barbecue sauce

SERVES 4

We are fortunate, as New Englanders, to have access to a lot of super-fresh striped bass—or "striper," as the locals call it—because it's a great fish to grill. This dish is a favorite at my (Chris's) restaurant in Westport, Massachusetts, the Back Eddy. We go with a medium-hot fire here in order to get a good sear, since this fish can stand up to it. If the flesh starts to become too dark, just move it to the cooler part of the fire until it finishes cooking. The sauce for the fish is like a thinned-out mango chutney; it goes particularly well with the meaty flavor of striped bass.

Serve this with Grilled Asparagus with Soy-Ginger Dressing (page 276) or Grilled Shiitake Mushrooms with Sherry, Soy, and Scallions (page 281).

For the sauce:
- 2 tablespoons olive oil
- 1 small red onion, peeled and diced small
- 2 tablespoons minced garlic
- 3 tablespoons peeled and minced fresh ginger
- 1 tomato about the size of a baseball, peeled and diced medium
- 2 ripe but firm mangoes, peeled, pitted, and diced medium
- 1/4 cup dry sherry
- 1/4 cup orange juice
- 1/4 cup white vinegar
- 3 tablespoons brown sugar
- 2 limes, halved
- Kosher salt and freshly cracked black pepper to taste

- 4 striped bass fillets, 8 ounces each (or substitute fillets of salmon, halibut, grouper, or even tuna)
- 3 tablespoons olive oil
- Kosher salt and freshly cracked black pepper to taste

1. Build a multi-level fire in your grill: Leaving one-quarter of the bottom free of coals, bank the coals in the remaining three-quarters of the grill so that they are three times as high on one side as on the other. When all the coals are ignited and the temperature has died down to medium (you can hold your hand about 5 inches above the grill grid, over the area where the coals are deepest, for 4 to 5 seconds), you're ready to cook.

2. In a large sauté pan or skillet over medium-high heat, heat the oil until it is hot but not smoking. Add the onion and sauté, stirring occasionally, until transparent, 7 to 9 minutes. Add the garlic, ginger, tomato, and mangoes and cook, stirring frequently, for 5 minutes more. Stir in the sherry, orange juice, vinegar, and brown sugar and bring just to a boil, then reduce the heat to medium and simmer vigorously until the mixture is reduced by about two-thirds, about 20 minutes. Remove from the heat, squeeze in the juice from the halved limes, and season to taste with salt and pepper.

3. Rub the fish fillets on both sides with the olive oil and sprinkle generously with salt and pepper. Place the fillets on the grill and cook until they develop a lovely dark sear

on the outside and are fully opaque on the inside, about 5 minutes per side, brushing with the barbecue sauce during the last 30 seconds of cooking on each side. If the flesh starts to become too dark, move the fillets to the cooler part of the fire and cover them with a pie plate or disposable foil pan to finish cooking. To check for doneness, poke the fish with your finger to check its firmness level (see page 13); if you're unsure, nick, peek, and cheat: Cut into one of the fillets at its thickest point and peek to be sure it is opaque all the way through.

4. Remove the fish from the grill and serve immediately, topping each fillet with a spoonful of the chunky sauce.

COOK TO COOK: This is one of those situations where the outside of the fish may start cooking too fast and you need to move the fillets to the side of the grill with fewer coals to finish cooking the inside. If you have to do that, cover the fish with a metal pie pan or foil pan to create an oven effect so it doesn't take too long.

mexican-style grilled mahi-mahi
with hearts of palm slaw and avocado sauce

SERVES 4

※ ※ ※ ※ ※ ※ ※ ※ ※ ※ ※ ※ ※ ※ ※ ※ ※

Mahi-Mahi is an excellent fish—mild in flavor with a flaky texture—and fortunately it is widely available these days. In this dish we cover it with a spice rub and grill it over a medium-hot fire, then serve it with a simple puréed avocado sauce and a crunchy, multicolored slaw featuring hearts of palm.

This fresh, colorful, brightly flavored dish is ideal for a hot summer day. Serve it with East Coast Grill Cornbread (page 322) and Fresh Margaritas (page 372).

For the slaw:
1/2 cup fresh lime juice (about 4 limes)
1/4 cup orange juice
1/4 cup red wine vinegar
8 dashes of Tabasco sauce, or to taste
1/2 cup roughly chopped fresh cilantro
Kosher salt and freshly cracked black pepper to taste
1 cup thinly sliced white cabbage
1 cup thinly sliced red cabbage
1/2 cup shredded carrots
5 hearts of palm, cut into long strips
———
2 tablespoons paprika
2 tablespoons ground cumin
2 tablespoons minced garlic

4 mahi-mahi fillets, 8 ounces each (or substitute fillets of salmon, halibut, or even cod)
3 tablespoons olive oil
Cilantro sprigs for garnish (optional)
1 lime, thinly sliced, for garnish (optional)

For the sauce:
1 very ripe avocado, halved and pitted
1 tomato about the size of a baseball, cored and quartered
1/2 small red onion, peeled and roughly chopped
1 tablespoon minced garlic
1/3 cup olive oil
Kosher salt and freshly cracked black pepper to taste

1. Build a multi-level fire in your grill: Leaving one-quarter of the bottom free of coals, bank the coals in the remaining three-quarters of the grill so that they are three times as high on one side as on the other. When all the coals are ignited and the temperature has died down to medium-hot (you can hold your hand about 5 inches above the grill grid, over the area where the coals are deepest, for 3 to 4 seconds), you're ready to cook.

2. In a large bowl, whisk together the lime juice, orange juice, vinegar, Tabasco, cilantro, and salt and pepper until blended. Add the two kinds of cabbage, carrots, and hearts of palm and toss to coat with the dressing. Cover and refrigerate until serving time.

3. In a small bowl, mix together the paprika, cumin, garlic, and salt and pepper to taste. Brush the mahi-mahi fillets on both sides with the oil, then rub them all over with the

spice mixture. Place the fillets on the grill over the coals and cook until just opaque all the way through, about 5 to 6 minutes per side. To check for doneness, poke the fish with your finger to check its firmness level (see page 13); if you're unsure, nick, peek, and cheat: Cut into one of the fillets at its thickest point and peek to be sure it is opaque all the way through.

4. While the fish is cooking, make the sauce: Scoop the avocado flesh into a food processor bowl along with the tomato, red onion, and garlic. With the processor running, pour in the olive oil in a thin stream until it is incorporated. Season with salt and pepper and transfer to a serving bowl.

5. When the fish is done, put a fish fillet on each plate along with a small mound of the slaw. Garnish with fresh cilantro sprigs and lime slices if desired and serve, passing the avocado sauce on the side.

COOK TO COOK: If you can't find hearts of palm for this salad (or if you have ecological objections to hearts of palm), make the slaw with endive instead.

grilled peppered skate wing
with tabasco-garlic butter and beet relish

SERVES 4

If you like skate and you can find it, you're in luck with this dish. Skate is a "by-catch," a fisherman's term for a fish caught by mistake when he's actually fishing for something else, so it can be hard to get hold of. Fortunately, though, as it becomes more popular in restaurants it is appearing more frequently in markets as well. Ask your fishmonger to remove the skin and the outside bones. What this leaves you with is a piece of cartilage with rich, stringy, delicious meat on the other side.

In this preparation the skate is coated with a black pepper crust before grilling, then served with a spicy butter and a beet relish that's got lots of horseradish in it. When you add in the flavorful sear from the fire, this is an unbeatable assemblage—and it's still excellent without the beet relish, if you don't have time to make it.

This dish is a particular favorite of our friend Bill Cramp, who likes to have it at least once or twice a year when we can get our hands on skate for him. He claims, though, that the beet relish is too powerful when it's first made and needs to sit for at least 24 hours. If you have the forethought to do that, it's actually not a bad idea.

You might serve this with plain grilled asparagus and a salad of bitter greens.

For the relish:
3 cups orange juice
1 1/2 cups red wine vinegar
1/3 cup prepared horseradish
3 tablespoons freshly cracked coriander seeds (or substitute 1 1/2
   tablespoons ground coriander)
1/2 cup roughly chopped fresh
   parsley
2 cups (about 3 medium) cooked,
   peeled, and diced beets
Kosher salt and freshly cracked black
   pepper to taste

For the butter:
1/2 cup unsalted butter, softened
1 tablespoon minced garlic
2 tablespoons fresh lemon juice
   (about 1/2 lemon)
3 tablespoons Tabasco sauce, or to
   taste
Kosher salt and freshly cracked black
   pepper to taste
———
4 skinless skate wings, 12 to 14
   ounces each
Kosher salt to taste
3/4 cup freshly cracked black pepper

1. Make the relish: In a medium saucepan over medium-high heat, bring the orange juice and vinegar to a boil. Reduce the heat slightly and simmer vigorously, skimming the scum from the surface periodically, until the mixture is reduced to 1 cup, about 40 minutes. Remove from the heat and cool to room temperature. Add the horseradish, coriander, and parsley and mix well. Place the beets in a medium bowl and pour the sauce over them. Season with salt and pepper and mix gently until combined, then cover and refrigerate until serving time.

2. Meanwhile, build a multi-level fire in your grill: Leaving one-quarter of the bottom free of coals, bank the coals in the remaining three-quarters of the grill so that they are three times as high on one side as on the other. When all the coals are ignited and the temperature has died down to medium (you can hold your hand about 5 inches above the grill grid, over the area where the coals are deepest, for 4 to 5 seconds), you're ready to cook.

3. In a small bowl, combine the softened butter, garlic, lemon juice, Tabasco, and salt and pepper and mix together until well blended. Scoop the butter onto an 8-inch square of plastic wrap, shape it into a short, fat cylinder, then fold the plastic wrap around it. Refrigerate until serving time.

4. Season the meat side of the skate wings with salt to taste and coat them with the black pepper. Place them on the grill over the coals and cook until they are just opaque all the way through, about 6 to 8 minutes per side. To check for doneness, poke a skate wing with your finger to check its firmness level (see page 13); if you're unsure, nick, peek, and cheat: Cut into a skate wing at its thickest point and peek to be sure it is opaque all the way through.

5. Unwrap the garlic butter and cut it crosswise into 4 slices. Serve each skate wing hot from the grill with a piece of the butter melting over it, and pass the beet relish on the side.

COOK TO COOK: It's particularly important with skate to be sure that it's fresh. The best way is to give it a sniff; if there's even a hint of ammonia, forget it.

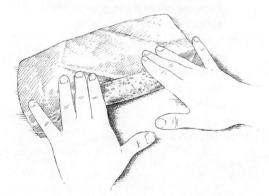

Shaping the cylinder of garlic butter

Grilled skate wings with garlic butter

spicy sausage-stuffed trout
with hoisin glaze and sesame crust

SERVES 4

ﭏ ﭏ ﭏ ﭏ ﭏ ﭏ ﭏ ﭏ ﭏ ﭏ ﭏ ﭏ ﭏ ﭏ ﭏ ﭏ ﭏ

You might think the combination of pork and fish is weird, but it has a long history. If you're familiar with the cooking of Boston's master chef Jasper White, for example, you probably know his famous pork chop and clams dish that was inspired by the classic Portuguese *Porco a Alentejana*, a homey preparation in which clams share a stewpot with cubes of marinated pork. Southeast Asian cooks are just as inventive with the pork-seafood combination. The Vietnamese dish Happy Pancake, for example, includes both shrimp and pork; squid stuffed with pork and *galangal* is wildly popular in Thailand; and one of the most common dishes we encountered in the street food stalls of Kuala Lumpur, Malaysia, was a tofu cake stuffed with minced white fish, pork, chiles, and shallots.

This recipe pays homage to the cooks of Southeast Asia. We use trout here because it is the easiest whole fish of good quality to find in American markets. We stuff it with a rich mixture of pork sausage, chiles, ginger, scallions, and garlic, then cook it by the indirect method, brushing it with hoisin and sesame during the last few minutes on the grill. It has a lot of spicy, smoky flavors going on, and it's also very attractive on the plate.

Serve with simple grilled eggplant, some Asian greens like tatsoi or mizuna, and white rice.

3 tablespoons vegetable oil
1 tablespoon sesame oil
1 red onion, peeled and thinly sliced
2 tablespoons peeled and minced
   fresh ginger
1 tablespoon minced garlic
2 tablespoons minced fresh chile
   peppers of your choice, or to
   taste
5 links sweet Italian sausage, casings
   removed

1/3 cup chopped scallions, both
   green and white parts, plus 2
   tablespoons more for garnish
Kosher salt and freshly cracked black
   pepper to taste
4 whole trout, 12 to 14 ounces each,
   cleaned and boned (head-on is
   cooler)
1/2 cup hoisin sauce
1/2 cup toasted sesame seeds

1. Start a fire well over to one side of a large kettle grill, using about enough coals to fill half a shoebox. When the fire dies down and the coals are well lit, you are ready to cook the fish.

2. Meanwhile, make the stuffing: In a large sauté pan or skillet over medium-high heat, heat the vegetable oil and sesame oil until hot but not smoking. Add the onion and sauté, stirring occasionally, until transparent, 7 to 9 minutes. Add the ginger, garlic, and chiles and sauté, stirring frequently, for 1 minute more, then add the sausage. Cook, breaking up the sausage until it is crumbled and no longer pink, about 5 minutes more. Remove from the heat, stir in the 1/3 cup scallions, sprinkle generously with salt and pepper, and taste for seasoning, then set aside to cool almost to room temperature.

3. When the stuffing is cool, sprinkle the fish inside and out with salt and pepper, spread one-quarter of the stuffing inside each fish, and then close each cavity using several toothpicks.

4. Place the trout on the side of the grill with no coals, being careful that no part of the fish is directly over the coals. Put the lid on the grill with the vents one-quarter of the way open and cook for 15 to 20 minutes. Carefully turn the fish over, add a handful of fresh charcoal to the fire, replace the lid, and cook 15 to 20 minutes more. Five minutes before the fish are done, brush them generously on both sides with the hoisin sauce and sprinkle them with the sesame seeds. To check for doneness, cut into the fish with a thin knife along the backbone and peek to be sure it is opaque all the way through.

5. Remove the fish from the grill, take out the toothpicks, arrange the fish on a platter, scatter the remaining scallions over the top, and serve.

COOK TO COOK: When you're cooking a whole fish on the grill, you want to be very gentle when you flip the fish over. In fact, don't flip it at all—roll it over with your tongs or a spatula as you would a sleeping bed partner. Remember, fish are delicate.

grilled swordfish and clams with black bean sauce

SERVES 4

※ ※ ※ ※ ※ ※ ※ ※ ※ ※ ※ ※ ※ ※ ※ ※ ※ ※

This is a kind of two-seafood riff on the "Clams Johnson" grilling method, which entails cooking clams right on the grill until they open, then bathing them in a sauce that we've kept warm on the cooler part of the grill. Here we grill meaty swordfish and succulent clams at the same time, popping the finished clams into a pan with a savory Chinese-inspired sesame–black bean combination. When all the seafood is done, we add several flavorful liquids to the black bean combination and let it heat up a bit, then serve both types of seafood liberally drizzled with the sauce.

Serve this dish with steamed rice and grilled asparagus or Aromatic Slaw with Southeast Asian Flavors (page 309).

3 tablespoons sesame oil	2 dozen (about 1 1/2 pounds)
3 tablespoons peeled and minced	littleneck clams, scrubbed
fresh ginger	2 tablespoons dry sherry
2 tablespoons minced garlic	1/3 cup white wine
2 tablespoons minced fermented	3 tablespoons soy sauce
black beans (or substitute black	5 dashes of Tabasco sauce, or to taste
bean paste)	1/2 cup thinly sliced scallions, both
4 swordfish fillets, 1 inch thick,	green and white parts
8 to 10 ounces each	
Kosher salt and freshly cracked black	
pepper to taste	

1. Build a multi-level fire in your grill: Leaving one-quarter of the bottom free of coals, bank the coals in the remaining three-quarters of the grill so that they are three times as high on one side as on the other. When all the coals are ignited and the temperature has died down to medium-hot (you can hold your hand about 5 inches above the grill grid, over the area where the coals are deepest, for 3 to 4 seconds), you're ready to cook.

2. In a shallow baking pan or disposable foil pan large enough to hold the clams in a single layer and sturdy enough to withstand the heat of a low fire, combine the sesame oil, ginger, garlic, and black beans and stir to mix. Place the pan over the side of the grill that has no fire.

3. Sprinkle the swordfish generously with salt and pepper, then put both the swordfish and clams on the hotter side of the grill. As the clams open, transfer them to the pan with the sesame–black bean mixture; discard any that do not open. Grill the swordfish until it is just opaque all the way through, about 4 to 6 minutes per side. To check for doneness, poke the fish with your finger to check its firmness level (see page 13); if you're unsure, nick, peek, and cheat: Cut into one of the fillets at its thickest point and

peek to be sure it is opaque all the way through. When the fish is done, transfer it to a large, rimmed platter and cover loosely with foil to keep warm.

4. When the clams have all been transferred to the pan, add the sherry, wine, soy, Tabasco, and scallions, stir a few times to combine, and place the pan over the hotter side of the grill for a moment to heat the sauce.

5. To serve, remove the clams from the sauce, arrange them around the swordfish on the platter, and drizzle both clams and swordfish generously with the sauce.

COOK TO COOK: Fermented black beans, which give this sauce its distinctive flavor, are black soy beans that have been carefully fermented, then dried and often salted. Their deep, winey flavor is a classic Chinese accompaniment to seafood. If you can't find the beans themselves, the jarred paste made from them is a fine substitute.

"blackened" grilled wolffish
with spicy corn tartar sauce and scallion grits

SERVES 4

Remember a few years ago when you couldn't go into a restaurant without finding a "blackened" this or that on the menu? Like most culinary crazes, this one ran its course quickly, leaving as its primary legacy the memory of many ill-considered and poorly prepared dishes. But blackening is a good thing when done right. In fact, there are obvious similarities between this technique and the spice-rubbed approach we favor—what you are "blackening" in this technique is actually a spice rub.

So this recipe is a tribute to the New Orleans style of cooking and to chef Paul Prudhomme, who popularized it. As the first regional American cuisine to fully capture the public's attention, it was important in helping us understand that we do have great food traditions in this country if you look on the local level.

For this rather rugged treatment we favor wolffish, also known as ocean catfish, because it has a texture that's firm enough to stand up to blackening. Then, for a combination of Southern flavors, we serve the fish with a jazzy tartar sauce and some good ol' grits, basically the Southern version of polenta but made from hominy corn.

Serve this with a salad, maybe a salad of bitter greens and apples.

For the grits:
5 cups water
1/2 teaspoon kosher salt
1 cup hominy 3 (not instant)
1/2 cup chopped scallions, both
    green and white parts
2 tablespoons unsalted butter
Kosher salt and freshly cracked
    black pepper to taste

For the tartar sauce:
2 egg yolks
1 cup vegetable oil
2 tablespoons red wine
    vinegar
2 tablespoons prepared brown
    mustard
3 tablespoons red hot sauce of your
    choice, or to taste

1/3 cup blanched corn kernels
    (blanch 1 ear in boiling salted
    water for 2 minutes, drain, and
    cut kernels off the cob)
1/4 cup sweet pickle relish
1/4 cup roughly chopped fresh
    parsley
1 tablespoon celery seeds

For the blackening rub:
3 tablespoons paprika
1 tablespoon dry mustard
2 tablespoons ground coriander
2 tablespoons ground black pepper
1 tablespoon cayenne pepper
2 tablespoons kosher salt
———
4 wolffish fillets, 8 to 10 ounces each
    (or substitute monkfish, blue-
    fish, mahi-mahi, or mackerel)

1. Build a multi-level fire in your grill: Leaving one-quarter of the bottom free of coals, bank the coals in the remaining three-quarters of the grill so that there are about three times as many one side as on the other. When all the coals are ignited and the temper-

ature has died down to medium (you can hold your hand about 5 inches above the grill grid, over the area where the coals are deepest, for 4 to 5 seconds), you're ready to cook the fish.

2. Meanwhile, make the grits: Bring the water to a full boil in a medium saucepan over high heat. Add the salt, then sprinkle the hominy into the water while stirring constantly. Reduce the heat to very low, then cover and cook, stirring frequently to prevent scorching, until the grits are about as thick as polenta, smooth, and have lost their raw taste, about 20 minutes. Remove the pan from the heat and stir in the scallions, butter, and salt and pepper to taste, then cover to keep warm until serving time.

3. While the grits are cooking, make the tartar sauce: Put the egg yolks in a blender or food processor, turn the motor on and, with the motor running, add the oil in a thin stream. When the oil is incorporated and the mixture has thickened to about the texture of mayonnaise, turn the motor off. Now add the vinegar, mustard, hot sauce, and half the corn kernels and pulse until well blended. Transfer the sauce to a bowl, fold in the remaining corn, the relish, chopped parsley, celery seeds, and salt and pepper to taste. Cover and refrigerate until serving time.

4. In a small bowl, combine all the ingredients for the blackening rub and mix well. Rub the fish all over with this mixture, pressing down gently to be sure it adheres. Put the fish on the grill and cook until just opaque throughout, about 3 to 4 minutes per side. To check for doneness, poke the fish with your finger to check its firmness level (see page 13), then if you're unsure, nick, peek, and cheat: Cut into the fish at its thickest point and peek to be sure it is opaque all the way through.

5. Serve the fish accompanied by the grits with tartar sauce on the side.

COOK TO COOK: The grill is ideal for the Cajun blackening technique. It gets much hotter than a sauté pan, so you can blacken the spice rub without overcooking the interior of, in this case, the fish.

grilled tautog with marcy's pesto, grilled tomatoes, and balsamic greens

SERVES 4

⚜ ⚜ ⚜ ⚜ ⚜ ⚜ ⚜ ⚜ ⚜ ⚜ ⚜ ⚜ ⚜ ⚜ ⚜ ⚜ ⚜

My (Chris's) wife, Marcy, has become a master of pesto. Not long ago she didn't have a clue as to how to make it, but one day she dug out a giant mortar and pestle that I had brought back from Mexico, picked a basketful of basil from the garden at our beach house, and went to work. That first pesto she made was fantastic, and it has gotten better over the years. I like to use it in every way I can think of.

Here we make a kind of breadless BLT in which the bacon becomes fish, the lettuce becomes wilted greens, the tomato is grilled, and pesto plays the part usually assigned to mayonnaise. For this dish I like to use tautog, a local New England fish also known as blackfish. It's mild-tasting and has off-white flesh with a firm texture and a medium flake. I think of tautog as a cross between snapper and striped bass, and it's my personal nominee for the single most underutilized fish in the Northeast.

You might serve this preceded by Ihsan's Grilled Cheese in Grape Leaves (page 34) and accompanied by rice or simple grilled new potatoes.

For the pesto:
3 garlic cloves, peeled
1/4 cup toasted pine nuts
2 cups whole basil leaves
3/4 cup extra-virgin olive oil
Kosher salt and freshly cracked black
   pepper to taste

For the greens:
2 tablespoons olive oil
1 teaspoon minced garlic
4 cups hearty baby cooking greens
   such as kale, mustard, collards,
   or beets (or substitute spinach)

3 tablespoons balsamic vinegar
1/2 teaspoon sugar
Kosher salt and freshly cracked black
   pepper to taste
———
4 tautog fillets, 8 ounces each (or
   substitute fillets of grouper,
   monkfish, or red snapper)
4 tablespoons olive oil
Kosher salt and freshly cracked black
   pepper to taste
2 ripe tomatoes about the size of
   baseballs, cored and halved
1 lemon, halved

1. Build a multi-level fire in your grill: Leaving one-quarter of the bottom free of coals, bank the coals in the remaining three-quarters of the grill so that they are three times as high on one side as on the other. When all the coals are ignited and the temperature has died down to medium (you can hold your hand about 5 inches above the grill grid, over the area where the coals are deepest, for 4 to 5 seconds), you're ready to cook.

2. Make the pesto: Mash the garlic to a paste in a mortar and pestle or purée in a blender. Add the pine nuts and basil and again mash or purée to a paste. Add the olive oil and mash or purée until smooth, add salt and pepper to taste, and set aside.

3. Make the greens: In a large sauté pan or skillet, heat the olive oil over medium-high heat until hot but not smoking. Add the garlic and cook for only about 5 seconds. Immediately add the greens, vinegar, and sugar and toss furiously until the greens are just wilted, about 1 minute. Remove from the heat, season to taste with salt and pepper, and divide among 4 individual plates.

3. Rub the fish all over with about 3 tablespoons of the olive oil and sprinkle generously with salt and pepper. Put on the grill directly over the coals and cook until opaque all the way through, about 3 to 4 minutes per side. To check for doneness, poke the fish with your finger to check its firmness level (see page 13); if you're unsure, nick, peek, and cheat: Cut into one of the fillets at its thickest point and peek to be sure it is opaque all the way through.

4. While the fillets are cooking, rub the tomato halves with the remaining tablespoon of oil, then put them on the grill on the side with fewer coals and cook until nicely seared, 2 to 3 minutes per side.

5. Place the fillets on top of the greens, smear a couple of tablespoons of the pesto over each fillet, then top each with a tomato half. Squeeze the lemon over the top and serve.

COOK TO COOK: We very highly recommend that you look around to find the most under-utilized but delicious fish in your region and use it in this recipe. You can be sure there will be one, and using it is a painless way to help preserve a sustainable supply of seafood.

grilled whole fish strategy with five sauce options

SERVES 4

※ ※ ※ ※ ※ ※ ※ ※ ※ ※ ※ ※ ※ ※ ※ ※ ※

This dish is a requirement for getting your Ph.G. (Doctorate of Grilling). You start out with clams and oysters, you move on to scallops and shrimp, you graduate to fish steaks such as tuna and swordfish, you tackle fish fillets—and then finally you reach the pinnacle, the zenith, the epitome of grilled fish technique and skill, the whole fish.

Truthfully, though, it's not really so difficult—or at least it's not if you look for a relatively small fish. We have stuffed a whole 20-pound striped bass and cooked it on the grill, but for that you need a professional commercial barbecue rig. On your standard backyard grill, you'd be smartest not to go over a 2-pounder. Under that limit there are plenty of options, from snapper to trout to fluke to striped bass.

Whichever whole fish you choose to grill, the critical features of the process are the same—"setting" the skin on both sides of the fish on a hot fire, then moving it to a cooler part of the fire and covering it to finish cooking. Within that dynamic, there are four basic things you need to remember: Don't put too much oil on the fish (it drips into the fire and causes flare-ups); make sure the grill grid is super-clean (the skin will stick more easily to greasy or dirty metal); don't move the fish around when you're setting the sear (you want the sear to have time to develop because otherwise you'll rip the skin); and use your tongs and a spatula to roll the fish over gently rather than flipping it (you'll need to ease the skin loose from the grill grid, and rolling is a less abrupt way to do so).

Because we know you'll want to try this technique often, we're providing you with five sauce options, basically variations on the theme of vinaigrettes. So get out there in the back yard and get your doctorate. Your mom will be proud.

4 small, dressed whole fish (red snapper, trout, black bass, bluefish, flounder, fluke, mackerel, striped bass, or tilapia), about 1 1/2 pounds each	4 tablespoons olive oil Kosher salt and freshly cracked black pepper to taste Sauce option of your choice, below

1. Build a multi-level fire in your grill: Leaving one-quarter of the bottom free of coals, bank the coals in the remaining three-quarters of the grill so that they are three times as high on one side as on the other. When all the coals are ignited and the temperature has died down to medium (you can hold your hand about 5 inches above the grill grid, over the area where the coals are deepest, for 4 to 5 seconds), you're ready to cook.

2. Make 3 diagonal cuts across each side of each fish, cutting all the way down to the bone. (This helps the fish cook evenly and makes it easier to gauge when they're done.) Brush each fish on both sides with oil and sprinkle generously with salt and pepper.

3. Put the fish on the grill over the side with more coals and cook until well charred on the first side, about 10 to 12 minutes. Carefully roll each fish over and cook until com-

pletely opaque, about 12 to 15 minutes more. To check for doneness, peek inside the slashes to be sure all the fish are just opaque all the way through.

4. While the fish are cooking, make one of the sauce options below.

5. To serve, place a fish on each plate and drizzle with sauce. Instruct your guests to lift off the top fillet of their fish and yank the spine up from the tail end, removing all the bones.

Your Five Sauce Options

1. Orange, Fennel, and Green Olive Vinaigrette

MAKES ABOUT 1 1/2 CUPS

1/2 cup fresh orange juice, simmered until reduced to 3 tablespoons, about 20 minutes
1/4 cup red wine vinegar
2 tablespoons fennel seeds

1/4 cup roughly chopped green olives
3/4 cup extra-virgin olive oil
Kosher salt and freshly cracked black pepper to taste

Combine all the ingredients in a small bowl and whisk together well.

2. Simple Greek Vinaigrette

MAKES ABOUT 1 1/4 CUPS

1/4 cup fresh lemon juice (about 1 lemon)
1 tablespoon minced garlic
1/4 cup roughly chopped fresh mint

3/4 cup extra-virgin olive oil
Kosher salt and freshly cracked black pepper to taste
Pinch of cinnamon

Combine all the ingredients in a small bowl and whisk together well.

3. Chunky Tomato-Caper Sauce

MAKES ABOUT 1 3/4 CUPS

1 ripe tomato about the size of a
    baseball, cored and diced small
1 tablespoon minced garlic
1/2 cup roughly chopped fresh
    parsley
1/3 cup red wine vinegar

1/4 cup capers, very well rinsed
1 teaspoon red pepper flakes, or to
    taste
3/4 cup extra-virgin olive oil
Kosher salt and freshly cracked black
    pepper to taste

Combine all the ingredients in a small bowl and whisk together well.

4. Spicy Mango-Lime Vinaigrette

MAKES ABOUT 1 3/4 CUPS

1 cup mango juice, simmered until
    reduced to 3 tablespoons, about
    30 minutes
1/4 cup fresh lime juice (about 2
    limes)
1/3 cup roughly chopped fresh
    cilantro

1 tablespoon minced fresh chile pep-
    per of your choice, or to taste
1 teaspoon minced garlic
1/2 teaspoon ground cinnamon
3/4 cup extra-virgin olive oil
Kosher salt and freshly cracked black
    pepper to taste

Combine all the ingredients in a small bowl and whisk together well.

5. Simple Sesame-Soy Sauce

MAKES ABOUT 1 1/4 CUPS

1/2 cup soy sauce
1/4 cup roasted sesame oil
1/4 cup rice wine vinegar
2 tablespoons peeled and minced
    fresh ginger

1 tablespoon sugar
Kosher salt and freshly cracked white
    pepper to taste

Combine all the ingredients in a small bowl and whisk together well.

COOK TO COOK: We can't emphasize this too much: For success when cooking a whole fish on a standard-size grill, make sure that the fish you choose is 2 pounds or less.

bacon-wrapped scallop tournedos with summer succotash

SERVES 4

Aaron DeRego, head chef at the Back Eddy, was cooking locally and seasonally long before it became fashionable. He created this extremely popular summer dish using the bounty of land and sea that makes it such a pleasure to be a cook in Westport, Massachusetts. We call the scallops "tournedos" because they are a seafood takeoff on the classic dish of that name, chunks of beef tenderloin wrapped in bacon and grilled.

8 slices thick-cut bacon

2 pounds (about 24) super-huge sea scallops

Kosher salt and freshly cracked black pepper to taste

3 tablespoons unsalted butter

2 cups corn kernels (from 2 ears)

2 cups fresh lima beans, peeled, blanched in boiling salted water for 30 seconds, and drained (or substitute thawed frozen lima beans)

1 tomato about the size of a softball, cored and diced small

3 tablespoons chopped fresh sage

1. Build a multi-level fire in your grill: Leaving one-quarter of the bottom free of coals, bank the coals in the remaining three-quarters of the grill so that they are three times as high on one side as on the other. When the coals are all ignited and the temperature has died down to medium (you can hold your hand about 5 inches above the grill grid, over the area where the coals are deepest, for 4 to 5 seconds), you're ready to cook.

2. In a large sauté pan or skillet, cook the bacon over medium-high heat until it has rendered a good amount of fat but has not yet begun to color or crinkle up, about 4 minutes. (You are looking to cook the bacon about halfway—you want it to remain pliable.) Remove from the heat.

3. Thread the scallops onto skewers, putting 3 on each skewer. Wrap a piece of bacon around each trio of scallops, securing it at the top and bottom with toothpicks. Sprinkle the skewers generously with salt and pepper, then put them on the grill over the side with fewer coals and cook until the scallops are opaque all the way through, about 5 to 7 minutes per side.

4. Meanwhile, melt the butter in a large sauté pan over medium heat. Add the corn, lima beans, tomato, sage, and salt and pepper to taste. Sauté, stirring occasionally, until all the ingredients are nice and hot, about 5 minutes.

5. Place about 1/4 of the succotash on each plate, top with 2 skewers, and serve.

COOK TO COOK: Be sure to use the largest scallops you can find in this recipe—and if you can find dry scallops, so much the better. Take it slow when cooking the bacon-wrapped skewers, putting them on the cooler side of the fire and watching carefully for flare-ups.

east coast grill grilled bouillabaisse with roasted red pepper mayo and toast

SERVES 6

This is the classic fish stew of Marseilles moved onto the grill. We make the broth first, then grill the seafood separately and add it to the broth later. This not only allows for each type of seafood to be properly cooked, it also ensures that each maintains its characteristic flavor even when it goes into the broth. This is a fun dish to make, and it's also impressive when you bring it to the table. Serve it with EZ Grilled Bread with Middle Eastern Salad (page 86) or with Caramelized Onions and Blue Cheese (page 82), or try it with Warm Grilled New Potato Salad with Corn and Chiles (page 316).

For the broth:
2 tablespoons olive oil
1 red onion, peeled and thinly sliced
1/2 fennel bulb, trimmed and cut into
    thin strips
3 tablespoons minced garlic
1 tomato about the size of a baseball,
    cored and diced small
1 bottle (750 ml) dry white wine
2 cups bottled clam juice
1 tablespoon anise seeds
1 tablespoon Pernod (optional)
2 cups water
Kosher salt and freshly cracked black
    pepper to taste

For the mayo:
2 roasted red peppers, page 290
    (or substitute jarred roasted
    peppers)
1 teaspoon minced garlic
2 large egg yolks
3 tablespoons fresh lemon juice
1/4 cup olive oil
1/2 cup vegetable oil

1/3 cup roughly chopped fresh
    parsley
Kosher salt and freshly cracked black
    pepper to taste

For the seafood:
6 jumbo (U/12) shrimp, peeled and
    deveined (about 1/2 pound)
1/2 pound large sea scallops
    (about 10)
1 1/2 pounds monkfish, membrane
    removed, cut into 6 equal pieces
1/3 cup olive oil
Kosher salt and freshly cracked black
    pepper to taste
24 mussels, scrubbed and debearded
    (about 2 pounds)
18 littleneck clams, scrubbed (about
    2 pounds)

4 slices crusty bread, 1 inch thick,
    lightly brushed with olive oil on
    both sides

1. Make the broth: In a large sauté pan or skillet over medium-high heat, heat the 2 tablespoons of oil until hot but not smoking. Add the onions and fennel and sauté, stirring occasionally, until the onions are transparent, 7 to 9 minutes. Add the garlic and tomato and cook, stirring frequently, 2 minutes more. Stir in the wine, clam juice, anise seeds, Pernod (if using), and water and bring just to a boil. Reduce the heat to low and simmer gently for 1/2 hour, skimming any film that rises to the surface. Season the

broth to taste with salt and pepper and cover to keep it warm while you grill the seafood. (The broth can be made up to a day ahead; let it cool to room temperature, then cover and refrigerate. Reheat the broth when you are ready to cook the seafood.)

2. While the broth is simmering, make the mayo: Place the red peppers, garlic, egg yolks, and lemon juice in a blender or food processor, cover, and turn it on. Slowly drizzle first the olive oil and then the vegetable oil in through the hole in the cover; as you do so, the mayonnaise will thicken. Add the parsley and season to taste with salt and pepper, then cover and refrigerate until you're ready to serve.

3. Build a fire on one side of your grill, using about enough charcoal to fill a large shoe-box. When all the coals are ignited and the fire has died down to medium-hot (you can hold your hand about 5 inches over the coals for 3 to 4 seconds), you're ready to cook. Place a shallow baking pan large enough to hold all the seafood (and sturdy enough to withstand the heat of a low fire) on the grill over the unheated side. Pour about 2 cups of the broth into the pan.

4. Now prepare the seafood: In a large bowl, combine the shrimp, scallops, and monk-fish with the olive oil and salt and pepper to taste, then toss gently. Put all of the seafood (including the mussels and clams) on the grill over the coals, transferring each piece when it is done to the pan of broth. The shrimp and scallops should take 3 to 4 minutes per side, the monkfish 6 to 8 minutes per side. To check for doneness for these three, cut into one of each and peek; they should be just opaque throughout. The mussels and clams are done when they open; discard any that do not.

5. When there is room on the grill, place the bread around the edge of the fire and toast lightly, about 2 minutes per side.

6. To serve, ladle one-sixth of the seafood and broth into each of 6 large, shallow soup bowls. Top each of the toast slices generously with the mayo and serve on the side for dunking.

COOK TO COOK: This is one of those recipes that include a period of about 15 minutes when you have to really look sharp. You will have some 60 pieces of seafood on the grill at the same time, and making sure each one gets properly cooked without burning is going to take a careful eye and a quick pair of tongs. So be sure to get your *mise en place* together before you put the first thing over the fire.

"roll your own" grilled shrimp and swordfish tacos with traditional garnishes

SERVES 6

This is a neat dish because you can cut up all the garnishes ahead of time, then grill the seafood and set both out on a buffet with the tortillas. We enjoy seeing people make their own tacos and eat them with their hands, so we're very partial to this dish. It also lends itself very well to a long period of intermittent eating interspersed with sipping and chatting. All in all, you won't find a better recipe for a relaxed, convivial summer meal.

We like to buy one large swordfish steak from the fishmonger if he has one and slice it up, since that's easier, and of course we prefer the humongous shrimp. If you can't find good-quality swordfish or have environmental objections to eating it, tuna is a fine substitute in this dish.

All you need to complete the meal is a couple of pitchers of White Sangria with Peaches and Grand Marnier (page 371) and a tropical fruit platter for dessert.

For the garnishes:
1 bunch arugula, well washed, dried, and cut into thin strips
2 red onions, peeled and thinly sliced
2 tomatoes about the size of base-balls, cored and diced small
1 bunch fresh cilantro, well washed, dried, and large stems removed
2 to 4 jalapeño peppers, sliced into super-thin circles
4 ears of corn, blanched in boiling salted water for 2 minutes, drained, and kernels cut off the cob (you should have about 2 cups of kernels)
1 cup small-diced fresh pineapple
1 cup sour cream
3 limes, quartered
2 cups of your favorite store-bought salsa, or make your own using the recipes on pages 328 to 332

2 ripe but firm avocados, peeled, pitted, diced small, and lightly spritzed with fresh lemon juice

———

2 tablespoons minced garlic
2 tablespoons ground cumin
2 tablespoons ground coriander
2 tablespoons ground paprika
1 to 2 tablespoons red pepper flakes
Kosher salt and freshly cracked black pepper to taste
1 pound colossal (U/12) shrimp, peeled and deveined, tails intact
1 1/2 pounds swordfish steak, about 1 inch thick (or substitute tuna)
1/4 cup olive oil
Kosher salt and freshly cracked black pepper to taste
12 corn or flour tortillas, 6 or 8 inches across

1. Build a multi-level fire in your grill: Leaving one-quarter of the bottom free of coals, bank the coals in the remaining three-quarters of the grill so that they are three times as high on one side as on the other. When all the coals are ignited and the temperature

has died down to medium-hot (you can hold your hand about 5 inches above the grill grid, over the area where the coals are deepest, for 3 to 4 seconds), you're ready to cook.

2. Put each of the garnishes in a separate small bowl and arrange the bowls on a platter, then cover and set aside until serving time.

3. In another small bowl, combine the garlic, cumin, coriander, paprika, pepper flakes, and salt and pepper and mix well to combine. Coat the shrimp and swordfish lightly with the olive oil, then rub them all over with this spice mixture. Place the shrimp and swordfish on the grill and cook until they are opaque all the way through, about 3 to 4 minutes per side for the shrimp and 4 to 6 minutes per side for the swordfish. To check for doneness, nick, peek, and cheat: Cut into one of the shrimp and into the thickest part of the fish and peek to be sure that both are just opaque throughout. Transfer the seafood to a platter and cover to keep warm.

4. Put the tortillas on the grill and cook briefly, flipping every 10 seconds or so, until they are soft and pliable, about 1 minute. Cut the shrimp in half and slice the fish into 6 pieces. Wrap the stack of warm tortillas in a large napkin or foil, then rush them to the table along with the platter of garnishes and the platter of seafood, so your guests can "roll their own."

COOK TO COOK: The garnishes for this dish require a fair amount of chopping. To make it easier to get everything to the table together, you can prepare all of the garnishes except the avocado up to 8 hours ahead of time, then cover and refrigerate them until an hour or so before serving time. The avocado is best if cut up just before serving.

barbecued "baked stuffed" spiny lobster with mango beurre blanc

SERVES 4

It's exciting to be a chef these days—some of the stuff that I (Chris) get to do as part of my work is amazing. This is a recipe I developed with my colleague Jimmy Burke on Petite St. Vincent in the Caribbean. Hayes and Lynn Richardson, who own this beautiful small island, invited Jimmy and me to cook with their chef, Marcus. We brought some ingredients of our own along, and Marcus introduced us to some of his favorites, among them spiny lobsters. Basically this is a lobster with a huge tail and no claws. I know it's heresy for a New Englander to say this, but I prefer the spiny lobster to the American version; the meat is not as sweet, and it has a little more texture and a bit more pronounced flavor.

This recipe is designed to take advantage of the incredible amount of tail meat in the spiny lobster. What you do is split the tails lengthwise and grill the halves just long enough to get a little sear on them, then lift the meat up from the shell and put some crab-avocado stuffing under it. You then put the tail halves back on the grill and cook them through over indirect heat, then serve them with a mango-flavored version of beurre blanc, the classic French "white butter" sauce. While we're not usually all that much in favor of "fusion" food, we think this one makes sense, particularly given the history of French influences in the Caribbean.

Serve this elegant dish with Warm Grilled New Potato Salad with Corn and Chiles (page 316) and a simple salad of tomatoes and avocados.

For the stuffing:
2 tablespoons olive oil
1 red onion, peeled and diced small
1 tablespoon prepared curry powder
12 ounces fresh lump crabmeat
1 ripe but firm avocado, peeled, pitted, and diced small
1/2 cup toasted unseasoned bread- crumbs
1/4 cup roughly chopped fresh parsley
Kosher salt and coarsely ground black pepper to taste

For the beurre blanc:
1 ripe but firm mango, peeled, pitted, and diced small

1/2 red onion, peeled and diced small
2 cups dry white wine
1 cup orange juice
1/4 cup fresh lime juice (about 2 limes)
1 cup cold unsalted butter, cut into small chunks
Kosher salt and freshly cracked white pepper (or substitute black) to taste

---

4 spiny lobster tails, 8 to 10 ounces each, cut in half lengthwise (or substitute regular lobster tails)
3 tablespoons vegetable oil
1 lime, cut into thin wedges, for garnish (optional)

1. Build a multi-level fire in your grill: Leaving one-quarter of the bottom free of coals, bank the coals in the remaining three-quarters of the grill so that they are three times as high on one side as on the other. When all the coals are ignited and the fire temperature is hot (you can hold your hand about 5 inches above the grill grid, over the area where the coals are deepest, for 2 seconds or less), you're ready to cook.

2. Make the stuffing for the lobster: In a large sauté pan or skillet over medium-high heat, heat the oil until it is hot but not smoking. Add the onion and sauté, stirring occasionally, until transparent, 7 to 9 minutes. Add the curry powder and cook, stirring frequently, 1 minute more. Remove the pan from the heat and let it cool for about 5 minutes, then gently fold in the crab, avocado, breadcrumbs, parsley, and salt and pepper and set aside.

3. Begin the beurre blanc: Combine the mango, red onion, white wine, orange juice, and lime juice in a small saucepan and bring to a boil over medium-high heat. Reduce the heat slightly and simmer vigorously until most of the liquid has evaporated, about 30 minutes. (Check it every 5 minutes or so after the first 15 minutes to be sure the liquid has not all disappeared, which would burn the other stuff.) Remove from the heat and set aside.

4. Rub the lobster tails all over with the oil, sprinkle them generously with salt and pepper, and place on the grill meat side down. Cook for just 3 minutes, then remove the tails from the heat. Holding one with your tongs, use a fork to gently lift up the meat at the large (head) end, being careful that it stays attached at the tail end. Tuck some of the stuffing under the meat all along the length of the shell. Lay the lobster meat back on top of the stuffing, and press gently to reshape the tail. Repeat with the remaining lobster tails.

5. Place the lobsters, meat side up, over the side of the grill that has no fire. Cover them with a foil pan and cook slowly until the stuffing is hot and the lobster meat is opaque throughout, about 6 to 8 minutes. To check for doneness, nick, peek, and cheat: Cut into one of the tails at its thickest point and peek to be sure it is opaque all the way through.

6. While the lobsters are cooking, finish the beurre blanc: Return the mango mixture to the stove over medium heat and whisk in the butter, chunk by chunk, until it is all incorporated. Season with salt and pepper and remove the sauce from the heat.

7. Arrange the lobster tails meat side up on a platter, spoon the sauce across them, and serve, garnished with lime wedges if you want.

COOK TO COOK: Spiny lobsters, also known as rock lobsters, are found in warm waters around the globe and in cold water in the southern hemisphere. Unlike Maine lobsters, they have no claws, so all of their meat is in the tail. In this country you usually have to buy them frozen, but that is fine.

GRILLED FRESH MOZZARELLA AND BREAD SKEWERS
WITH TOMATOES, RED ONION, AND PESTO VINAIGRETTE . . . P. 30

NEW-SCHOOL GRILLED BUFFALO WINGS WITH BLUE CHEESE DRESSING
AND CUCUMBER SPEARS . . . P. 51

EZ GRILL BREAD WITH ASIAGO, PROSCIUTTO, AND SUN-DRIED TOMATOES (IN BACK);
WITH SHRIMP, ARTICHOKE HEARTS, AND BACON (IN FRONT) . . . PP. 83 AND 84

GRILLED PEEL-AND-EAT COLOSSAL SHRIMP
WITH GARLIC-TABASCO BUTTER . . . P. 99

GRILLED CLAMS ON
THE HALF SHELL
WITH TABASCO,
LEMON, AND GARLIC
. . . P. 116

GRILLED THAI-
STYLE SQUID WITH
LIME, CHILE, AND
PEANUTS OVER
ASIAN NOODLES
. . . P. 125

GRILLED GIANT PORTERHOUSE (OR T-BONE)
AND GRILLED POTATO STEAKS . . . PP. 144 AND 298

GRILLED GIANT PORK CHOPS WITH SWEET PEACH BARBECUE SAUCE
AND ASH-ROASTED CORN . . . PP. 166 AND 287

SMOKE-ROASTED WHOLE FRESH HAM WITH ORANGE-PINEAPPLE CHUTNEY
AND A HOBO PACK OF BEETS, CARROTS, AND APPLES . . . PP. 180 AND 300

GRILLED BUTTERFLIED LEG OF LAMB WITH GREEK GARNISHES . . . P. 196

SPICE-CRUSTED BLUEFISH "NEW BEDFORD"
WITH MUSSELS, CHOURICO, AND TOMATOES . . . P. 208

EAST COAST GRILL GRILLED BOUILLABAISSE
WITH ROASTED RED PEPPER MAYO AND TOAST . . . P. 234

BACON-WRAPPED SCALLOP TOURNEDOS WITH SUMMER SUCCOTASH . . . P. 233

GRILLED CHICKEN AND SAUSAGE TOSSED WITH PEACHES, PEPPERS, PECORINO, AND BLACK OLIVE VINAIGRETTE . . . P. 250

SIMPLE GARLIC- AND HERB-CRUSTED SMOKE-ROASTED FLATTENED
WHOLE CHICKEN AND CORN PUDDING . . . PP. 252 AND 254

GRILLED PEPPERED PORTOBELLO STEAKS
WITH PARMESAN DRESSING . . . P. 282

GRILLED PEACHES WITH VANILLA ICE CREAM AND
FRESH STRAWBERRY SAUCE . . . P. 378

back eddy–style grilled lobster
with three topping options

SERVES 4

Partly because lobsters are so expensive, I (Chris) have always been a crab guy. But over the past few years, thanks to Cheryl and Bob Gifford, owners of Lee's Wharf in Westport, Massachusetts, who buy from all the local lobstermen and sell to the public as well as to restaurants like the Back Eddy, we have come to be more appreciative of the virtues of this luxe crustacean. I also put out some of my own lobster traps this past summer, and of course I ended up cooking the ones that I caught, along with my nephew Tommy, who often helped me haul up the traps. Since food always tastes better when you have gathered it yourself, these were the best lobsters I'd ever had.

In the course of cooking so many lobsters, we found that they're particularly delicious when grilled, since the slight smoky sear from the grilling fire complements the rich meat beautifully. Although we tend to prefer our lobsters served very simply, with nothing more than salt and pepper and lemon butter, here we're providing a couple of slightly more complicated topping options as well. They're all good choices, depending on your mood.

Serve this with corn on the cob (see Four Grilled Corn Strategies, page 286) and boiled potatoes with butter and parsley.

4 live lobsters, 2 to 2 1/2 pounds each	The topping option of your choice, below
Kosher salt and freshly cracked black pepper to taste	

1. Build a multi-level fire in your grill: Leaving one-quarter of the bottom free of coals, bank the coals in the remaining three-quarters of the grill so that they are three times as high on one side as on the other. When all the coals are ignited and the temperature has died down to medium (you can hold your hand about 5 inches above the grill grid, over the area where the coals are deepest, for 4 to 5 seconds), you're ready to cook.

2. Select and prepare your topping option of choice, below. Set it aside while you deal with the lobsters.

3. Place each lobster on its stomach and insert the point of a large knife into the head just below the eyes. Bring the knife down through the body and tail to split the lobster lengthwise, making sure to cut just through the meat and to leave the shell connected. Lay the lobster open, leaving the two halves slightly attached. Now pull off the claws and attached legs from the lobsters and crack them slightly with the handle of a knife. You want to fracture the shells a bit here, not disintegrate them; one good whack should do the job on each claw and leg.

4. Place the claws and legs on the grill right over the coals, cover with a pie pan, and cook until the meat is just opaque all the way through, about 5 to 7 minutes per side. At the same time, sprinkle the lobster bodies generously with salt and pepper to taste, place them flesh side down on the grill, and cook for 8 to 10 minutes. To check for doneness, lift the tail meat from the shell of one of the lobsters—the exposed meat should be completely opaque, not translucent.

5. Remove the lobsters from the grill and brush, drizzle, or otherwise top them with your accompaniment of choice, then serve, providing nutcrackers for opening the claws and legs.

COOK TO COOK: If you're not into killing lobsters with a knife, you can boil them briefly first (about 2 minutes), then remove the tails and claws and legs and put them on the grill. (Discard the bodies or save them for stock.)

Topping Options

Option 1: Simple Lemon Butter

MAKES 1 CUP

1 cup unsalted butter, melted
Juice of 1 lemon

Stir together the butter and lemon juice. To serve, brush the mixture generously over the lobster meat, then pass the rest separately.

Option 2: Crispy Garlic Olive Oil with Parsley and Capers

MAKES 1 CUP

6 garlic cloves, thinly sliced
1/2 cup extra-virgin olive oil
3 tablespoons capers, well rinsed
1/4 cup flat parsley leaves, well
    washed and dried

Juice of 1 lemon (about 1/4 cup)
Kosher salt and freshly cracked black
    pepper to taste

Combine the garlic and oil in a small sauté pan or skillet and sauté over medium heat until the garlic is browned but not burned, about 2 to 3 minutes. Remove from heat and stir in the remaining ingredients. To serve, drizzle the mixture over the lobster meat.

Option 3: Sweet Corn Relish

MAKES 1 CUP

2 ears of corn, blanched in boiling
    salted water for 2 minutes,
    drained, and kernels cut off the
    cob (about 1 cup of kernels)
1/3 cup cider vinegar
2 tablespoons sugar

2 tablespoons celery seeds
3 tablespoons roughly chopped fresh
    chervil or parsley
Kosher salt and freshly cracked black
    pepper to taste

In a small bowl, combine all the ingredients and toss them together well. Cover and let stand at room temperature at least an hour if possible, to blend the flavors. To serve, spoon some of the relish over the lobster meat.

cumin-crusted grilled chicken breasts with orange-chipotle barbecue sauce

SERVES 4

In this quick treatment, boneless chicken breasts are coated before grilling with whole cumin seeds, resulting in a crunchy and very flavorful crust. It's worth a trip to the store for the whole seeds for this one. We finish the dish with a full-on barbecue sauce featuring our favorite chile pepper, the dried and smoked jalapeño known as chipotle. As always when dealing with sauces that contain sugar, you brush it on each side of the chicken only during the last 30 seconds or so of cooking.

Serve this chicken with Pan-Fried Sweet Plantains with Sour Cream (page 293) and Smoky Corn and Tomato Salad with Cilantro Vinaigrette (page 319).

For the sauce:
2 tablespoons olive oil
1 small red onion, peeled and diced small
2 tablespoons minced garlic
2 to 3 tablespoons mashed chipotle peppers in adobo sauce, or to taste
1 ripe tomato about the size of a baseball, diced small
2 cups orange juice
1 cup white vinegar
1/2 cup catsup
1/4 cup light or dark brown sugar

1/4 cup molasses
Kosher salt and freshly cracked black pepper to taste
Juice of 1 lime (about 2 tablespoons)
1/2 cup roughly chopped fresh cilantro

———

4 boneless, skin-on full chicken breasts, 10 to 12 ounces each
1/3 cup toasted whole cumin seeds (or substitute 1 1/2 tablespoons ground cumin)
Kosher salt and freshly cracked black pepper to taste

1. Build a multi-level fire in your grill: Leaving one-quarter of the bottom free of coals, bank the coals in the remaining three-quarters of the grill so that they are three times as high on one side as on the other. When all the coals are ignited and the temperature has died down to medium (you can hold your hand about 5 inches above the grill grid, over the area where the coals are deepest, for 4 to 5 seconds), you're ready to cook.

2. In a large sauté pan or skillet over medium-high heat, heat the oil until it is hot but not smoking. Add the onion and sauté, stirring occasionally, until golden brown, 11 to 13 minutes. Add the garlic, chipotles, and tomato and cook, stirring frequently, for 3 minutes more. Stir in the orange juice and vinegar, bring to a boil, then reduce the heat

to medium and simmer vigorously, stirring occasionally, until the mixture is reduced by about two-thirds, about 30 minutes. Stir in the catsup, sugar, molasses, and salt and pepper to taste and cook for 5 minutes more. Transfer the sauce to a blender and purée until smooth (be careful with the hot liquid). Allow the sauce to cool slightly, then stir in the lime juice and cilantro. Reserve 1/4 cup sauce for basting the chicken and pour the remaining sauce into a small serving bowl.

3. Rub the chicken breasts on both sides with the cumin seeds, pressing down gently to be sure they adhere, and sprinkle generously with salt and pepper. Place the breasts, skin side down, on the grill directly over the coals and cook, turning over once, until the chicken is opaque all the way through, about 7 to 9 minutes per side, brushing with the barbecue sauce during the last 30 seconds of cooking on each side. To check for doneness, poke one of the breasts with your finger to test its firmness level (see page 13); if you're unsure, nick, peek, and cheat: Make a small cut in the thickest part of one of the breasts and check to be sure that it is opaque all the way through, with no red near the bone.

4. Serve the chicken hot, passing the remaining sauce on the side.

COOK TO COOK: You want to be sure to cook the chicken all the way through without burning it on the outside. So don't rush—be certain that your fire has died down to medium before you put the chicken on the grill.

grilled chicken breasts over fresh corn risotto with parmesan-tomato relish

SERVES 4

This is an inside-outside situation: risotto is cooking on the stove inside and chicken is on the grill outside. If you have got two cooks, have one start the chicken when the other is about halfway on the risotto so both get done at about the same time. If you're on your own, the order goes like this: start the fire, throw together the relish (unless you did that yesterday), make the risotto, keep it warm, grill the chicken.

This is a wonderful menu for late summer when fresh corn and garden tomatoes appear at farmers' markets. All you need to round out the feast is an arugula salad. Or you could also serve it with Parsley Salad with Tomatoes and Bulgur (page 311) or Crispy Prosciutto-Wrapped Asparagus (page 75).

For the relish:
1 cup diced ripe tomato (about 1 large tomato)
1/3 cup extra-virgin olive oil
1/4 cup roughly chopped fresh basil
Juice of 1 lemon (about 1/4 cup)
Kosher salt and freshly cracked black pepper to taste
1/2 cup freshly grated Parmesan cheese

For the risotto:
4 to 6 cups chicken stock
3 tablespoons unsalted butter
1 small onion, peeled and diced small

1 1/2 cups arborio rice
3 ears of corn, blanched in boiling salted water for 2 minutes, drained, and kernels cut off the cob (about 1 1/2 cups of kernels)
1/4 cup freshly grated Parmesan cheese
Kosher salt and freshly cracked black pepper to taste

4 boneless, skin-on full chicken breasts, 10 to 12 ounces each
Kosher salt and freshly cracked black pepper to taste

1. Build a multi-level fire in your grill: Leaving one-quarter of the bottom free of coals, bank the coals in the remaining three-quarters of the grill so that they are three times as high on one side as on the other. When all the coals are ignited and the temperature has died down to medium (you can hold your hand about 5 inches above the grill grid, over the area where the coals are deepest, for 4 to 5 seconds), you're ready to cook.

2. Make the relish: In a small bowl, toss together the tomatoes, olive oil, basil, lemon juice, and salt and pepper until well mixed. Just before serving, stir in the Parmesan cheese.

3. Make the risotto: In a medium saucepan, bring the chicken stock to a boil, then reduce the heat to low and keep it at a simmer. In a large sauté pan or skillet, melt the butter over medium heat. Add the onion and cook, stirring occasionally, until it is translucent, 7 to 9 minutes. Add the rice, stirring to coat with the butter, and cook until

the rice just begins to color, 3 to 4 minutes. Add the simmering stock 1/2 cup at a time, stirring constantly until all the liquid is absorbed each time before adding more, until the rice is tender but still has a bit of chew and the liquid is very creamy. It should take 25 to 30 minutes. About 5 minutes before the rice is finished, stir in the corn. When the rice is done, remove the pan from heat, then stir in the Parmesan and season to taste with salt and pepper. Cover the pan to keep the risotto warm while you grill the chicken.

4. Sprinkle the chicken breasts generously with salt and pepper, put them on the grill skin side down, and cook, turning once, until they are opaque all the way through, about 7 to 9 minutes per side. To check for doneness, poke the chicken with your finger to test its firmness level (see page 13); if you're unsure, nick, peek, and cheat: Make a small cut in the thickest part of one of the breasts and check to be sure that it is opaque all the way through, with no red near the bone.

5. To serve, divide the risotto among 4 shallow pasta bowls. Slice the chicken on the bias and fan the slices over the risotto. Top with a spoonful of the relish, garnish with a sprig of fresh basil if desired, and serve hot.

COOK TO COOK: Be sure to get the skin side of the breasts nice and crisp, then flip them over to finish cooking. If you need to move the breasts off to the side and cover them with a disposable foil pan to get them cooked all the way through without burning, go right ahead and do that. It's always okay.

grilled bone-in garlic chicken breasts with lemon, parsley, and grilled figs

SERVES 4

※ ※ ※ ※ ※ ※ ※ ※ ※ ※ ※ ※ ※ ※ ※ ※ ※ ※

Here's a little secret: A bone-in chicken breast is just about the hardest thing to grill properly. In fact, grilling is not the ideal technique for bone-in chicken. Like sautéing, it is a high-heat cooking method best suited to foods that can be cooked through quickly without burning on the outside. With that bone in the center, a breast in no way qualifies. But for some reason everybody thinks it's perfect for the grill and cooks it directly over the coals for the whole time, just like a burger—which results in its being one of the most consistently screwed-up grill dishes around.

But here's another secret: A bone-in chicken breast properly cooked over live fire is a real treat, considerably more flavorful than its boneless counterpart. So this is the deal: You build a multi-level fire and sear the chicken over the hottest part (which is at medium heat), then move it to a cooler part, cover it with a disposable foil pan, and let it finish cooking all the way through. (If you have got time and want to ensure that the chicken stays moist, let it sit in brine for a couple of hours before it goes over the flames.) To enhance the flavor, we dip the smoky, juicy chicken in a garlicky, lemony vinaigrette, then garnish it with one of our bedrock favorites, grilled figs.

Serve this with Orange-Raisin Couscous with Almonds and Parsley (page 321) and Smoky Acorn Squash with Maple-Vanilla Butter (page 296).

For the brine (optional):
1 quart water
3/4 cup sugar
3/4 cup kosher salt
_____

4 bone-in, skin-on split chicken
    breasts, about 10 ounces each
4 tablespoons plus 1 teaspoon
    minced garlic

Kosher salt and freshly cracked black
    pepper to taste
1/4 cup extra-virgin olive oil
Juice of 1 lemon
1/3 cup roughly chopped fresh
    parsley
8 fresh ripe but firm figs, halved
    lengthwise
2 tablespoons vegetable oil

1. For the brining (optional step): In a bowl or pot large enough to hold the chicken, stir together the water, sugar, and salt until the sugar and salt completely dissolve. Add the chicken breasts, making sure they are submerged in the liquid; add additional water if necessary to cover. Place in the refrigerator for 2 to 5 hours, then remove the breasts from the brine, discard the brine, and pat the breasts dry with paper towels.

2. Build a multi-level fire in your grill: Leaving one-quarter of the bottom free of coals, bank the coals in the remaining three-quarters of the grill so that they are three times as high on one side as on the other. When all the coals are ignited and the temperature has died down to medium (you can hold your hand about 5 inches above the grill grid,

over the area where the coals are deepest, for 4 to 5 seconds), you're ready to cook the chicken.

3. Rub the chicken breasts with the 4 tablespoons of garlic and sprinkle them generously with salt and pepper. Place them skin side down on the hottest part of the grill and cook until the skin is very brown and crisp, about 4 minutes; flip and cook on the other side for an additional 4 minutes. Now move the breasts to the cooler side of the grill, place them skin side down, cover them with an inverted foil pan, and cook until they are completely opaque but not dried out, about 10 to 12 minutes. To check for doneness, poke the chicken with your finger to test its firmness level (see page 13); if you're unsure, nick, peek, and cheat: Make a small cut in the thickest part of one of the breasts and check to be sure that it is opaque all the way through, with no red near the bone.

4. While the chicken is cooking, make the vinaigrette: Whisk together the olive oil, lemon juice, parsley, and the remaining teaspoon of garlic in a large bowl. When the breasts are done, place them one at a time in the bowl with the vinaigrette. Turn each breast over a couple of times with your tongs to coat, then transfer it to a serving platter. Drizzle any remaining dressing over the chicken. Cover loosely with foil to keep warm while you grill the figs.

5. Rub the fig halves with the vegetable oil and sprinkle them with salt and pepper. Place them on the grill cut side down and cook until just nicely browned, about 2 to 3 minutes.

6. Remove the foil from the chicken, arrange the figs around the breasts on the platter, and serve.

COOK TO COOK: Chicken breast terminology is a little confusing. When you say "breast," you are properly referring to a double breast, while a single breast is correctly referred to as a "cutlet." However, most consumers call a single breast just that—a "breast." To make our meaning clear, we refer to the double breast as a "full breast" and the single breast, or cutlet, as a "split breast." Just so you know.

grilled chicken and sausage tossed with peaches, peppers, pecorino, and black olive vinaigrette

SERVES 4 TO 6

In this country we are used to meals that consist of a big piece of protein accompanied by side dishes. But in much of the rest of the world, a fairly small amount of meat or fish or fowl is combined with other ingredients to create a healthful dish with lots of different individual flavors. Here we showcase that approach. What we do is grill a bunch of stuff—chicken breasts, sausages, onions, and bell peppers—and then cut it all up and toss it with peaches and a vinaigrette with the loamy taste of black olives, topping it all off with a shower of shaved Pecorino. It's easy, light, and flavor-packed—a great summer lunch.

All you need to make this a meal is some crusty bread and maybe Grilled Eggplant Steaks with Minted Yogurt-Cucumber Relish (page 279).

1/3 cup extra-virgin olive oil	2 pounds boneless, skin-on split
1/4 cup balsamic vinegar	chicken breasts
1 teaspoon minced garlic	1 pound hot Italian sausage links
1/4 cup pitted, chopped, good-quality	2 red bell peppers, halved and
black olives	seeded
Kosher salt and freshly cracked black	1 red onion, peeled and sliced thick
pepper to taste	1/4 cup vegetable oil
2 ripe but firm peaches, pitted and	1/2 pound very thinly shaved
each cut into 8 chunks	Pecorino Romano cheese
1 cup flat parsley leaves, well washed	
and dried	

1. Build a multi-level fire in your grill: Leaving one-quarter of the bottom free of coals, bank the coals in the remaining three-quarters of the grill so that they are three times as high on one side as on the other. When all the coals are ignited and the temperature has died down to medium (you can hold your hand about 5 inches above the grill grid, over the area where the coals are deepest, for 4 to 5 seconds), you're ready to cook.

2. In a large bowl, whisk together the extra-virgin olive oil, vinegar, garlic, black olives, and salt and pepper to taste. Stir in the peaches and parsley and set aside.

3. Sprinkle the chicken generously with salt and pepper and place over the coals skin side down. Grill until the breasts are just opaque throughout, about 7 to 9 minutes per side. To check for doneness, nick, peek, and cheat: Cut into one of the breasts at the thickest point and peek to be sure it is opaque all the way through, with no pinkness. Soon after you start grilling the chicken, put the sausages on the grill and cook, rolling around occasionally, until they are heated through, 8 to 12 minutes, moving the sausage briefly to the side with no coals if there are flare-ups. When the chicken and

the sausage are both done, cut them into bite-size pieces and add to the bowl with the vinaigrette and peaches.

4. Coat the pepper halves and onion slices with the vegetable oil and sprinkle generously with salt and pepper. Place on the grill and cook until both are well browned, about 2 to 3 minutes per side. Cut into bite-sized pieces and add them to the bowl with the meat and peaches.

5. Toss all the ingredients together until everything is well coated with the dressing. Transfer to a serving bowl, sprinkle with the shaved Pecorino, and serve.

COOK TO COOK: Make sure your fire is medium here—if it's hotter, the skin of the chicken will scorch; if it's cooler, you won't get enough of a sear.

simple garlic- and herb-crusted smoke-roasted flattened whole chicken

SERVES 6

If you're among those folks who find smoke-roasting a little intimidating, then this is the dish for you. There's nothing quite so easy as cooking a whole chicken in a kettle grill, because it cooks pretty quickly and you don't have to worry about getting it tender. It is a sure-fire confidence builder; we're willing to bet that you'll start using the technique a lot after you try it on this dish. And it's a guaranteed crowd pleaser—most everybody likes chicken, particularly when it's got a little smoke on it. Even if we are cooking for only two or three people, we still like to smoke-roast two chickens so we can have one to take with us to the beach or for chicken salad the next day.

Serve with any hobo pack (pages 300 to 305) and grilled corn made by the strategy you prefer (page 286). And make some nice Cheesy Chipotle Cornbread (page 323) to go along.

For the spice rub:
1/4 cup minced garlic
1/4 cup crushed coriander seeds (or substitute 2 tablespoons ground)
1/2 cup roughly chopped mixed fresh herbs of your choice (oregano, sage, rosemary, parsley)

1/4 cup olive oil
Kosher salt and freshly cracked black pepper to taste
———
2 whole chickens, 3 pounds each
Kosher salt and freshly cracked black pepper to taste

1. Light a fire well over to one side of a large kettle grill, using about enough charcoal to fill 1 1/2 large shoeboxes.

2. In a small bowl, combine all the ingredients for the spice rub and mix well.

3. Dry the chickens with paper towels, put them on a cutting board breast side up, and push down hard on their backbones to flatten them as much as possible. Sprinkle them generously with salt and pepper, then rub them all over with the spice mixture, pressing down gently to be sure it adheres.

4. When the fire has died down and all the coals are covered with white ash, place the chickens on the side of the grill with no coals, breast side down, with the legs facing toward the coals, being careful that none of the meat is directly over the coals. Put the lid on the grill with the vents open one-quarter of the way. Cook for 30 minutes, then turn the chicken to breast side up, add another 1/2 shoebox full of fresh charcoal, and continue cooking until the bird is opaque all the way through, about 30 to 45 minutes more. To check for doneness, nick, peek, and cheat: Cut into the thickest part of one of

the thighs, all the way to the bone; there should be no pinkness. (It's hard to use a thermometer with a flattened bird, but if you choose to, you're looking for a final temperature of 160°F.)

5. When the chickens are done, remove them from the heat, cover them loosely with foil, and let them rest for about 10 minutes. Then split each one down the backbone and serve.

COOK TO COOK: Smoke-roasting is basically cooking by indirect heat just as you do in classic barbecuing but at a somewhat higher temperature and in much less time. This technique comes in handy when you have a lot of people coming to dinner. You just put the food on the grill, close the cover, and refuel once during the process while you hang out and socialize. You can even throw a hobo pack or two onto the coals so your side dish is cooking at the same time.

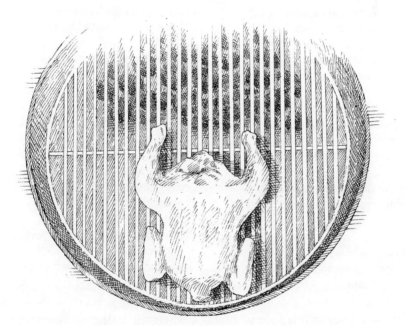

barbecue-style smoke-roasted flattened whole chicken with corn pudding

SERVES 6

We're so fond of smoke-roasted flattened chicken that we want you to have two options. Once you've got your confidence up with the simple version (page 252), give this one a try. It's actually no more complicated, it just takes a little more time to put together. But with a classic barbecue rub, a quick and easy barbecue sauce, and a sweet and tender corn pudding to go along with the smoky chicken, this is a Southern feast all ready to go. Just add salad.

For the spice rub:
4 tablespoons ground paprika
2 tablespoons ground cumin
2 tablespoons chili powder
2 tablespoons white sugar
2 tablespoons light or dark brown
    sugar
2 tablespoons kosher salt
2 tablespoons freshly cracked black
    pepper
1 tablespoon cayenne pepper

———

2 whole chickens, 3 pounds each
Kosher salt and freshly cracked black
    pepper to taste

For the corn pudding:
2 cups fresh corn kernels (from about
    4 ears of corn)

2 cups milk, warmed slightly
2 large eggs, lightly beaten
2 tablespoons unsalted butter,
    melted
4 or 5 dashes of Tabasco sauce, or
    to taste
1 teaspoon sugar
1 teaspoon kosher salt
1/2 teaspoon freshly cracked black
    pepper

For the sauce:
1 cup catsup
2 tablespoons cider vinegar
3 tablespoons molasses
3 tablespoons steak sauce of your
    choice
Kosher salt and freshly cracked black
    pepper to taste

1. Light a fire well over to one side of a large kettle grill, using about enough charcoal to fill half of a large shoebox.

2. In a small bowl, combine all the rub ingredients and mix well.

3. Dry the chickens with paper towels, put them on a cutting board breast side up, and push down on their backbones to flatten them as much as possible. Sprinkle them generously with salt and pepper, then rub them all over with the spice mixture, pressing down gently to be sure it adheres.

4. When the fire has died down and all the coals are covered with white ash, place the chickens on the side of the grill with no coals, breast side down, with the legs facing toward the coals, being careful that none of the meat is directly over the coals. Put the lid on the grill with the vents one-quarter of the way open and cook the bird for 30 minutes, then turn it breast side up, add another 1/2 shoebox full of fresh charcoal, and continue cooking until the bird is opaque all the way through, about 30 to 45 minutes more. To check for doneness, nick, peek, and cheat: Cut into the thickest part of one of the thighs, all the way to the bone; there should be no pinkness. (It's hard to use a thermometer with a flattened bird, but if you choose to, you're looking for a final temperature of 160°F.)

5. While the chickens are on the grill, make the corn pudding: Preheat the oven to 350°F. In a medium bowl, combine all the pudding ingredients and mix well. Pour the batter into a buttered oven-proof casserole, set the casserole into a larger roasting pan, and fill the roasting pan with enough hot water to come halfway up the sides of the casserole. Place in the preheated oven and bake until the pudding is firm but still jiggles very slightly in the center, about 40 to 45 minutes.

6. While the pudding is baking, make the sauce: In a small saucepan over medium-high heat, combine all of the sauce ingredients and bring just to a boil. Reduce the heat to low and simmer until the flavors are melded and the sauce is slightly thickened, about 15 minutes.

7. When the chickens are done, remove them from the grill, cover them loosely with foil, and allow them to rest for about 10 minutes. Then split each one down the backbone and serve, accompanied by the barbecue sauce and corn pudding.

COOK TO COOK: Make sure the legs of the bird are closest to the fire here, since they take longer to cook than the breast.

slow-grilled mustard-crusted butterflied game hens with smoky, lemony red onion rings

SERVES 4

We're going to confess something—we think poultry is the hardest thing to get just right on the grill, perfectly cooked through but not burned on the outside. If you use small birds like these game hens, butterfly them so they lie flat, and grill them slowly, you'll have a better shot at hitting the mark. Even so, this dish is a little tricky. But it tastes fantastic, it looks beautiful, and if you're a serious grill person you need to accept the challenge, because this is another requirement for your Ph.G. (Doctorate of Grilling).

Get your butcher to butterfly the birds for you if possible. Use a medium-low fire to cook the birds slowly, starting out skin side down so they get very crisp, then flipping them and finishing the cooking. It's important to watch carefully here, being prepared at a moment's notice to move the birds to the side of the fire with fewer coals if they start to burn. You also should keep an eye on the onions, which get tossed with lemon and herbs and are on the grill at the same time. They make a flavorful complement to the tender hens.

You might serve these birds with Grilled Fingerling Potatoes with Blue Cheese (page 297) or Grilled Broccoli Rabe with Sun-Dried Tomatoes, Balsamic Vinegar, and Pine Nuts (page 283).

4 Rock Cornish game hens, about
    1 1/2 pounds each, butterflied
    with backbone removed
6 tablespoons olive oil, divided
Kosher salt and freshly cracked black
    pepper to taste
3 tablespoons minced garlic
1/4 cup lightly cracked mustard
    seeds

2 large red onions, peeled and sliced
    1 inch thick
1/4 cup fresh lemon juice (about
    1 lemon)
3 tablespoons extra-virgin olive oil
1/4 cup roughly chopped fresh herbs:
    any one or a combination of
    thyme, parsley, and oregano

1. Build a multi-level fire in your grill: Leaving one-quarter of the bottom free of coals, bank the coals in the remaining three-quarters of the grill so that they are three times as high on one side as on the other. When all the coals are ignited and the temperature has died down to medium-low (you can hold your hand about 5 inches above the grill grid, over the area where the coals are deepest, for 5 seconds), you're ready to cook.

2. Rub the butterflied hens with 3 tablespoons of the olive oil and sprinkle them generously with salt and pepper. In a small bowl, combine the garlic and mustard seeds and mix well. Coat the hens with this mixture, pressing down gently so it adheres, and set them aside.

3. Rub the onions with the remaining 3 tablespoons of olive oil and sprinkle them generously with salt and pepper.

4. Place the hens on the grill, skin side down, over the side with more coals. Place the onions on the grill over the side with fewer coals. Cook the onions until they are brown and soft, about 15 minutes per side. Cook the hens until the skin is nicely browned on the first side, about 15 minutes. (If the skin starts to get too dark, move the hens to the side with fewer coals and continue to cook for the remainder of the 15 minutes.) Flip them over and cook until the second side is also brown and crisp, about 15 minutes more, again moving the hens to the side with fewer coals if the skin starts to get too black. Now check for doneness: Cut into one of the hens in the thigh or where the wing meets the breast; there should be no pink. Remove the hens from the grill, cover them loosely with foil, and set them aside.

5. When the onions are done, transfer them to a medium bowl. Add the lemon juice, extra-virgin olive oil, and herbs, then toss to coat the onions and separate them into rings. Season to taste with salt and pepper.

6. Serve each game hen topped with a pile of the grilled onion rings.

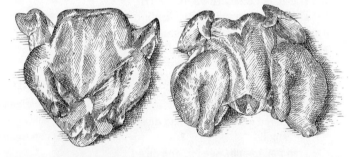

COOK TO COOK: The key to success with the onions is making sure they stay together on the grill; we suggest using a spatula to turn them and remove them from the grill. If you don't have room for the onions and the game hens on your grill at the same time, cook the hens first, then cover them with foil while you cook the onions.

hens get small

* * *

Although they may sound exotic and even a bit weird, Rock Cornish game hens are actually just a cross of two types of chicken, the White Rock and the Cornish. What makes them distinctive is that they are bred specifically to be eaten very young and therefore very small, usually weighing in at between 1 and 1 1/2 pounds. A Rock Cornish game hen is almost as tender as a poussin, the name given to a baby chicken about a month old. But because of its breeding, the game hen has better flavor. We like them because you serve one to each person, which always seems very luxurious and celebratory.

smoke-roasted game hens with linguiça-apricot stuffing and basil-balsamic sauce

SERVES 4 HUNGRY FOLKS

Here's another option for those cool little game hens, a bit fancier because it includes a stuffing. If you're in a hurry, of course, you can either smoke-roast the hens with no stuffing or just stuff them with onion quarters and orange segments. But the linguiça and apricot stuffing brings a lot of flavor to the dish, plus the sausage (a very garlicky variety, pronounced "lin-GWEE-suh") helps keep the bird moist as it slowly roasts over the indirect heat and smoke of the fire. As always when smoke-roasting, make sure that no part of the hens is actually over the coals, since the birds need to stay on the grill quite a while to cook through. Unlike chickens, these guys are small enough to cook breast up the whole time, so you don't need to mess around with them as they cook. But since the legs need to cook a little longer than the breasts, it's helpful to place the birds with the legs facing toward the fire.

This is a great little dinner dish. Serve it with Warm Salad of Grilled Eggplant, Summer Squash, and Zucchini (page 315) or Grilled Peppered Portobello Steaks with Parmesan Dressing (page 282).

For the stuffing:
3 tablespoons olive oil
1 large red onion, peeled and diced small
1 red bell pepper, seeded and diced small
1 cup small-diced dried apricots
1/2 pound linguiça, diced small (or substitute chourico or kielbasa)
Kosher salt and freshly cracked black pepper to taste

For the sauce:
1 cup catsup

1/2 cup balsamic vinegar
2 tablespoons light or dark brown sugar
1/2 cup roughly chopped fresh basil
———
4 Rock Cornish game hens, 1 to 1 1/2 pounds each, rinsed inside and out and patted dry
2 tablespoons vegetable oil
4 tablespoons freshly cracked coriander seeds (or substitute 2 tablespoons ground coriander)
4 tablespoons minced garlic

1. Start a fire well over to one side of your grill, using about enough coals to fill a shoebox.

2. In a large sauté pan or skillet over medium-high heat, heat the olive oil until hot but not smoking. Add the onion and bell pepper and sauté, stirring occasionally, until the onion is transparent, about 7 to 9 minutes. Add the apricots, linguiça, and salt and pepper to taste and mix well, then remove from the heat and allow to cool to room temperature.

3. While the stuffing cools, make the sauce: In a small saucepan over medium heat, combine the catsup, vinegar, and brown sugar and bring to a simmer, stirring until the sugar dissolves. Remove the pan from the heat, stir in the basil, and set aside.

4. When the stuffing has come down to room temperature, divide it evenly among the birds, filling each cavity loosely and pinning it closed with a toothpick or skewer. Rub the birds all over with the vegetable oil, sprinkle generously with salt and pepper, and then rub with the coriander and garlic, pressing down gently to be sure they adhere.

5. When the fire dies down and the coals are covered with white ash, put the birds on the side of the grill with no coals underneath, with the breasts facing away from the fire. Be careful that none of the meat is directly over the coals. Brush the birds with the sauce, then put the lid on the grill with the vents one-quarter of the way open and cook, adding a handful of fresh charcoal after 30 minutes, until the birds are opaque throughout, about 1 to 1 1/2 hours, brushing the hens with the sauce every 20 minutes or so. To check for doneness, pierce one of the birds with a fork at the thigh; if the juices run clear, the bird is done.

6. Remove the birds from the grill and serve one to each person, passing any remaining barbecue sauce separately.

COOK TO COOK: Rules are made to be broken, and here we break the maxim that you never put sauces with sugar onto food until the last few minutes of grilling. But we're cooking with indirect heat here, so it's a lot easier to keep the sauce from burning. Just be careful not to overdo it—you don't want any of the sauce dripping into the bottom of the grill and possibly making it over to the coals, where it would cause flare-ups.

grilled spicy duck breast and mango skewers with souped-up soy sauce

SERVES 4

Asian-inspired is our favorite way to go with duck, and duck is also wonderful with fruit, so here we put those two together in what are basically duck and mango kebabs with Asian flavors. For a simple but flavor-packed drizzling and dipping sauce, we pep up some soy sauce with a few other Asian ingredients and a bit of sugar. This is a great sauce to make in advance and keep on hand in the refrigerator; it works very well with fish as well as poultry.

You'll notice that we're marinating here, a process we usually avoid. But with duck, the marinating process seems to draw out some of the fat, so we're going for it.

These skewers make excellent appetizers as well as entrées. Serve them with Aromatic Slaw with Southeast Asian Flavors (page 309) and the rice of your choice.

1/2 cup soy sauce
1/2 cup dry sherry
1/2 cup white vinegar
2 tablespoons sugar
1/4 cup cracked toasted coriander seeds (or substitute 2 tablespoons ground coriander)
3 tablespoons freshly cracked white pepper (or substitute black pepper)
2 pounds boneless duck breast (about 6 single breasts), most of the fat removed, cut into 1 1/2-inch chunks
2 ripe but firm mangoes, peeled and cut into 1-inch chunks
Kosher salt to taste

For the sauce:
3/4 cup good-quality soy sauce
1/4 cup dry sherry
1 tablespoon light or dark brown sugar
3 tablespoons peeled and minced fresh ginger
3 tablespoons minced fresh chile pepper of your choice (or substitute red pepper flakes)
1 teaspoon minced garlic
1/3 cup roughly chopped fresh cilantro (or substitute the green part of scallions)

1. In a bowl large enough to hold the duck, combine the soy sauce, sherry, vinegar, sugar, coriander, and pepper and whisk until the sugar is fully dissolved. Add the duck meat and toss until all the pieces are well coated. Cover and refrigerate for at least 1 hour and up to 12 hours.

2. About 30 minutes before you're ready to cook, build a multi-level fire in your grill: Leaving one-quarter of the bottom free of coals, bank the coals in the remaining three-quarters of the grill so that they are three times as high on one side as on the other. When all the coals are ignited and the temperature has died down to medium (you can hold your hand about 5 inches above the grill grid, over the area where the coals are deepest, for 4 to 5 seconds), you're ready to cook.

3. Remove the duck from the marinade with your tongs, shaking it lightly to get rid of any excess. Discard the marinade. Alternate duck and mango chunks as you thread 4 skewers, then sprinkle them lightly with salt. Put the skewers over the coals and grill until they are nicely browned but not charred, about 5 to 7 minutes per side. To check for doneness, poke the duck with your finger to check its firmness level (see page 13); if you're unsure, nick, peek, and cheat: Make a 1/4-inch cut in one of the chunks and peek at the center to be sure it is just slightly less done than you like it, since it will continue to cook after it is removed from the fire. (We like duck breast medium-rare to medium.)

4. While the skewers are cooking, combine all the sauce ingredients in a small bowl and whisk until the sugar is fully dissolved.

5. To serve, slide the mango and duck off the skewers onto plates, drizzle generously with the sauce, and serve hot.

COOK TO COOK: The key to making this dish hassle-free is to buy the duck breasts already separated; it's a lot of work carving up whole ducks to get them. Fortunately, it is increasingly easy to find duck breasts. Also, use a sharp knife to trim about eighty percent of the fat away, leaving just enough to keep the duck moist over the flames but not enough to cause flare-ups.

smoke-roasted whole duck with
orange-peach marmalade and a sweet potato hobo pack

SERVES 2

When you cook a whole duck, your two main goals are to get the fat out and get the skin crisp. The Chinese, of course, have mastered that with their Peking duck technology. The way we attack the problem is to punch a number of holes into the side of the duck between the wing and the breast, being careful to poke only into the fat layer that sits under the skin, not into the meat itself. Then we rub the duck all over with sherry and let it sit in the refrigerator uncovered overnight. This is one case in which you really shouldn't skip the advance preparation, because it both dries the skin and gets rid of some of the fat.

To accompany the duck, we make a simple orange-peach marmalade (fruit and duck go well together) and an aromatic sweet potato hobo pack. You might serve it with a simple green salad or a green vegetable like steamed green beans, sautéed spinach, or roasted asparagus. To us, this seems like a great menu for a romantic fall afternoon.

1 whole duck, about 5 pounds, all
    excess fat carefully removed
1/2 cup dry sherry
Kosher salt and freshly cracked black
    pepper to taste

For the hobo pack:
1 large sweet potato, peeled and
    diced large
1/2 cup raisins
4 tablespoons unsalted butter,
    cut into small pieces
2 tablespoons light or dark brown
    sugar

2 tablespoons maple syrup
1 cinnamon stick (or substitute
    1 teaspoon ground cinnamon)
Kosher salt and freshly cracked black
    pepper to taste

For the marmalade:
2 cups peaches, pitted and diced
    large
2 cups dry white wine
1 cup orange juice
1 cup light or dark brown sugar
Pinch of ground cloves

1. Use a fork to prick a dozen or so holes through the duck skin down to the layer of fat in the area between the wing and the breast, being careful not to puncture the meat underneath. Pat the duck dry with paper towels, then rub it all over with the sherry. Put it on a plate and refrigerate it overnight.

2. Start a fire well over to one side of a large kettle grill, using about enough coals to fill 2 large shoeboxes.

3. To make the hobo pack: Tear off 4 sheets of heavy-duty foil, each about 2 feet long, and stack them one on top of the other. Arrange the sweet potatoes and raisins on the center of the top sheet. Dot with the butter and top with the brown sugar, maple syrup,

and cinnamon stick or ground cinnamon, then sprinkle generously with salt and pepper. Fold up the sheets of foil around the potatoes, one after the other, turning the package one-quarter turn each time and making sure that each sheet is well sealed around the potatoes. Or put all the hobo pack ingredients into a disposable foil pan and cover tightly with a double layer of heavy-duty foil.

4. When the fire is fully lit, pat the duck dry again and sprinkle it generously with salt and pepper. Place the duck on the grill over the side with no coals with the legs closest to the coals, being careful that none of the duck is directly over the coals. Put the lid on the grill with the vents one-quarter of the way open and cook for 70 to 90 minutes, adding 1/2 shoebox full of fresh charcoal after the first 30 minutes of cooking and shifting the position of the duck after 40 minutes so the breast is closer to the fire. To check for doneness, pierce the leg of the duck and make sure the juices run clear; the leg bone should also wiggle slightly in its socket.

5. Meanwhile, when the duck has cooked for about 30 minutes, place the hobo pack in the coals around the periphery of the fire, where the heat is less intense. Pile the coals up around the pack and cook until the potatoes are tender, about 45 minutes. Remove the pack from the coals and cut open the foil.

6. While the duck and hobo pack are cooking, make the marmalade: Combine the peaches, white wine, orange juice, brown sugar, and cloves in a medium saucepan and bring to a boil over medium-high heat. Reduce the heat to low and simmer gently, skimming any foam that forms on the surface, until the peaches are falling apart and the marmalade is thick, about 25 to 35 minutes. Remove from the heat and set aside to cool.

7. To serve, cut the duck in half. Serve each half topped with a generous spoonful of marmalade and accompanied by half of the sweet potato mixture along with a sharp knife for personal carving.

COOK TO COOK: To carve the duck:
1. Slice straight down on one side of the breastbone, following the shape of the carcass. Repeat on the other side of the breastbone.
2. Keep cutting down the back on either side of the breastbone until you come to the joint that holds the thigh and the wing to the carcass.
3. Cut right on through these joints and you will have cut the bird in half.

straight-on smoke-roasted turkey

SERVES 6

Let's face it, plain old roast turkey is just not that interesting. But you're probably going to end up cooking and serving this big bird at least once a year anyway, so here's a way to bring real flavor to its rather bland meat. First we soak it in brine, which not only makes it more tender but also amplifies its flavor. Then we slowly smoke-roast it in a covered grill so that it picks up all the smokiness from the fire. If you want, you can add some aromatics to the fire (see page 120 for more details), because this is one of those situations in which the food spends enough time over the coals to become infused with the character of the smoke. When this turkey comes off the fire, you're going to be amazed at how much more tasty and exciting it is than the standard version.

We like to serve this with the traditional turkey fixings. For us, that means mashed sweet potatoes, cranberry relish, Susan's spoonbread, and creamed onions, but feel free to stick with your own.

1 gallon water	2 apples of your choice, cored and
2 cups kosher salt	quartered
1 1/2 cups sugar	2 oranges, quartered
Freshly cracked black pepper to taste	12- to 15-pound turkey

1. In a large bucket or other container that the turkey will easily fit into, combine the water, salt, and sugar and stir to dissolve the salt and sugar. Remove the giblets from the turkey cavity and rinse the turkey well, then place it in the container, making sure there is enough brine to cover it completely. Refrigerate 24 to 48 hours, turning every 12 hours or so.

2. Start a fire well over to one side of a large kettle grill, using about enough coals to fill a shoebox. When the fire dies down and the coals are well lit, remove the turkey from the brine. Rinse the bird and dry it well, then sprinkle the inside of the cavity generously with pepper and put in the apples and oranges.

3. Place the turkey on the side of the grill away from the coals, being careful that no part of the bird is directly over the coals. Put the lid on the grill with the vents one-quarter of the way open and cook, adding a handful of fresh charcoal about every 30 minutes, for about 2 1/2 to 3 hours. Turn the turkey around at least twice during the cooking time, or more often if the side facing the fire seems to be getting too done. To check for doneness, pierce the thigh with a fork. When the juices run clear, the turkey is done. (If you want to use a meat thermometer, place it in the pit between the breast and the leg to check the temperature: when the thermometer reads 160°F, the bird is done.) Remove the bird from the grill, cover it loosely with foil, and allow it to rest at least 15 minutes before carving. Serve with the usual pomp and ceremony.

COOK TO COOK: If you don't have room in your refrigerator, you can brine the turkey in a large cooler, as long as you keep the water cold. The easiest way to do that is to add about 4 freezer packs to the brine when you first put the turkey in, then keep rotating with another set of 4 freezer packs every 4 hours or so. And speaking of room, you're going need a big grill to make this recipe.

pasta with grilled portobellos, fire-roasted peppers, and goat cheese

SERVES 4 TO 6 AS A LIGHT MAIN DISH OR PASTA COURSE

We love to make simple pastas in the summer. If we're grilling meat or fish tonight, we might throw a couple of portobellos and red or yellow bell peppers on the fire to use in a pasta dish tomorrow night. Fire-roasted bell peppers are one of the great vegetable preparations around, and with their meaty, almost steaklike texture, portobellos are excellent on the grill, particularly if you're one of those people who are trying to cut down on meat.

Serve this with a simple salad up front or EZ Grill Bread with Tomatoes, Parmesan, and Basil (page 85) or Prosciutto-Wrapped Grilled Peaches with a Balsamic Drizzle (page 40).

2 pounds portobello mushrooms,
   stems removed
3 red or yellow bell peppers
1/4 cup olive oil
Kosher salt and freshly cracked black
   pepper to taste
12 ounces spaghetti (or substitute
   another dried pasta of your
   choice)

1/4 cup extra-virgin olive oil
1/2 cup roughly chopped fresh
   parsley
1/2 pound goat cheese, crumbled

1. Build a multi-level fire in your grill: Leaving one-quarter of the bottom free of coals, bank the coals in the remaining three-quarters of the grill so that they are three times as high on one side as on the other. When all the coals are ignited and the temperature is medium-hot (you can hold your hand about 5 inches above the grill grid, over the area where the coals are deepest, for 3 to 4 seconds), you're ready to cook.

2. Rub the mushrooms and peppers with the oil and sprinkle them generously with salt and pepper. Put the peppers over the coals and grill, rolling them around occasionally, until the skin is completely black and well blistered on all sides, about 8 to 13 minutes. While the peppers are roasting, place the mushrooms on the part of the grill with fewer coals and grill them about 6 to 8 minutes on each side, or until the inside of one of the mushrooms looks moist all the way through.

3. Remove the vegetables from the grill. Cut the mushrooms into large dice and put them in a medium bowl. Pop the peppers into a brown paper bag, tie the bag shut, and set it aside. When the peppers are cool enough to handle—after about 10 minutes—remove them from the bag and peel off the skins. Now tear them in half, remove the ribs and seeds, and run the peppers gently under cold water to remove any remaining charred pieces of skin. Cut the peppers into large dice, place them in the bowl with the mushrooms, add the olive oil and parsley, and cover loosely with foil to keep warm.

4. In a large pot, bring 4 quarts of water to a boil. Add the pasta and some salt and cook until the pasta is al dente, 8 to 10 minutes. Drain the pasta, immediately add it to the bowl with the mushrooms and peppers, and season to taste with salt and pepper. Add the goat cheese, gently toss, and serve immediately.

COOK TO COOK: Be sure to check the doneness of the mushrooms by slicing into one; it is done when it has lost that dry, white look and instead is dark and moist all the way through.

grilled shrimp linguine
with smoky prosciutto, sun-dried tomatoes, and basil

SERVES 6

※ ※ ※ ※ ※ ※ ※ ※ ※ ※ ※ ※ ※ ※ ※ ※ ※

Including a grilled component in a pasta dish is a cool thing to do because the mild background flavor of the pasta really accentuates the smoky char of the grilled food. Here we include not only grilled shrimp but also grilled prosciutto, which is a little more unusual. Serve this with EZ Grill Bread with the flavored oil of your choice (page 77) and a salad of watercress and Boston lettuce.

1 pound dried linguine	Kosher salt and freshly cracked black
1 cup sun-dried tomatoes, sliced thin	pepper to taste
1/4 cup extra-virgin olive oil	1/2 pound very thinly sliced
1 1/2 pounds (about 16) extra-large	prosciutto
(U/12) shrimp, peeled and	1 cup fresh basil leaves, cut into
deveined, tails intact	thin strips
2 tablespoons olive oil	Juice of 1 lemon
1 tablespoon minced garlic	

1. Build a multi-level fire in your grill: Leaving one-quarter of the bottom free of coals, bank the coals in the remaining three-quarters of the grill so that they are three times as high on one side as on the other. When all the coals are ignited and the temperature is hot (you can hold your hand 5 inches above the grill grid, over the area where the coals are deepest, for 2 seconds or less), you're ready to cook.

2. Cook the linguine in 4 quarts of boiling salted water until al dente, 8 to 10 minutes. Drain the pasta and transfer it to a large bowl, then add the sun-dried tomatoes and olive oil and toss until well mixed. Cover the bowl loosely with foil to keep warm and set aside.

3. While the pasta is cooking, in a large bowl toss together the shrimp, olive oil, garlic, and salt and pepper. Thread the shrimp onto skewers, place on the grill, and cook until just opaque throughout, about 3 to 4 minutes per side. To check for doneness, peek inside one of the shrimp to be sure it is opaque all the way through. Push the shrimp off the skewers into the bowl with the pasta.

4. Put the prosciutto slices on the grill and cook until they are just crisp, about 1 minute.

5. Add the prosciutto to the pasta along with the basil, lemon, and more salt and pepper to taste. Toss until well combined and serve immediately.

COOK TO COOK: Be careful not to leave the prosciutto over the fire too long here; you don't need to cook it, you just want to crisp it up and give it a little smokiness.

pasta from hell: "the next generation" with curried grilled chicken

SERVES 4

Stop here. Do not cook this dish. In fact, do not even consider reading any farther unless you are a certifiable chile-head. This dish is totally out of control, a punishment designed for the customers who always told me (Chris) at the East Coast Grill, "Oh, that's good and spicy, but it's not really hot." Now, as a chef I like cooking full-flavored food and using a little bit of heat, but I don't like to go crazy with chiles. At least not now I don't, although I admit that in my youth I walked that fine chile-powered edge between pleasure and torture, like looking down the barrel of a gun just to see whether it will go off. It was at that time that I devised the original Pasta from Hell so my customers would never again be able to look me in the face and say, "Your food isn't hot enough."

But if you are in fact a chile fanatic, then this is the dish for you. We ask only that you sign the Release Form (see below) before you share in the agony and wallow in the fiery torpor that results from over-ingestion of Scotch bonnet peppers.

(And here's a secret message from Doc: If you are a chile pepper wimp like me, you can make this dish with only a single jalapeño or other mild chile, and it tastes fantastic. Just don't let Chris know you did it.)

Serve this with East Coast Grill Cornbread (page 322).

4 boneless, skinless split chicken breasts (cutlets), 8 ounces each
2 tablespoons vegetable oil
3 tablespoons curry powder
Kosher salt and freshly cracked black pepper to taste

For the pasta:
3 tablespoons olive oil
1 red onion, peeled and diced small
2 ripe but firm mangoes, pitted, peeled, and diced small

4 tablespoons minced fresh Scotch bonnet chile peppers
2 tablespoons peeled and minced fresh ginger
1/2 cup pineapple juice
12 ounces dried fettuccine
1/4 cup fresh lime juice (about 2 limes)
1/2 cup roughly chopped fresh cilantro
Kosher salt and freshly cracked black pepper to taste

1. Build a multi-level fire in your grill: Leaving one-quarter of the bottom free of coals, bank the coals in the remaining three-quarters of the grill so that they are three times as high on one side as on the other. When all the coals are ignited and the temperature is hot (you can hold your hand about 5 inches above the grill grid, over the area where the coals are deepest, for 2 seconds or less), the fire is ready for cooking this dish.

2. Coat the chicken breasts with the vegetable oil, rub them with the curry powder, and sprinkle them generously with salt and pepper. Place on the grill and cook until they

are browned on the outside and just cooked through, about 4 to 6 minutes per side. To check for doneness, poke the chicken with your finger to test its firmness level (see page 13); if you're unsure, nick, peek, and cheat: Make a 1/4-inch cut in the thickest part of one of the breasts and check to be sure that it is opaque all the way through. When they're done, transfer the breasts to a plate and cover them loosely with foil to keep warm while you make the pasta.

2. In a large sauté pan or skillet over medium-high heat, heat the oil until it is hot but not smoking. Add the onion and sauté, stirring occasionally, until transparent, 7 to 9 minutes. Add the mangoes, chiles, and ginger and sauté, stirring frequently, for 2 minutes more. Stir in the pineapple juice and simmer, stirring occasionally, for 3 minutes. Remove from the heat and set aside.

3. Meanwhile, bring 4 quarts of salted water to a boil, add the fettuccine, and cook until just al dente, 8 to 10 minutes for dried pasta or 3 to 4 minutes for fresh. Drain the pasta and return it to the pot. Pour the sauce over the pasta, then add the lime juice, cilantro, and salt and pepper. Toss until everything is well combined and divide among 4 pasta bowls.

4. Slice the chicken on the bias into strips, arrange it on top of the pasta, and serve.

COOK TO COOK: In case you overestimate the strength of your heat resistance and have to call for an antidote, here are the . . .

five most popular heat quenchers

1. *Rice or ice*
2. *Beer*
3. *Cornbread*
4. *Creamsicle*
5. *Vintage port*

official burning hell release form

* * *

I, the undersigned, do hereby agree to hold harmless Chris and Doc and all their employees and successors for any "problems" that may occur from the consumption of "Pasta from Hell" (hereinafter referred to as "the Dish").

These problems may include, but are not limited to: discoloration of the skin or clothing, emission-induced impacts on the ozone layer, reduced capabilities of the left side of the brain, and so on and so forth.

I, the undersigned, further testify that I am eating the Dish of my own free will.

Signed _____ this day of _____ .

YOU KNOW HOW LOTS OF TIMES IN A RESTAURANT YOU END up ordering a particular dish not so much because you crave the steak or halibut but because you really want to try the spicy Thai-style slaw or the smoky grilled asparagus that comes with it? Well, that's what this chapter is all about—side dishes that are every bit as enticing, flavor-packed, and satisfying as any entrée.

Most of the recipes here are grilled, of course, or at least have a grilled component to them, adding an edge of smoky sear. We look at this as a kind of updating of the long-time American tradition of using cured pork products to add depth to a dish, only we're using fire rather than pig to boost the flavor quotient.

And speaking of meat, this chapter is a haven for vegetarians: With a couple of exceptions that use a little bacon, these are wholly meat-free dishes. As with the recipes in the Starters chapter, you can easily put several of these together to make a fully gratifying meatless meal. You can also use the dishes in this chapter as appetizers or even midday snacks if you like.

Any of you who have read our other books know that we are big fans of ash roasting, otherwise known as hobo pack cookery, and there are plenty of hobo packs to choose from here. There are also some prime examples, such as Four Grilled Corn Strategies (page 286) and Fire-Roasted Peppers with Five Flavor Options (page 290), of our stratagem of providing many options for the same dish, since not everyone likes the exact same taste or texture.

Some of the dishes here use slightly unfamiliar ingredients, such as hearts of palm or shiitake mushrooms or fermented black beans. But most of them consist of familiar foods that are put together in ways you may not have thought of. There's nothing unusual about acorn squash, maple syrup, or vanilla, for example, but when you combine them with a little butter and some time over the flames, you've got a whole new taste experience.

However you use them, the dishes in this chapter are bound to expand your grill repertoire as well as providing you some basic go-alongs for any grilled feast.

grilled asparagus with parmesan cheese and sweet-and-sour bacon dressing

SERVES 6

We're big fans of grilled asparagus, which we associate with the opening of the outside grilling season in our part of the country. Recently we've had good success using very thin, young, tender asparagus spears and putting them straight on the grill rather than blanching them first. Not surprisingly, they hold both their texture and their flavor better if they don't have to go through the boiling water bath. The deciding factor here is whether the spears are thicker or thinner than a pencil—if thicker, blanch; if thinner, just toss them right on the grill.

Here we serve the asparagus with an old-school sweet-and-sour bacon dressing and a sprinkling of Parmesan. This dish is a pinch hitter: It can be either an appetizer or a side dish.

2 pounds asparagus, bottom ends trimmed or snapped off	3 tablespoons balsamic vinegar
4 slices bacon, slab (the unsliced kind you slice yourself) if possible	1/2 teaspoon sugar
	Kosher salt and freshly cracked black pepper to taste
1/4 cup olive oil	3 tablespoons olive oil
	1/4 cup grated Parmesan cheese

1. Build a multi-level fire in your grill: Leaving one-quarter of the bottom free of coals, bank the coals in the remaining three-quarters of the grill so that they are three times as high on one side as on the other. When the coals are all ignited and the temperature has died down to medium (you can hold your hand about 5 inches above the grill grid, over the area where the coals are deepest, for 4 to 5 seconds), you're ready to cook.

2. Unless the asparagus spears you are using are thinner than pencils, blanch them: In a medium sauté pan or skillet, blanch the spears in boiling salted water until they turn bright green, about 2 minutes. Immediately plunge them into ice water to stop the cooking and drain well.

3. Dry the sauté pan or skillet and return it to the stove. Add the bacon and cook over medium heat until crisp, about 6 to 8 minutes. Set aside 2 tablespoons of the bacon drippings from the pan, then transfer the bacon to paper towels or brown paper to drain. When the bacon has drained, crumble it coarsely and set it aside.

4. In a small bowl, combine the olive oil, vinegar, sugar, the 2 tablespoons of bacon drippings, and salt and pepper to taste. Whisk until the sugar has dissolved, then set aside.

5. Brush the asparagus spears all over with the olive oil and place them on the grill, rolling them around occasionally for even cooking, until golden brown and slightly charred, 2 to 3 minutes (3 to 4 minutes if unblanched).

6. When the asparagus spears are done, arrange them on a platter. Whisk the dressing again, drizzle it over the hot asparagus, sprinkle with Parmesan cheese and the reserved bacon, and serve immediately.

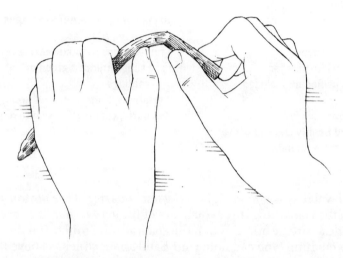

Snapping asparagus

grilled asparagus
with soy-ginger dressing on a bed of cabbage

SERVES 4

ﾊ ﾊ ﾊ ﾊ ﾊ ﾊ ﾊ ﾊ ﾊ ﾊ ﾊ ﾊ ﾊ ﾊ ﾊ ﾊ ﾊ

As long as your spears of asparagus are pencil-thin, you can put them right on the grill without blanching them, which of course makes the dish that much easier. You can also skip the bed of cabbage if you like, but we think the crunchiness of the cabbage really sets off the tenderness of the asparagus.

For the dressing:
2 tablespoons roasted sesame oil
2 tablespoons olive oil
2 tablespoons soy sauce
2 tablespoons white vinegar
2 tablespoons peeled and minced
    fresh ginger
1 teaspoon sugar
Kosher salt and freshly cracked white
    pepper to taste (or substitute
    black pepper)

30 medium (not large) asparagus
    spears, trimmed
3 tablespoons roasted sesame oil
1 1/2 cups shredded green or red
    cabbage
8 scallions, both white and green
    parts, cut lengthwise into narrow
    strips

1. Build a multi-level fire in your grill: Leaving one-quarter of the bottom free of coals, bank the coals in the remaining three-quarters of the grill so that they are three times as high on one side as on the other. When the coals are all ignited and the temperature has died down to medium (you can hold your hand about 5 inches above the grill grid, over the area where the coals are deepest, for 4 to 5 seconds), you're ready to cook.

2. Meanwhile, whisk together all the dressing ingredients in a small bowl, then set aside.

3. Place the asparagus, the 3 tablespoons of sesame oil, and salt and pepper to taste in a shallow dish and roll the asparagus around in the oil to coat. Put the asparagus on the grill and cook until the spears are browned and tender, 4 to 6 minutes.

4. Place the shredded cabbage on a serving platter. Arrange the grilled asparagus on top, pour the dressing over, garnish with the scallions, and serve.

sesame-crusted grilled zucchini with honey-soy glaze

SERVES 4 TO 6

Zucchini have a bad name because they are so unbelievably plentiful in late summer. But they are magnificent on the grill, particularly if you cut them into long, thick planks so they can develop a nice, dark sear on the outside at the same time they cook through on the inside. (Incidentally, you'll know they are done when the interior looks kind of moist rather than raw and translucent.) This simple side dish with Asian flavors may well give you a whole new outlook on this maligned vegetable.

1/3 cup honey

4 tablespoons soy sauce

4 medium zucchini, unpeeled, halved lengthwise to make 8 planks about 1 inch thick (see illustration on next page)

2 tablespoons roasted sesame oil

Kosher salt and freshly cracked white pepper to taste (or substitute black pepper)

1/3 cup toasted sesame seeds

1/4 cup finely chopped scallions, both green and white parts

1. Build a multi-level fire in your grill: Leaving one-quarter of the bottom free of coals, bank the coals in the remaining three-quarters of the grill so that they are three times as high on one side as on the other. When the coals are all ignited and the temperature has died down to medium (you can hold your hand about 5 inches above the grill grid, over the area where the coals are deepest, for 4 to 5 seconds), you're ready to cook.

2. In a small bowl, combine the honey and soy sauce, whisk until well blended, and set aside.

3. Rub the zucchini planks all over with the sesame oil and sprinkle them generously with salt and pepper. Put on the grill and cook, turning once, until they are nicely browned and the inside has lost its raw, translucent look, about 3 to 4 minutes per side. During the last 20 to 30 seconds of grilling, brush the honey mixture over both sides of the zucchini, flipping it after 15 seconds or so to do the second side.

4. Arrange the zucchini on a serving dish, sprinkle with the sesame seeds and scallions, and serve.

COOK TO COOK: Cutting oblong squashes such as zucchini and summer squash into what we call planks—thick lengthwise slices—exposes a lot of the interior to the flame while still keeping the flesh thick enough that it doesn't cook too fast. The result? Well-cooked squash with an exquisite exterior sear. (See illustrations on the next page.)

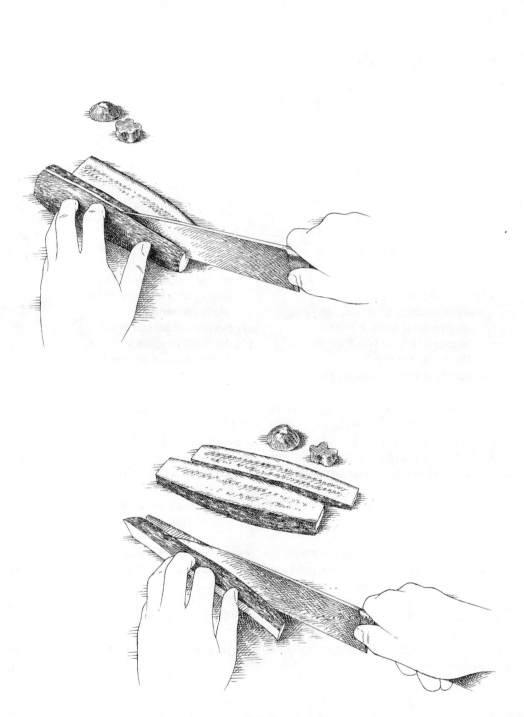

Making zucchini planks

grilled eggplant steaks
with minted yogurt-cucumber relish

SERVES 4

One of the great benefits of grilling eggplant is that you don't need to go through all that salting and draining business. If you cut the eggplant into thick slices and put it over the fire with just a bit of oil and salt and pepper, the eggplant develops a great sear on the outside and still maintains some texture on the inside, plus it has none of the bitterness that people often associate with this vegetable. The key is to use a medium-hot rather than a low fire, and not to overdo it—don't leave the eggplant on the grill so long that it gets mushy.

1 large eggplant, cut into 1-inch-thick
    slices
3 tablespoons olive oil
Kosher salt and freshly cracked black
    pepper to taste
1/2 cup plain yogurt (whole-milk
    if possible)

1 cucumber, peeled, seeded, and
    diced small
1/3 cup roughly chopped fresh mint
1 teaspoon minced garlic
Juice of 1 lemon

1. Build a multi-level fire in your grill: Leaving one-quarter of the bottom free of coals, bank the coals in the remaining three-quarters of the grill so that they are three times as high on one side as on the other. When the coals are all ignited and the temperature has died down to medium-hot (you can hold your hand about 5 inches above the grill grid, over the area where the coals are deepest, for 3 to 4 seconds), you're ready to cook.

2. Rub the eggplant slices on both sides with the oil and sprinkle them generously with salt and pepper. Place on the grill and cook, turning once, until the interior has lost its raw, translucent look, about 3 to 4 minutes per side. Remove the eggplant slices to a platter.

3. In a small bowl, combine the yogurt, cucumber, mint, garlic, lemon juice, and salt and pepper and mix well. Top the eggplant slices with the yogurt relish and serve warm or at room temperature.

grilled eggplant with spicy black bean sauce

SERVES 4

Try this dish on your friends who think they don't like eggplant. When you cut it thick and put it straight on the grill without salting and draining it first, eggplant takes on a rich flavor and a meaty texture that has converted many former foes. Asian flavors work especially well with grilled eggplant.

Spicy black bean paste, which not only packs a kick but also has a deep and distinctive flavor, is available in most Asian stores. If you can't find it, though, you can substitute a slightly smaller amount of chile-garlic paste.

3 tablespoons roasted sesame oil
2 tablespoons olive oil
1 large eggplant, cut lengthwise into
    planks about 1 inch thick
Kosher salt and freshly cracked white
    pepper to taste (or substitute
    black pepper)

3 tablespoons spicy black bean paste
    (or substitute hoisin sauce)
1 tablespoon brown sugar
3 tablespoons rice wine vinegar (or
    substitute white wine vinegar)
1/2 cup finely chopped scallions,
    both green and white parts

1. Build a multi-level fire in your grill: Leaving one-quarter of the bottom free of coals, bank the coals in the remaining three-quarters of the grill so that they are three times as high on one side as on the other. When the coals are all ignited and the temperature has died down to medium (you can hold your hand about 5 inches above the grill grid, over the area where the coals are deepest, for 4 to 5 seconds), you're ready to cook.

2. In a small bowl, combine the sesame oil and the olive oil and mix well. Brush the eggplant on both sides with the oil and sprinkle generously with salt and pepper, then put on the grill and cook, turning once, until the eggplant is tender and the inside has lost its translucent look, about 3 to 4 minutes per side.

3. While the eggplant is cooking, whisk together the black bean paste, brown sugar, vinegar, and salt and pepper in a small bowl. Top the grilled eggplant slices with the black bean sauce, garnish with the chopped scallions, and serve.

COOK TO COOK: There are scores of varieties of eggplant, each with its own virtues. For this preparation, though, the best choice is the plump, oblong purple variety most familiar to American cooks.

grilled shiitake mushrooms
with sherry, soy, and scallions

SERVES 4

Here's a side dish that is quite simple but packs a lot of flavor. We just trim the mushrooms a bit, coat them with an Asian-inspired wet rub, grill them up, and dress them with a sherry-soy-vinegar dressing that really picks up the flavor. The result is an awesome side dish for roasted chicken or pork; it's also brilliant as part of a grilled vegetarian experience.

For the dressing:
1/4 cup dry sherry
1/4 cup dark soy sauce
2 tablespoons white vinegar
1 teaspoon sugar
2 tablespoons peeled and minced
    fresh ginger
1/4 cup finely chopped scallions,
    both white and green parts

———

2 tablespoons roasted sesame oil
2 tablespoons vegetable oil

1 tablespoon minced garlic
1 teaspoon red pepper flakes
2 tablespoons freshly cracked
    toasted coriander seeds (or
    substitute 1 tablespoon ground
    coriander)
2 pounds large shiitake mushrooms,
    tough bottom part of stems
    trimmed off
Kosher salt and freshly cracked black
    pepper to taste

1. Build a multi-level fire in your grill: Leaving one-quarter of the bottom free of coals, bank the coals in the remaining three-quarters of the grill so that they are three times as high on one side as on the other. When the coals are all ignited and the temperature has died down to medium-hot (you can hold your hand about 5 inches above the grill grid, over the area where the coals are deepest, for 3 to 4 seconds), you're ready to cook.

2. In a small bowl, whisk together the dressing ingredients until the sugar dissolves, then set aside.

3. In a bowl large enough to hold the mushrooms, combine the sesame oil, vegetable oil, garlic, red pepper flakes, and coriander seeds and mix well. Add the mushrooms, sprinkle generously with salt and pepper, and toss until well coated. Put the mushrooms on the grill and cook until they are browned and crisp and have grill marks on them, about 3 to 4 minutes per side. (To check for doneness, nick, peek, and cheat: Cut into one of the mushrooms and peek to be sure it looks moist all the way through, rather than dry at the center.)

4. When the mushrooms are done, take them off the grill and put them back into the bowl you originally tossed them in. Pour the dressing over them, toss gently, and serve.

grilled peppered portobello steaks
with parmesan dressing

SERVES 4 TO 6

Sometimes you see portobellos in the market that are just monsters, and this is the place to use them—the bigger the cap, the better. All you do is rub them with a little oil, pepper them up as much as possible, then grill them over a medium fire and serve them with a simple oil-vinegar-Parmesan combination that perfectly suits the meaty mushroom steaks. It's very easy to check these big 'shrooms for doneness; just cut into the middle of one, and if it looks moist all the way through, it's done.

2 pounds portobello mushrooms, as
    large as you can find, stemmed
1/3 cup extra-virgin olive oil
1/4 cup freshly cracked black pepper
Kosher salt to taste

For the dressing:
1/2 cup extra-virgin olive oil
1/4 cup red wine vinegar
1/4 cup grated Parmesan cheese

1. Build a multi-level fire in your grill: Leaving one-quarter of the bottom free of coals, bank the coals in the remaining three-quarters of the grill so that they are three times as high on one side as on the other. When the coals are all ignited and the temperature has died down to medium (you can hold your hand about 5 inches above the grill grid, over the area where the coals are deepest, for 4 to 5 seconds) you're ready to cook.

2. Rub the mushrooms with the olive oil and then with the black pepper, then sprinkle generously with salt. Put them on the grill and cook until they are tender and slightly seared, 6 to 8 minutes per side. (To check for doneness, nick, peek, and cheat: Cut into one of the mushrooms and peek to be sure it looks moist all the way through, rather than dry at the center.)

3. While the mushrooms are cooking, whisk the dressing ingredients together in a medium bowl.

4. When the mushrooms are done, take them off the grill, cut them into thick slices, add to the bowl with the dressing, toss gently to coat, and serve warm.

grilled broccoli rabe with sun-dried tomatoes, balsamic vinegar, and pine nuts

SERVES 4

Although it may seem a little odd, broccoli rabe on the grill actually works great—the inherent bitterness of the rabe is a good foil for the smoky grilled flavor. Here we toss the rabe with some other classic Italian ingredients for a quick and flavorful side dish.

2 bunches broccoli rabe, blanched in boiling salted water for 1 minute and well drained
3 tablespoons olive oil
Kosher salt and freshly cracked black pepper to taste

3 tablespoons finely chopped sun-dried tomatoes
1/4 cup balsamic vinegar
1 teaspoon minced garlic
1/4 cup toasted pine nuts, coarsely chopped

1. Build a multi-level fire in your grill: Leaving one-quarter of the bottom free of coals, bank the coals in the remaining three-quarters of the grill so that they are three times as high on one side as on the other. When the coals are all ignited and the temperature has died down to medium (you can hold your hand about 5 inches above the grill grid, over the area where the coals are deepest, for 4 to 5 seconds), you're ready to cook.

2. In a large bowl, combine the broccoli rabe with the olive oil and salt and pepper to taste and toss well to coat. Put the rabe on the grill and cook, turning once, until it is tender, about 2 to 3 minutes per side. Remove the rabe from the grill and put it back in the same large bowl.

3. Add the sun-dried tomatoes, vinegar, and garlic, adjust the seasoning, and toss well. Place on a serving platter, garnish with the pine nuts, and serve.

COOK TO COOK: When choosing rabe, we like to pick the bunches that have the greatest number of those miniature broccoli-type heads.

grilled leeks with chunky artichoke and sun-dried tomato dressing

SERVES 4

Leeks, which are a slightly refined member of the onion family, not only taste wonderful grilled but also smell fantastic while they're over the flames. So here we have a kind of upscale version of the old truck-stop axiom that you should always have some onions cooking on the flat-top grill because the smell will make customers really hungry. Leeks have a more subtle aroma than onions, but it will do the trick. Once you've got people's hunger aroused you don't want to disappoint them, so to complement the leeks we use cheese, artichokes, and sun-dried tomatoes in a nice, chunky dressing with lots of Mediterranean flavors going on.

8 medium leeks, white parts only, trimmed and very well washed
2 tablespoons olive oil
Kosher salt and freshly cracked black pepper to taste

For the dressing:
1/4 cup grated Parmesan cheese
8 fresh or jarred artichoke hearts, chopped medium

8 sun-dried tomato halves, diced small
1 teaspoon minced garlic
1/4 cup extra-virgin olive oil
Juice of 1 lemon
1/2 cup (loosely packed) roughly chopped parsley leaves

1. Build a multi-level fire in your grill: Leaving one-quarter of the bottom free of coals, bank the coals in the remaining three-quarters of the grill so that they are three times as high on one side as on the other. When the coals are all ignited and the temperature has died down to medium (you can hold your hand about 5 inches above the grill grid, over the area where the coals are deepest, for 4 to 5 seconds), you're ready to cook.

2. Rub the leeks with oil and sprinkle them generously with salt and pepper, then place them on the grill and cook, rolling them around occasionally for even cooking, until they are golden brown and slightly charred, 8 to 12 minutes. Remove from the grill, halve them lengthwise, and arrange them cut side up on a serving plate.

3. While the leeks are cooking, combine the cheese, artichoke hearts, tomatoes, garlic, oil, lemon, and parsley leaves in a medium bowl and mix well. Pour the dressing over the hot leeks and serve immediately, or allow to cool and serve at room temperature.

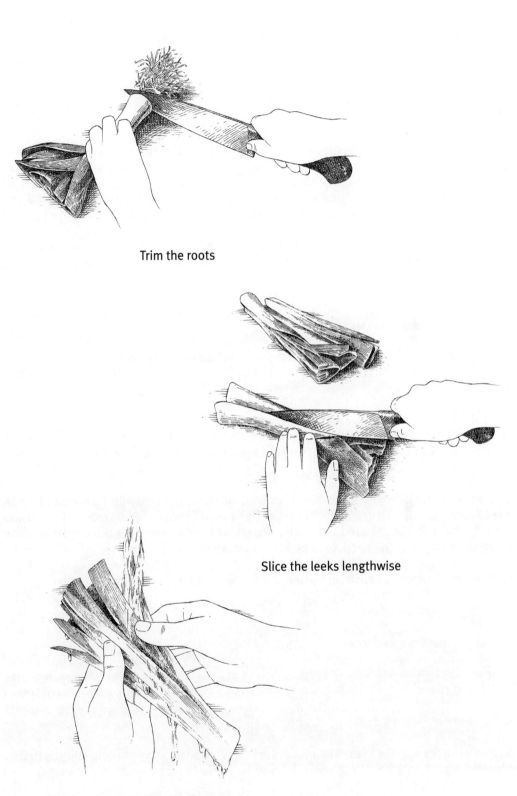

Trim the roots

Slice the leeks lengthwise

Clean very well under running water

four grilled corn strategies with latin flavor modifiers

There are any number of methods for dealing with corn on the grill, each with its own merits. We decided to give you not just one method but four. That way, you can take your choice depending upon which aspect is most important to you. Or you might like one method for one meal, another for a different meal. In any case, here they all are. We've also included three Latin-inspired flavor modifiers to brush onto the ears after they're cooked.

Incidentally, you need to start your fire about half an hour before you plan to cook the corn, to be sure the fire has time to come to a peak and then die down to medium or medium-low.

Option 1: Incredibly Intricate

This is the most difficult method. We don't recommend it, but we include it here because some people are inexplicably fond of it. We think they just like to do a lot of work.

1. Peel down the outer husk of each ear of corn without actually removing it, remove the inner silky threads, and wrap the outer husk back up around the ear. Run all the ears under water for a couple of seconds before putting them on the grill, to keep them from burning.

2. Place the ears of corn on the grill over medium heat (you can hold your hand about 5 inches above the grill grid for 4 to 5 seconds) and grill until the husks look brown and slightly charred, about 10 to 12 minutes. (To check for doneness: Peel back the husk on one ear and poke at the kernels to be sure they are tender.)

3. Remove the husks, brush on butter, season with salt and pepper, and serve.

Option 2: Husk-on and Soaked

This method gives very tender corn, and it's very easy. On the other hand, it ties up a lot of grill space for a while, because it's relatively slow. The soaking takes time too.

1. Soak the ears in water for 15 minutes.

2. Place the ears on the grill over a medium fire (you can hold your hand about 5 inches above the grill grid for 4 to 5 seconds) and let them steam until they are just cooked

through, about 15 to 20 minutes. (To check for doneness, peel back the husk and silk on one ear and poke at the kernels to be sure they are tender.)

3. Remove the husks and silk, brush on a little butter, season with salt and pepper, then roll the ears around on the grill ever so slightly to add a little char. Now they're ready to eat.

Option 3: Naked Corn

This is our favorite top-of-the-grill method. It's easy, it's quick, and you get good corn flavor plus a nice smokiness.

1. Shuck and de-silk the ears.

2. Place the ears over a medium-low fire (you can hold your hand about 5 inches above the grill grid for 5 seconds) and let them cook for 3 to 5 minutes, rolling them around for even cooking, until they are just golden brown.

Option 4: Ash-Roasted

This approach, which we like because the corn cooks with some of the butter, salt, and pepper already on it, produces a very smoky flavor. It's our favorite method of the four.

1. Shuck and de-silk the corn.

2. Wrap each ear, along with butter, salt, and pepper to your liking, in a double layer of foil. (Or place all the ears in a disposable foil pan and cover the pan tightly with a double layer of foil.) Place the packages in the coals of your grill fire for 12 to 15 minutes. (To check for doneness, peel open one of the packages and poke at the kernels to be sure they are tender.)

3. Remove the corn from the foil packages, brush on more butter, season with more salt and pepper, and serve.

latin flavor modifiers

Each of these should be enough for a dozen or more ears of corn.

Orange Chipotle Butter

1/2 cup orange juice
2 tablespoons puréed chipotle peppers in adobo sauce
1/2 cup unsalted butter

1. In a small saucepan, bring the orange juice to a boil over high heat. Reduce the heat to medium-low and simmer vigorously until the orange juice is reduced by two-thirds, about 15 to 20 minutes.

2. Remove from heat and add the chipotles and butter, stirring until the butter melts and blends with the orange juice. Drizzle over the grilled corn.

Lime Juice and Roasted Cumin Salt

1/2 cup kosher salt
1/4 cup cumin seeds
3 limes, cut in wedges

1. In a small sauté pan or skillet over low heat, combine the salt and cumin seeds and cook, stirring constantly, until the salt starts to smoke slightly and becomes fragrant, 2 to 3 minutes.

2. Squeeze the lime wedges over the corn and sprinkle liberally with the salt.

Cilantro-Lime Butter

1/4 cup roughly chopped fresh cilantro
2 tablespoons lime juice (about 1 lime)
1 tablespoon Tabasco sauce
1/2 cup unsalted butter, softened

1. In a small bowl, work the cilantro, lime juice, and Tabasco into the butter until well mixed. You can use the butter right away, or you can wrap it in plastic wrap, shape it into a square log, and place it in the refrigerator until firm. When you're ready to serve it, place the butter, unwrapped, in a butter dish.

2. Allow your guests to roll their own corn on the butter (the way most people do at home when they eat corn on the cob and no one's watching).

colorful grilled peppers
with thyme, sherry, and toasted garlic

SERVES 6

I (Chris) love pulling up to Cole Walker's roadside stand in Little Compton, Rhode Island, on a summer day and seeing those bright, fresh peppers—red, yellow, orange, purple, green—stacked up in huge piles. I have often thought it would be fun to try to use them in a dish that would deliver all that color right to the table. So here it is.

Despite its kaleidoscopic appearance, it's pretty simple. You just halve the peppers, grill them, and combine them with a little garlic, olive oil, thyme, and sherry. The result is a great dish to eat today, a great dish to put on your sandwiches tomorrow, even a great dish to turn into a relish if you choose.

5 assorted bell peppers of your choice (red, yellow, purple, and orange), halved lengthwise, cored and seeded	1/3 cup olive oil
	5 cloves garlic, peeled and thinly sliced
1/4 cup olive oil	1/4 cup fresh thyme leaves
Kosher salt and freshly cracked black pepper to taste	2 tablespoons dry sherry

1. Build a multi-level fire in your grill: Leaving one-quarter of the bottom free of coals, bank the coals in the remaining three-quarters of the grill so that they are three times as high on one side as on the other. When the coals are all ignited and the temperature has died down to medium (you can hold your hand about 5 inches above the grill grid, over the area where the coals are deepest, for 4 to 5 seconds), you're ready to cook.

2. Coat the pepper halves lightly with the olive oil and sprinkle them generously with salt and pepper, then put them on the grill and cook until they are golden brown but still crisp, about 2 to 3 minutes per side. (You're not going to peel these peppers, so don't char them as you would when making fire-roasted peppers.) When the peppers are done, cut them into strips 1/2 inch wide and transfer them to a large bowl.

3. In a small sauté pan or skillet over medium-high heat, heat the olive oil until hot but not smoking. Add the garlic slices and sauté, stirring, until just lightly browned, about 1 minute. Pour the garlic and oil over the peppers.

4. Add the thyme and sherry to the bowl, season to taste with salt and pepper, and toss well. The peppers can be served at room temperature or chilled.

fire-roasted peppers with five flavor options

MAKES 6 ROASTED PEPPERS

You see roasted bell peppers so often these days that they are almost a cliché. But when you have a lot of peppers on hand, it's hard to think of anything better than taking five or six of them, roasting them up over a wood fire until they're totally black, and then working with them out on the deck to get them clean. At that point your choices are many. You can simply sprinkle these smoky little guys with extra-virgin olive oil and balsamic vinegar and eat them like that; you can flavor them with a slightly more complex flavored oil; or you can combine them with a few other ingredients to make a kind of relish.

Here we give five options for flavor combinations that we think go great with these fire-roasted beauties. You can make as many peppers as you have room for on the grill, but bear in mind that each of our flavoring options will season about six of them.

6 red, yellow, or orange bell peppers

1. Build a multi-level fire in your grill: Leaving one-quarter of the bottom free of coals, bank the coals in the remaining three-quarters of the grill so that they are three times as high on one side as on the other. When the coals are all ignited and the fire is hot (you can hold your hand about 5 inches above the grill grid, over the area where the coals are deepest, for 2 seconds or less), you're ready to cook.

2. Place the peppers on the grill and cook, rolling around occasionally, until the skin is completely black and well blistered on all sides, about 8 to 13 minutes. Remember, in this case burned is good.

3. Remove the peppers from the grill, pop them into a brown paper bag, tie the bag shut, and set it aside while the peppers cool enough to handle, about 15 minutes.

4. Remove the partially cooled peppers from the bag. Tear them in half, remove the ribs and seeds, and peel off the skin; you may have to run the peppers gently under cold water to remove the final charred bits of skin. Combine the peppers with the flavor option of your choice.

five flavor options

option 1: garlic-thyme oil

1/4 cup extra-virgin olive oil
1 tablespoon minced garlic
3 tablespoons fresh thyme
Kosher salt and freshly cracked black pepper to taste

In a bowl large enough to hold the peppers, combine all the ingredients and mix well. Add the roasted, peeled, halved peppers, tossing to coat thoroughly. Serve warm or at room temperature.

option 2: basil-garlic vinaigrette

1/4 cup extra-virgin olive oil
3 tablespoons balsamic vinegar
1/2 cup julienned fresh basil
1/2 teaspoon minced garlic
Kosher salt and freshly cracked black pepper to taste

In a bowl large enough to hold the peppers, combine all ingredients and mix well. Add the roasted, peeled, halved peppers, tossing to coat thoroughly. Serve warm or at room temperature.

option 3: green olive–red onion mix

1 red onion, peeled and diced small
1/4 cup roughly chopped pitted green olives
1/4 cup extra-virgin olive oil
Juice of 1/2 lemon
Kosher salt and freshly cracked black pepper to taste

Dice the roasted peppers small and place in a medium bowl, along with the onion and olives. Drizzle with the olive oil and lemon juice, sprinkle generously with salt and pepper, and toss until well mixed. Serve warm or at room temperature.

option 4: peach-fennel mix

1 ripe but firm peach, halved, pitted, and diced small
1 bulb fennel, trimmed, cored, and thinly sliced
1 red onion, peeled and very thinly sliced
1/4 cup extra-virgin olive oil
Juice of 1 lemon
Kosher salt and freshly cracked black pepper to taste

Dice the roasted peppers small and place in a medium bowl, along with the peach, fennel, and onion. Drizzle with the olive oil and lemon juice, sprinkle generously with salt and pepper, and toss until well mixed. Serve warm or at room temperature.

option 5: goat cheese–black olive mix

3 ounces sliced goat cheese
Freshly cracked black pepper to taste
1/4 cup roughly chopped black olives
Extra-virgin olive oil

Sprinkle the roasted pepper halves and goat cheese slices generously with pepper. Layer the peppers, cheese, and olives in a glass jar just large enough to hold everything. Fill the jar to the top with olive oil, cover, and refrigerate for about 1 hour. Serve the marinated peppers and cheese with the oil.

pan-fried sweet plantains with sour cream

SERVES 4

Next time you're in a Latin or Caribbean grocery store, look over on the floor and you'll see a bunch of once-green plantains that are now partly yellow but mostly black. If they were bananas they'd be so far gone you might not want to eat them, but for plantains they're perfect. They're called *maduro* (mature), which basically means ripe, and the black skin is a sign that most of the starch in the plantain has changed to sugar. It's kind of like a potato turning into a banana but retaining a little of its potato-ness as well.

What we like to do with maduros is slice them on the bias, pan-fry them in a little butter, and serve them with sour cream on the side. It makes a delicious and unusual starch dish, and it's also an excellent breakfast item.

2 wicked-ripe plantains	Kosher salt to taste
2 tablespoons unsalted butter	1 lime, cut into 4 wedges
1/2 cup sour cream	

1. Cut the plantains on the bias into sections about 1 1/2 to 2 inches long, then peel the sections.

2. Melt the butter in a medium-sized sauté pan or skillet over medium heat, then add the plantains and cook until golden brown, about 2 minutes per side. (Cook them in batches if necessary, to avoid crowding the pan.)

3. Sprinkle the hot plantains with salt and serve right away, accompanied by a spoonful of sour cream and a lime wedge on the side.

COOK TO COOK: If you want to make this dish a little fancier, you can use crème fraîche in place of sour cream—and for a real tropical treat, spread some guava paste or jelly on top.

extra-large grilled sweet potato fries with shiitake-parsley butter sauce

SERVES 4

This might seem like an odd combination, sweet potatoes with shiitake mushrooms, but somehow the dish really comes together. I (Doc) think it's because the sweetness of the sweet potatoes works well against the earthiness of the mushrooms, which exhibit that quality of "meatiness" or "savoriness" that the Japanese call *umami*. (Many taste scientists now believe it is a fifth basic taste, along with sweet, sour, salty, and bitter.) On the other hand, maybe it's just two things that happen to taste good together.

In either case, this is an unusual but very delicious side dish that's particularly easy to put together if you've got the grilling fire lit for another dish, anyway.

2 large sweet potatoes, peeled and
    quartered lengthwise
2 tablespoons vegetable oil
Kosher salt and freshly cracked black
    pepper to taste

For the sauce:
3 tablespoons unsalted butter

1/2 pound shiitake mushrooms
    (or substitute white mushrooms),
    thinly sliced
1/2 teaspoon ground allspice
Small pinch of ground mace
1/4 cup roughly chopped fresh
    parsley
2 tablespoons dry sherry

1. Build a multi-level fire in your grill: Leaving one-quarter of the bottom free of coals, bank the coals in the remaining three-quarters of the grill so that they are three times as high on one side as on the other. When the coals are all ignited and the temperature has died down to medium (you can hold your hand about 5 inches above the grill grid, over the area where the coals are deepest, for 4 to 5 seconds), you're ready to cook.

2. Boil the sweet potato quarters in a large pot of boiling salted water until just tender, about 6 to 10 minutes (you should be able to pierce them with a toothpick but still feel some resistance). Drain and run under cold water to stop the cooking process. Rub the blanched sweet potatoes with oil and sprinkle them generously with salt and pepper, then place them on the grill and cook until golden brown, about 4 to 5 minutes per side. Remove from the grill and arrange on a platter, cut side up.

3. Meanwhile, melt the butter over medium heat in a large sauté pan or skillet. Add the mushrooms and cook until they are moist all the way through, about 6 to 8 minutes. Remove the pan from the heat, stir in the spices, parsley, and sherry, and season to taste with salt and pepper. Spoon the mushrooms and their liquid over the hot potatoes and serve hot.

cinnamon soy-glazed grilled sweet potatoes

SERVES 4

In this dish it's really important to get the blanching of the sweet potatoes just right. You want them to boil enough that they don't have to spend a long time on the grill (the outside will burn if they do), but not boil so long that they become mushy. The best way to check them is to stick one with a fork after about 6 minutes in the boiling water; it should be rather easy to pierce while still offering a good deal of resistance.

The sweetened rice wine called mirin contributes a beguiling flavor as well as sweetness to the glaze here. If you don't have it, though, you can substitute sweet vermouth or sweet sherry.

1/3 cup mirin (or substitute sweet vermouth or sweet sherry)
1/3 cup dark soy sauce
2 tablespoons molasses
1 tablespoon peeled and minced fresh ginger
1 teaspoon ground cinnamon

Kosher salt and freshly cracked black pepper to taste
3 sweet potatoes, peeled and cut on the bias into slices about 1 inch thick
2 tablespoons olive oil

1. Build a multi-level fire in your grill: Leaving one-quarter of the bottom free of coals, bank the coals in the remaining three-quarters of the grill so that they are three times as high on one side as on the other. When the coals are all ignited and the temperature has died down to medium (you can hold your hand about 5 inches above the grill grid, over the area where the coals are deepest, for 4 to 5 seconds), you're ready to cook.

2. In a small bowl, whisk together the mirin, soy sauce, molasses, ginger, cinnamon, and salt and pepper to taste. Set aside while you cook the potatoes.

3. Cook the sweet potato slices in boiling salted water until barely tender, about 6 to 8 minutes. Drain the slices and pat them dry with paper towels, then brush them on both sides with the oil and sprinkle them generously with salt and pepper.

4. Place the slices on the grill and cook, turning once, until they are nicely browned and tender, about 3 to 4 minutes per side. During the last 15 seconds of grilling, brush the sweet potato slices with the soy glaze. Serve hot or at room temperature.

smoky acorn squash with maple-vanilla butter

SERVES 4

When you see all those bright, beautiful acorn squashes at your local vegetable stand in the fall, it's very inspiring. And they taste as good as they look, with a distinctly autumnal flavor. The only problem is, it's a big pain to peel these guys, so we're always looking for ways to bypass that step when we cook them. Here we cut the squashes in half, clean them out, roast them until they're just tender, and then put them on the grill to give them a little smoky char. When they come off the grill, we put a little maple-vanilla butter in the cavities for that sweet holiday squash experience.

2 acorn squashes, halved, strings and
    seeds removed
2 tablespoons vegetable oil
Kosher salt and freshly cracked black
    pepper to taste
4 tablespoons unsalted butter,
    softened

2 tablespoons pure maple syrup
1 vanilla bean, split lengthwise
    (or substitute 1/2 teaspoon
    vanilla extract)

1. Preheat the oven to 350°F.

2. Place the squash halves cut side down on a baking sheet and roast them until just tender, 35 to 40 minutes.

3. Meanwhile, build a multi-level fire in your grill: Leaving one-quarter of the bottom free of coals, bank the coals in the remaining three-quarters of the grill so that they are three times as high on one side as on the other. When the coals are all ignited and the temperature has died down to medium-low (you can hold your hand about 5 inches above the grill grid, over the area where the coals are deepest, for 5 seconds), you're ready to put the squashes on.

4. Rub the squash halves with the vegetable oil and salt and pepper to taste. Grill them, cut side down, until golden brown and slightly charred, about 10 to 15 minutes.

5. While the squashes are on the grill, combine the butter and maple syrup in a small bowl. With the tip of a sharp knife, scrape the vanilla seeds into the bowl. Mix until the seeds are well distributed in the butter, then set aside.

6. When the squash halves are done, put a spoonful of the butter in each cavity, brushing a little along the edges as it melts.

COOK TO COOK: You can use vanilla extract here if you can't get your hands on a vanilla bean, but the bean does create a more satisfying flavor.

grilled fingerling potatoes with blue cheese

SERVES 4

This is an interesting dish that I (Chris) got from a friend and colleague of mine, Terry Bell. When Terry worked at a Boston-area restaurant called Not Your Average Joe's, he came up with this unbelievably simple dish, which features the great combination of potatoes and blue cheese. You just blanch the potatoes until they are tender but still have enough texture to hold together on the grill, then halve them, grill them, and melt a little blue cheese on top of them on the cooler side of the grill. Couldn't be much easier, but it tastes fantastic.

We like Maytag blue cheese with this dish, but any type will work, so just choose your favorite. And try whatever variety of fingerlings you find in your local market. The name refers only to the long, slender, fingerlike shape of the potatoes; other than sharing that characteristic, fingerlings may vary widely in texture, taste, even color. With farmers now growing all kinds of interesting and flavorful potatoes, there are plenty of choices to play with.

1 pound fingerling potatoes	Kosher salt and freshly cracked black
2 tablespoons olive oil	pepper to taste
	1/3 cup crumbled blue cheese

1. Build a multi-level fire in your grill: Leaving one-quarter of the bottom free of coals, bank the coals in the remaining three-quarters of the grill so that they are three times as high on one side as on the other. When the coals are all ignited and the temperature has died down to medium (you can hold your hand about 5 inches above the grill grid, over the area where the coals are deepest, for 4 to 5 seconds), you're ready to cook.

2. While the fire is heating up, blanch the potatoes in boiling salted water until just tender (you should be able to stick a toothpick into them but still feel some resistance), about 5 to 8 minutes.

3. Cut the potatoes in half lengthwise, rub them lightly all over with the oil, and sprinkle them generously with salt and pepper. Arrange them, cut side down, over the side of the grill with the deepest coals and cook until the potatoes are crusty and brown, about 3 to 4 minutes per side.

4. Meanwhile, place a sturdy foil pan large enough to hold all the potatoes in a single layer on the side of the grill away from the fire. Transfer the grilled potatoes to the pan, placing them cut side up, and scatter the blue cheese over them. Allow the cheese to melt slightly, then serve hot.

grilled potato steaks with bacon, sour cream, and chives

SERVES 4

This dish is one of our favorites. It's kind of a grilled play on the classic baked potato, so naturally it goes perfectly with a big, juicy steak.

The butter is optional here, but we recommend it. After all, this is a pretty decadent dish, so why not go all the way? We don't have it often, but when we do we definitely want the real deal.

4 large baking potatoes, scrubbed well, unpeeled	Kosher salt and freshly cracked black pepper
8 slices bacon, diced small	1 cup sour cream
1/4 cup olive oil	1 bunch chives, minced
	1/2 cup unsalted butter (optional)

1. Build a multi-level fire in your grill: Leaving one-quarter of the bottom free of coals, bank the coals in the remaining three-quarters of the grill so that they are three times as high on one side as on the other. When the coals are all ignited and the fire has died down to medium (you can hold your hand about 5 inches above the grill grid, over the area where the coals are deepest, for 4 to 5 seconds), you're ready to cook.

2. Cut thin slices lengthwise off 2 parallel sides of each potato so you can lay it flat. Now cut each potato in half lengthwise to make 2 planks; you want each plank to be about 1 1/2 inches thick. (No need to peel the potatoes; trimming the sides will take off some of the skin, and it's fine to leave the rest on.)

3. In a large sauté pan or skillet, gently cook the potatoes in simmering salted water about 8 to 9 minutes, until they are just done but still very firm. Test them by poking a toothpick into one; it should go in quite easily, but meet with a fair amount of resistance. Carefully transfer the potatoes to a colander to drain.

4. While the potatoes are cooking, cook the bacon in a small sauté pan or skillet over medium heat until crisp, about 6 to 8 minutes, then transfer to paper towels or newspaper to drain.

5. Rub the potato planks all over with the olive oil and sprinkle them generously with salt and pepper. Place on the grill and cook until they are really crispy and brown, about 4 to 5 minutes per side.

6. Arrange the potatoes on a serving platter and top with the bacon, sour cream, chives, and butter if desired.

HOBO PACKS AND OTHER ASH-ROASTED SIDES

THE JOYS OF ASH COOKERY

In our opinion, most people just don't cook hobo packs often enough. Making them is an incredibly painless way to come up with great, exciting side dishes. They're easy to assemble, they're even easier to cook—how much work is it to wrap some stuff in foil and stick the packet in the ashes?—and they're the ultimate make-ahead dishes. You can assemble them in the morning and then just put them in the fire that afternoon or evening. To make the whole process even easier, you don't have to wrap the food in layers and layers of foil wrap—you can just toss everything into a disposable foil pan and cover it tightly with a couple layers of foil.

The only thing you have to be careful about when making hobo packs is not to puncture the foil; if you do, the juices will run out and the food will end up dry and probably burned. Also, be sure that you follow our system of always making a multi-level fire, with one area that has few coals. This is where the hobo packs go. There will be plenty of heat to cook them through but not so much that they will be incinerated.

The recipes here are just examples. By the time you're finished trying these, you'll be going into your refrigerator to see what you've got, then improvising your own hobo packs. That's how simple they are.

hobo pack of beets, carrots, and apples with orange and ginger

SERVES 4

We love using beets in hobo packs, because it's just about the easiest way to cook them and they taste so wonderful with that smoky edge they acquire from sitting in the coals. Here we combine them with sweet carrots and sweet-tart Granny Smith apples, then flavor the whole batch with ginger and orange. The result is an earthy side dish with sweet and spicy undercurrents.

2 oranges, thinly sliced
3 beets about the size of baseballs, peeled and quartered
2 medium carrots, peeled and cut in large chunks
2 Granny Smith apples, cored and diced large

2 tablespoons peeled and minced fresh ginger
1/4 cup fresh orange juice
1/3 cup olive oil
Kosher salt and freshly cracked black pepper to taste

1. Combine all the ingredients in a large bowl and toss gently to mix well.

2. Tear off 4 sheets of heavy-duty foil, each about 2 feet long, and stack them one on top of another. In the center of the top sheet, arrange the orange slices on the bottom and pile the combined vegetables and apples on top. Fold up the sheets around the mixture, one after another, turning the package a quarter turn each time and making sure that each sheet is well sealed around the filling. If necessary, split the ingredients and make 2 hobo packs. Or arrange the orange slices on the bottom of a deep disposable foil pan, pile the combined vegetables and apples on top, and cover tightly with a double layer of heavy-duty foil.

3. Place the hobo pack (or packs) in the coals around the periphery of the fire, where the heat is less intense. Pile the coals up around the pack and cook until the vegetables are tender, about 45 minutes. Remove the pack from the coals, unroll the foil, and serve hot.

COOK TO COOK: Be sure to use plenty of salt and pepper on the vegetables and fruits here to really bring out the flavors.

hobo pack of plantains and onions with raisins, garlic, and lime

SERVES 4

Mellow-flavored plantains are a wonderful choice for hobo packs. Here we mix them with red onions, sweet raisins, and thin slices of unpeeled lime for a sweet-tart component. Be sure to use plantains that are at the proper stage of ripeness, usually indicated by yellow skin with a few black spots. If they're overripe (mostly black skin), they'll turn to mush, but if they're under-ripe (green skin), they'll emerge from the coals with centers that are still too hard. Ripe but firm plantains will come out soft, tender, and sweet, with just a little resistance to the bite.

3 ripe but still firm plantains, peeled
    and cut in 3-inch chunks
2 medium red onions, peeled and cut
    in 3-inch chunks
1/2 cup raisins
2 heads garlic, separated into cloves,
    peel left on

1/3 cup olive oil
Kosher salt and freshly cracked black
    pepper to taste
2 whole limes, thinly sliced

1. Combine all the ingredients except the limes in a large bowl and toss gently to mix well.

2. Tear off 4 sheets of heavy-duty foil, each about 2 feet long, and stack them one on top of another. Arrange the lime slices on the bottom of the top sheet and then pile on the rest of the ingredients. Fold up the sheets around the vegetables, one after another, turning the package a quarter turn each time and making sure that each sheet is well sealed around the filling. If necessary, split the ingredients and make 2 hobo packs. Or arrange the lime slices on the bottom of a deep disposable foil pan, pile the plantain and onion mixture on top, and cover tightly with a double layer of heavy-duty foil.

3. Place the hobo pack (or packs) in the coals around the periphery of the fire, where the heat is less intense. Pile the coals up around the pack and cook until the vegetables are tender, about 30 minutes. Remove the pack from the coals, unroll the foil, and serve hot.

COOK TO COOK: The skin of all but the ripest plantains clings very closely to the fruit. To peel, slice a bit off the top and bottom of the plantain, run your knife down the three lengthwise "seams," and then do a kind of prying/slicing maneuver to take the peel off.

hobo pack of yuca, corn, and tomatoes with cumin, chile, and oregano

SERVES 4

❧ ❧ ❧ ❧ ❧ ❧ ❧ ❧ ❧ ❧ ❧ ❧ ❧ ❧ ❧ ❧ ❧

This Latin-inspired hobo pack features one of our favorite Caribbean tubers, the yuca (pronounced *yook*-ah). Also known as manioc or cassava, yuca is shaped like a long, narrow sweet potato. Its rough outer skin looks like scaly bark, often thickly coated with wax applied to keep it fresh during shipping. When cooked, the stark-white flesh has a slightly sweet, rather buttery flavor and a somewhat glutinous, chewy texture that works particularly well in situations like a hobo pack. Yuca takes a bit of preparation before you can combine it with the other ingredients, since it has both an underskin and a fibrous central core, both of which need to be removed.

2 yuca (about 1 pound), skin and pink underskin peeled, center core removed, and flesh cut in chunks

2 ears of corn, shucked, desilked, and cut in thirds

1 ripe tomato about the size of a baseball, diced large

3 tablespoons toasted cumin seeds (or 1 1/2 tablespoons ground cumin)

1 to 2 tablespoons minced chile pepper of your choice

1/4 cup roughly chopped fresh oregano

1/2 cup olive oil

Kosher salt and freshly cracked black pepper to taste

1. Combine all the ingredients in a large bowl and toss gently to mix well.

2. Tear off 4 sheets of heavy-duty foil, each about 2 feet long, and stack them one on top of another. Arrange the combined ingredients in the center of the top sheet. Fold up the sheets around the vegetables, one after another, turning the package a quarter turn each time and making sure that each sheet is well sealed around the vegetables. If necessary, split the ingredients and make 2 hobo packs. Or put the vegetables into a deep disposable foil pan and cover tightly with a double layer of heavy-duty foil.

3. Place the hobo pack (or packs) in the coals around the periphery of the fire, where the heat is less intense. Pile the coals up around the pack and cook until the vegetables are tender, about 30 minutes. Remove the pack from the coals, unroll the foil, and serve hot.

hobo pack of winter squash, bacon, and red onions

SERVES 4

※ ※ ※ ※ ※ ※ ※ ※ ※ ※ ※ ※ ※ ※ ※ ※ ※ ※

This is a perfect fall dish that takes advantage of the range of squashes in the market. We particularly like butternut, Hubbard, buttercup, and acorn, not only because they are usually the easiest to get hold of, but because of their rich flavors. But Sweet Dumpling, Delicata, Golden Nugget, or any of the other winter squashes are also really good in this dish, as is pumpkin. And anything that contains bacon is okay with us.

4 thick strips bacon, slab if available	3 cups large-diced winter squash of
2 tablespoons unsalted butter	your choice
2 oranges, sliced into thick disks	3 tablespoons roughly chopped fresh
(don't peel them)	thyme or oregano
2 red onions, peeled and quartered	Kosher salt and freshly cracked black
lengthwise	pepper to taste

1. In a medium sauté pan or skillet over medium heat, cook the bacon until crisp, about 6 to 8 minutes. Remove the pan from the heat. Transfer the bacon to paper towels or a brown paper bag to drain, then discard all but 2 tablespoons of the drippings from the pan. Add the butter to the pan and stir until it has melted into the hot drippings. When the bacon is well drained, crumble it coarsely and set it aside.

2. Tear off 4 sheets of heavy-duty foil, each about 2 feet long, and stack them one on top of another. Arrange the orange slices on the center of the top sheet, then put on the onions, then the squash. Drizzle the butter mixture over the top and sprinkle with the fresh herbs and bacon. Fold up the sheets around the vegetables, one after another, turning the package a quarter turn each time and making sure that each sheet is well sealed around the vegetables. If necessary, split the ingredients and make 2 hobo packs. Or layer the ingredients—orange slices first, then onions, then squash, with the butter mixture and herbs on top—in a deep disposable foil pan and cover tightly with a double layer of heavy-duty foil.

3. Place the hobo pack (or packs) in the coals around the periphery of the fire, where the heat is less intense. Pile the coals up around the pack and cook until the onions are tender and the squash is cooked through, about 25 to 30 minutes.

4. Remove the pack from the coals and unroll the foil; if the squash needs more time, rewrap the pack and put it back in the coals until the squash is done.

COOK TO COOK: Slab bacon is simply bacon that comes in a large slab rather than in slices. The big advantage is that you can slice it as thick as you like, instead of having to settle for the thin slices you get with the presliced version. If the slab bacon comes with a thick outer rind, as it sometimes does, you should cut the rind off and discard it.

hobo pack of sweet potatoes, apples, and sage

SERVES 4

With its Boy Scout origins and somewhat haphazard nature, the hobo pack is a very casual affair. But this one, quite sweet and a little sophisticated, is a kind of holiday version, well-suited to the Thanksgiving or Christmas table. As it cooks in the heat of the coals, the sweet apples and raisins mingle with the earthy sweet potatoes and sage while the butter supplies richness and the brandy gives it extra style. Of course, there's no need to save it for a holiday—why deprive yourself?—because it's great for any autumn or winter dinner.

2 large Golden Delicious apples,
unpeeled, cored and quartered
2 sweet potatoes, well scrubbed,
peeled, and quartered length-
wise
1 red onion, peeled and sliced thin

1/4 cup raisins
1/4 cup finely chopped fresh sage
3 tablespoons unsalted butter
3 tablespoons brandy
Kosher salt and freshly cracked black
pepper to taste

1. Tear off 4 sheets of heavy-duty foil, each about 2 feet long, and stack them one on top of another. Arrange the apples and sweet potatoes in the center of the top sheet, then top with the onion slices, shower with the raisins and sage, dot with the butter, drizzle with the brandy, and (finally) sprinkle generously with salt and pepper. Fold up the sheets around the ingredients, one after another, turning the package a quarter turn each time and making sure that each sheet is well sealed around the food. If necessary, split the ingredients and make 2 hobo packs. Or arrange the ingredients in the order described above in a deep disposable foil pan and cover tightly with a double layer of heavy-duty foil.

2. Place the hobo pack (or packs) in the coals around the periphery of the fire, where the heat is less intense. Pile the coals up around the pack and cook until the apples are tender and the potatoes are cooked through, about 30 minutes.

3. Remove the pack from the coals and unroll the foil; if the sweet potato needs more time, put the pack back in the coals or in a 300°F oven until the sweet potato is done.

hobo pack of tomato and broccoli rabe with garlic and lemon

SERVES 4

A Mediterranean mixture, this dish gets its flavor punch from pleasantly bitter broccoli rabe and thinly sliced lemons, which actually turn sweet as they cook in the heat of the coals. Garlic, thyme, and tomatoes round out the mix, all bound together by the indispensable olive oil.

2 lemons, sliced very thin
2 ripe tomatoes about the size of
   baseballs, quartered
2 bunches broccoli rabe, trimmed
2 tablespoons minced garlic

2 tablespoons fresh thyme leaves
1/2 cup olive oil
Kosher salt and freshly cracked black
   pepper to taste

1. Combine all the ingredients in a large bowl and toss gently to mix well.

2. Tear off 4 sheets of heavy-duty foil, each about 2 feet long, and stack them one on top of another. In the center of the top sheet, arrange the lemon slices and the tomato on the bottom and put the broccoli rabe on top. Fold up the sheets around the vegetables, one after another, turning the package a quarter turn each time and making sure that each sheet is well sealed around the vegetables. If necessary, split the ingredients and make 2 hobo packs. Or arrange the lemon slices and tomato in a deep disposable foil pan, put the broccoli rabe on top, and cover tightly with a double layer of heavy-duty foil.

3. Place the hobo pack (or packs) in the coals around the periphery of the fire, where the heat is less intense. Pile the coals up around the pack and cook until the vegetables are tender, about 20 minutes. Remove the pack from the coals, unroll the foil, and serve hot.

blue cheese–stuffed, ash-roasted red onions with raisins and pine nuts

SERVES 4

※ ※ ※ ※ ※ ※ ※ ※ ※ ※ ※ ※ ※ ※ ※ ※ ※

This is a rich dish, perfect to nestle into the ashes while you're smoke-roasting a pork, beef, or lamb roast. It has got a little sweetness from the raisins, tanginess from the blue cheese, and earthiness from the pine nuts, so it has enough flavors going on to make it a very dynamic side dish. It takes some work to blanch and partially hollow out the onions, but the end result is worth it.

4 medium red onions, peeled	1/4 cup raisins, steeped in 1/4 cup
1/2 pound blue cheese, crumbled	heated dry sherry for 15 minutes
1/4 cup toasted pine nuts	Freshly cracked black pepper to taste

1. Cut a thin slice off the root end of each onion so that it will stand upright. Cut off the top one-quarter or so of the other end (it's called the bud end, if you wanted to know). Bring a large pot of water to a boil and drop in the onions. Reduce the heat to low, simmer for about 10 minutes, then transfer the onions to a large bowl filled with ice water.

2. While the onions are cooking, toss the blue cheese, pine nuts, sherry-soaked raisins, and pepper together in a medium bowl until well mixed. Set aside.

3. Tear off 2 sheets of heavy-duty foil, each about 2 feet long, and stack them one on top of another. When the onions are cool enough to handle, remove the inner third of each onion, leaving a stuffable shell, and arrange them in the center of the top sheet of foil. Divide the filling among the onion shells. Fold up the sheets of foil around the stuffed onions, one after the other, turning the package a quarter turn each time and making sure that each sheet is well sealed around the onions. Or place the onion shells in a deep disposable foil pan, divide the filling among them, and cover tightly with a double layer of heavy-duty foil.

4. Place the hobo pack in the coals around the periphery of the fire, where the heat is less intense. Pile the coals up around it and roast about 30 to 40 minutes.

5. Remove the pack from the coals, cut open the foil, and serve the onions hot.

COOK TO COOK: We tried a number of other options (a fork, tongs, a grapefruit spoon) and found that the easiest way to remove the inner third of a blanched onion is to cut it out with a paring knife.

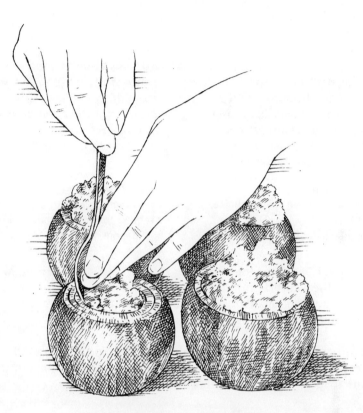

Hollow the onions with a paring knife,
then use a spoon to fill them

ash-roasted pears
with blue cheese–walnut stuffing and a balsamic drizzle

SERVES 4

⚒ ⚒ ⚒ ⚒ ⚒ ⚒ ⚒ ⚒ ⚒ ⚒ ⚒ ⚒ ⚒ ⚒ ⚒ ⚒ ⚒

The inspiration for this particular dish came from my (Doc's) habit of a few years ago, when I roasted Bosc pears for breakfast every morning and took to trying them with different flavor combinations. With Chris's help it morphed into this variation on the hobo pack, which involves hollowing out the pears and stuffing them with some cheese and walnuts, then wrapping them up in foil and tossing the packets into the coals to cook. We like it as an unusual side dish, particularly with pork, but it also works really nicely as a cheese dessert course.

4 very firm Bosc pears
1/2 pound blue cheese of your choice,
    crumbled
1/3 cup chopped toasted walnuts

1 cup balsamic vinegar
1 teaspoon sugar
1 tablespoon freshly cracked black
    pepper

1. Core the pears through the top, stopping 1/4 inch from the bottom. Mix together the blue cheese and the walnuts and then push one-quarter of the mixture into the center of each pear. Fold up 2 sheets of foil around each of the pears, making sure that each sheet is well sealed.

2. Place the foil-wrapped pears in the coals around the periphery of the fire, where the heat is less intense. Pile the coals up around the packages and cook until the pears are tender, about 20 to 30 minutes.

3. While the pears are roasting, bring the vinegar, sugar, and pepper to a boil over high heat, then reduce the heat to medium and simmer vigorously until the mixture is reduced by two-thirds and is somewhat syrupy, about 15 to 20 minutes.

4. When the pears are tender, remove the packages from the coals, unroll the foil, drizzle the pears with the balsamic glaze, and serve warm.

COOK TO COOK: Bosc pears really are the best choice here. Of the other varieties readily available, Anjous are too juicy and lack the sturdiness to stand up to the heat of the coals. Bartletts are an acceptable second choice, but even they tend to get a little mushy.

aromatic slaw with southeast asian flavors

SERVES 6

We love making slaws—they're a great vehicle for presenting all kinds of different textures and tastes. When traveling in Southeast Asia, we discovered that cooks in that part of the world are particularly adept at combining raw greens and whole leaves of herbs with other intensely flavored ingredients like limes, chiles, ginger, and fish sauce to create brightly spiced, lively salads that are easy to make despite their flavor complexity.

The only trick here is to toss everything together at the last minute so the herbs stay fresh and bright. This slaw is a perfect accompaniment to any type of grilled food, but we particularly like it with seafood.

1 cup shredded green cabbage
1 cup shredded red cabbage
1 cup shredded carrots
1 cup loosely packed fresh whole
    mint leaves
1 cup loosely packed fresh whole Thai
    basil leaves (or substitute regu-
    lar basil leaves)
1 cup loosely packed fresh whole
    cilantro leaves (stems are okay,
    too)

For the dressing:
1/2 cup fresh lime juice (about
    4 limes)

1/4 cup *nam pla,* Southeast Asian fish
    sauce (available in Asian mar-
    kets or large supermarkets)
3 tablespoons peeled and minced
    fresh ginger
2 tablespoons Asian chile-garlic
    paste (or substitute 1 tablespoon
    minced red chiles)
2 tablespoons light or dark brown
    sugar
3 tablespoons freshly cracked white
    pepper (or substitute 1 1/2 table-
    spoons ground)
Kosher salt to taste

1. In a large bowl, combine the cabbage, carrots, mint, basil, and cilantro, and mix well.

2. In a small bowl, whisk the dressing ingredients until blended.

3. Just before serving, pour the dressing over the slaw and toss until all the vegetables and herbs are well coated. Season to taste with salt and additional white pepper.

slaw "a la playa" with avocados, hearts of palm, and orange-cumin dressing

SERVES 4 TO 6

Every winter we try to get away for a week or two with a group of friends to Tamarindo, a town on the Pacific coast of Costa Rica with spectacular beaches and a couple of great surf breaks. Everyone in the group is in the food business, so we always bring along several suitcases loaded with good meats and favorite wines. But we also like to cook with the typical ingredients of the country. This is our *ensalada tipica*, the slaw that we make and take down to the beach with us just about every day. (Thus "a la playa"—to the beach.) It's colorful, crunchy, and flavorful, and we can almost guarantee you'll find it tasty and refreshing even if you've never been to the tropics.

For the dressing:
1 ripe tomato about the size of a
    baseball, cored and diced small
2 cups orange juice, simmered until
    reduced to 1/2 cup, about
    20 minutes
2 tablespoons cumin seeds (or sub-
    stitute 1 tablespoon ground
    cumin)
1/4 cup olive oil
1/4 cup red wine vinegar
1/4 cup roughly chopped fresh
    cilantro
Kosher salt and freshly cracked black
    pepper to taste

1 cup julienned red cabbage
1 cup julienned green cabbage
1/2 cup julienned carrots
1 cup julienned hearts of palm (either
    the jarred kind, drained, or, if you
    can find them, fresh)
2 avocados, peeled, pitted, and
    sliced thin

1. In a large bowl, whisk together all the dressing ingredients.

2. Add the cabbage, carrots, hearts of palm, and avocado and toss to coat thoroughly with the dressing. Serve immediately or chill slightly in the refrigerator first.

COOK TO COOK: If you can't locate (or don't like) hearts of palm, you can leave them out, but in that case you might want to up the number of avocados to 3.

parsley salad with tomatoes and bulgur

SERVES 6

¾ ¾ ¾ ¾ ¾ ¾ ¾ ¾ ¾ ¾ ¾ ¾ ¾ ¾ ¾ ¾ ¾

This is actually one of our favorite grilling go-alongs. A lot of people don't give parsley much respect as an herb, largely because its prowess as a garnish has given it a reputation as a mere decoration. But one of my (Chris's) favorite kitchen snacks has always been a nice big sprig of parsley liberally sprinkled with salt. So we've started using this neglected herb, in both its curly and flat-leaf incarnations, as a green, and it works really well.

Here we display parsley's virtues in our version of taboulleh, the classic Middle Eastern salad. It's particularly good with grilled food because the slight bitter bite of the parsley, the aromaticity of the mint, and the sourness of the lemon provide an excellent counterpart to the rich, smoky grilled taste.

2 cups fine bulgur

2 ripe tomatoes about the size of
    baseballs, cored and diced
    medium

2 bunches flat parsley leaves (a few
    stems are okay), roughly
    chopped

1/4 cup finely chopped fresh mint

1/3 cup extra-virgin olive oil

Juice of 1 lemon

Kosher salt and freshly cracked black
    pepper to taste

1. Put the bulgur in a large, heatproof bowl. Pour 4 1/2 cups boiling water over the bulgur, cover the bowl, and let it sit for 20 minutes.

2. While the bulgur is soaking, combine the remaining ingredients in a large bowl.

3. After 20 minutes, drain the bulgur through a fine sieve and add it to the bowl with the other ingredients. Mix well, then cover and refrigerate until serving time.

COOK TO COOK: Don't try to substitute cracked wheat for the bulgur in this recipe; bulgur is a precooked product, while cracked wheat is uncooked. If you can't find fine bulgur (often labeled #1), you can substitute medium (#2), but coarse (#3) is really too large to mingle properly with the other ingredients.

black bean and pineapple salad
with orange-chipotle vinaigrette (for a crowd)

SERVES 8

꽃 꽃 꽃 꽃 꽃 꽃 꽃 꽃 꽃 꽃 꽃 꽃 꽃 꽃 꽃 꽃

We prefer black beans to white because they have a deeper, more distinctive taste, so you can combine them with other intensely flavored tropical ingredients. Here we do just that. Like other black bean dishes, this one can be served hot, cold, or at room temperature.

This recipe makes enough to feed a good-sized group, but even if you are feeding only a couple of people we recommend that you make the whole amount, because this salad holds very well, covered and refrigerated. If you keep it for more than a day, refresh it by mixing in a bit more lime juice and freshly chopped cilantro.

2 cups dried black beans (or substitute 3 cans of black beans, 15 ounces each, drained and rinsed well)

For the vinaigrette:
Juice of 1 orange
1/2 cup fresh lime juice (about 4 limes)
2 tablespoons molasses
2 tablespoons cider vinegar
2 tablespoons chipotle peppers in adobo sauce
2 tablespoons toasted cumin seeds (or substitute 1 tablespoon ground cumin)

Kosher salt and freshly cracked black pepper to taste
1/4 cup olive oil
___

1/2 small pineapple, peeled, cored, and diced medium
1/2 red bell pepper, cored, seeded, and diced medium
1/2 green bell pepper, cored, seeded, and diced medium
1/2 red onion, diced small
3 tablespoons roughly chopped fresh cilantro
3 tablespoons roughly chopped fresh oregano
Kosher salt and freshly cracked black pepper to taste

1. If using dried beans, soak them in cold water overnight or for at least 5 hours, then drain and rinse well. Put them in a saucepan with cold water to cover by about 2 inches. Bring to a boil over high heat, then reduce the heat to medium-low and simmer until the beans are soft to the bite but not mushy, about 1 1/2 to 2 hours, adding the salt after the first 1/2 hour. Drain the beans and put them in a large bowl.

2. While the beans are cooking, make the dressing: In a blender or food processor, combine the orange and lime juices, molasses, vinegar, chipotles, cumin, and salt and pepper to taste and process until smooth. With the machine running, add the oil through the feed tube in a thin stream until the dressing is well blended.

3. To the bowl with the beans, add the pineapple, bell peppers, onion, cilantro, oregano, and salt and pepper to taste. Pour the dressing over the salad, toss well until combined, and serve.

white bean salad with grilled squash, zucchini, and roasted red pepper dressing (for a crowd)

SERVES 8 TO 10

We have become champions of the lowly zucchini and summer squash, crops that all home gardeners seem to grow an overabundance of, to the point that sometimes you wonder why they plant them at all. Well, we'll tell you why—because they're delicious. Grilling is a great way to cook them, because they pick up a lot of flavor on the outside but keep that nice, juicy, squashy thing going on inside.

Here we use grilled squash to give substance and flavor to a Mediterranean-style white bean salad with a roasted red pepper dressing. Easy, quick, and generous enough to feed a crowd, this salad is good for tonight, good for tomorrow night, and good for the next night, too.

1 pound dried cannellini, Great Northern, navy, or other white beans (or substitute 3 cans white beans, 15 ounces each, drained and rinsed well)
1 large bay leaf
1 tablespoon kosher salt

For the dressing:
2 roasted red peppers, jarred or homemade (see page 290)
3/4 cup olive oil
1/4 cup balsamic vinegar
1 teaspoon minced garlic
1/4 cup roughly chopped fresh herbs: any one or a combination of basil, thyme, and oregano

Kosher salt and freshly cracked black pepper to taste

2 medium zucchini, cut lengthwise into 1/2-inch planks
2 medium summer squash, cut lengthwise into 1/2-inch planks
1 small red onion, peeled and quartered lengthwise
1/4 cup olive oil
2 ripe plum tomatoes, cored and diced small
3 scallions, white and green parts, sliced thin

1. If using dried beans, soak them in cold water overnight or for at least 5 hours, then drain and rinse well. Place them in a saucepan with the bay leaf and fresh water to cover by about 2 inches. Bring to a boil over high heat, then reduce the heat to medium-low and simmer until the beans are tender, about 45 minutes to 1 hour, adding the salt after the first 30 minutes. Drain the beans and put them in a large bowl.

2. While the beans are cooking, make the dressing: In a blender or food processor, purée the roasted peppers until smooth. Add the vinegar, garlic, and herbs and blend for a few more seconds. With the machine running, add the olive oil in a steady stream. Season to taste with salt and pepper.

3. Build a multi-level fire in your grill: Leaving one-quarter of the bottom free of coals, bank the coals in the remaining three-quarters of the grill so that they are three times as high on one side as on the other. When the coals are all ignited and the temperature has died down to medium (you can hold your hand about 5 inches above the grill grid, over the area where the coals are deepest, for 4 to 5 seconds), you're ready to cook.

4. Brush the planks of zucchini and summer squash and the onion quarters lightly with the olive oil and sprinkle them generously with salt and pepper. Arrange them on the grill and cook until well browned, about 3 to 5 minutes per side. When the vegetables are done, dice them coarsely and add them to the beans along with the tomatoes and scallions.

5. Pour the dressing over the salad and toss until well combined, then allow the salad to cool to room temperature before serving.

warm salad of grilled eggplant, summer squash, and zucchini

SERVES 10

Here's a grilled dish that you can make before you start to grill the entrée, because it's best served just barely warm or even at room temperature. It's a perfect dish for late summer, when you're innundated with all that eggplant, summer squash, and zucchini. Just combine the vegetables with garlic and red pepper flakes, set them on the grill until they are browned and tender, and then toss them in a vinaigrette.

Served with EZ Grill Bread with Personality (page 77), this makes an excellent side dish for steak. It is also a fine vegetarian entrée.

For the dressing:
1/2 cup extra-virgin olive oil
1/4 cup fresh lemon juice (about 1 lemon)
1/4 cup balsamic vinegar
3 tablespoons freshly cracked corian-der seeds
1/2 cup roughly chopped fresh parsley
Kosher salt and freshly cracked black pepper to taste

2 large eggplants, cut into slices about 1 inch thick
3 medium summer squash, cut lengthwise into planks about 1 inch thick
3 medium zucchini, cut lengthwise into planks about 1 inch thick
1/4 cup olive oil
2 tablespoons peeled and minced garlic
1 tablespoon red pepper flakes
Kosher salt and freshly cracked black pepper to taste

1. Build a multi-level fire in your grill: Leaving one-quarter of the bottom free of coals, bank the coals in the remaining three-quarters of the grill so that they are three times as high on one side as on the other. When the coals are all ignited and the temperature has died down to medium (you can hold your hand about 5 inches above the grill grid, over the area where the coals are deepest, for 4 to 5 seconds), you're ready to cook.

2. In a small bowl, combine all the dressing ingredients, whisk together well, and set aside.

3. In a large bowl, combine the eggplant slices, summer squash and zucchini planks, oil, garlic, pepper flakes, and salt and pepper to taste. Toss gently to coat the vegetables. Place them on the grill and cook, turning once, until well browned, about 3 to 4 minutes per side. (To check for doneness, cut into one slice of each vegetable; it should look moist all the way through.) Remove the vegetables to a cutting board and cut them up into large chunks, then put them back into the bowl you originally tossed them in.

4. Stir the dressing again, then add it to the bowl with the vegetables and toss gently. Serve the salad warm or at room temperature.

warm grilled new potato salad with corn and chiles

SERVES 4

Grilled potatoes don't match up all that well with mayo, but they are fantastic tossed in a kind of vinaigrette with a few other ingredients like fresh corn. With that inimitable grilled flavor, potatoes can also stand up to chiles, so we add puréed chipotles to the mix. It may not be quite the potato salad that Grandma used to make for the family reunion picnic, but it sure is good.

1 ripe tomato about the size of a baseball, diced small

3 ears corn, blanched in boiling salted water for 2 minutes, drained, and kernels cut off the cobs (about 1 1/2 cups)

1 to 2 tablespoons puréed chipotle peppers in adobo sauce (or substitute minced fresh chile pepper of your choice)

1/4 cup red wine vinegar

1 teaspoon sugar

1/3 cup roughly chopped fresh cilantro

Kosher salt and freshly cracked black pepper to taste

16 new potatoes about the size of golf balls, scrubbed but not peeled

3 tablespoons olive oil

1. Build a multi-level fire in your grill: Leaving one-quarter of the bottom free of coals, bank the coals in the remaining three-quarters of the grill so that they are three times as high on one side as on the other. When the coals are all ignited and the temperature has died down to medium (you can hold your hand about 5 inches above the grill grid, over the area where the coals are deepest, for 4 to 5 seconds), you're ready to cook.

2. Meanwhile, blanch the potatoes for 10 minutes in a large pot of boiling salted water, then drain and chill in running cold water.

3. While the potatoes are blanching, get the rest of the dish ready: In a bowl large enough to hold the potatoes, combine the tomato, corn, chile purée, vinegar, sugar, cilantro, and salt and pepper to taste. Toss gently.

4. Thread the blanched potatoes onto skewers, brush them with the olive oil, and sprinkle them generously with salt and pepper. Put the skewers on the grill and cook, turning once, until the potatoes are nicely browed and can easily be pierced with a fork but still offer some resistance, about 3 to 4 minutes per side. When the potatoes are done, transfer them to the bowl of dressing, toss well to coat, and serve.

COOK TO COOK: Round items like new potatoes sometimes flip around on skewers when you move them. To prevent this if it bothers you, thread each potato onto *two* skewers held parallel and about half an inch apart.

white bean and artichoke heart salad with charred tomato dressing

SERVES 4 TO 6

Next time you have a grilling fire lit, set a cored and quartered tomato over the fire for about five minutes and get it nicely charred. Then you can make this flavorful, smoky dressing right away, or you can put the tomato in the refrigerator for a couple days and use it to make the dressing any time you like.

This salad, which pairs the earthy but still rather subtle flavors of artichoke hearts and white beans, fits into any summer meal.

For the dressing:
1 ripe tomato about the size of a
    baseball, cored and quartered
1 tablespoon vegetable oil
Kosher salt and freshly cracked black
    pepper to taste
2 cloves garlic, peeled
1/2 cup extra-virgin olive oil
2 tablespoons brown mustard

1/4 cup red wine vinegar

2 cups cooked white beans of your
    choice
1 cup artichoke hearts, quartered
    (thawed frozen are okay)
2 stalks celery, diced small
1/2 cup roughly chopped fresh thyme
    or parsley

1. Build a multi-level fire in your grill: Leaving one-quarter of the bottom free of coals, bank the coals in the remaining three-quarters of the grill so that they are three times as high on one side as on the other. When the coals are all ignited and the temperature had died down to medium (you can hold your hand about 5 inches above the grill grid, over the area where the coals are deepest, for 4 to 5 seconds), you're ready to cook.

2. Make the dressing: Coat the tomato quarters with the vegetable oil, sprinkle them generously with salt and pepper, and grill them until well charred, about 4 to 5 minutes. Remove the tomato from the grill, put it in a blender or food processor along with the garlic, olive oil, mustard, and vinegar, and pulse until not quite smooth.

3. In a serving bowl, combine the dressing with the beans, artichoke hearts, celery, and salt and pepper to taste, garnish with the chopped herbs, and serve.

COOK TO COOK: Go carefully when blending or processing the dressing. It has a much more satisfying character if you leave it slightly chunky rather than fully puréeing it.

black bean, avocado, and tomato salad with mango-lime dressing

SERVES 4 TO 6

I (Chris) love beans. There's just something about their earthy flavors that I find uniquely satisfying. Many people think of them primarily as a cold-weather staple, but I like to get them out in the summer too. So here's a salad featuring the classic Latin combination of black beans, avocado, and mango.

1 cup cooked or well-rinsed canned black beans

2 ripe medium avocados, peeled, pitted, and diced large

2 ripe tomatoes about the size of baseballs, cored and diced large

1/2 cup chopped scallions, both green and white parts

1/2 cup roughly chopped fresh cilantro

2 tablespoons cumin seeds (or substitute 1 tablespoon ground cumin)

2 tablespoons freshly cracked coriander seeds (or substitute 1 tablespoon ground coriander)

Kosher salt and freshly cracked black pepper to taste

For the dressing:

1 mango, peeled, pitted, and diced small

1/2 cup olive oil

1/4 cup red wine vinegar

2 tablespoons minced red or green chile peppers of your choice

1/4 cup roughly chopped fresh cilantro

Juice of 2 limes

Kosher salt and freshly cracked black pepper to taste

1. In a large bowl, combine the beans, avocados, tomatoes, scallions, cilantro, cumin, coriander, and salt and pepper to taste. Toss gently to mix.

2. In a small bowl, combine the ingredients for the dressing and whisk to mix well. Pour the dressing over the salad, toss gently to coat, and serve.

smoky corn and tomato salad with cilantro vinaigrette

SERVES 4 TO 6

In August and September the markets in New England are bursting with excellent locally grown corn and tomatoes. We like to combine the two, along with a little smoke flavor, in as many dishes as we can. This straightforward salad has been an important part of many a satisfying late-summer meal.

6 ears corn, shucked and de-silked
3 ripe tomatoes about the size of
   baseballs, cored and diced large
1 red onion, peeled and sliced thin
1/3 cup olive oil
Juice of 3 limes

1/2 cup roughly chopped fresh
   cilantro
2 tablespoons puréed chipotle peppers in adobo sauce
Kosher salt and freshly cracked black
   pepper to taste

1. Build a multi-level fire in your grill: Leaving one-quarter of the bottom free of coals, bank the coals in the remaining three-quarters of the grill so that they are three times as high on one side as on the other. When the coals are all ignited and the temperature has died down to medium (you can hold your hand about 5 inches above the grill grid, over the area where the coals are deepest, for 4 to 5 seconds), you're ready to cook.

2. Put the ears of corn on the grill and cook, rolling them around occasionally, until they are just slightly browned and a little tender, about 4 minutes. Remove them from the heat and slice the kernels off the cobs into a large bowl. (You should have about 3 cups of kernels.) Add the tomatoes and red onion to the bowl.

3. In a small bowl, combine the oil, lime juice, cilantro, chipotles, and salt and pepper and whisk to mix well. Pour the dressing over the salad, toss gently to coat well, and serve.

COOK TO COOK: In this salad you are not looking to cook the corn through. You're just toasting it on the grill so it gets a little smokiness on it but stays slightly crunchy.

cucumber, tomato, and mango salad with lime, chiles, and peanuts

SERVES 6 TO 8

Cucumbers and tomatoes are an ultra-familiar combination to American cooks, but mango brings a touch of the exotic to the mix. To keep that theme going, we combine these three with flavors common to Southeast Asia to create a salad that is easy to put together but has many layers of tastes. Perhaps because of this dynamic, it pairs wonderfully with any grilled food.

2 tablespoons sesame oil
1/3 cup fresh lime juice (about 3 limes)
3 tablespoons peeled and minced fresh ginger
3 tablespoons minced red or green chile peppers of your choice
Kosher salt and freshly cracked black pepper to taste
2 medium cucumbers, peeled, seeded, and diced medium

2 ripe mangoes, peeled, pitted, and diced medium
2 ripe tomatoes about the size of baseballs, cored and diced medium
1/4 cup roughly chopped fresh cilantro
1/4 cup roughly chopped fresh mint
1/2 cup roughly chopped unsalted peanuts

1. In a small bowl, combine the oil, lime juice, ginger, chiles, and salt and pepper and whisk to mix well.

2. In a large bowl, combine the cucumbers, mangoes, and tomatoes. Add the dressing and toss to coat well.

3. Arrange the salad on a platter, garnish with the cilantro, mint, and peanuts, and serve.

orange-raisin couscous with almonds and parsley

SERVES 4

Instant couscous is a real boon to the cook who needs a quick but tasty starch side dish. Here we flavor it with orange juice (use fresh-squeezed here, since it is an important flavor component of the dish and you need to squeeze only a couple of oranges), raisins, almonds, and coriander seeds, ingredients typical of North African cooking. This is ideal for buffets, since it is equally good warm or at room temperature.

1 cup orange juice (fresh-squeezed is best)
1/2 cup olive oil
1 cup instant couscous
1/3 cup raisins
1/3 cup toasted chopped almonds

3 tablespoons crushed toasted coriander seeds
1/2 cup roughly chopped fresh parsley
Kosher salt and freshly cracked black pepper to taste

1. In a small saucepan over medium heat, bring the orange juice to a simmer. Remove from the heat and stir in the olive oil. Place the couscous in a medium bowl and pour the hot orange juice mixture over it. Cover and allow to sit for 15 minutes.

2. Uncover the bowl and fluff the couscous with a fork. Stir in the raisins, almonds, coriander, and parsley, and season to taste with salt and pepper. Serve the couscous warm or at room temperature.

east coast grill cornbread

MAKES 12 THICK PIECES

This cornbread, which is on the sweet and cakey side of its traditional Southern cousin, has been a stone-cold favorite at the East Coast Grill since the restaurant first opened its doors in 1985. It's the perfect accompaniment to all kinds of barbecue, works great dunked in soups, stews, or pot licker, and makes an excellent snack all by itself. We like to eat it topped with some butter and maple syrup or drizzled with chile honey, which you make by stirring a teaspoon or so of dried red pepper flakes into about 1/3 cup of honey.

If by any chance you happen to have any of this bread left over, cut it into big cubes and dry them in a 350°F oven for around 10 minutes, and you'll have excellent croutons to use in salads.

4 cups all-purpose flour
2 cups yellow cornmeal
1 1/2 cups sugar
1 teaspoon salt
2 tablespoons baking powder

4 large eggs
3 cups milk
2 1/2 tablespoons vegetable oil
1/2 cup melted butter

1. Preheat the oven to 350°F.

2. Lightly oil a 12 × 8 × 2-inch pan and put it in the oven to heat up.

3. In a large bowl, sift together the flour, cornmeal, sugar, salt, and baking powder. In a separate large bowl, whisk together the eggs, milk, and vegetable oil. Pour the wet ingredients over the dry ingredients, then add the melted butter and stir just until mixed.

4. Using oven mitts, take the pan out of the oven, quickly spread the batter in it, give it a smack against the counter to even it out, and pop it back into the oven. Bake until the cornbread is browned on top and a cake tester comes out clean, about 1 hour.

cheesy chipotle cornbread

MAKES 12 THIN PIECES

For a little more serious flavor, we add some hot and smoky chipotles, creamy Jack cheese, and tangy buttermilk to our cornbread, along with cream-style corn to give it a more varied texture. It may not be as versatile as the standard bread, but it's more distinctive and stands on its own very well. We like to serve this doctored-up version with barbecue or as a brunch bread.

1 1/4 cups all-purpose flour
1 1/4 cups yellow cornmeal
3 tablespoon sugar
2 teaspoons baking powder
1 teaspoon salt
1 cup canned cream-style corn
3/4 cup buttermilk

3 tablespoons mashed chipotle peppers in adobo sauce
1 small yellow onion, peeled and grated
1 cup grated Monterey Jack cheese
1 large egg, lightly beaten
4 tablespoons vegetable oil

1. Preheat the oven to 350°F.

2. Lightly oil an 8 × 8 × 2-inch pan and put it in the oven to heat up.

3. In a large mixing bowl, sift together the flour, cornmeal, sugar, baking powder, and salt.

4. In a small saucepan over medium heat, combine the corn and buttermilk and mix well. When the mixture is hot but not boiling, remove it from the heat and stir in the chiles and grated onion. Add the cheese and egg, stirring quickly until blended. Pour the mixture over the dry ingredients along with the oil, and mix just until combined.

5. Using oven mitts, take the pan out of the oven, quickly spread the batter in it, smack it once on the counter to even it out, and stick it back in the oven. Bake until the cornbread is browned on top and a cake tester comes out clean, about 30 minutes.

FLAVOR SPIKES

Chutneys, Relishes, Catsups,
Mustards, Spice Rubs, Salsas, Pickles,
and Other Condiments

IF YOU LOOKED INTO EITHER OF OUR REFRIGERATORS ON any given day, you would find them mostly taken up with condiments. We tend to shop meal by meal for produce, meat, seafood, and poultry, because that way we get the freshest stuff and we're free to be inspired by whatever is best at the supermarket, butcher shop, or produce stand that day. But this approach works much better when there's a salsa or two, a flavorful homemade mustard, or a chutney waiting at home in the refrigerator plus a couple of spice rubs stored in the pantry, ready to add a ton of flavor to the meal at the drop of a hat.

In addition to their big flavors and their convenience, there is another reason the recipes in this chapter make perfect sense with grilled food. Unlike sautéing or roasting, grilling doesn't have a natural starting point for sauces—the *fond*, or tasty brown bits left in the pan after roasting or sautéing. So these spice rubs and intensely flavored little dishes, from pickles to sambals, can fill in, serving the function of accompanying food when it comes off the fire.

And why not mix and match, using different condiments with different dishes as you please? These little dishes work equally well with today's grilled pork, tomorrow's grilled steak, and the next day's leftover grilled lamb. With powerful flavors and a wide variety of culinary inspirations—chutneys from India, salsas from Mexico, sambals from Indonesia, pickles from all over—these "sauces" for grilled food are wild, fun, and easy.

salsa fresca with late summer tomatoes, lime, and jalapeños

MAKES ABOUT 4 CUPS

ॐ ॐ ॐ ॐ ॐ ॐ ॐ ॐ ॐ ॐ ॐ ॐ ॐ ॐ ॐ ॐ ॐ

This is a pretty straight-up tomato salsa, designed to take advantage of the luscious tomatoes of August. It is best eaten the day you make it, without refrigeration, so that the flavor of the tomatoes can shine. Serve it alongside pork, fish, or steak or as a dip with some fried plantains.

3 ripe tomatoes about the size of baseballs, cored and diced small

1/2 cup scallions, both green and white parts, diced small

2 tablespoons roughly chopped jalapeños, or to taste

1/4 cup fresh lime juice (about 2 limes)

2 tablespoons freshly cracked toasted cumin seeds (or substitute 1 tablespoon ground cumin)

1/2 cup roughly chopped fresh cilantro

Kosher salt and freshly cracked black pepper to taste

In a large bowl, combine all ingredients and toss gently until well mixed. Serve within a few hours.

COOK TO COOK: We like this particular salsa very hot, but as always you can adjust the jalapeño quotient to suit your own capacity for heat.

the world's hottest salsa, rojo de loco

MAKES ABOUT 4 CUPS

This is for the crazy people. It's always fun to have something super-hot around that can be brought out from hiding to challenge those nuts who swear they like things really, really hot. The key to the blazing nature of this dish is to get hold of Scotch bonnets or habaneros. To bring out their flavor as well as their heat, we roast them along with the garlic and onions before combining them with the other ingredients.

10 to 15 Scotch bonnet or habanero
    peppers, stemmed and halved
    but not seeded
4 garlic cloves, peeled
1 red onion, peeled and diced medium
3 tablespoons olive oil
Kosher salt and freshly cracked black
    pepper to taste
2 cups canned tomatoes with their
    juice

1/2 cup roughly chopped fresh
    cilantro
2 tablespoons ground coriander
2 tablespoons ground cumin
2 tablespoons chili powder
1 tablespoon sugar
1/2 cup fresh lime juice (about
    4 limes)

1. Preheat the oven to 400°F.

2. In a small bowl, combine the peppers, garlic cloves, onion, olive oil, and salt and pepper and toss to combine well. Scatter the mixture in a small roasting pan and roast, turning over once or twice, until the vegetables are soft and golden brown, about 30 minutes. Remove from the oven and allow to cool a bit.

3. Put the slightly cooled mixture into a food processor or blender with all the remaining ingredients, season with salt and pepper, and process or blend until the salsa is well mixed but still slightly chunky. This salsa will keep, covered and refrigerated, for up to 4 days.

pineapple-chipotle salsa

MAKES ABOUT 4 CUPS

Sweet, exotic, yet readily available, pineapple is ideal for salsas. It goes particularly well, we think, with the smoky heat of chipotles. This is a good salsa to set out with Fried Plaintain Rounds (page 334) or tortilla chips for something to munch on at a cocktail party or during a ball game.

- 1/2 fresh pineapple, peeled and diced small
- 1/2 red bell pepper, seeded and diced small
- 1/2 large red onion, peeled and diced small
- 2 tablespoons chipotle peppers in adobo sauce, mashed (or substitute 1 tablespoon dried)
- 1/4 cup orange juice
- 1/4 cup fresh lime juice (about 2 limes)
- 1/3 cup roughly chopped fresh cilantro
- 1 tablespoon cracked toasted cumin seeds (or substitute 1/2 tablespoon ground cumin)
- 1 tablespoon cracked toasted coriander seeds (or substitute 1/2 tablespoon ground cumin)
- Kosher salt and freshly cracked black pepper to taste

In a medium bowl, toss everything together until well mixed. The salsa is best served right away, but will keep, covered and refrigerated, for about 3 or 4 days.

peach-chipotle salsa

MAKES ABOUT 4 CUPS

Okay, we admit that this is a little bit of a fusion approach. Chipotles are a specialty of Mexico, where peaches are definitely not a big item. But we love both of them and can't help combining two of our favorites. If the lack of authenticity bothers you, substitute Mexican mangoes for the peaches. Either way, this salsa is excellent with chicken and pork.

3 ripe but firm peaches, diced small
1/2 red onion, peeled and diced small
1 1/2 tablespoons chipotle peppers in adobo sauce, mashed
1 1/2 tablespoons freshly cracked toasted coriander seeds (or substitute 2 teaspoons ground coriander)
1 1/2 tablespoons freshly cracked toasted cumin seeds (or substitute 2 teaspoons ground cumin)

2 scallions, both green and white parts, diced small
1 tablespoon fresh lime juice
1/4 cup pineapple juice
1/2 cup roughly chopped fresh cilantro
Kosher salt and freshly cracked black pepper to taste

In a medium bowl, combine all the ingredients and mix together well. Serve immediately or cover and refrigerate up to 3 or 4 days.

mango–black bean salsa

MAKES ABOUT 5 CUPS

This salsa takes off from the classic Mexican combination of fruit and lime juice, adds other Mexican flavors in the form of cilantro and cumin, then mixes in some black beans for earthiness and, of course, chiles for heat. As with most salsas, it is ideal to serve this one freshly made, but you can store it, covered and refrigerated, for several days if you want. We like this salsa best with pork or chicken, or served as a dip with Fried Plantain Rounds (page 334) for scoops.

1 cup cooked or well-rinsed canned black beans

3 ripe mangoes, peeled, pitted, and diced small

1/2 red bell pepper, seeded and diced small

1/2 green bell pepper, seeded and diced small

1/2 red onion, peeled and diced small

3/4 cup pineapple juice

1/2 cup fresh lime juice (about 4 limes)

1/2 cup roughly chopped fresh cilantro

2 tablespoons ground cumin

1 tablespoon minced red or green chile pepper of your choice, or to taste

Kosher salt and freshly cracked black pepper to taste

In a large bowl, combine all the ingredients and mix together well. Serve right away or cover and store in the refrigerator up to 4 days.

COOK TO COOK: Although some varieties of beans get mushy when canned, we have found that canned black beans offer a decent alternative to home-cooked.

smoky-hot guacamole

I (Chris) was always down on grilling avocados—I thought they, like soft-shell crabs, were one of the few things that really didn't work well on the grill. But one day, Mark Hall, a chef at the Blue Room, grilled up some avocados to use in a dish he wanted to make. I tasted them and was immediately hooked on the rich, smoky flavors. Since then I've used them quite a lot.

This salsa makes a very nice little side dish as well as a dip. You simply grill the avocado for a few minutes, then scoop out the flesh and combine it with other ingredients, ending up with a variation on traditional guacamole that has a little smoke flavor to it.

4 ripe avocados, halved and pitted but not peeled
1/4 cup olive oil
Kosher salt and freshly cracked black pepper to taste
1 ripe tomato about the size of a baseball, cored and diced small
1/2 cup chopped scallions, both green and white parts
3 tablespoons chipotle peppers in adobo sauce, mashed

1/2 cup fresh lime juice (about 4 limes)
1/3 cup roughly chopped fresh cilantro
1 tablespoon ground coriander
2 tablespoons chili powder, or to taste

1. Build a multi-level fire in your grill: Leave one-quarter of the bottom free of coals, bank the coals in the remaining three-quarters of the grill so that they are three times as high on one side as on the other. When the coals are all ignited and the temperature has died down to medium (you can hold your hand about 5 inches above the grill grid, over the area where the coals are deepest, for 4 to 5 seconds), you're ready to cook.

2. Brush the cut sides of the avocado halves with olive oil and sprinkle them generously with salt and pepper. Put them on the grill, cut side down, and cook for about 3 to 4 minutes, until you can see the grill marks and the avocados are nicely softened. Remove them from the grill and, as soon as they are cool enough to handle, scoop the avocado pulp out of the skins into a medium bowl.

3. Mash the pulp well with a fork, then add all the remaining ingredients, toss gently until well mixed, season to taste with salt and pepper, and serve.

fried plantain rounds

SERVES 4 AS A SIDE DISH

It may seem odd to have a side dish in this chapter, but these rounds are so delicious served with salsas and chutneys that we decided to put them right here where you wouldn't forget them. Be sure to use green rather than ripe plantains here; the ripe ones will not crisp up properly.

2 green plantains

2 cups vegetable oil

Kosher salt and freshly cracked black pepper to taste

1. Peel the plantains and cut them crosswise into rounds about 2 inches long. In a small saucepan, heat the oil until very hot but not smoking, and drop in the plantain rounds in groups of 3. Cook the rounds until they're well browned, about 2 or 3 minutes, then remove them from the oil and drain them on a flattened brown paper bag or paper towel.

2. Stand each fried section upright on a table, and with a heavy object and steady pressure, squash it flat as a pancake. (We use a small cutting board for this, but a frying pan will do fine.)

3. Put the smashed sections back into the hot oil, two or three at a time, and cook them 2 minutes more, until the whole surface is golden brown. Fish them out, drain them again, and sprinkle them generously with salt and pepper. Serve with any of the salsas or chutneys in this chapter.

banana-apricot chutney

MAKES ABOUT 5 1/2 CUPS

৺ ৺ ৺ ৺ ৺ ৺ ৺ ৺ ৺ ৺ ৺ ৺ ৺ ৺ ৺ ৺

If you can't find fresh apricots, which admittedly is a challenge because of their short season and extreme perishability, you can substitute two ripe peaches or ripe mangoes in this recipe. This chutney is particularly good with pork chops, pork roast, pork tenderloin—basically, any cut of pork.

3 tablespoons olive oil
1 small red onion, peeled and diced small
1 tablespoon peeled and minced fresh ginger
Generous pinch of ground allspice
5 ripe apricots, peeled, pitted, and quartered

1 ripe but firm banana, peeled and cut into large chunks
1/2 cup pineapple juice
1/3 cup red wine vinegar
1/4 cup molasses
2 tablespoons light or dark brown sugar
Kosher salt to taste

1. In a large sauté pan or skillet over medium-high heat, heat the oil until hot but not smoking. Add the onion and sauté, stirring occasionally, until transparent, 7 to 9 minutes. Add the ginger and allspice and cook, stirring, for 1 minute more. Add the apricots and banana, cook for 2 more minutes, stirring occasionally, then add the pineapple juice and vinegar.

2. Bring the mixture to a simmer, stirring occasionally, then reduce the heat to low and continue to simmer gently, stirring frequently, until the mixture has thickened slightly, about 10 minutes. Add the molasses and brown sugar and stir until both are well blended in.

3. Remove from the heat, season with salt to taste, and allow to cool to room temperature before serving. This chutney will keep, covered and refrigerated, for up to 1 week.

aromatic apple-date chutney

MAKES ABOUT 5 CUPS

We really like dates in chutneys, since they contribute not only a unique flavor but a deep sweetness. This version, which goes particularly well with red meat, is a very good one to have on hand in the refrigerator all year round.

3 tablespoons olive oil

1 large red onion, peeled and diced small

3 tablespoons peeled and minced fresh ginger

3 tablespoons freshly cracked toasted coriander seeds (or substitute 1 1/2 tablespoons ground coriander)

1 teaspoon ground allspice

5 Granny Smith apples, cored and diced small

1/2 cup finely chopped dates

1 cup mango juice (or substitute fresh orange juice)

1 cup balsamic vinegar

1/3 cup molasses

1/2 cup roughly chopped fresh mint

Kosher salt and freshly cracked black pepper to taste

1. In a large sauté pan or skillet over medium-high heat, heat the oil until hot but not smoking. Add the onion and sauté, stirring occasionally, until transparent, 7 to 9 minutes. Add the ginger, coriander, and allspice and sauté, stirring frequently, 2 minutes more. Stir in the apples and dates and sauté, still stirring frequently, another 2 minutes.

2. Add the mango juice and vinegar and bring to a simmer, then reduce the heat to low and simmer gently, stirring frequently, until the mixture thickens a bit, about 10 minutes. Add the molasses and brown sugar and stir until it all blends in.

3. Remove from the heat, stir in the mint, and season to taste with salt and pepper. Allow the chutney to come to room temperature before serving. It will keep, covered and refrigerated, up to 10 days.

dried fruit chutney with lime and mint

MAKES ABOUT 5 CUPS

This Indian-inspired, slightly sweet chutney is very versatile. You can skip one of the three sweeteners (brown sugar, white sugar, and molasses) if you like, but we are quite fond of the complex layers of sweetness that you get if you use all three. This chutney is very good with any kind of roasted meat, particularly lamb, or spread on sandwiches.

2 tablespoons vegetable oil
2 onions, peeled and diced small
2 cups roughly chopped assorted
  dried fruits (apricots, peaches,
  pears, prunes, etc.)
1/4 cup raisins
1 medium red bell pepper, seeded and
  diced small
6 tablespoons light or dark brown
  sugar
1/4 cup white sugar
1 tablespoon molasses

1/2 cup orange juice
1 teaspoon kosher salt
1/2 teaspoon freshly cracked black
  pepper
1/2 teaspoon cracked toasted coriander seeds
1/2 cup white vinegar
2 tablespoons fresh lime juice (about
  1 lime)
1 teaspoon roughly chopped fresh
  mint

1. In a large sauté pan or skillet over medium-high heat, heat the oil until hot but not smoking. Add the onions and sauté, stirring occasionally, until transparent, about 7 to 9 minutes. Add the dried fruits, raisins, and bell pepper and sauté, stirring frequently, for 3 more minutes.

2. Add the two kinds of sugar, molasses, orange juice, salt, pepper, and coriander and bring to a simmer, then reduce the heat to low and simmer gently, stirring occasionally, for about 30 minutes. If the mixture starts to stick to the pan, add a little water or more orange juice.

3. Remove the pan from the heat and let the mixture cool slightly, then stir in the vinegar, lime juice, and mint and mix well to blend everything in. This chutney will keep, covered and refrigerated, for about 1 week.

COOK TO COOK: If you can locate unsulphured dried fruits, they really do have a clearer, fresher flavor. Check the Sources section (page 401) for mail-order options.

papaya-horseradish chutney

MAKES ABOUT 5 CUPS

Sort of a chutneyized version of the classic papaya salsa, this spicy condiment gets its heat not from chile peppers but from the horseradish root, which imparts a nice, earthy flavor. We like to serve this one with steak, roasted or grilled pork, or grilled lamb.

3 tablespoons vegetable oil
1 red onion, peeled and diced small
2 tablespoons peeled and minced fresh ginger
2 tablespoons toasted cumin seeds (or substitute 1 1/2 tablespoons ground cumin)
3 papayas, peeled, pitted, and diced large
1/2 cup orange juice

1 cup cider vinegar
1 cup light or dark brown sugar
1 cup freshly grated horseradish (or substitute half jarred, see Part-Fresh, Extra-Pungent Home-made Horseradish, page 356)
1/4 cup fresh lime juice (about 2 limes)
Kosher salt and freshly cracked black pepper to taste

1. In a large sauté pan or skillet over medium-high heat, heat the oil until hot but not smoking. Add the onions and sauté, stirring occasionally, until golden brown, 11 to 13 minutes. Stir in the ginger and cumin and sauté, stirring frequently, 2 minutes more. Add the papaya and sauté 1 minute, stirring.

2. Add the orange juice and vinegar and bring to a simmer, stirring occasionally, then turn down the heat and simmer gently until the mixture thickens slightly, about 10 minutes. Add the brown sugar, stirring until it is completely incorporated, then remove the pan from the heat.

3. Stir in the horseradish, lime juice, and salt and pepper to taste. Cool to room temperature before serving, or cover and refrigerate up to 1 week.

peach–red pepper relish with basil and black olives

MAKES ABOUT 6 CUPS

※ ※ ※ ※ ※ ※ ※ ※ ※ ※ ※ ※ ※ ※ ※ ※ ※

We think of this fresh, lively mixture as a kind of all-purpose Mediterranean relish, with all the factors that make the cuisines of that region so attractive. You can substitute apricots or even mangoes for the peaches if you want.

5 ripe but firm peaches, pitted and sliced into eighths	1/3 cup extra-virgin olive oil
2 red bell peppers, seeded and cut into thin strips	1/3 cup balsamic vinegar
1 red onion, peeled and thinly sliced	Juice of 1 lemon
1/2 cup fresh basil leaves, cut into thin strips	Kosher salt and freshly cracked black pepper to taste
1/2 cup roughly chopped pitted brine-cured black olives such as Kalamata	

In a medium bowl, combine all of the ingredients and mix well. It's that simple. This relish will keep, covered and refrigerated, for 3 days.

tomato-basil relish

MAKES ABOUT 5 CUPS

※ ※ ※ ※ ※ ※ ※ ※ ※ ※ ※ ※ ※ ※ ※ ※ ※

The Mediterranean flavors in this relish are particularly delicious with grilled fish or chicken, but they also go very well with pork.

3 large ripe tomatoes, cored and diced small	3 tablespoons freshly cracked toasted coriander seeds
1/2 cup extra-virgin olive oil	Pinch of sugar
Juice of 1 lemon	Kosher salt and freshly cracked black pepper to taste
1 cup fresh basil leaves, cut into thin strips	

In a medium bowl, combine all the ingredients and mix well. This one is best served immediately, but you can cover and refrigerate it up to 3 days.

mediterranean eggplant and olive relish

MAKES ABOUT 5 CUPS

Grilled eggplant, one of our favorite vegetables, provides the bulk of this mild but fla-vorful relish, with briny capers and earthy olives setting off the flavor sparks. This is an excellent relish to serve when you have guests coming over who aren't into hot food. Try serving it with EZ Grill Bread (page 77) or with grilled pork chops or chicken breasts.

2 medium-size eggplants, cut in
    1-inch thick slices
1 onion, halved
6 tablespoons vegetable oil
Kosher salt and freshly cracked black
    pepper to taste
1/2 cup whole cooked peeled toma-
    toes, diced medium

1/3 cup capers, rinsed and drained
12 pitted brine-cured black olives
    such as Kalamata
1/4 cup red wine vinegar
1 tablespoon minced garlic
3 tablespoons fresh thyme leaves

1. Build a multi-level fire in your grill: Leaving one-quarter of the bottom free of coals, bank the coals in the remaining three-quarters of the grill so that they are three times as high on one side as on the other. When the coals are all ignited and the temperature has died down to medium (you can hold your hand about 5 inches above the grill grid, over the area where the coals are deepest, for 4 to 5 seconds), you're ready to cook.

2. Rub the eggplant slices and the onion halves with the oil and sprinkle them gener-ously with salt and pepper. Place on the grill over the coals and cook, turning once, until tender, about 3 to 4 minutes per side for the eggplant and 8 to 10 minutes per side for the onion. Transfer to a cutting board and cut them up into large chunks.

3. In a large bowl, combine the eggplant and onions with all the remaining ingredi-ents, adjust the seasoning, and toss gently until well mixed. Serve warm or chilled. This relish will keep, covered and refrigerated, for about 3 days.

southeast asian–style fresh tomato relish with ginger, basil, and mint

MAKES ABOUT 6 CUPS

We could call this a salsa but we're not going to, because they actually have condiment-style dishes very much like these all over Southeast Asia and they don't call them salsas. But here's a simple, very aromatic, salsa-like combo that goes great with fish, pork, or even beef.

4 ripe tomatoes about the size of baseballs, cored and diced small
1/2 cup finely chopped scallions, both green and white parts
1/2 cup roughly chopped fresh basil (Thai basil if possible)
1/4 cup roughly chopped fresh mint
3 tablespoons peeled and finely chopped fresh ginger
2 tablespoons chile-garlic paste (see Sources, page 401, or substitute 1 garlic clove minced with 1 tablespoon fresh chile)

2 tablespoons *nam pla,* Southeast Asian fish sauce (available in Asian markets or large supermarkets)
1 tablespoon light or dark brown sugar
3 tablespoons roasted sesame oil
1/4 cup fresh lime juice (about 2 limes)
3 tablespoons white vinegar
Kosher salt and freshly cracked black pepper to taste

In a medium bowl, combine all the ingredients and toss gently until well mixed. This relish will keep, covered and refrigerated, up to 4 days.

COOK TO COOK: Here's a hint for those of you who are not familiar with fish sauce—don't sniff it. The aroma, much more powerful than the flavor, may dissuade you from using it. When used in relative small amounts, the sauce has a subtle taste and deepens all the other flavors in the dish. Give it a try.

red onion–ginger jam

MAKES ABOUT 3 CUPS

This chutney-like jam is outstanding with roasted meat, whether beef, pork, or lamb. It also keeps quite well, so you can make it days in advance and then just bring it out of the refrigerator when you put the roast in the oven or the chops on the grill. Bring it up almost to room temperature before serving.

2 tablespoons olive oil
2 small red onions, peeled and very thinly sliced
2 tablespoons peeled and minced fresh ginger
1 tablespoon minced garlic
2 whole star anise, crushed
1 tablespoon ground coriander
1/8 teaspoon ground mace (or substitute ground cinnamon)

2 tablespoons light or dark brown sugar
2 tablespoons orange juice
2 tablespoons white vinegar
Kosher salt and freshly cracked white pepper to taste (or substitute black pepper)

1. In a large sauté pan or skillet over medium-high heat, heat the oil until hot but not smoking. Add the onions and sauté, stirring occasionally, until golden brown, about 9 to 11 minutes. Add the ginger and garlic and sauté, stirring frequently, 1 more minute.

2. Add the remaining ingredients and cook, stirring frequently, until the mixture thickens slightly, about 5 minutes. Remove from the heat and allow the jam to cool to room temperature before serving, or cover and refrigerate for up to 1 week.

spicy peach-tomato jam

MAKES ABOUT 6 CUPS

Tomatoes and peaches make a very interesting flavor combination, an exciting mix of tart and sweet, earthy and aromatic. Here we add some ginger and cumin and a whole lot of fresh chile peppers along with vinegar and brown sugar, and we simmer it all into a hyper-flavorful jam that's good not only with red meat but even with fish. If you don't like your condiments hot, you can always cut down on the amount of chiles to suit your taste.

3 tablespoons olive oil
1 large red onion, peeled and diced small
3 tablespoons peeled and minced fresh ginger
3 tablespoons minced fresh chile pepper of your choice, or to taste
3 tablespoons toasted cumin seeds (or substitute 1 1/2 tablespoons ground cumin)

2 ripe tomatoes about the size of baseballs, cored and diced small
5 ripe peaches, pitted and diced large
1/2 cup tomato juice
1 cup cider vinegar
1/2 cup light or dark brown sugar
Kosher salt and freshly cracked black pepper to taste

1. In a large sauté pan or skillet over medium-high heat, heat the oil until hot but not smoking. Add the onion and sauté, stirring occasionally, until golden brown, 11 to 13 minutes. Add the ginger, chiles, and cumin and sauté, stirring frequently, 2 minutes more. Stir in the tomatoes and peaches and sauté, still stirring frequently, another 2 minutes.

2. Add the tomato juice and vinegar and bring to a simmer, stirring occasionally, then reduce the heat to low and simmer gently, stirring frequently, until the mixture thickens slightly, about 10 minutes. Add the brown sugar and stir until it dissolves and blends into the jam.

3. Remove from the heat and season to taste with salt and pepper. Allow to cool to room temperature before serving. This jam will keep, covered and refrigerated, up to 1 week.

mango-chipotle catsup

MAKES ABOUT 4 1/2 CUPS

Today, we think of catsup only as the familiar tomato-based sauce without which French fries and hamburgers would not be complete. But it is only over the past hundred years or so that the word has come to mean just this one sauce. Previously, making catsup out of something was seen primarily as a way of preserving the ingredient in vinegar and spices, so catsups were concocted using everything from mushrooms to walnuts to horseradish root. This particular version, a sweet-hot combination that resembles a puréed mango chutney, is excellent with pork or any strong-flavored dish.

1 tablespoon vegetable oil
1 large onion, peeled and thinly sliced
3 ripe mangoes, peeled, pitted, and roughly chopped
3 tablespoons chipotle peppers in adobo sauce, mashed
1/4 cup light or dark brown sugar, packed

3 tablespoons molasses
2 tablespoons white sugar
1 teaspoon kosher salt
1/2 teaspoon freshly cracked black pepper
1/4 teaspoon ground allspice
1/2 cup white vinegar
2 tablespoons lemon juice (about 1/2 lemon)

1. In a large sauté pan or skillet over medium-high heat, heat the oil until hot but not smoking. Add the onion and sauté, stirring occasionally, until transparent, about 7 to 9 minutes. Add the mangoes and sauté, stirring frequently, for about 4 minutes.

2. Stir in the chipotles, brown sugar, molasses, white sugar, salt, pepper, and allspice and bring to a simmer. Reduce the heat to low and simmer gently, stirring occasionally, until the catsup is somewhat thickened, about 30 minutes. Be sure you check to see if the mixture is starting to scorch on the bottom of the pan at any point; if it does, stir in a bit of water or orange juice.

3. Transfer the catsup to a blender or food processor, add the lemon juice, and purée until smooth. This catsup will keep, covered and refrigerated, for about a week.

no-so-mean mr. mustard

* * *

Mustard is one of the great underrated condiments. Most of us have the impression that the only choices in this department are the inexpensive bright yellow kind used on ballpark franks and the Dijon style that has become popular for more upscale uses lately. Delicious as those are, however, they are only the beginning of mustard possibilities. By making them yourself, you can have a wide variety of flavored mustards in the refrigerator ready to spice up just about any meal.

The basis of any good mustard, of course, is the mustard seed. We think that you'll be surprised at the potent pungency of these little seeds when you grind them up yourself. Whether in the form of powder or crushed seeds, mustard has to be mixed with liquid in order for the enzyme that makes it spicy to be released. To add more flavor to the mixture, we use not only water but a range of liquids—different vinegars, orange juice, beer, sherry, what have you.

You'll notice that some of the recipes call for brown mustard seeds, some for yellow, and some for a mix of the two. This is really just to add variety to the recipes. Brown seeds are more powerful than yellow, with a sharper heat, but you can basically use whatever is available to you. Whichever you use, be sure to let the finished mixtures sit at room temperature, uncovered, for several hours before you cover and refrigerate them. This helps take the jagged edge off their pungency. Then leave them in the refrigerator for a week or so before you use them, giving them a chance to mellow a bit more.

One thing to be aware of when making these mustards is that you probably don't want to buy mustard seeds in those little bottles you find in the grocery store—not because of quality issues, but because they are ridiculously expensive. You can order seeds from mail order spice houses such as Penzey's (see Sources, page 401) for as little as one-quarter of the supermarket cost if you order a fairly large amount. An even better option would be an Indian grocery store, if you have one in your area.

five serious mustard options

❧ ❧ ❧ ❧ ❧ ❧ ❧ ❧ ❧ ❧ ❧ ❧ ❧ ❧ ❧ ❧ ❧ ❧

Sweet-and-Hot Balsamic Mustard

MAKES ABOUT 2 CUPS

1 cup brown mustard seeds
3/4 cup balsamic vinegar
1/4 cup water
3 tablespoons light or dark brown
    sugar

Kosher salt and freshly cracked black
    pepper to taste

With a mortar and pestle or a spice grinder, coarsely grind the mustard seeds. Put them in a medium bowl. Add the vinegar and the water slowly, stirring to combine. Add the brown sugar and salt and pepper, then stir until the sugar has dissolved and the mixture is of uniform texture. Set aside, uncovered, to cure for about 3 hours. Cover and refrigerate for at least 1 week. Bring to room temperature and stir well before serving.

Exotic Ginger, Sherry, and Coriander Mustard

MAKES ABOUT 2 1/2 CUPS

1/2 cup yellow mustard seeds
1/4 cup toasted coriander seeds
3 tablespoons peeled and minced
    fresh ginger
1/2 cup dry mustard

3/4 cup white vinegar
1/2 cup dry sherry
Kosher salt and freshly cracked black
    pepper to taste

With a mortar and pestle or a spice grinder, coarsely grind the mustard seeds and coriander seeds. Transfer to a food processor, add the ginger and dry mustard, and purée until smooth. With the machine running, slowly add the vinegar and sherry through the feed tube and mix until blended. Season with salt and pepper and set the mixture aside, uncovered, to cure for about 3 hours. Cover and refrigerate for at least 1 week. Bring to room temperature and stir well before serving.

Orange-Cumin Mustard

MAKES ABOUT 2 1/2 CUPS

1/2 cup yellow mustard seeds
1/2 cup brown mustard seeds
1 cup orange juice
1/2 cup white vinegar

3 tablespoons ground cumin
Kosher salt and freshly cracked black
    pepper to taste

With a mortar and pestle or a spice grinder, coarsely grind the two kinds of mustard seeds and put them in a medium bowl. Slowly add the orange juice and vinegar, stirring to combine. Stir in the cumin and salt and pepper, then set the mixture aside, uncovered, to cure for about 3 hours. Cover and refrigerate for at least 1 week. Bring to room temperature and stir well before serving.

Apricot-Basil Beer Mustard

MAKES ABOUT 2 1/2 CUPS

1/2 cup brown mustard seeds
1/3 cup dried apricots, snipped into
    small pieces
1 1/2 cups roughly chopped basil
    leaves
1/2 cup roughly chopped parsley

1/2 cup dry mustard
1 cup dark beer of your choice
1/2 cup water
2 tablespoons molasses
Kosher salt and freshly cracked black
    pepper to taste

With a mortar and pestle or a spice grinder, coarsely grind the mustard seeds. Transfer them to a food processor, add the apricots, basil, parsley, and dry mustard, and purée until smooth. With the machine running, slowly add the beer, water, and molasses through the feed tube and mix until blended. Season with salt and pepper, then set the mixture aside, uncovered, to cure for about 3 hours. Cover and refrigerate for at least 1 week. Bring to room temperature and stir well before serving.

COOK TO COOK: In general we like our mustards hot, but sometimes we mix in a little dry mustard to get the mustard flavor with less heat. If you're a heat fan, though, you can substitute seeds for the dry mustard when we wimp out like that.

Horseradish Mustard

1/2 cup yellow mustard seeds
1/2 cup dry mustard
1/2 cup prepared horseradish
1 tablespoon light or dark brown
   sugar

1/2 cup cider vinegar
1 cup water
Kosher salt and freshly cracked black
   pepper to taste

With a mortar and pestle or a spice grinder, coarsely grind the mustard seeds. Transfer them to a food processor, add the dry mustard, horseradish, and brown sugar, and purée. With the machine running, slowly add the vinegar and water through the feed tube and mix until combined. Season with salt and pepper, then set the mixture aside, uncovered, to cure for about 3 hours. Cover and refrigerate for at least 1 week. Bring to room temperature and stir well before serving.

ten excellent spice rub options

* * *

When food coated with a spice rub is put over a grilling fire, a fantastic reaction takes place and a super-flavorful crust develops on the exterior. We think it's the best and easiest way to get deep, intense flavors. We also like the contrast created with the interior of the food, which keeps its original taste. So we are, and have long been, huge fans of spice rubs of all varieties. We always have several mixed up and ready to go in our kitchens, because that way it takes almost no time to get ready to grill some awesome food.

While spice rubs produce very complex flavors, the technique for using them could not be simpler. Just take small handfuls of whatever spice combo you have chosen and rub it over the entire surface of the food you are going to cook, using a bit of pressure to make sure that a good layer adheres to the food. That's all there is to it. Once the food has started to cook, don't worry when the rub begins to turn dark brown. This is what happens to spices when they are cooked, particularly with a high-heat cooking method like grilling. As long as the spices don't turn black or begin to smoke, you're in the clear.

In order to get the most out of spices, it is important to buy them whole, then toast and grind them yourself. This may seem a little precious, but it's really worth it. You're probably familiar with the tremendous flavor difference between preground and freshly ground black pepper. Well, it makes just as big a difference when you grind any other spice yourself. And toasting spices, particularly the ones that are seeds, brings out their volatile oils and intensifies their flavor quite a bit. Just put the seeds in a small sauté pan over medium heat and cook them, shaking or stirring frequently, until they darken and become fragrant, which usually takes about 2 minutes. If you see a little wisp of smoke, take the seeds off the heat right away. Once the seeds are toasted, add them to any other spices in the mixture and grind them. You can do this either in a mortar and pestle or in a spice grinder (which can be an electric coffee grinder that you keep for this purpose). In the absence of these tools, spices can be crushed by grinding them against a cutting board with the bottom of a small sauté pan.

The wet rubs here will keep, covered and refrigerated, for several weeks. If kept in a tightly sealed jar in a cool, dark place, the dry rubs will keep almost indefinitely. After a couple of months, though, they will have lost a fair amount of their aromaticity, so it's best not to keep them longer than that.

simple cumin seed rub

MAKES ABOUT 3/4 CUP

This is about as simple as it gets, but you will be surprised at how much flavor it brings to fish, meat, or even vegetables when rubbed on before grilling.

1/2 cup cracked toasted cumin seeds
2 tablespoons kosher salt

3 tablespoons freshly cracked black pepper

In a small bowl, combine all the ingredients and mix well.

simple cracked coriander rub

MAKES ABOUT 3/4 CUP

Like cumin, coriander is a great base spice for rubs. Simply combined with salt and pepper, it gives a very aromatic edge of flavor to fish, chicken, or pork.

1/2 cup cracked toasted coriander seeds
2 tablespoons kosher salt

3 tablespoons freshly cracked black pepper

In a small bowl, combine all the ingredients and mix well.

easy, universal, and always appropriate rub

MAKES ABOUT 1 CUP

This simple rub may be our favorite, combining as it does the virtues of cumin and coriander, two spices that are exotic enough to be interesting but familiar enough not to be intimidating. It is an excellent full-flavored rub that works well on just about any food. We particularly like it with fish such as tuna or bluefish.

1/2 cup cracked toasted coriander
   seeds
1/4 cup cracked toasted cumin seeds

2 tablespoons kosher salt
3 tablespoons freshly cracked black
   pepper

In a small bowl, combine all the ingredients and mix well.

traditional bbq rub

MAKES ABOUT 1 3/4 CUPS

Rub this mixture on meat or fowl, put it on the grill away from the flames, and in an hour or two you've got your classic barbecue. This all-purpose rub is especially good on pork and chicken.

1/2 cup paprika
1/4 cup chili powder
3 tablespoons ground cumin
2 tablespoons ground coriander
1 tablespoon curry powder

1 tablespoon cayenne pepper
1/4 cup light or dark brown sugar
1/4 cup kosher salt
1/4 cup freshly cracked black pepper
1 teaspoon ground allspice

In a small bowl, combine all the ingredients and mix well.

spicy pepper rub

MAKES ABOUT 1 1/2 CUPS

We like this very aromatic rub because it combines three types of heat—white pepper, black pepper, and chile pepper—and you can feel each one in a different part of your mouth. Use it liberally or sparingly depending on your taste for heat. It is particularly good on red meats.

1/2 cup freshly cracked black pepper
1/4 cup freshly cracked white pepper
1/3 cup cracked toasted coriander
　　seeds

2 tablespoons red pepper flakes
1 tablespoon ground ginger
3 tablespoons kosher salt

In a small bowl, combine all the ingredients and mix well.

west indies hot dry rub

MAKES ABOUT 2 CUPS

Chicken and pork are our favorites for this rub, which combines the many intense flavors of West Indian cooking.

1/3 cup curry powder
1/4 cup ground cumin
1/4 cup ground coriander
1/4 cup dry mustard

1/4 cup freshly cracked white pepper
1/4 cup ground ginger
1/4 cup red pepper flakes
1/4 cup kosher salt

In a small bowl, combine all the ingredients and mix well.

the "real deal" west indies hot wet rub

MAKES ABOUT 2 1/2 CUPS

Here's another one for you chile-heads. Don't try it unless you have an asbestos palate. But if you are a heat fanatic, this is going to deliver the real deal to any chicken, pork, or fish that you rub it on.

- 1/3 cup cheap yellow mustard
- 1/4 cup red wine vinegar
- 1/2 cup chopped Scotch bonnet or habanero chile peppers, or to taste
- 1/2 cup roughly chopped scallions, both green and white parts
- 2 tablespoons peeled and roughly chopped fresh ginger
- 1/4 cup light or dark brown sugar
- 3 tablespoons curry powder
- 3 tablespoons ground cumin
- 1 teaspoon ground cloves

Combine all ingredients in a blender or food processor and purée.

COOK TO COOK: You can use high-quality mustard in this dish if you want, but to get the most authentic flavor, use the cheap kind that comes in the glaring yellow squeeze bottle.

spicy latin wet rub

MAKES ABOUT 2 1/2 CUPS

If you use the full amount of chipotles in this Latin-inspired rub, it will be plenty hot. You can reduce the amount considerably, though, and still have a very robust and flavorful rub. We like this with chicken, pork, or beef.

- 1/2 cup olive oil
- 1 cup fresh cilantro leaves
- 3 garlic cloves, peeled
- 1/2 cup chipotle peppers in adobo sauce
- 1/4 cup toasted cumin seeds
- 1/4 cup toasted coriander seeds
- Kosher salt and freshly cracked black pepper to taste

Combine all ingredients in a blender or food processor and purée.

aromatic southeast asian wet rub

MAKES ABOUT 3 1/2 CUPS

Rub this on fish, chicken, or pork and you'll have the intensely aromatic flavors of Southeast Asia on your table in no time. If you choose to omit the fish sauce—which would be a mistake, but it's better to make the rub without it than not to make it at all—substitute an equal amount of soy sauce.

1/4 cup roasted sesame oil
1/2 cup roughly chopped fresh mint
1/2 cup roughly chopped fresh cilantro
1/2 cup roughly chopped basil (preferably Thai)
1/4 cup minced fresh ginger
3 tablespoons chile-garlic paste (see Sources, page 401; or substitute 1 large garlic clove minced with 1 small chile pepper)

3 tablespoons *nam pla*, Southeast Asian fish sauce (available in Asian markets or large supermarkets)
1 tablespoon light or dark brown sugar
Kosher salt and freshly ground black pepper to taste

Combine all ingredients in a blender or food processor and purée.

most exotic rub

MAKES ABOUT 1 CUP

There is something about even the simplest spice rub that seems a bit exotic, a link to the romance and mystery of the ancient Spice Road and all of that. But if you're looking for the full, highly aromatic, somewhat esoteric, completely exotic treatment, this is the rub for you. It combines some of the world's most aromatic spices in a rub that will transform chicken, pork, or (our favorite for this rub) duck into a rare treat.

1/2 cup toasted coriander seeds
15 allspice berries
Seeds from 10 cardamom pods
5 whole cloves
1 small stick of cinnamon

1 tablespoon ground ginger
1 tablespoon dry mustard
3 tablespoons kosher salt
3 tablespoons white peppercorns

Combine all the ingredients and grind together with a mortar and pestle or a spice grinder.

way-hot pineapple chile sambal

MAKES ABOUT 1 1/2 CUPS

In Indonesia and Malaysia, sambals are indispensable accompaniments to just about every meal. But exactly what constitutes a sambal depends very much on where it's being served. It may be (and very often is) as simple as chile peppers ground up with lime juice and spices, or it may be more like a relish, with coconut or fruit or vegetables in it. The one constant is that it is hot, spicy, and very strong-flavored. So here is our version of a pineapple sambal, powerful and hot and superb with grilled fish or chicken.

1 cup peeled and small-diced fresh pineapple

2 tablespoons peeled and minced fresh ginger

2 tablespoons minced jalapeño or other chile pepper of your choice, or to taste

3 tablespoons roasted sesame oil

3 tablespoons *nam pla*, Southeast Asian fish sauce (available in Asian markets or large supermarkets)

In a medium bowl, combine all the ingredients and mix well. Serve this one right away; it won't keep too well.

part-fresh, extra-pungent homemade horseradish

MAKES ABOUT 2 CUPS

If you can solve this mystery, you will be my (Chris's) guest for dinner at the East Coast Grill. Here it is: How do you make the hottest, most pungent horseradish? Hm?

If you say that the way to do it is to grate it fresh yourself, I have to tell you that you're wrong. In fact, fresh-grated horseradish turns out to be not that hot—and I know, because I've spent a lot of time researching this issue. I love horseradish with oysters and shrimp cocktail and beef and a lot of other foods, and I like it really hot. As it turns out, the way to get the best flavor and the most heat from horseradish is to combine freshly grated with a smaller amount of bottled prepared. For some reason, there is something in the prepared horseradish that ignites the fresh; it's a mystery, but like all great mysteries it works its magic every time.

Make this and I guarantee you will have the hottest, most pungent, most nasal-clearing horseradish you've ever experienced. Serve it on roasted meats, add a bit to chutneys to give them a little extra life, mix it into your cocktail sauce, or combine it with grainy mustard for a lovely sauce for sandwiches.

1 cup peeled and coarsely grated fresh horseradish	1/2 cup white wine vinegar
1/2 cup prepared (jarred) horseradish	1 teaspoon kosher or other coarse salt

Combine all the ingredients in a blender or food processor and purée well. Pack into a jar with a nonreactive lid and store, covered, in the refrigerator. The horseradish is ready to eat immediately, but it will keep, covered and refrigerated, for months. It is best eaten within 3 or 4 weeks, however, before the flavor and kick start to fade.

chutney-horseradish sauce

MAKES 1 CUP

This recipe is something I (Chris) learned back in my short stint at a catering outfit in Milford, Michigan, quite a few years ago. I know it sounds a little odd, and it may seem even odder to you that we're giving you a recipe that involves little more than mixing together some packaged ingredients, but give it a try and you'll be happy. Sweet, hot, and pungent, it makes an excellent all-purpose dipping sauce for chicken wings, lamb skewers, or tenderloin tips.

1/3 cup honey
1/3 cup jarred horseradish

1/3 cup jarred chutney such as Major Grey's

Place all ingredients in a food processor or blender and purée. This will keep, covered and refrigerated, for several weeks.

refrigerator pickles

* * *

When it comes to adding spikes of flavor to a meal, every culture in the world relies, at least to some extent, on pickles. Originally developed as a way of preserving fruits and vegetables, pickling became over the centuries a way of adding distinctive taste as well. Pickles have a characteristic sweet-sour-salty flavor profile that comes from the sugar, vinegar or citrus juice, and salt typically used in preservation. In addition, because they are generally used to add sharp accents to the meal rather than provide the primary nourishment, pickles tend to be very highly spiced.

Today we don't have to worry about preservation—we've got refrigerators. But by using the same basic ingredients to make "quick pickles," meant to remain refrigerated for a few days or weeks until eaten, we can get the swagger and snap of old-fashioned pickles without the work.

We've always been big fans of quick pickles, and the pickle passion of our friend Dan George has only increased our enthusiasm. We urge you to make batches of these pickles to use as appetizers, as cocktail snacks, as accompaniments to meals, as something to give as a gift, or just as something to munch on whenever you feel the urge.

rosemary pickled peaches

MAKES ABOUT 5 CUPS

A jar of these pickles makes an excellent present, particularly if you use white balsamic vinegar so the peaches keep much of their color. They look beautiful on any holiday table, and they're delicious with any kind of meat.

1 cup white balsamic vinegar (see Sources, page 401; or substitute regular balsamic)	1 cup orange juice
	8 ripe but firm peaches, pitted and cut into 6 to 8 wedges each
3/4 cup dry vermouth	3 tablespoons rosemary needles

In a large nonreactive saucepan, combine the vinegar, vermouth, and orange juice and bring to a boil over high heat. Remove the pan from the heat and add the peaches and rosemary. Allow to cool to room temperature, uncovered, then cover and refrigerate. These pickles are best if left to sit for at least 48 hours before eating. They will keep, covered and refrigerated, for up to 6 weeks.

winter tomato pickles with ginger and two seeds

MAKES ABOUT 1 QUART

Despite the name, this recipe is actually designed to make use of tomatoes in late fall, ones that are still hard but not totally green—so maybe we should call the recipe "In-Between Tomato Pickles." In any case, these pickles are excellent with mild-flavored fish and are nice to put out on the table with any Asian-style dinner.

4 almost-ripe tomatoes about the size of baseballs, cored and cut into wedges about 1/8 inch thick
2 medium-size red onions, cut into rounds about 1/2 inch thick
2 tablespoons kosher salt
1 piece of fresh ginger about 2 inches long, peeled and sliced into thin disks

1 tablespoon peeled and minced ginger
1 1/2 cups red wine vinegar
3/4 cup sugar
4 teaspoons toasted coriander seeds
2 tablespoons yellow or brown mustard seeds

1. In a medium-size nonreactive bowl, combine the tomatoes and onions with the salt and toss to mix well. Cover, refrigerate, and allow to stand for at least 4 hours or overnight. Drain, then rinse and drain twice to remove the salt, then set aside.

2. In a nonreactive saucepan, combine all remaining ingredients and bring to a boil over medium-high heat, stirring once or twice to dissolve the sugar. Reduce the heat to low and simmer for 5 minutes, stirring occasionally. Remove from the heat and allow the mixture to cool for 5 minutes, then pour over the tomatoes and onions. Allow to cool to room temperature uncovered, then cover and refrigerate. These pickles will keep, covered and refrigerated, for about 2 weeks.

pickled corn on the cob

MAKES ABOUT 4 QUARTS

At first you may think pickling corn is odd, but you're going to end up loving these pickles if you make them. They look beautiful in the jar, they taste great, and it's fun to suck on the cob after you've eaten off all the kernels. They were inspired by a visit to a pickle store—that's right, a store devoted exclusively to homemade pickles—in Istanbul, where huge jars of whole pickled ears of corn, among many other things, had been set in the window to attract customers.

These pickles are ideal as snacks before dinner or with cocktails.

2 teaspoons vegetable oil

8 garlic cloves, peeled and crushed

4 red, orange, and/or yellow bell peppers, seeded and cut into thin rings

2 large onions, peeled and cut into thin rings

4 teaspoons prepared Dijon mustard mixed with 2 teaspoons water

4 cups white wine vinegar

2 cups water

1 cup orange juice

1 1/2 cups sugar

2 tablespoons kosher salt

2 tablespoons cracked toasted coriander seeds

1 tablespoon whole cloves

5 small fresh chile peppers of your choice, or to taste, slit down the side but left whole

6 ears of corn, husked, desilked, and cut into rounds about 1/2 to 3/4 inch thick

1. In a large sauté pan or skillet, heat the oil over medium-high heat until it is hot but not smoking. Add the garlic, peppers, and onions and cook, stirring occasionally, until all the vegetables are slightly softened and the peppers have brightened in color, about 5 minutes. Be careful not to overcook or brown; they should be crisp-tender. Remove from the heat and set aside.

2. In a large nonreactive pot, combine all the remaining ingredients except the corn and bring to a boil over high heat.

3. Add the corn rounds. (There should be enough liquid to cover them; if not, add a bit more water.) Bring back to a boil, reduce the heat to low, and simmer for 5 minutes. Add the reserved vegetables and bring back to a simmer again. Turn off the heat and allow to cool to room temperature, uncovered, then cover and refrigerate. These pickles taste good as soon as they've cooled, but they will last for 2 weeks, covered and refrigerated. We like them best served chilled.

COOK TO COOK: If you use any of the new super-sweet corn varieties in this recipe, consider cutting back the sugar by about 1/4 cup or so.

cantaloupe pickles with scorched coriander seeds

MAKES ABOUT 1 1/2 QUARTS

This is an example of the oil pickles very popular in India, much of Southeast Asia, and parts of Africa. The oil serves both as a preservative and as a medium for distributing flavor. Here we intensify the flavor of the coriander by toasting it darker than usual, then cooking it even more in a little oil.

You can substitute peaches for the cantaloupe if you like, but the melon is more unusual and really tastes quite exotic. Come to think of it, an even better substitute might be a firm honeydew or Persian melon. In fact, why not seize this chance to explore all those melons that you don't quite know how to pick out? If you bring one home that is not perfectly ripe, you can just turn it into delicious pickles.

1 medium-size, not-quite-ripe can-
    taloupe, seeded, peeled, and cut
    into 1/2-inch cubes
Zest and juice of 3 limes
1/4 cup peeled and grated fresh
    ginger
3 tablespoons minced garlic
2 jalapeños or other small chile pep-
    pers of your choice, with seeds,
    cut into thin slices

2 teaspoons kosher salt
2 dashes of Tabasco sauce
Freshly cracked black pepper to taste
3 tablespoons coriander seeds
1/2 cup vegetable oil

1. In a medium bowl, combine the cantaloupe and lime juice and mix well. Set aside for 1 hour, tossing occasionally to coat. Drain the cantaloupe (discard any liquid) and add the lime zest, ginger, garlic, jalapeños, salt, hot sauce, and black pepper to taste. Mix well and set aside.

2. In a dry sauté pan or skillet over medium-high heat, cook the coriander seeds, shaking the pan frequently, until the seeds begin to crackle and jump. Add just enough oil to coat the seeds (about 2 tablespoons) and continue cooking, shaking the pan frequently, for 3 minutes more. Add the remaining oil to the pan and cook for 1 more minute. Remove the pan from the heat, pour the oil and coriander over the peaches, and mix well. These pickles can be eaten right away, but they are actually better after a few weeks. They will keep, covered and kept in a cool dark place, for 3 weeks, or for 3 to 4 months if covered and refrigerated.

OH, GO AHEAD:
DRINKS AND DESSERTS

WE ALWAYS ASSOCIATE GRILLING WITH ESPECIALLY TASTY beverages. Maybe that's because grilling goes along with summer, hot weather, and the relaxed atmosphere that lends itself to hanging out and enjoying a few drinks. Or maybe it's because the right liquid concoction is crucial for maintaining the proper frame of mind when the food is over the flames and the pressure is on to avoid incinerating it.

Whatever the reason, we enjoy coming up with all kinds of special drinks to imbibe both at the grill and at the table, some with alcohol and some without, and in this chapter we give you a number of our favorites. The white sangria and iced tea seem to go particularly well with lunch, the limeades are unbelievably good at all times, the coolers are always refreshing, and the shake and the yogurt drink are excellent for a mid-afternoon break. And of course there are margaritas in all of their guises, ideal for that late afternoon or early evening cocktail hour.

Desserts are not our specialty, but we do like them, and we've come up with recipes for a handful that we particularly enjoy. Most of them have some grilled component, of course, but we also include a cake and two kinds of brownies to pop in the oven on those occasions when you don't mind the heat in the kitchen. Any one of the desserts is an excellent ending to a grilled dinner.

ginger-pineapple iced tea

MAKES 1/2 GALLON

It's fun to have a range of different cooling nonalcoholic drinks around the house in the summer. It's even more fun if, instead of going to the store and buying drinks in a bottle, you make your own. We highly recommend it. You'll like them better, and your guests will be impressed and feel welcomed by your hospitality. This version of that old standby, iced tea, is particularly nice because it has a little tropical edge to it from the pineapple and ginger.

2 cups pineapple juice
6 cups water
4 slices peeled ginger, each about the
    size of a quarter
1/2 cinnamon stick (or 1 teaspoon
    powdered cinnamon)

5 whole cloves
1/2 cup sugar
6 to 8 tea bags of your choice

1. In a medium-size nonreactive saucepan, combine all the ingredients except the tea bags and bring to a boil over medium-high heat, stirring frequently to dissolve the sugar. Remove the pan from the heat and toss in the tea bags. Allow them to steep for 10 minutes, then strain the mixture, discard the spices and tea bags, and let the tea cool to room temperature.

2. To serve, fill a pitcher with plenty of ice and pour in the tea. Stir until cold, and serve in glasses filled with additional ice.

COOK TO COOK: We like orange pekoe or English Breakfast tea here, but use whatever you prefer. If you can find high-quality tea bags (cloth instead of paper), check them out—you might find them worth the extra money.

lemon limeade

MAKES 1/2 GALLON

This is the real, honest-to-goodness, homemade version of those carbonated lemon-lime drinks that are so popular in cans. If you're not fond of carbonization, of course, you can do it the old-fashioned way and just use plain old tap water. It takes a little bit of time to squeeze this many lemons and limes, but that's part of the whole summer relaxation thing. Just slow down, take your time, and enjoy the process. If you want, you can add some rum and get really relaxed.

1 1/2 cups sugar
1 cup water
Grated zest of 2 lemons
Grated zest of 2 limes
Grated zest of 1 orange

1 cup fresh lemon juice (about 4 lemons)
1 cup fresh lime juice (about 8 limes)
1 quart cold soda water

1. In a small nonreactive saucepan, combine the sugar, water, and three kinds of zest and bring to a boil over medium-high heat. Reduce the heat to low and simmer for about 10 minutes, stirring frequently. Remove from the heat and set aside to cool to room temperature.

2. Fill a large pitcher halfway with ice, add the lemon juice, the lime juice, and the cooled syrup. Stir until well blended, then add the cold soda water and mix well.

orange limeade with watermelon

SERVES 4

What with squeezing the limes and oranges and puréeing the watermelon, you'll find that you need a few minutes to make this drink. But the layers of flavor—which you don't really get unless you have fresh juice—make it a particularly nice option for those who want something with a satisfying, complex taste but no alcohol.

1 cup lime juice (about 8 limes)
2 cups fresh orange juice (about 2 or 3 oranges)

3 cups watermelon juice
3/4 cup sugar
1 quart water

Combine all ingredients in a large pitcher with plenty of ice. Stir until the juices are well mixed and the sugar has dissolved. Divide among 4 glasses and serve immediately.

COOK TO COOK: To make watermelon juice, just cut a watermelon into big chunks, remove the rind, and cut the chunks into cubes, slipping out the seeds as you do. Then purée the cubes in a blender or food processor, and there's your juice. Yum.

peach yogurt drink

SERVES 4

I (Doc) love the yogurt-based Indian drink called lassi. Cooling and healthful, it's just exotic enough to seem like a special treat on a really hot day. In our version of lassi, we've added peaches for additional flavor and some classic Indian spices that can be omitted if you prefer.

2 ripe peaches, peeled and pitted	1 teaspoon each ground cumin, fennel
2 cups plain whole-milk yogurt	seeds, and ground cardamon
1/2 cup water or apple juice	(optional)
1/4 cup light or dark brown sugar	10 ice cubes
2 tablespoons white sugar	4 sprigs of fresh mint for garnish

Place all ingredients except the mint in a blender and purée until smooth. Divide among 4 tall glasses and garnish with mint sprigs.

mango milk shake

SERVES 4

Among the world's great experts on tropical fruit, our friend Michael Seigal has to rank high. Be it mangosteen, jackfruit, or loquat, Michael is there. Often after he and I (Chris) finish playing tennis, he gives me a couple of mangoes. I like to let them sit on the table in my kitchen until they are ripe enough that the whole house is filled with their delicate fragrance, then put them in a milk shake and have them for breakfast. If you are feeling in a healthful frame of mind, you can skip the ice cream—but including it sure does make for a satisfying morning.

2 ripe mangoes, peeled and pitted	1 cup milk
2 scoops vanilla ice cream	5 ice cubes
2 cups fresh orange juice	Juice of one lime

Place all ingredients in a blender and purée until smooth. Divide among 4 tall glasses and serve immediately.

watermelon-raspberry cooler

SERVES 4

≝ ≝ ≝ ≝ ≝ ≝ ≝ ≝ ≝ ≝ ≝ ≝ ≝ ≝ ≝ ≝ ≝

One of the things we really enjoyed when we were traveling in Southeast Asia was the seemingly omnipresent watermelon juice. You could get it at any of the innumerable fruit stands on the streets or along the highways, and it was never absent from break-fast buffets at tourist hotels. We started drinking it a lot after we got home, too. Here we purée the watermelon along with raspberries, lime juice, and ginger to create an excellent nonalcoholic cooler—although of course we wouldn't stop you from adding alcohol should you choose to.

4 cups cubed and seeded watermelon
1 pint fresh or thawed frozen
    raspberries
1 tablespoon peeled and minced fresh
    ginger

Juice of 2 limes
2 tablespoons sugar
1 quart soda water
Sprigs of fresh mint leaves and lime
    slices for garnish

Place the watermelon, berries, ginger, lime juice, and sugar in a blender and purée until smooth. Strain into a pitcher and add plenty of ice. Add the sparkling water, stir until cold and well blended, and divide among 4 glasses. Garnish with mint sprigs and lime slices and serve

mango-raspberry wine cooler with fresh mint

SERVES 4 TO 5

These days a fair number of people seem to be avoiding beer and wine and going to more unusual, slightly alcoholic drinks along the lines of spiked iced teas. So here's our own little wine cooler with fresh raspberries and mangoes, which is very refreshing when you want something light with just a little bit of kick and some good flavor. We like it with Alsatian white wines, but it works with a wine like pinot gris, too.

1 pint fresh raspberries
1 cup mango juice
Plenty of ice cubes
1 bottle (750 ml) white wine such as
    Gewürztraminer, Riesling, or
    pinot gris

1 cup soda water
Juice of 1 lime
Mint sprigs for garnish

1. In a blender, combine the raspberries and mango juice and purée until smooth.

2. Fill a large pitcher halfway with ice, then pour in the fruit purée, wine, soda water, and lime juice. Stir until the mixture is well blended and cold.

3. Pour into glasses and garnish each with a fresh sprig of mint.

orange-rosé wine cooler with green grapes

SERVES 4

Largely because of an advertising campaign in the 1960s that resulted in the widespread popularity of rosé wines that managed to be overly sweet and unpleasantly harsh at the same time, rosé came to have a very bad name in this country. But as more and more wine drinkers are learning, there are of course many excellent rosés. We wouldn't recommended that you use an ultra-high-quality bottle here, since you're going to be mixing it with many other ingredients, but a dry rosé works best. Try this one on a very hot summer afternoon or a breezy summer evening.

1 bottle (750 ml) dry rosé	1/2 orange, sliced thin (not peeled)
1/2 cup Grand Marnier	1/2 lime, sliced thin (not peeled)
1 cup fresh orange juice	1 cup green grapes, halved
Juice of one lime	

Combine all ingredients in a large pitcher with plenty of ice. Stir until well mixed and divide among 4 glasses.

white sangria with peaches and grand marnier

SERVES 4 TO 5

This is another version of a wine cooler, perfect for a hot August day when peaches are in season. Any crisp, relatively dry white wine will do the trick here; just avoid Chardonnays.

Plenty of ice cubes	2 ripe peaches, pitted and cut into 8
1 bottle (750 ml) crisp white wine	wedges each
such as pinot gris	1/2 cup Grand Marnier
1 cup tropical fruit juice such as	1 orange, thinly sliced (not peeled)
mango, papaya, or guava	1 lime, thinly sliced (not peeled)

1. Fill a large pitcher halfway with ice, then pour in the wine, fruit juice, peach wedges, Grand Marnier, and about three-quarters of the orange and lime slices. Stir until cold and well mixed.

2. Pour into glasses, adding a few of the reserved fruit slices to each.

fresh margaritas with ten variations

MAKES 1 QUART; SERVES 4 TO 6

To us, the margarita is the official cocktail of cooking outdoors. There's a story behind this version, a tribute to the fact that no matter what you know about a subject, you can always learn something more. I (Chris) was a big fan of the margaritas we served at the East Coast Grill, and I was not alone in this admiration—our version of this classic cocktail had won Best of Boston awards on several occasions. Then one day my friend Kay Rentschler and her associate Bridget from *Cook's Illustrated* magazine called and asked for a conference. They had been working on a margarita recipe and wanted to come over and see what they could learn from me, the Margarita Master. So they came to the restaurant, we did an impromptu tasting, and—well, it takes a big man to admit it, but their recipe was better than mine. Theirs was a bit more laborious, but the results made it well worth the effort.

So here's my version of their drink. I've simplified it a bit, because their recipe required 24 hours of marinating, and who wants to think ahead when cocktails are involved? And let me seize this chance to extend my thanks to the bartenders at the East Coast Grill—Meg, Kiki, and John—for the thousands of margaritas they've made in perfecting the recipe.

1 cup lime juice (about 8 limes)
1/3 cup lemon juice (about 1 lemon)
1/2 cup water
2 tablespoons grated lime zest
1 tablespoon grated lemon zest
1 tablespoon grated orange zest

1/4 cup sugar (superfine if you have it)
3 tablespoons coarse salt (optional)
1 1/2 cups tequila (preferably *reposado*)
1 1/2 cups Triple Sec or other sweet orange liqueur

1. In a small nonreactive saucepan, combine the two kinds of juice, water, three kinds of zest, and sugar. Bring to a boil over medium-high heat, then reduce the heat to low and simmer, stirring occasionally, for 10 minutes. Remove from the heat and allow to cool to room temperature.

2. If you want your glasses salted, pour the salt out onto a plate, rub the rims of the glasses with the leftover lime rinds (from making the juice), then dip the rims into the salt. Fill each glass about halfway with ice.

3. Strain the juice through a fine sieve into a 1-quart pitcher or cocktail shaker. Add the tequila, the Triple Sec, and the remaining crushed ice, then stir or shake until the mixture is thoroughly combined and well chilled, 20 to 30 seconds. Strain into the ice-filled glasses and garnish each drink with a slice of lime. Serve immediately.

COOK TO COOK: It may seem obvious, but be sure to grate the fruits first, then juice them. Use the fine holes of your grater to harvest the zest.

ten margarita variations

And here are some variations on the margarita, so you never have to drink the same cocktail twice in a row.

1. *Martin's Famous Margaritas:* This is the favorite of the jovial Martin Berry, an East Coast Grill alumnus who is Cambridge's most popular bartender. Add 1/2 cup fresh orange juice to the basic recipe.

2. *Mango Margaritas:* Add 1 cup puréed mango (about 1 large mango, pitted and peeled) to the basic recipe.

3. *Blue Margaritas:* The single most popular margarita at the East Coast Grill, this was introduced by Smiley Singleton, our original bartender, and was instrumental in the success of the restaurant. The clever part of it is that Blue Curaçao is an orange liqueur, so substituting it for Triple Sec doesn't really change the flavor of the drink.
   Substitute 1/2 cup Blue Curaçao liqueur for 1/2 cup of Triple Sec in the basic recipe.

4. *Blue-Green Mangoritas:* Substitute 1/2 cup Blue Curaçao and 1 cup puréed mango for the Triple Sec in the basic recipe.

5. *Watermelon Margaritas:* Add 1 cup watermelon juice to the basic recipe.

6. *One-Eyed Jake Margaritas:* Invented by John and Sally, bartenders at the Back Eddy, this margarita was served at the memorial service for Jake, my (Chris's) one-eyed dog.
   Substitute Grand Marnier for the Triple Sec in the basic recipe, and use Patron tequila or another super-high-quality tequila of your choice.

7. *Mescal Margaritas:* To get a margarita with Chris's favorite smoky flavor, substitute Bacardi Tropico rum for the Triple Sec and use mescal in place of the tequila in the basic recipe.

8. *Raspberry Margaritas:* Substitute Chambord for the Triple Sec in the basic recipe and garnish with fresh raspberries.

9. *Grand Gold Margaritas:* Substitute Grand Marnier for the Triple Sec, and use Gold tequila in the basic recipe.

10. *Doc's Quick and Easy Playa Negra Special Margarita:* We offer this drink in memory of the time that we were all down in Costa Rica and our friend Ihsan asked me (Doc) to mix him a martini. I figured we were in the tropics and little ceremony was required, so I poured some gin in a glass, mixed in a little vermouth and a bunch of ice, and handed it to him. He was a bit shocked, but he drank it anyway, and he found that it wasn't too bad after it had a chance to cool down. So when you want a quick Margarita without a lot of fuss, here's your recipe:

Combine 1 part tequila of your choice, 1 part Triple Sec, 1 part lime juice, and a little sugar. Shake it up, pour it out, and drink it down.

tequila and mescal

* * *

Let's get one thing straight right from the beginning: There's no worm in tequila. What you are thinking of is mescal. And although both drinks are made from the juice of Mexico's agave plant, they are quite different.

There are two basic types of tequila. The first is 100% blue agave. The second is mixed or **mixta**, in which sugar solutions are added to the fermented agave juice just before distillation. By law, all 100% blue agave must be made and bottled in Mexico. It is like single-malt versus blended Scotches.

That's not the whole tequila story, though. There are also three different varieties of 100% agave tequilas—**blanco** or "silver," which is not aged at all; **reposado** or "rested," which is aged not less than two months in wooden barrels; and **anejo** or "old," which is aged not less than one year in wooden barrels that may be no larger than 600 liters. Many people confuse the long-aged *anejo* with gold tequila. In fact, gold tequila may have been aged only a month or so, or it may even simply have been tinted with an additive, usually some type of caramel. The caramel or other additives are used to take some of the harshness out of this, the lowest-common-denominator tequila.

Mescal, a similar but less refined and elegant liquor, is made from other varieties of agave and, since it is distilled over a wood fire, has a different, more smoky flavor. Like the now-popular Italian drink grappa, mescal has a pretty harsh edge. As fans of harshness in alcohol, we are quite fond of it.

vanilla-flavored ash-roasted apples with maple whipped cream

SERVES 6

🌿 🌿 🌿 🌿 🌿 🌿 🌿 🌿 🌿 🌿 🌿 🌿 🌿 🌿 🌿 🌿 🌿

We're not big on sweets, but this is one dessert that gets us going. And it's easy, too. Get your hands on some good cooking apples and core them, then throw some butter, pecans, and half a vanilla bean into each one, wrap them in foil, and toss them in the coals for 20 minutes or so. After you unwrap them, serve them hot, topped with maple syrup and whipped cream. The only part that can be complicated is coring the apples from the top without breaking through the bottom. If you have a large melon baller knocking around in your kitchen drawer, it does the job easily.

6 large, firm cooking apples such as
    Golden Delicious, Cortlands,
    Baldwins, or Northern Spys
6 tablespoons unsalted butter, cut
    into 6 pieces
1/2 cup chopped toasted pecans

3 vanilla beans, each split lengthwise
    (or substitute 1 tablespoon
    vanilla extract)
2 cups whipped cream
1/4 cup pure maple syrup

1. Tear off 4 sheets of heavy-duty foil, each about 2 feet long, and stack them one on top of the other. Core the apples through the top, stopping 1/2 inch from the bottom. Arrange the apples in the center of the top sheet of foil. Now push 1 piece of butter and 1/6 of the pecans into the center of each apple, along with 1/2 a vanilla bean folded in

half (or 1/2 teaspoon vanilla extract if you don't have vanilla beans). Fold up the sheets of foil around the apples one after the other, turning the package one-quarter turn each time and making sure that each sheet is well sealed around the apples. Or you can place the apples in a deep disposable foil pan, cover with a double layer of heavy-duty foil, and seal well.

2. Place the foil-wrapped apples in the coals at the periphery of the fire, where the heat is less intense. Pile the coals up around the package and cook until the apples are tender, about 20 to 30 minutes. Remove from the coals, unroll the foil, and remove the vanilla beans. Top each apple with a big spoonful of whipped cream and a generous drizzle of maple syrup and serve warm.

apples of our eyes

* * *

The key to finding a good apple for ash-roasting—or for baking, for that matter—is to find one that combines good flavor and a high calcium content. Calcium is important because it helps the apple retain its shape during roasting or baking. After trying lots of apples in this and other recipes, we decided that our favorites include Golden Delicious, Cortlands, and Baldwins. Granny Smiths and Red Delicious are too dry, McIntoshes too mushy. But we also encourage you to try any locally available varieties, particularly heirlooms—you might find something fantastic that you can share with other cooks from your part of the country.

fire-roasted banana goop sundaes with rum, raisins, and butter

SERVES 6

You know those bananas that are so dark and overripe that all you can think of to do with them is make banana bread? Well, think again. Instead, throw them on the grill over a medium fire and just let them cook. What you'll end up with is a super-sweet banana purée. Squeeze that over some ice cream, add a little flavored butter, and you've got a truly delicious dessert.

But why should you have all the fun? To let your guests make their own Banana Goop Sundaes, put out a butter dish, a bowl of raisins, and a small pitcher of rum. Pile the hot bananas on a plate where everyone can reach them, and give each guest a bowl of ice cream, a knife, and a spoon.

6 super-ripe bananas	6 tablespoons unsalted butter
Your favorite ice cream—you know how much	1/2 cup raisins
	3 tablespoons dark rum

1. Place the bananas, still in their skins, over a medium-hot to dying-down fire and cook until they are practically liquefied inside—about 5 to 15 minutes, depending on the heat and the ripeness of the bananas.

2. Scoop the ice cream into 6 dessert dishes. When the bananas have turned to mush inside (you can tell by poking them gently), remove them from the grill. Cut the tip off one of the bananas and squeeze the hot goop over a bowl of ice cream. Top with 1 tablespoon butter, a few raisins, and a drizzle of rum. Repeat with the remaining bananas and ice cream.

grilled peaches with vanilla ice cream and fresh strawberry sauce

SERVES 4

❦ ❦ ❦ ❦ ❦ ❦ ❦ ❦ ❦ ❦ ❦ ❦ ❦ ❦ ❦ ❦ ❦

Grilling fruit is no longer considered weird, as it was when we first started tossing peaches, plums, and apples on the grill fifteen or so years ago. It is now widely recognized as a great way to bring out the inherent sweetness and amplify the flavors of fruits. This dessert couldn't be easier—just grill some peach halves and top them with ice cream and a very simple strawberry sauce—but it's got great flavor and it manages to be simultaneously rich and refreshing.

2 cups fresh strawberries, washed, hulled, and quartered
1 tablespoon sugar
1 teaspoon fresh lime juice
2 ripe peaches, halved and pitted

2 tablespoons unsalted butter, melted
1 quart really good vanilla ice cream, or other flavor of your choice

1. Build a multi-level fire in your grill: Leaving one-quarter of the bottom free of coals, bank the coals in the remaining three-quarters of the grill so that there are about three times as many on one side as on the other. When the coals are all ignited and the temperature has died down to medium (you can hold your hand about 5 inches above the grill grid, over the area where the coals are deepest, for 4 to 5 seconds), you're ready to cook.

2. In a small bowl, combine the strawberries, sugar, and lime juice and mix well.

3. Put the peaches on the grill, cut side down, and cook just until lightly seared, about 6 to 8 minutes. Flip them over, brush the tops with the butter, and cook until the butter begins to caramelize, another 2 or 3 minutes.

4. Put a small scoop of ice cream on top of each peach half, spoon on some of the strawberry sauce, and serve.

s'more hobo pack

SERVES 4

Easy to make, this dessert brings back memories for adults and is great for kids, too. The little bit of smokiness that the marshmallows have on them when they come out of the coals adds a nice touch.

4 whole graham crackers, broken in half to make 8 squares

2 Hershey's milk chocolate bars, each broken into quarters
12 marshmallows

1. Tear off 4 sheets of heavy-duty foil, each about 2 feet long, and stack them one on top of the other. Lay out 4 graham crackers to make 1 large square in the center of the top sheet of foil. Using half of the chocolate, place a piece of chocolate on each cracker. Top with marshmallows, then with the rest of the chocolate, and finally with the graham cracker squares, making 4 "sandwiches."

2. Fold up the sheets of foil one after the other, turning the package one-quarter turn each time and making sure that each sheet is well sealed around the square of crackers.

3. Place the foil-wrapped package in the coals at the periphery of the fire, where the heat is less intense. Pile the coals up around the package and cook for 5 minutes; flip the package over and cook for another 5 minutes, so that both layers of chocolate and the marshmallows are partially melted. Remove from the coals, unroll the foil, and hand out the squares.

banana-carrot cake with guava frosting

SERVES 8

Here's a little semitropical turn on that old American standby, carrot cake. To improve the texture and get rid of the vegetal flavor that sometimes mars this type of cake, we borrow the *Cook's Illustrated* method of mixing the carrots with sugar at the beginning of the process, letting them sit so the sugar pulls some of the liquid out of the carrots, and then draining them. It takes almost no extra time, and it definitely makes for a better cake.

2 1/2 cups finely grated carrots	4 large eggs
1 cup white sugar	1/2 cup mashed very ripe banana
2 cups all-purpose flour	1/2 cup plain yogurt (whole-milk
1 tablespoon cinnamon	if possible)
2 teaspoons baking soda	1 teaspoon vanilla extract
1/2 teaspoon salt	3/4 cup chopped toasted pecans or
1 1/2 sticks unsalted butter, melted	macadamia nuts
and cooled slightly	1/2 cup toasted shredded coconut
1/2 cup packed light brown sugar	(optional)

1. Preheat the oven to 350°F. Grease and flour two 8-inch round cake pans.

2. Place the carrots in a colander over a large bowl. Sprinkle with 1/4 cup of the white sugar and toss to coat. Allow the carrots to stand while you prepare the rest of the recipe.

3. In a large bowl, whisk together the flour, cinnamon, baking soda, and salt. Set aside.

4. In another large bowl, whisk together the remaining white sugar with the brown sugar and butter until well blended. Add the eggs one at a time, mixing well after each addition, then stir in the mashed banana, yogurt, and vanilla. Toss the carrots lightly in the colander to drain well, then add to the batter and mix until evenly blended. Fold in the dry ingredients and nuts. Divide the batter between the pans.

5. Place the pans in the preheated oven and bake until a tester inserted near the center of the cakes comes out clean, 30 to 40 minutes. Cool the cakes 10 minutes in the pans, then invert onto a rack to cool completely. Wrap and store at room temperature overnight.

6. Fill and frost with Guava Frosting, and sprinkle with toasted coconut if desired.

guava frosting

Not surprisingly, if you can find fresh guavas for the frosting you will get a better flavor. But they can be hard to locate and are always expensive, so the guava paste is a perfectly fine option.

- 4 ounces (1 stick) unsalted butter at room temperature
- 1/2 cup canned guava paste or 3/4 cup fresh ripe guava pulp (mash and press through a fine sieve before measuring)
- 8 ounces cream cheese at room temperature

- 3 to 3 1/2 cups sifted confectioners' sugar
- 1/8 teaspoon salt
- 1 teaspoon vanilla extract
- 2 to 3 teaspoons fresh lemon juice
- 1/2 cup toasted unsweetened shredded coconut (optional)

Blend the butter and guava with an electric mixer until smooth. Add the cream cheese and blend until smooth. Gradually add the sugar, then add the salt, vanilla, and lemon juice to taste. If the frosting is very soft, refrigerate for 1 hour or until it reaches spreading consistency.

COOK TO COOK: This cake tastes better on the second day, so you should wrap and store the layers (separately) overnight. Frost the cake on the day you are serving it.

macadamia nut brownies

MAKES 1 DOZEN

Everybody loves brownies, and here's an excellent version with macadamia nuts to give it that little tropical flair. Of course, you can substitute walnuts if you're a stickler for tradition.

4 ounces unsweetened chocolate
1 1/2 sticks unsalted butter
2 cups sugar
4 large eggs
1 1/2 teaspoons vanilla

2 tablespoons strong brewed coffee
1 cup all-purpose flour
1 cup coarsely chopped toasted
    macadamia nuts

1. Preheat the oven to 350°F. Line an 8 × 8-inch baking pan with aluminum foil with a 2-inch overhang on 2 opposite sides. Butter or grease the foil well.

2. In a small saucepan over low heat, melt the chocolate and butter together until smooth. Remove from the heat and transfer to a large mixing bowl. Stir in the sugar until well mixed.

3. Add the eggs to the chocolate mixture one at a time, blending well after each addition. Add the vanilla and coffee, stirring until smooth. Stir in the flour and 3/4 cup of the nuts, mixing until incorporated, and transfer the batter to the prepared pan. Sprinkle the batter with the remaining nuts.

4. Bake until a tester inserted near the center of the brownies comes out with moist crumbs, about 30 to 40 minutes. Cool for 20 minutes in the pan, then use the foil to unmold the brownies. Cool completely on a rack before cutting into bars.

macadamia nut brownies with mildly creative additions

MAKES 1 DOZEN

This rendition of our brownies goes just a bit more in the tropical direction. If you like, you can use low-fat coconut milk, but since you're already putting in all that butter, eggs, and chocolate, what the heck, you might as well use the real thing.

4 ounces unsweetened chocolate
1 1/2 sticks unsalted butter
2/3 cup coconut milk
2 cups sugar
4 large eggs
1 1/2 teaspoons vanilla
2 tablespoons Kahlua

1 1/4 cups all-purpose flour
1 cup coarsely chopped toasted
macadamia nuts
6 ounces white chocolate, coarsely
chopped
2 tablespoons unsweetened shredded coconut

1. Preheat the oven to 350°F. Line an 8 × 8-inch baking pan with aluminum foil with a 2-inch overhang on 2 opposite sides. Butter or grease the foil well.

2. In a small saucepan over low heat, melt the chocolate and butter together until smooth. Remove from the heat and transfer to a large mixing bowl. Add the coconut milk and then the sugar, mixing well.

3. Add the eggs to the chocolate mixture one at a time, blending well after each addition. Add the vanilla and Kahlua, stirring until smooth. Stir in the flour, 3/4 cup of the nuts, and the white chocolate, mixing until incorporated. Transfer the batter to the prepared pan and sprinkle with the remaining nuts and the coconut.

4. Bake until a tester inserted near the center of the brownies comes out with moist crumbs, about 30 to 40 minutes. Cool for 20 minutes in the pan, then use the foil to unmold the brownies. Cool completely on a rack before cutting into bars.

THE FLAMING PANTRY

AS YOU LOOK THROUGH THE RECIPES IN THIS BOOK, YOU'LL notice a handful of ingredients coming up over and over. Some of them, like garlic or basil, are probably very familiar to you; others, such as fish sauce or coriander seeds, may seem more exotic. We figured you might like to know a bit about each. This chapter isn't a complete "pantry" for all the ingredients in the book, or even for all the unusual ones. Instead, it's an explanation of the nature of some of our favorites, why we like them so much, and how to keep them in good shape. You might think of it as our personal Desert Island Shopping List. (If you need help locating any of these ingredients, check out the Sources section, page 401.)

SEASONINGS, HERBS, AND SPICES

THE BIG TWO

Salt

It used to be that the one ingredient you never had to think much about was salt. I mean, salt was salt, right? Well, not anymore. As with so many other foods and seasonings, salt has become much more interesting and complex as we have learned more about it, and cooks are starting to use different salts for different purposes.

In fact, I (Chris) keep five kinds in my kitchen at all times. I like superfine iodized salt for corn on the cob. Kosher salt is my everyday, all-purpose choice for brining, seasoning meat, and cooking pasta. For flavoring beyond kosher salt, I like gray salt. But when I really want to dress up a dish, I use exotic salts as a garnish: fleur de sel adds a clean, bright flavor to steak and oysters, and Hawaiian red clay salt sparks up pale foods like chicken, fish, or baked potatoes.

Here are some designer salts you might want to try, just for the fun of it. But beware: They are definitely not cheap. To help alleviate the pain caused by laying out this kind of cash, you might think of them not as seasonings but as condiments in their own right.

Fleur de sel: Hand-skimmed from the surface of evaporating seawater in the salt beds off the pristine Atlantic coast of France, this is a top-of-the-line sea salt with a price to match. Its fine white crystals are tinged with pink and have a faint scent of violets.

Sel gris, or gray salt: This salt is what's left after they skim off the fleur de sel. Naturally it's less expensive and not as white (hence the name), but many people think its flavor is just as good or even better. Sel gris tends to be large-grained and moist.

Maldon: This sea salt from Essex, England, is a dry, white salt with a clean, pronounced flavor. While it's fine for cooking, it's especially nice eaten raw so that you can feel its signature snowflake-like crystals on your tongue.

Halen Môn: An organic Welsh sea salt from the Isle of Anglesey, this one has pure white, crunchy crystals that are almost sweet.

Trapani: A Sicilian sea salt farmed from a Mediterranean nature reserve, trapani has a clean, intense, bright flavor.

Hawaiian red clay ("Alaea") salt: More orange or salmon-colored than red, this salt gets its striking color from the volcanic clay that runs into the sea from Kauai. Once dried, the clay is blended into the salt, improving the flavor as well as the color. Sprinkle it on after cooking—it's especially nice on pale foods where you can appreciate its wild color.

Hawaiian black lava salt: Like Alaea salt, this variety gets its color from an unusual ingredient. The salt is dried with purified black lava rock, then activated charcoal is added.

Kala namak: This is India's own "black" salt, a pinkish-brown powder that is only mildly salty but has a smoky, complex flavor so pronounced that it plays the role of a spice in cooking.

Sindhalu: With its opaque white and orange stripes, this rock salt from Pakistan is pretty to look at. It's even said to be an aphrodisiac. But it is sold in large, inconvenient chunks and is not very flavorful.

Blue Dragon: This Korean sea salt has a clean, fresh taste and unusually large grains. It's particularly nice for making salt crusts for roasting.

Pepper

Over the past couple of decades, most home cooks have begun to recognize the incredible difference between freshly ground pepper and the preground stuff. The next step, which is certainly not necessary but is a lot of fun, is to differentiate among various types of peppercorns. Despite what most of us think, it's not true that pepper is pepper is pepper. Like chocolate or coffee beans, pepper has individual varieties that gain specific flavor profiles from the climate, soil, and growing conditions where they are raised.

Two of the most highly valued peppercorns, Malabar and Tellicherry, come from pepper's original home in southern India. Malabar is the smaller peppercorn of the two, with a resinous aroma, a spicy citrus tang, and a rather biting heat that licks the back of the throat. Tellicherry peppercorns come from the same plant as Malabar but are larger fruits that have been allowed to ripen more completely, so they have a more complex flavor. With their full, almost fruity flavors, pungent aroma, and mild bite, Tellicherry peppercorns are widely considered the finest of all.

Indonesia is the source of the other two most prominent pepper varieties. Sarawak peppercorns, grown on the island of Borneo, tend to have a pleasantly musty, woodsy flavor and a relatively mild heat that develops slowly. Lampong peppercorns, from the island of Sumatra, have balanced fruity flavors and a bright, rather pronounced heat. If you are looking for a strong, even, spreading heat in a dish, Lampong is the pepper of choice.

Whichever peppercorns you choose, buy them whole and grind them just before use.

Storage: Keep in a cool, dark, dry place no longer than a year.

White Pepper

White pepper is made by allowing peppercorns to ripen fully before the skin is removed and the inner corn is dried. The result is a smaller, smooth-skinned, milder-flavored pepper with a more floral flavor than its black brethren. It is quite popular in various Asian cuisines. Since we are big fans of aromaticity, we use white pepper quite a lot, particularly in Asian-style dishes.

Storage: Keep in a cool, dark, dry place no longer than a year.

A FEW OTHERS

Basil

I (Chris) very clearly remember tasting fresh basil for the first time back in 1975, when my Italian chef at the Culinary Institute made me go to the garden and pick basil to make pesto. I've been intoxicated with the herb since that day. Its distinctive sweet, licorice-tinged flavor is a key element in the cuisines of Southeast Asia as well as the Mediterranean. There are many varieties, from the readily available sweet basil that most cooks are familiar with to opal basil, Thai basil, even lemon and cinnamon basil. It's fun to play around with all the varieties, but the best bet, as always, is to buy whatever is of highest quality. All varieties of basil can easily be grown in your garden.

Storage: Basil will keep for almost a week if stored in the refrigerator with the stems in water and the leaves covered with a plastic bag.

Chipotle Peppers

Anyone who has ever used any of our other cookbooks already knows that this is our absolute favorite chile. A dried, smoked jalapeño, the chipotle imparts a unique hot, smoky, deep flavor to anything you add it to. Chipotles are available in two forms, either dried or packed in adobo sauce, which is a mixture of tomatoes, vinegar, onions, and spices. We prefer the latter because the chipotles packed in adobo sauce are ready to use without any further ado, but dried chipotles are also excellent. If you do buy your chipotles dry, look for some with a warm, reddish-brown color, not gray or dusty-looking, and reconstitute them before use by soaking them in boiling-hot water for 40 minutes.

Storage: Either type keeps indefinitely on the shelf in a cool, dark place.

Cilantro

Okay, so some people say it tastes like soap. It seems as if that idea must spring from a genetic predisposition, because we just don't get it. To us, the pungent, very distinctive, highly aromatic flavor of cilantro is fantastic. (Maybe we just like the whole parsley clan—cilantro, like cumin and coriander, is a member of this family.) In any case, cilantro is probably the most widely used herb in the world. It's very important in cooking not only throughout Mexico and Latin America but also in Southeast Asia, where it is typically combined with mint and basil. Because we are partial to all of those cuisines, we use this herb a lot. But if you are one of those people who *really* don't like it, you can substitute its milder cousin, parsley.

Since drying destroys the aromatic nature of cilantro, it is worth the effort to get the fresh herb. Almost unknown in the United States a couple of decades ago, it is now readily available. You can also grow cilantro easily in your own garden.

Storage: Store cilantro in the refrigerator with the stems in water and the leaves covered with a plastic bag. It will keep that way for almost a week.

Coriander Seed

Coriander is integral to the cuisines not only of the Middle East but also of North Africa, Spain, Portugal, South America, and Mexico. It's one of the few spices that we really couldn't do without, because it adds a complex, very evocative flavor to a whole range of foods.

Coriander seeds come from a plant that originated in the southern and eastern Mediterranean, the leaves of which are the herb cilantro. (If you do try growing your own cilantro, experiment with the fresh berries—they have a unique fruity pungency.). The dried seeds are round, slightly smaller than black peppercorns, and yellowish tan in color, with tiny ridges running around them. Their flavor is nutty, intensely aromatic, and rather sweet, with echoes of orange peel. The taste will probably be more familiar to most Americans than they expect, since coriander is the primary flavoring for hot dogs.

Coriander is often preground so that the rather fibrous outer portion of the seed is completely pulverized. Don't assume that the fibrous part makes it impossible to deal with whole seeds, however. Toast the seeds first to bring out their flavor and aroma, and then use an electric grinder (or even the bottom of a sauté pan) to grind them. The process takes only a couple of minutes for the amount used in most recipes.

Storage: Store tightly sealed in a cool, dry place for no more than 6 months.

Cumin Seed

Along with coriander, cumin is one of the basic spices used in almost all equatorial cuisines. These greenish yellow "seeds," with their distinctive nutty flavor, are actually the dried fruit of an annual herb indigenous to Egypt. Slightly darker than coriander, with an oval shape punctuated by tiny vertical ridges, cumin seeds are also widely used in Indian, Latin American, African, and Middle Eastern cuisines. (There is also a black variety of cumin, which has a sweeter, more refined, and more complex flavor, but it is expensive and difficult to locate.)

Like coriander, cumin has an aromatic, slightly nutty flavor, but cumin's flavor has a sharper edge, a hint of lemon, and a medicinal tinge. Again like coriander, cumin adds a distinctive flavor that resonates with many culinary associations the instant you taste it. And like coriander once again, cumin will be recognized by most Americans—in this case because it's almost always used in that national favorite, chili con carne.

As with other spice seeds, toasting cumin and grinding it yourself just prior to use really brings out its flavor and aroma.

Storage: Store in a cool, dry place for no more than 6 months.

Garlic

What can we say about garlic? In 1950s America, using these pungent little cloves in your cooking marked you as either adventurous or (that all-purpose term) "ethnic." Our national culinary maturity is demonstrated by the fact that today garlic is probably the single most indispensable flavoring in American cooking after salt and pepper. But that doesn't distinguish us from the rest of the world; there are few cuisines that can properly be cooked without at least some garlic. Personally, we like to make chips out of it, mash it into a paste, wrap it in foil and roast it in the coals to give it a smoky flavor, and in general toss it into just about everything that's not a dessert.

There are a number of kinds of garlic on the market right now. Generally speaking, the less readily available hardneck varieties have a deeper, richer flavor than the softneck types found in most supermarkets, but either will do fine. We recommend, though, that you stay away from the huge heads of so-called "elephant garlic"—this is not true garlic, and its flavor is way too mild for our taste. When you're buying garlic, look for plump, heavy heads. Avoid those that are light for their size and those with soft or shriveled cloves.

Storage: Stored in a cool, dry place—not in the refrigerator—garlic will keep for up to 1 month.

Ginger

The underground stem, or rhizome, of a perennial tropical plant, ginger is the epitome of aromatic pungency. We love it for its sweet, sharp, almost floral flavor, and there's no way you can cook Asian-influenced foods without it. Because fresh ginger can be fibrous, be sure to mince it well unless it's going to be strained out of the final dish. Powdered dry ginger, which increases in pungency when heated, is very useful for smoothing out spice mixtures.

Storage: Wrap fresh ginger in plastic wrap and store in the refrigerator for up to 3 weeks, or freeze for up to 6 months. Powdered dry ginger can be kept, tightly sealed in a cool, dark place, for up to 6 months.

Mint

Part of the Southeast Asian herb trio (along with basil and cilantro), mint has a slightly astringent quality that makes it particularly refreshing. Although there are more than 30 species of mint, and over 600 varieties, the two most commonly available are peppermint (quite pungent; it has a peppery flavor, bright green leaves, and purplish stems) and spearmint (not as pungent as peppermint; it has gray-green to green leaves). Either works fine in our recipes, or if you feel like it you can experiment with such offbeat entries as chocolate mint or lemon mint. Mint is also a prolific garden plant, thriving even in rock gardens and other unpromising locations.

Storage: Stored in the refrigerator with the stems in water and the leaves covered with a plastic bag, mint will keep for up to a week.

Oregano

Usually thought of as a Mediterranean herb, oregano is actually a very important element of Latin American cooking, and in fact most of the oregano imported into the United States comes from Mexico. The Mexican varieties have a stronger flavor than the Mediterranean ones. Unlike basil or mint, oregano dries well without losing too much of its character, so you can substitute dried for fresh in recipes in which the herb is cooked, using about half the amount.

Storage: Stored in the refrigerator with the stems in water and the leaves covered with a plastic bag, oregano will keep for up to a week.

A Few Fruits and Vegetables

Asparagus

Asparagus may be our very favorite grilled side dish, for three reasons: It's incredibly easy to cook—just put a little oil on it, toss it on the grill, and roll it around; its flavor is distinctive enough to be fully satisfying but mild enough to complement almost any main course; and spring asparagus season coincides with "whip out the grill" season.

Storage: Asparagus should be used the day it's bought if possible, but it can be kept in the refrigerator, wrapped in plastic, for a couple of days.

Avocados

Perhaps the top non-starch vegetable of Latin American cooking, avocados are among our favorites, too. They are surprisingly delicious grilled, and wonderful in salsas. For both of those uses, it's best to use avocados that are ripe but still quite firm; they should give just slightly when pushed with your finger. In general, we prefer the Hass avocados from California to the larger, more smooth-skinned Fuertes.

Storage: Most avocados found in supermarkets are not yet ripe; you can ripen them by keeping them in a paper bag at room temperature for several days. Ripe avocados will keep for a couple of days in the refrigerator.

Figs

To us, a grilled fig is a perfect example of how the right cooking method can improve even the best fruits. Fresh figs are delicious raw, but they are fantastic when grilled—the little edge of sear they get from the fire intensifies their mellow flavor, and the heat sort of melts their already tender interior to give them a wonderful, soft texture. Fresh figs can be difficult to locate even when they are in season, from June through October. So pick up good-quality figs of whatever variety you can find. For grilling, though, our favorites are the deep purplish black Mission figs with their red interior and sweet flavor, or the reddish brown Brunswicks, which have amber-pink flesh.

Storage: Figs keep in the refrigerator for no more than a few days.

Limes

With their complex sour flavor, limes are definitely the most dynamic of all the citrus fruits. Maybe that's because, by weight, a lime has 50 percent more acid than a lemon. In any case, limes are indispensable in the tropical larder, even more than lemons are in the European pantry. A lot of our food gets finished with lime juice, whether it's a soup that has lime squeezed into it at the end of cooking or a grilled chicken that gets lime spritzed over it as it comes off the fire. That last-minute jolt adds a freshness and also brings up many of the other flavors of the dish.

Of course, we are talking here about the relatively large, shiny, dark green fruit variously known as the Persian or Tahitian lime. In other parts of the world, "lime" most often refers to what we in America know as the Mexican or "key" lime, a smaller, yellow-green fruit with many seeds and a somewhat more pungent flavor. But regular Persian limes are just fine in all of our recipes. When you're in the market, choose brightly colored, smooth-skinned limes that are heavy for their size. Small brown areas on the skin won't affect flavor or juiciness, but avoid limes with hard or shriveled skins.

Storage: Limes keep in the refrigerator for up to 2 weeks.

Mangoes

This luscious, fragrant fruit, which originated somewhere in Southeast Asia, is a daily staple in more than half of the world. One of the reasons we are so fond of using mangoes in our cooking is that they have echoes of so many other tropical fruits—bananas, lichees, pineapple, and sometimes even guava and passion fruit.

Although you would never know it from the paucity of varieties available in our supermarkets, there are more varieties of mangoes than of apples. In this country, the most commonly used varieties are the yellow, rather mild-flavored Tommy Atkins and the somewhat richer-flavored Haden. If you can get your hands on them, you should also try the large, lemony Keitt, the sweet Palmer, and the pineappley Van Dyke.

When shopping for mangoes, choose full, heavy fruits with some yellow or red showing on the skin. Fully ripe fruits will be as tender as a ripe avocado, with skin that is taut against the flesh. Avoid mangoes with soft or wrinkled spots. Brown spots are fine. A pleasant aroma from the stem end is a good indicator of quality and ripeness.

Storage: To ripen partially ripe mangoes, keep at room temperature until tender. Do not store for more than a couple of days in the cold.

Peaches

We use peaches often in our cooking because they are the closest thing we have in this country to a tropical fruit, with all the sweet, musky, mellow, juicy virtues that implies.

Plus we find peaches to be versatile—they're wonderful on the grill and pair very well with Mediterranean flavors, particularly herbs such as basil. Fortunately, there are hundreds of varieties of peaches grown in the United States, with skin that varies in color from pink-blushed white to red-blushed yellow, and flesh that ranges from pink to gold. Our recommendation for peaches, as for most produce, is that you use whichever variety grows closest to you or—if you live in an area like Iowa, far from peach-growing country—whichever variety your local store can get in the best quality.

Storage: Ripen underripe fruit at room temperature in a paper bag with an apple for a couple of days. Store ripe peaches in the refrigerator for no more than 5 days.

Sweet Potatoes

We find sweet potatoes much more dynamic than white potatoes, and we like to use them in all kinds of ways—made into fries, cut into rounds and grilled, mashed, in salads, what have you. It's possible to use "sweets" in all these ways because their rich, deep, distinctive flavor is not only great by itself but also combines very well with other strong tastes, such as lime juices or chiles or even olives.

Not so long ago you would find only one type of sweet potato even in the best produce markets, but these days there are often several varieties even in supermarkets. The best sweet potatoes for cooking are known in this country as yams. (This misnomer—in the rest of the world, yams are a large, very starchy, and quite different tuber—originated as a marketing ploy but really caught on.) The variety you are most likely to be buying if the bin is simply labeled "yams" is the Beauregard. Beauregards are particularly sweet and don't get stringy when baked, as some other varieties may. Other popular varieties include Jewel, a short, blocky, gold-skinned potato with deep orange flesh that is quite sweet and very creamy in texture; Hernandez, a rather fat and irregularly shaped tuber that is less sweet than most; and Garnets, which have a violet or dusky red skin (hence the name), with flesh that is a slightly mottled bright orange, medium sweet, and particularly soft. We encourage you to try them all, along with any other varieties you find, and see which you like best.

Storage: Sweet potatoes don't keep as well as white potatoes do. Keep them in a cool, dark place for about a week or so, but do not refrigerate them.

Watermelon

Watermelon is found everywhere in the tropics. Americans are very fond of it, too—they consume some three billion pounds of the melon each year, and no less an authority than Mark Twain called it "what angels eat." Sweet but not cloying, inexpensive, and thirst-quenching, it's a wonderful fruit. Following in the footsteps of our grandfathers, who preferred to eat their watermelon sprinkled with salt and pepper, we like to use watermelons in savory preparations such as salsas and salads. But our true favorite is watermelon juice, which is a standard on buffet lines throughout Southeast Asia.

When you buy a melon, look for a symmetrical one with no flat sides. If the melon sounds hollow when you whack it on the side, it's probably ripe. It should be firm and heavy, with no soft spots or blemishes.

Storage: Keep a whole watermelon in the refrigerator for no more than a week.

SOME PREPARED PRODUCTS

Balsamic Vinegar

We like to think of balsamic as the catsup of grilled food. Maybe that's because it spends time in a charred oak barrel at one point in its development, so it has a faint underlying charcoal flavor. For whatever reason, it really does match up well with the smoky sear of grilled food. We recommend that you keep two kinds in your pantry: a small bottle of the real thing, true aged *aceto balsamico* that you can drizzle sparingly over grilled foods, and a big bottle of the cheaper mass-produced variety that you can reduce (boil down) to form a mahogany-colored sweet-sour glaze to coat fish, meat, fruit, or whatever.

Storage: Keeps indefinitely.

Chile-Garlic Paste

This spicy fermented paste, also known as Saigon paste, is made from nothing more than chiles, salt, oil, and garlic. The Chinese and the Koreans use it as an ingredient in cooking, while for the Vietnamese it is a ubiquitous table condiment. In fact, an English-speaking waiter in Saigon once told us that this paste is "more exciting than Atlantic City." While that might be considered damning with faint praise, you get the drift: This is great stuff.

Storage: This paste keeps indefinitely in the refrigerator.

Fish Sauce (*Nam Pla*)

An essential ingredient in the cooking of Southeast Asia, this thin brown liquid is made by packing anchovies or other small fish in salt and allowing them to ferment for three months or more, drawing off the liquid as it seeps out. To fully appreciate fish sauce, you have to understand that its aroma, which largely disappears during cooking, is its most uncompromising property, outpacing its flavor by several degrees of intensity. The second key to enjoyment is understanding that fish sauce is not meant to occupy center stage. Instead, the sauce should play a strong supporting culinary role, providing a subtle, rich, and elusive undertone of flavor that is beguiling and ultimately addictive.

Each Southeast Asian country makes its own fish sauce: *nam pla* in Thailand, *nuoc mam* in Vietnam, *tuk trey* in Cambodia, *ngan-pya-ye* in Burma, and fish gravy or *patis* in the Philippines. Even the finest fish sauces are inexpensive, costing no more than a couple of dollars for a 24-ounce bottle. The best are reputedly from an island off Vietnam called Phu Quoc—this name has evolved into a generic term for high quality.

Storage: Fish sauce keeps indefinitely on the shelf.

Hoisin Sauce

Hoisin is a thick, sweetish, dark red mixture that is particularly well liked in southern China. Made from soybeans, garlic, vinegar, sugar, flour, chile peppers, and various spices, it is widely used as a table dipping sauce and in marinades. It can be found in all Chinese markets and many supermarkets. Different brands vary in sweetness, spiciness, and viscosity. The best way to find the brand you prefer is to taste a few, but the order of the ingredient list will clue you in as to which flavors are predominant. Also called Peking sauce.

Storage: Hoisin sauce should keep almost indefinitely even without refrigeration, but it's best kept tightly covered in the refrigerator.

Olive Oil

Olive oil has to a large extent replaced butter both in cooking and on the table in modern American cuisine. As with balsamic vinegar, we recommend that you keep two types on hand: a very high quality, full-flavored, artisanal extra-virgin for drizzling on salads or over a piece of grilled fish or meat, and a standard supermarket-variety for cooking purposes.

Storage: Olive oil will keep for up to a year if tightly covered and stored in a cool, dark place.

Soy Sauce

As anyone who is even a moderate fan of Chinese or Japanese food knows, soy sauce is as indispensable to those cuisines as salt and pepper are to ours. A fermented product, soy sauce has a deep, complex flavor that, like salt, deepens the flavors of other ingredients as well as adding its own. There are more than 285 individual flavor components in a good soy sauce, including nearly 20 amino acids. These amino acids are what enables the sauce to heighten the flavor of other foods without masking them.

There are two main types of soy sauce, Chinese and Japanese. Chinese varieties tend to be thicker, darker, and more powerfully flavored, while Japanese are sweeter, less salty, and more refined. We recommend that you try both and decide for yourself which you prefer. In general, we have a preference for the Japanese. "Lite" soy sauces are low-sodium versions sold in this country, which in our opinion you should use only if you need to reduce the salt in your diet.

When looking for a soy sauce, avoid supermarket brands like La Choy, which are made from hydrolyzed vegetable protein, hydrochloric acid, caramel, and corn syrup and have a chemical/metallic taste. Stick with imported, all-natural brands. We like Pearl River Bridge for Chinese, Kikkoman or San-J for Japanese.

Storage: Soy sauce keeps in a cool, dark place for over a year.

Tabasco Sauce

With the increased popularity of chile peppers in the United States over the past couple of decades, hundreds and hundreds of hot sauces have come onto the market. Many of them are very good, but our favorite is still this old standby. Made by combining the fiery Tabasco chile pepper with vinegar and salt, then fermenting the mixture in barrels for three years, this mega-popular sauce has a nice flavor, packs a respectable punch, and, since it is available everywhere, makes a good substitute for fresh chiles in a pinch.

Storage: Tabasco sauce keeps just about forever.

SOURCES

Almost all of the ingredients in our recipes can be found in well-stocked supermarkets or ethnic stores. But in case you don't have access to either of those, here are mail-order sources for some of the more hard-to-find ingredients, in roughly alphabetical order.

ASIAN INGREDIENTS

Found in Asian markets and some supermarkets

AsiaFoods.com
(877) 902-0841
www.asiafoods.com
A good source for: nori, wasabi powder, nam pla (fish sauce), chile-garlic paste

Formaggio Kitchen
(888) 212-3224
244 Huron Avenue, Cambridge, MA
www.formaggiokitchen.com
A good source for: spicy black bean paste

Katagiri & Company, Inc.
(212) 755-3566
224 East 59th Street, New York, NY
www.katagiri.com
A good source for: nori, pickled ginger, hijiki seaweed

Kitchen/Market—The Cook's Catalog
(888) 468-4433
218 Eighth Avenue, New York, NY
www.kitchenmarket.com
A good source for: wasabi powder, nam pla (fish sauce), fermented black beans

Quickspice.Com
(800) 553-5008
www.Quickspice.Com
A good source for: nori, pickled ginger, wasabi powder, nam pla (fish sauce), fermented black beans, chile-garlic paste, spicy black bean paste, hijiki seaweed

Rafal Spice Company
(800) 228-4276
2521 Russell Street, Detroit, MI
www.rafalspicecompany.com
A good source for: nori, pickled ginger, wasabi powder, nam pla (fish sauce), fermented black beans, chile-garlic paste
Also: bbq mops, mortars and pestles, skewers, spice grinders, guava paste, lots of hot sauces and pickled peppers

BACON, SLAB

Found in well-stocked supermarkets and specialty food stores

D'Artagnan
(800) 327-8246
280 Wilson Avenue, Newark, NJ
www.dartagnan.com

New Braunfels Smokehouse
(830) 625-2416
Corner of Highway 46 and I-35, New Braunfels, TX
www.nbsmokehouse.com

Nodine's Smokehouse
(860) 491-4009
Route 63/North Street, Goshen, CT
www.nodinesmokehouse.com

CHEESES

Found in specialty food stores

Balducci's
(800) 225-3822
424 Sixth Avenue, New York, NY

Dean & Deluca
(800) 221-7714
560 Broadway, New York, NY
www.dean-deluca.com

Formaggio Kitchen
(888) 212-3224
244 Huron Avenue, Cambridge, MA
www.formaggiokitchen.com

Zingerman's
(888) 636-8162
620 Phoenix Drive, Ann Arbor, MI
www.zingermans.com

CHIPOTLE PEPPERS IN ADOBO SAUCE

Found in Latino markets and some supermarkets

Chile Today—Hot Tamale
(800) 468-7377
31 Richboynton Road, Dover, NJ
www.chiletoday.com

Formaggio Kitchen
(888) 212-3224
244 Huron Ave, Cambridge, MA
www.formaggiokitchen.com

Kitchen/Market—The Cook's Catalog
(888) 468-4433
218 Eighth Avenue, New York, NY
www.kitchenmarket.com

Rafal Spice Company
(800) 228-4276
2521 Russell Street, Detroit, MI
www.rafalspicecompany.com

CHOURICO SAUSAGE
Found in Latino and Portuguese markets

D'Artagnan
(800) 327-8246
280 Wilson Avenue, Newark, NJ
www.dartagnan.com

Dean & Deluca
(800) 221-7714
560 Broadway, New York, NY
www.dean-deluca.com

Zingerman's
(888) 636-8162
620 Phoenix Drive, Ann Arbor, MI
www.zingermans.com

DRIED FRUIT, UNSULPHURED

Found in natural food stores

American Spoon Food
(800) 222-5886
411 East Lake Street, Petoskey, MI
www.spoon.com

BulkFoods.com
(email orders only, but great selection)
355 Morris Street, Suite 200, Toledo, OH
www.bulkfoods.com

Kitchen/Market—The Cook's Catalog
(888) 468-4433
218 Eighth Avenue, New York, NY
www.kitchenmarket.com

GRAPE LEAVES

Found in Middle Eastern markets and well-stocked supermarkets

Formaggio Kitchen
(888) 212-3224
244 Huron Avenue, Cambridge, MA
www.formaggiokitchen.com

Rafal Spice Company
(800) 228-4276
2521 Russell Street, Detroit, MI
www.rafalspicecompany.com

QUAIL

Found in specialty food stores, Asian markets, some supermarkets

D'Artagnan
(800) 327-8246
280 Wilson Avenue, Newark, NJ
www.dartagnan.com

Got to be Gourmet, Inc.
(866) 820-FOOD
www.gottobegourmet.com

SALTS (THE EXPENSIVE ONES)

Found in specialty food stores

Dean & Deluca
(800) 221-7714
560 Broadway, New York, NY
www.dean-deluca.com

Formaggio Kitchen
(888) 212-3224
244 Huron Avenue, Cambridge, MA
www.formaggiokitchen.com

Zingerman's
(888) 636-8162
620 Phoenix Drive, Ann Arbor, MI
www.zingermans.com

SPICES (BULK AND SPECIALTY)

Found in Indian and Middle Eastern markets

The British Express
(888) 840-1280
2880 SW 42nd Avenue, Palm City, FL

www.britishfood.com
Sherwood curry

Caravanserai: The Spice Traders
(707) 220-2458
P.O. Box 85, San Mateo, CA
www.caravanserai.net
Bulk spices

Formaggio Kitchen
(888) 212-3224
244 Huron Avenue, Cambridge, MA
www.formaggiokitchen.com
Urfa, Maras, Aleppo, and other such peppers

Penzey's Spices
(800) 741-7787
18900 West Bluemound Road, Brookfield, WI
www.penzeys.com
Bulk spices

Rafal Spice Company
(800) 228-4276
2521 Russell Street, Detroit, MI
www.rafalspicecompany.com
Sherwood curry, bulk spices

WHITE TRUFFLE OIL
Found in specialty food stores

Dean & Deluca
(800) 221-7714
560 Broadway, New York, NY
www.dean-deluca.com

Earthy Delights
(800) 367-4709
1161 East Clark Road, Suite 260, DeWitt, MI
www.earthy.com

Formaggio Kitchen
(888) 212-3224
244 Huron Avenue, Cambridge, MA
www.formaggiokitchen.com

Zingerman's
(888) 636-8162
620 Phoenix Drive, Ann Arbor, MI
www.zingermans.com

WOOD CHIPS AND CHUNKS

Found where grills are sold

Barbeques Galore
(800) 752-3085
15041 Bake Parkway, Suite A, Irvine, CA
www.bbqgalore-online.com

The Hot Shoppe
(888) 468-3287
311 South Clinton Street, Syracuse, NY
www.hotshoppe.com

Rafal Spice Company
(800) 228-4276
2521 Russell Street, Detroit, MI
www.rafalspicecompany.com

INDEX

with blue cheese, grilled, 33

fresh, prosciutto-stuffed grilled
chicken tenderloins with
pesto butter and, 49–50

grilled, grilled bone-in garlic
chicken breasts with lemon,
parsley and, 248–49

lightly grilled hearts of romaine
with blue cheese, honey-
mustard dressing and, 32

fire extinguishers, 23

fires:

fuels for, 18–20

multi-level, 7–8, 19, 23, 24

right type of, 23

safety concerns and, 23

starting of, 9–11

fish, 201–32

oily, learning to love, 203

prevention of sticking, 202

strategy for grilled whole, with
five sauce options, 230–32

see also specific kinds of fish

fish sauce (nam pla), 398–99

flank steak, 145

mustard-slathered grilled, with
smoky jalapeño-honey
sauce, 139–40

tenderizing of, 141

flare-ups, 23–24

flavor boosters, smoke, 120

flavoring methods, 15–17, 23

flounder with oranges, fennel, and
artichoke hearts, wine-
steamed, 206–7

fluke:

Johnson, grilled with a
Provençal-style hobo pack,
201–2

spicy raw, with mangoes, lemon,
and lime, 134

foil pans, disposable, 22

"fork test," for barbecuing, 6

French-style dishes:

barbecued "baked stuffed" spiny
lobster with mango beurre
blanc, 238–40

East Coast Grill grilled bouillabaisse with roasted red

pepper mayo and toast,
234–35

frosting, guava, 381

banana-carrot cake with, 380–81

fruit, see specific fruits

fruit, dried:

chutney with lime and mint, 337

unsulphured, sources of, 405

fruitwoods, 120

fuels, 18–20

aromatic, 5, 19–20

game hens, Rock Cornish, 256–59

with linguiça-apricot stuffing
and basil-balsamic sauce,
smoke-roasted, 258–59

slow-grilled mustard-crusted
butterflied, with smoky,
lemony red onion rings,
256–57

garlic(ky), 391–92

-basil vinaigrette, 291

bone-in grilled chicken breasts
with lemon, parsley, and
grilled figs, 248–49

-chile paste, 398

crispy, olive oil with parsley and
capers, 243

and herb-crusted smoke-
roasted flattened whole
chicken, simple, 252–53

–green grape sauce, hot-smoked
salmon with, 118–20

grilled clams on the half shell
with Tabasco, lemon and,
116

grilled lamb skewers with
tomato-feta relish, 188–89

hobo pack of plantains and
onions with raisins, lime
and, 301

hobo pack of tomato and broccoli
rabe with lemon and, 305

new potatoes with shrimp puttanesca, grilled, 102–3

and parsley-rubbed skirt steak
with sweet-and-sour mari-
nated red onions, 152–53

spinach, grilled bone-in beef rib

eye with aged balsamic and,
150–51

-Tabasco butter, grilled peel-
and-eat colossal shrimp
with, 99–100

-Tabasco butter, grilled peppered skate wing with beet
relish and, 220–21

-thyme oil, 291

toasted, colorful grilled peppers
with thyme, sherry and, 289

toasted, grilled squid with lemon
and, 123–24

gas grills, 20–21

gasoline, avoiding use of, 23

ginger(ed), 392

-chile dressing, Thai-style
grilled scallops with aromatic greens and, 106–7

-coconut curry sauce, grill-
steamed Thai-style mussels
with, 114–15

cucumber relish, curry-rubbed
grilled shrimp with minted
yogurt and, 97–98

curried grilled quail with dried
grapes, mint and, 42–43

and curry-rubbed grilled lamb
shoulder chops with apricot-
lime barbecue sauce, 192–93

hobo pack of beets, carrots, and
apples with orange and, 300

-mango barbecue sauce, chunky,
grilled striped bass with,
216–17

-peanut sauce, grilled chile
chicken wings with cucum-
ber spears and, 44–45

-pineapple iced tea, 365

raw striped bass salad with
sesame, soy and, 133

–red onion jam, 342

sherry, and coriander mustard,
exotic, 346

Southeast Asian–style fresh
tomato relish with basil,
mint and, 341

-soy dressing, grilled asparagus
on a bed of lettuce with, 276

CHRIS SCHLESINGER is the chef/owner of the nationally prominent East Coast Grill in Cambridge, Massachusetts, as well as of the Back Eddy, a waterfront restaurant in Westport, Massachusetts. He received the James Beard Award for Best Chef in the Northeast in 1996.

A highly regarded cooking teacher, Chris has taught courses in technique at his alma mater, the Culinary Institute of America, at both the New York and Napa Valley campuses. He is a founding member of the national organization Chefs 2000, which supports local farmers in New England.

JOHN WILLOUGHBY is executive editor of *Gourmet* magazine. Prior to joining the staff at *Gourmet* in February of this year, John was the senior editor of *Cook's Illustrated* magazine for seven years and the coauthor of a monthly feature in the *New York Times* dining section for six years. He is also a frequent contributor to national magazines, among them *GQ, Martha Stewart Living,* and *Metropolitan Home.*

A much sought after lecturer and teacher, John appears weekly on the PBS television show "America's Test Kitchen" and teaches a graduate course in food writing at the Radcliffe Institute for Advanced Studies at Harvard University.